D1272178

The Revolutionary Reign of Terror

To Harriet

The Revolutionary Reign of Terror

The Role of Violence in Political Change

Rosemary H.T. O'Kane
Department of Politics
University of Keele

Edward Elgar

Published by
Edward Elgar Publishing Limited
Gower House
Croft Road
Aldershot
Hants GU11 3HR
England

Edward Elgar Publishing Company
Old Post Road
Brookfield
Vermont 05036
USA

British Library Cataloguing in Publication Data
O'Kane, Rosemary H. T. *1947–*
    The revolutionary reign of terror.
    1. Politics. Violence
    I. Title
    322.42

Library of Congress Cataloguing in Publication Data
O'Kane, Rosemary H.T.
        The revolutionary reign of terror: the role of violence in
    political change/Rosemary H.T. O'Kane.
            p. cm.
        Includes bibliographical references and index.
        1. Revolutions. 2. Terrorism. 3. Violence. I. Title.
    JC491.044   1991
    321.09'4–dc20   91–9171
                                                                          CIP
ISBN 1 85278 082 7

Printed in Great Britain by
Billing & Sons Ltd, Worcester

Contents

Preface   vii

PART I   REVOLUTIONARY REIGNS OF TERROR AND
          THEORY

1   Violence at the Centre of Revolution: Civil Wars and
    Policy Choice   3
2   Terror and the State: Totalitarian, Proto-Totalitarian and
    Revolutionary Regimes   16
3   Reigns of Terror and the Lessons of Comparative History   36

PART II   THE CLASSIC REIGNS OF TERROR

4   The Archetypal Case: The Reign of Terror in the French
    Revolution   57
5   Revolutionary Terror in the Russian Revolution: The
    Second Classic Case   86
6   Old Revolutions, New Lessons: The American War of
    Independence and the Puritan Revolution   117

PART III   GUERRILLA MOVEMENTS AND CIVIL WAR
            TO REVOLUTION

Introduction   149

7   Cuba 1959: A Different Type of Revolution   152
8   Nicaragua 1979: Resisting Terror   169
9   China 1949: A Counter-Case?   192

PART IV   CLASSIC REVOLUTIONS IN MODERN TIMES

Introduction   209
10   The Ethiopian Revolution: The Military Institute Terror   211
11   The Iranian Revolution: Terror in the Islamic State   228

PART V   CONCLUSIONS

12   Comparative Lessons from Revolutionary Terrors: The
      Establishment of the Revolutionary State   253

      Appendix: Mexico 1911–34   270

Bibliography   279

Index   291

Preface

Revolutionary reigns of terror are critical events of political change. So much can be learnt from studying change which cannot be understood from research into peaceful political transition. Revolutions are the most exciting of all aspects of politics. My interest in the subject was first opened, as is true for so many, by reading Barrington Moore Jr's *Social Origins of Dictatorship and Democracy.* For cultivating my interest I am greatly indebted to Michael Freeman at Essex University whose course on revolutions it was my privilege to take many years ago. It was he who opened my eyes to the broader issues of politics, societies undergoing dramatic change and the overlap between political science and morals.

I have tried hard in this study to be objective, in the sense that I have endeavoured to lay out hard criteria – laws, institutions, executions, prison conditions – which permit me to decide whether or not a Terror has been present or absent. The attempt to be objective has not been easy in a study which draws comparisons across three and a half centuries, where information is often patchy and evidence often disputed. I can but say that I have tried my best.

The application of objective criteria to revolutionary terrors does not however rule out moral questions, questions of excess in particular, and in seeking to be objective I have not aimed to shake away all moral values. To do so is neither possible for people nor desirable. I do not hide the fact that terror and violence hold no fascination to me in themselves and that I am repulsed by terroristic and violent behaviour. At the same time, it seems pointless to deny that such events take place, indeed they abound in politics throughout the world. It also seems unworldly not to accept that violence must occur in revolutions and that revolutionary governments face a damnably difficult time in which the attraction of resorting to violence, indeed terror, must at times seem overwhelming. It is easy to sit in a comfy chair in a comfortable Western democracy and condemn revolutionary violence. Revolutions fight against violence as much as they use it and they occur in violent societies. Their attraction exists in the fact that they bring hope to the oppressed who suffer violence against humanity in their daily lives. That the violence of reigns of terror occurs within such violent events generated from such violent societies is not surprising and condemnation of revolutionary terrors out of hand, however strong the repulsion felt at the acts involved, is simply unrealistic. I do not conceal my admiration for the Nicaraguan Revolution and my shock for Cromwell's treatment of Ireland. To praise and condemn these cases was, however, neither the purpose nor the inspiration for this study – in neither case was I in fact particularly aware of their detail before. There was too much in the press about the Contra–Nicaragua War to develop a clear understanding and books on the building of the revolutionary government in Nicaragua were yet to be published. Whatever may be read into my surname I have always held a great admiration for Cromwell too.

In generating the initial ideas which led to this book I am indebted to my students here at Keele University. I have taken pleasure in teaching them a course on revolutions over the years. They have given me endless reward, stimulation and fun. They can read this book only if they continue to challenge what I say. My gratitude for the stimulation I have received goes also to my colleagues in the Department of Politics at the University, and for their care and understanding I am forever indebted to my family, Les and Harriet. For their endless goodwill and efficiency I extend my grateful thanks to Kim Johnson and Pauline Weston who have typed this book for me and even after endless changes have continued smiling and still been willing to change things again without complaint. For his encouragement and patience my thanks are due also to Edward Elgar, without whom this book would not have been possible.

Rosemary H.T. O'Kane
Keele

PART I
Revolutionary Reigns of Terror and Theory

1. Violence at the Centre of Revolution: Civil Wars and Policy Choice

The study of revolutions has, at last, found its rightful place as a central topic of social science (Taylor 1984). The study of politics should be as much concerned with conflict and violence as with consensus and order, with illegitimate rule as with legitimate authority. Whilst rather uncommon before 1960, articles and books on revolution have since proliferated. Almost without exception, however, they have concentrated on the causes of revolution. It is understandable; the explanation for events naturally gives priority to the discovery of causes. Explanation does not, however, stop there; the revolutionary process and the outcomes of revolutions are also important.

Most contemporary writers on revolution pay scant attention to the product of the upheaval because they hold that discovery of the causes of revolutions naturally involves explanation for their outcomes. Comparative history approaches stand out for considering the relationship between the causes of revolution and their different natures. Barrington Moore Jr, in *The Social Origins of Dictatorship and Democracy* (first edition 1966), is expressly tentative, and debates throughout the possibility that the reactionary route (fascism) could have been taken if things had gone differently at various crucial points: if, for example, the Guomindang had won in China; or in America, the western farmers had aligned with the southern plantation owners in the Civil War. Theda Skocpol, *States and Social Revolutions* (1979) whilst arguing that particular structures (agrarian bureaucracies) are susceptible to revolutions, brings in additional factors, global factors in particular, to explain revolutionary outcomes. Thus whilst structural conditions were generally similar in France, Russia and China, their outcomes differed because over more than a century the international situation had changed significantly.

It is, however, exactly Moore's and Skocpol's arguments about the outcomes of revolutions which have been most heavily criticized (see,

3

for example, Weiner (1975) and Smith (1983) on Moore, Taylor (1984) on Skocpol). In particular both theories and Moore's most especially have come under attack for giving inadequate attention to the role of ideology and the effect of ideologically motivated revolutionary leaders and organizations (Lowenthal 1968; Femia 1972). The argument goes essentially: Communism and democracy (and fascism for Moore) are ideologies and the appeal of communism to the peasantry in China, the new proletariat in Russia and of the ideas of *les philosophes* to the new bourgeoisie/middle classes in France cannot be subsumed under structural arguments. Most importantly, in respect of the outcomes of those revolutions, the shaping of the new governments and development of the new societies and economies cannot be explained without taking into consideration the role of ideology: the new bourgeois ideas about property and merit in Napoleon's France, the importance of Marxism-Leninism in Russia and of Maoism in China.

The debate about whether ideas are dependent on or independent of material conditions represents a major divide in the social sciences, and in view of the crucial part played by revolution in Marxist theory, the debate has special poignancy for theories of revolution. In being neither democratic nor communist the Iranian Revolution, which occurred whilst Skocpol's book was being published, has thrown new light on the parts played by ideas. Indeed Skocpol has since accepted this (Skocpol 1982). This classic revolution in modern times with its new Islamic dimension has re-awakened an aspect of revolutions which has fallen out of favour, namely the stages of revolution between causes and outcomes and for this study in particular, the stage termed the reign of terror.

In the earlier writings on revolution, Lyford Edwards, *The Natural History of Revolutions* first published in 1927 and Crane Brinton, *The Anatomy of Revolution* first published in 1938, it was argued that a reign of terror was a necessary stage of revolution because all revolutions involve a period of crisis. Edwards drew attention to the remarkable similarity of problems faced by new revolutionary regimes, 'foreign invasion', and 'domestic insurrection' most especially (Edwards 1970: 156) and Brinton largely accepted Edwards' diagnosis. Edwards' book, written over fifty years before Skocpol's, bears a striking resemblance to the latter's conclusions about state-building in respect of her emphasis on the dictates of wars and the need to defeat 'foreign enemies' and 'domestic counter-revolutionaries' (Skocpol 1979: 234). Specific concentration on reigns of terror seems, however, to provide greater insight into the full process of revolution.

Skocpol (1979: 293) ends her book with a quotation from Franz Neumann: 'the struggle for political power – i.e., the struggle for the control of the coercive organisations, for police, justice, army, bureaucracy, and foreign policy – is the agent of historical progress'. This is essentially the proposition from which this book begins. Revolutions are about the struggle for political power and, once grasped by the new revolutionary regime, the struggle to hang on to power. Revolutions are, though, unlike almost every other political circumstance, for whilst they are about the struggle for power they do not stop at control over existing coercive forces. Revolutions are born out of the decay or destruction of old coercive institutions. The process of revolution involves a new struggle to replace and establish those institutions. This breakdown of the old order and establishment of the new is the stuff of revolutions, the struggles to gain power, to shape the institutions of the new order and to maintain control over them are at their heart.[1] As such the 'middle' of revolutions, the interlude between cause and outcome, which has mostly been neglected, turns out to be a crucial period to study.

The attraction of studying revolutionary reigns of terror follows naturally. Reigns of terror seem to herald the critical turning-point of revolution. This is so for essentially two reasons. The violence involved in Terrors and the destruction which they wreak ensures that there is no turning back. Once a reign of terror has occurred, even if those who presided over it have failed to hang on to power, the old ways of doing things, social, political, economic, cultural, can never be as they were before the revolution. Too many individuals have been killed, and probably even more importantly far too many new experiences have been undergone by people at all levels of society. Turned upside down, later rolled in sometimes several directions, things will have settled differently than before. In addition to the destruction of old ways, reigns of terror also represent the process by which oppositions, many of them new and not necessarily therefore representative of the old order, are defeated. Those which are not defeated will come to inherit the new order. This defeat of oppositions provides the conditions under which the new order can begin to be built. The end of this crisis of opposition creates the conditions from which a new government can be formed to tackle the crucial task of righting the effects of chaos, wrought by change, made worse by the terror itself.

TOWARDS A TENTATIVE THEORY

Hypotheses can be generated from reading the histories and noting comparisons. They can also be sparked from reading existing theories, here those concerned with revolutions, terror or the state; they can, of course, also be formulated through experience. With its proponent fortunate enough not to have experienced a revolutionary reign of terror at first hand, the initial hypothesis for explaining revolutionary reigns of terror grew, as do most theories of revolution, from a distillation of histories and theories. At the same time, recent cases, those of Iran and Ethiopia in particular, seemed to strike a chord. Classic reigns of terror appeared to be taking place in modern times. The poignancy of Christmas 1989 in Romania was to come later.

Modern examples did not, however, all appear to point in the same direction. The Cuban revolution, perhaps that of China, and most definitely the Nicaraguan revolution which coincided with the Iranian revolution seemed different. In these revolutions, the notion of a reign of terror seemed far less appropriate, possibly inappropriate. In addition to France and Russia, Edwards and Brinton included in their studies the earlier cases of the American and English revolutions. These they offered as mild cases of Terrors. This provided a potential way forward. On the other hand, the alternative possibility existed that contrary to Edwards' and Brinton's claims, reigns of terror were not a necessary stage of revolution. If true, this possibility seemed doubly attractive: on the one hand, it gave more scope to the importance of revolutionary governments' policy decisions and therefore increased the importance of the ideological complexion of the group which triumphed over chaos; at the same time, the possibility that reigns of terror were not a necessary stage opened the way for looking critically at the existing proposed general causes of Terrors.

Through a broad consideration of the points of comparison between France, Russia, Cuba, Nicaragua, China, Iran and Ethiopia, such as they were known to me in greater and lesser depth, an initial proposition arose. Reigns of terror could be avoided, or at least greatly reduced in their violence, if countries had civil wars before the revolutionary government came to power and more particularly so if guerrilla warfare provided the initial motor for the revolution.[2] The proposition seemed to fit the cases. Furthermore, whilst Edwards and Brinton had given several causes and proposed that all had to be present for a reign of terror to occur, the civil wars in both France (the region around the Vendée especially) and Russia (1918–21) seemed especially important to these terrors. Interestingly, this observation also went against Skocpol's prime emphasis on foreign wars as the historical basis of nation-building in revolutions. The proposition was not that civil war was the only cause of reigns of terror, but simply that it held prime importance as the factor most closely associated with the terror's virulence and the end of civil war a crucial period for the outcome of the revolution. Other general factors, especially foreign wars and economic problems, would also have an effect, as too might a host of factors specific to each case, but standing above all of these, in both the general and the specific case, would be the presence and virulence of civil war, or its absence.

The proposition also held potential significance as a theory. The advantage of having a civil war before a revolution would be that the opposition forces would have been weakened, in some cases even destroyed. In the context of revolutions seen as a process of struggle for reconstruction and maintenance of power, the reduction in potential counter-revolutionary activity would lessen the need for coercion. In this sense it would seem to follow that the most violent reigns of terror would be likely to be found where domestic counter-revolution was at its worst, that is where full-blown civil war was being fought. Such views seemed in line with Tilly's (1978: ch.7) approach to the outcomes of revolutions.

There seemed though to be more in this importance of civil war than a straightforward proposition about the strength of the counter-revolution. In Nicaragua, Cuba and China the civil wars which had raged in the prelude to the overthrow of the old order rather than in its aftermath had been preceded by guerrilla movements. Importantly, these guerrilla movements had contained within them codes of practice governing behaviour towards others, including opposition forces. In broad terms these practices can be described as humane. Castro let captured soldiers go, food was never to be stolen from peasants but was to be exchanged for medical assistance or the like. Honesty, courtesy and politeness were the orders given to the Red Soldiers in China (see Fairbairn 1974: 271 and 99–100). To some extent such acts were good practice for reducing the chances of betrayal, but there was more to it than that. Repulsion at the repression and abuses perpetrated by the regimes under attack by the guerrilla forces provided a focus for contrasting behaviour. In addition, through the civil war process experience had also been gained which brought greater understanding of the people's needs to the new revolutionary government.

Policy choice had played a part in the behaviour adopted by these guerrilla forces. It seemed reasonable, therefore, to suppose that the choice of policies adopted would continue to play a part once in power too. If so, then choice could affect the intensity of the reign of terror, that is the level of coercion applied and the nature of the violence used. Indeed policy choice might more broadly have a bearing on whether or not a reign of terror occurred at all.

The view put forward by existing social science theories for the causes of revolutionary reigns of terror is that such Terrors are a necessary response to circumstances directly encountered. Those circumstances, such as foreign invasion, sabotage, civil war or economic crisis, are seen as inherited crises, not ones provoked or stoked by the revolutionaries in power. The complexion of even a peacetime government is surely likely, though, to have a significant effect both on the type of legislation introduced and on the level of coercion used to implement it. It seems unreasonable to deny that the same might also be true for governments in times of change and upheaval. Whilst it might be that revolutionary governments face especially pressing problems, even where such problems have been entirely uninvited, choices may still be made in their handling. In troubled times, how much more likely it is too that ill-considered policies will be rushed through. Where revolutionaries are in power, how much more likely again that policies will have wide-ranging effects and provoke hostility from those disadvantaged by policies introduced or angered by the method of their implementation. As Hobsbawm (1968: 12) remarks

> Irrespective of their general character as phenomena of historic rupture, concretely revolutions are also episodes in which groups of people pursue intended goals, whatever the causes and motives which make them act or the – inevitable – difference between their intentions and the results of their action. They belong to the realm of politics as well as to that in which political decisions are unimportant.

Hobsbawm argues that these 'political decisions', normally of lesser importance before the revolutionary overthrow, can take on primary significance once the revolutionaries take over and turn 'a changing situation to their advantage' (ibid: 13). On balance, it seemed to go against common conceptions of the way all governments work, and not just revolutionary governments either, to rule out the view that policies introduced by new revolutionary regimes would affect opposition (mostly provoking but sometimes ameliorating it) and adopt the view that policies would play at most only an incidental role in the process of revolution.

Revolutionary reigns of terror occur within the post-revolutionary period of crisis when revolutionary regimes seek to hang on to political power in the face of opposing forces contending for that power. Revolutionary governments do not simply face opposition from the overthrown regime of the old order; they can also create new forces of counter-revolution in opposition to policies enacted. Such developing oppositions do not, though, conform to Krejci's perception:

> Once the *ancien régime* loses the decisive confrontation, the coalition of revolutionary forces falls apart and individual revolutionary factions begin to engage in in-fighting...The political differentiation can be conceptualised in terms of a fivefold political spectrum: supporters of the *ancien régime* on the one hand, and revolutionaries on the other, with the latter divided into right, centre, left and extreme left. (Krejci 1983: 213)

In practice such divisions amongst revolutionaries, if present as potential oppositions, may or may not be turned into actual oppositions posing a real threat against the regime in the sense of actually taking up arms against those in control at the time.

Policies aimed at fundamental change are bound to have greater potential for provoking opposition than those aimed at less far-reaching reforms. Decisions to implement policies through coercion rather than persuasion or inducement are also likely to provoke greater resistance. Such policies, like the need to raise and feed an army, could be a straightforward reaction to problems directly encountered, though choice exists in how these problems are to be faced – whether the army is to be voluntary or conscripted, for example, or whether and how producers are to be paid for the food required for the army. However pressing problems may be, an element of choice over how exactly the problem should be handled remains in all but the rarest circumstances.

Other radical policies might also be introduced which could themselves provoke new sources of counter-revolution. Such policies may be a reaction to conditions encountered directly (severe economic problems, for example) but they need be neither entirely nor even inherently so. Both the choice of means to tackle unexpected and unprovoked problems and the decision to restructure the post-revolutionary society in one way rather than another are policy decisions, both have the potential to exacerbate opposition. These decisions will be constrained by the complexion of the particular revolutionary regime. In practice, the constraint may not match up to an ideology (such as Marxism–Leninism), it may be a loose set of ideals or a programme for reform as yet in outline only. However nascent or fully-fledged these revolutionary programmes and ideas are, they set limits on policy formation. Sartre (1960), comparing the French and Cuban revolutions, described Cuba's programme for reform worked out through practical discovery rather than philosophical writings as a 'primitive ideology' as compared with the 'elaborate ideology' of the French revolution.

All revolutions must be affected to some degree by the ideas, primitive or elaborate, which fuel revolutionary fervour and colour the complexion of revolutionary government. If so, then it follows that the relationship between civil wars and reigns of terror cannot be straightforward. Full understanding of the relationship between civil wars and reigns of terror can only be achieved if examination of the policy decisions made by the revolutionaries is included. In particular, it is necessary to consider the extent to which chosen policies stirred up opposition rather than quietening it and whether practical alternatives to policies actually pursued existed in the face of pressing problems not of the revolutionaries' own making. Naturally study of such problems is inherently of interest to the explanation for reigns of terror and their claimed relationship to civil wars.

If the proposition that civil wars are of primary significance for Terrors holds, it follows that the outcome of a revolution is more especially in the balance for revolutions not propelled through civil war to power, normally by guerrilla warfare, but plunged into violent civil war after the overthrow of the old order. For these revolutions, the reign of terror is, indeed, the crux of the revolution. The period after revolutionary takeover is, though, a critical one for all revolutions and the study of this period is essential to a general understanding of the outcomes of revolutions. It follows too that it is important to differentiate between the two types of revolution, those where guerrilla movements have played a part before the revolutionary overthrow and those where they have not.

THE APPROACH

The propositions about the special importance of the timing and virulence of civil war and the boundaries put on policy decisions by the revolutionary government's ideology, whether primitive or elaborate, were first formed tentatively. The ideas needed to be developed and tested. As a consequence, the method chosen was, in as far as prior knowledge and expectations would permit, to adopt an open-minded, part deductive, part inductive approach, to allow theoretical interest to direct investigation whilst at all times trying to learn from cases studied, too. On the one hand, the aim was to avoid the imposition of a preconceived interpretation which could lead to the suppression of interesting features and the distortion of reality; on the other hand, the aim was to avoid the false assumption of pure case history studies that 'history speaks for itself'.

History cannot alone generate understanding for accounts of history are themselves a series of interpretations some of which are competing interpretations which need to be decided between, not assimilated into one overview.[3] The collection of new evidence can decide in favour of one view rather than another but usually that evidence itself turns out to be compatible with more than one possible analysis of the broader context in which that new evidence is placed. With respect to the general study of revolutions which have taken an historical approach, examining case studies in detail (Leiden and Schmitt 1973, Dunn 1989, Moore 1969, Skocpol 1979, Wolf 1973), analysis has taken the form of using the history books to support the interpretation presented. The effect of this has been to conceal the debate within the history literature itself. Whilst it may offer comfort to learn that there is general agreement within the literature on this or that point, more recent research indicating a contrary view can easily be concealed.

Moore (1969) stands out for systematically grappling with the disputes within the history books, wrestling with alternatives to his preferred approach, arguing for challenging views to be relegated to secondary importance. In as far as his general analysis arises allegedly from the case studies he has quite naturally been challenged by critics for displaying a partial analysis (Weiner 1975). Such criticism reflects the impossibility of making a complete separation in practice between the inductive and deductive methods, the construction of a theory from the evidence as opposed to using the evidence to test hypotheses deduced from a theory. To compare like with like requires a preconceived basis for assuming them to be similar in the first place. Furthermore, comparison of like with like is not enough. Any similarities found need also to be checked against cases alike in their preconditions but differing in their outcomes. The findings must also be tested against cases where outcomes have been similar but where pre-conditions have differed. Without these checks and counter-checks it is impossible to begin to evaluate the significance of the generalizations made. For example, it is not difficult to demonstrate that poverty amongst large sections of the population is a condition which is present before revolutions; it is also the case, however, that such poverty exists in many countries which do not have revolutions. With respect to outcomes, change brought by revolution, for example the construction of a communist party state, has also been found where a revolution had not occurred (in East Germany 1945–89 for example).

These considerations of counter examples require not only the presence of common phenomena (revolutions, poverty and Communist parties) but also the possibility that a phenomenon could have been present (the failure to have a revolution when conditions looked poor enough, the failure to have a revolution yet the development of a single party state like ones following Communist revolutions). This notion that a phenomenon could have been present requires that a theoretical perspective be adopted. This need not imply that a fully thought through theory exists before the comparison of case histories is embarked upon (the deductive method); it could be just an hypothesis or even a notion of what might be found. Otherwise there would be no point in undertaking the study. It follows that as more is learnt about each case new hypotheses will be developed and as the material used will itself be influenced by theoretical perspectives (histories offer competing analyses, historians sometimes explicitly employing theories, Marxist historians for example) theories cannot but impinge on comparative studies.[4]

MacIntyre (1973: 333–7) has argued that the use of counter examples for the rejection or modification of theories requires the existence in the social sciences of law-like generalizations equivalent to those of the natural sciences. Such theories, he argues, we neither have nor can we achieve. For the study of revolutions this is certainly fair. These are events in which people play a part and where unpredictable things happen. The differences between two revolutions can always be put down to specific rather than general factors and as there are too few cases anyway there is little chance of building towards statistically significant generalizations. Facing these problems, the method proposed here has virtues. MacIntyre argues that progress can be achieved in the social sciences through information gathering, conceptual clarification and the like so long as the social scientist strives to be conscious of personal, cultural and time-specific ideological constraints.

The method proposed here seems best described as theoretically informed comparative history. Keeping an open mind, all cases are investigated against a background of theory and hypotheses, not only the tentative proposal which gave pre-eminence to the study of civil war and policy choices but also the alternative propositions concerning reigns of terror found in Edwards' and Brinton's works and the related propositions concerning state building found in Skocpol's work. Support for any new theory must always come in part from rejection of alternative explanations. Competing theories have the potential to correct the refraction caused by the author's preferred theoretical perspective. Of course it is impossible not to view past events from a present perspective and other cultures through Western eyes but in drawing comparisons across time and place the very method itself can help to correct such preconceptions. The inclusion of existing theoretical propositions is crucial also in a direct way, for the civil war and policy choice hypothesis which guides this study is concerned with primary importance amongst several relevant factors.

ON WHAT IS TO COME

The intention of this study is to extend and deepen understanding of revolutionary reigns of terror and through investigation of that crucial period of revolutions, when the use of violence by the revolutionary state reaches its peak, to gain a better understanding of the nascent state. As discussion will reveal, a view of the mature state as resting on a balance of coercion and support emerges from the cases and their study directs attention towards the relative ease of establishing central control over the revolutionary forces of coercion afforded by the period of civil war before the revolutionary overthrow. There is no guarantee that the generalizations which emerge will satisfy others. It is hoped at the very least, however, that information will be seen from a new perspective and that more will be known, both factually and conceptually, about the relationship between politics and society and, most particularly, the revolutionary reign of terror.

Of their nature, terror and violence disgust. They involve deplorable acts by one individual, sometimes several individuals against another. The terrors considered here involve such horrific examples. It is the policy of this book not to make mention of individual details. This has been decided upon for two reasons. In view of the fact that anarchistic terrors mostly run alongside reigns of terror, the notion that any single example, or even several such examples, can be made to characterize terrors is false; such characterization is better made through drawing attention to the scale of events. The second reason is perhaps more personal. The use of examples to shock does not lend poignancy to the study of terrors, it debases it. To dwell on the particular anchors attention to the violence for itself rather than as part of the wider set of events, the subject matter of political science.[5] Human suffering is ever part of society, force ever part of the state (see, for example, Moore 1972). It would be wrong, therefore, in concentrating on revolutionary reigns of terror to give the impression that they have a monopoly on vileness; as the following chapter will show, terrors do not.

NOTES

1. The above amounts to a view of what a revolution is but it does not constitute a definition. There are many around in the literature and I share with Hobsbawm (1986: 9) a view of revolution as a 'combination of symptoms' which separates out the generally accepted large-scale revolutions which have a shocking impact both nationally and internationally. Revolutions include large-scale mass movements and shake society at its roots so that life can never settle the same again. In addition to shaking the social, economic and cultural bases of society, they bring down and replace the political system at the very least (the entire social, economic and cultural system at the very most) and reverberate beyond the nation state. The scale of the mass movement itself signals the fact that a revolution is probably going on, though a proper assessment takes time and must await the actual rather than potential impact of the revolutionary situation. It is possible and reasonable therefore usefully to consider both why large-scale mass movements have not fulfilled their revolutionary potential and why, outside of shocking mass upheavals, fundamental transformation has occurred. The adjective 'revolutionary' can be applied to both types of situation but the pure classification of revolution must remain the preserve of the total event.

2. For the notion of guerrilla warfare as a motor of revolution see Debray (1968). Modern revolutionary wars of independence were not included in this study for foreign war and civil war lose their distinction when a country is a colony. As will be shown this proves a problem for the American Revolution.

3. See Carr (1964: ch.4) and Mills (1970: ch.8). The argument is essentially that historians approach history with some theory of what it is important to study which is itself a reflection of the age in which the researcher lives. This is in line with MacIntyre (1973) on social scientists, discussed below.

4. For a discussion of the comparative history method see Skocpol (1979: ch.1), though as Smith (1973: 160–2) points out when favourably contrasting Moore (1969) with Skocpol (ibid), Skocpol fails to include cases which directly contradict, in having outcomes the same but preconditions different or vice versa. For a good and concise discussion of these issues for comparative politics, see DeFelice 1980.

5.   See, for example, Geras (1989) where the use of two extremely unpleasant examples, though valuable for making a philosophical point about excessive use of violence, in practice swamp the imagination. Leggett (1981) too gives specific individual examples of the horrific behaviour of one particular Cheka official. Of course such knowledge must not be suppressed but when the particular official turns out to be mentally deranged and dismissed from the Cheka as a consequence, the potential problem for individual examples to mislead the general view is evident.

2. Terror and the State: Totalitarian, Proto-Totalitarian and Revolutionary Regimes

It is naturally important to begin a comparative investigation into revolutionary reigns of terror (or revolutionary terrors, Terrors or reigns of terror as they will sometimes be referred to here) with a consideration of their essential nature. In order not to prejudge the findings and invite tautology, it is necessary to seek their essence not through the comparison of case histories later to be explained but through consideration of the broader literature on terror.

TERRORISM AND FEAR

In practice, the literature concentrates mostly on 'terrorism', and furthermore on insurgent terrorism rather than state terrorism (see Price 1977; Lacqueur 1979, Lodge 1981, Wilkinson 1986, Wardlaw 1989). The tendency, and recent works offer no exception to this, is to give crucial emphasis to the fear that terrorism induces in people and through this to generalize a definition for both state and insurgency terror. Wardlaw (1989: 16), the most respected recent authority offers the following:

> Political terrorism is the use, or threat of use, of violence by an individual or a group, whether acting for or in opposition to established authority, when such action is designed to create extreme anxiety and/or fear-inducing effects in a target group larger than the immediate victims with the purpose of coercing that group into acceding to the political demands of the perpetrators.

This is in line with Thornton's (1964: 73) view, much quoted in the literature, that 'terror is a symbolic act designed to influence political behaviour by extranormal means entailing the use or threat of violence'. Certainly this emphasis on the creation of fear has been part of the classic explanation for revolutionary reigns of terror (see Edwards 1970, whose work is discussed in Chapter 3). Such definitions of state terror will not do, for they involve part explanation for what is to be explained. The purpose of state terrorism, they suggest, is to create fear such that people will surrender to demands, but state terrorism is itself defined in terms of fear creation.

Walter (1972: 5), one of the few who concentrates on state terror rather than insurgency terror, argues that terror 'may mean, on the one hand, the psychic state – extreme fear – and, on the other hand, the thing that terrifies – the violent event that produces the psychic state'. In recognition of this he concentrates on the 'process of terror, the act and the fear together in reaction to each other'. Wilkinson (1986: 56) includes both of these elements: 'political terrorism' is the 'systematic use of murder and destruction in order to terrorise individuals, groups, communities or governments into conceding to the terrorists' political demands'. The second part, however, seems both tautological (terrorism is the act of terrorizing) and redundant. If 'murder and destruction' is being carried out 'systematically' it is hard to believe that fear and anxiety will not result. The only condition under which such a reaction would be stopped would be if arbitrariness and injustice were absent and horror removed from the public eye. In other words, if the targets were picked out carefully such that the innocent did not fall victim and everyone other than the guilty went unpunished with even their punishment being concealed. Otherwise, following Townshend (1986), the two sides would need to be equals, both armed, capable of turning 'terror' into war.

Townshend writing on twentieth-century Ireland has focused on what is missing from most definitions: 'Terrorism is a one-way relationship between unlikes. It might most straightforwardly be defined as the use of violence by the armed against the unarmed. Only because the targets are unarmed, undefendable, unprepared by organisation or training to cope with the shock of violence, are they put into terror' (Townshend 1986: 90). This is an important point and one, furthermore, to which far too little attention has been paid in the literature on terror. It draws attention away from intention to create fear which is inherently unmeasurable to the tangible differences between victim and perpetrator. These inequalities especially contrast in revolutionary reigns of terror.

Wardlaw offers five explanations for the concentration of recent literature on 'insurgent terrorism':

- Institutionalized terrorism is simply less likely to make the headlines in comparison with an exciting newsworthy event such as the hijacked aeroplane.
- States have some control over how they appear to others and so state repression can be made to appear rational whilst rebel terrorism is portrayed as irrational.
- 'Reigns of terror' occur in the main in authoritarian states which have control over the media anyway.
- The problems faced by researchers; quoting Groom (1978), he notes that 'it is dangerous to conduct field research in contemporary reigns of terror' (this is something of an understatement); he also remarks that understanding dictators such as Robespierre and Stalin is especially difficult for social researchers with whom they contrast so sharply in outlook.
- Rebel terrorism has the attraction of danger and it is a more immediate danger too:

State terrorism may be brutal and unjust but, in general, one knows what activities not to indulge in in order to escape its immediate and personal intrusion. Individual terrorism by contrast bears no necessary relation to one's own behaviour. It appears random and therefore more dangerous. (Wardlaw 1989: 11)

Leaving aside his first comment, all of these points reflect Wardlaw's recognition that state terrors differ crucially from insurgent terrors: terroristic states have at least some control over their image, usually having complete control over the media; such states are also both more dangerous and more incomprehensible to the researcher; and lastly the type of danger faced in those states differs from that of insurgent terrorism. The fifth point is quoted in full for good reason as it has an important bearing on this study. If state terrorism is, as Wardlaw argues, 'brutal and unjust' then many of the innocent must fall victim. If so then there is a contradiction in Wardlaw's statement for it follows that for some it is not possible to escape its immediate and personal intrusion by avoiding indulgence in certain 'activities'. This is particularly important for revolutionary reigns of terror.

STATE TERRORS

Outside of the upheaval of revolutions it may perhaps be possible to avoid arrest by abiding by the laws of a terroristic state, though such was not the case for Jews in Germany; neither was it the case in Stalin's Soviet Union where every member of the population was 'held under immediate threat' (Conquest 1971: 11). In all terroristic states, some arbitrariness must remain. Gregor has argued strongly that it is exactly this arbitrariness which distinguishes terror regimes from repressive regimes, where acts of violence are straightforwardly used. In the latter case the individual is able, after intimidation, to avoid acts forbidden by the government:

> Terrorism on the other hand, does not intimidate its victims because it offers them no escape from deadly coercion or loss. There is no schedule of behaviours to which the prospective victim might conform. The victim is an 'innocent' – he has neither done anything proscribed nor can he undertake compliance behaviours to avoid threat. (Gregor 1982: 159)

In support of his argument Gregor offers the cases of innocents executed and sent to camps in both Stalin's Russia and Hitler's Germany and draws as a contrast the case of Mussolini's Italy as a repressive rather than a terroristic regime. In these claims Gregor is entirely in line with both Friedrich and Brzezinski's (1965) and Arendt's (1958) views of totalitarianism.

In revolutionary upheaval the chances of the innocent falling victim to the terror are multiplied yet higher. For the very newness of the regime, its very lack of established procedure and the crisis of the situation produce laws against counter-revolution which are open to broad interpretation. Laws against hoarding, for example, introduced in most revolutions, could easily be made to apply to any peasant who withheld a little grain or a worker who bought on the black market. Such acts in times of scarcity when people are faced with starvation are not activities in which 'not to indulge'. When a counter-revolutionary act becomes survival itself then a revolutionary reign of terror can become every bit as dangerous as the bomb hidden beneath the park bench, or the hijacking which involves those who just happened to book a flight on that particular day.

The agents of the Terror inexperienced in their tasks and, in the exceptional circumstances of revolution, given wide rein operate in uncertainty and so carry dread. In such circumstances, too, terror appears officially sanctioned whilst at the same time the regime seems either incapable or unwilling to punish those who take the law into their own hands (particularly if spontaneous action looks to be directed against government-defined enemies). Under such circumstances anarchistic terror is likely to flourish. The mob that burns the home of a hoarder or ransacks the home of a one-time landlord and then kills him for his past exploitation adds to the terror of the Terror. The revolutionary reign of terror is, ironically, likely to be made worse by the very incapacity of the reign to keep full control.[1] The upheaval of the revolutionary situation prevents for many the possibility of engaging only in acts which are safe, in Wardlaw's sense of not leading to arrest. As the example of the landlord suggests, it may be past not present action which is the crime. In general, the danger of the innocent being drawn into Terrors is high simply because of the uncertainty of the times.

As Wardlaw (1989: 7–8) points out though, state terror contrasts with insurgent terrorism because official terror 'usually involves a bureaucracy (police, armed services, intelligence agencies, secret police, immigration control, information control, etc.) which, in essence, is the administration of terror (either directly or indirectly) by large numbers of citizens'. Indeed the very fact that laws such as those against counter-revolutionary activity are passed by a government and implemented through state organizations such as police forces and courts supports this view. Wardlaw recognizes, however, that similar sorts of procedures can exist within rebel terrorist organizations too. He mentions the case of the Irish Republican Army but emphasizes that these courts are contained within the organization itself rather than applied to society as a whole (Wardlaw 1989: 8).

THE TERROR OF TOTALITARIAN REGIMES

The important problem is not that of differentiating insurgent terrorism from state terror for the fact that it is the government which is legitimizing the terror is really rather easy to grasp. What is important is the differentiation of revolutionary reigns of terror from terror used by governments in other circumstances and in particular (given the reputation of reigns of terror such as those associated with Robespierre and Stalin) the differentiation of revolutionary reigns of terror from totalitarian regimes. This too ought to be rather easy, for revolutionary reigns of terror occur within the revolutionary upheaval whilst totalitarian regimes do not. Using this distinction, however, the end of this period of upheaval becomes crucial. The problem is that one of the classic cases of totalitarianism (the other being Nazi Germany) is

Stalin's Russia which grew out of a revolution. Definitions of revolution (as distinct from riots, rebellions and the like) often include the existence of an ideology or 'value-orientation' (for example, Smelser 1962, Gurr 1972). Ideology is also emphasized in state terrors. At risk of confusing the cause of terroristic states with their definition, Walter (1972: 341–2) puts top of his list of 'functional prerequisites' for a terroristic regime, 'a shared ideology that justifies violence'. In this he links Nazi Germany and Stalin's Russia with the French revolutionaries. An official, elaborate, ideology is also top of Friedrich and Brzezinski's (1965: 22) list of the characteristics of the totalitarian syndrome.[2]

Certainly state terrors are bound to be given some sort of public justification, though whether such justification amounts to an ideology is rather less clear. In Walter's claim, the word 'ideology' seems potentially redundant. A government might present a justification for declaring a state of emergency in reaction, for example, to actual insurgency or assassinations but such justification would not amount to an ideology. In revolutions, similarly, any act counter to the revolutionary regime's survival could be used to justify the use of violence, as too could fear of counter-revolution. Such acts of terror, taken to ensure the survival of a regime, need not amount to the pursuance of ideological objectives.[3] With respect to totalitarianism, furthermore, Arendt is careful to separate ideology (totalitarian regimes she argues derive their actions from pre-existing ideologies) from terror which she considers to be 'the essence' of totalitarian government (Arendt 1958: 474). It is usual to include a secret police force as most especially important to a totalitarian regime. Arendt, however, goes beyond the consideration of state surveillance to the physical horrors of totalitarian rule and highlights concentration camps, where people were shut off from the world, tortured and killed in great numbers (pp. 437–59).

It is surely Arendt who captures in this the quintessence of terror. It exists not simply in the use of force and violence and the threat which emanates from it once used – all regimes rest to some degree on the threat of force, and violence is used by an overwhelming proportion of states (see O'Kane 1989, Sivard 1985, and also Calvert 1986, for some glaring examples, past as well as present). In the concentration camp, the state has constructed a situation every bit as dangerous and arbitrary for the individuals within it as the bomb beneath the park bench. People are made powerless in its presence, without control over its effects, and its effects are total. People are stripped of dignity, of humanity. Torture, mental, physical or both, is part of their existence and their destiny is death, either from execution or as the consequences of internment, disease, starvation or suicide.[4]

Such is the terror of revolutionary Terrors, but there is a difference between them and totalitarian states. It lies not just in the degree of their establishment, the length of time that they have had to perfect their organization and sharpen their operation to achieve the deepest reach into society, though certainly the lack of establishment of revolutionary regimes is part of the difference. The difference lies also in the way in which the terror operates. In totalitarian regimes there exists a formality of organization over society. The agents of the organization, the secret police, ordinary police, bureaucrats, concentration camp personnel, prison officers, judges, counsellors, torturers, are all accountable to the state. Crucially, too, the terror in totalitarian regimes is organized by the state; there is no scope for spontaneous, anarchical terror to break out amongst the people.

THE NATURE OF REVOLUTIONARY TERROR

In revolutionary reigns of terror, the revolutionary crisis itself prevents total state control and invites lawlessness. All structures of terror are new and essentially untried. Revolutionary tribunals or courts are hurriedly constructed, without the benefit of proper training and consultation, to try crimes committed on the basis of laws against counterrevolution which are themselves untested. Inevitably, differences in performance are bound to arise, reflecting differences between the officers involved and special local factors. To an extent, therefore, power is bound to be devolved. In contrast to the organized arrests, show trials and mechanical concentration camps of totalitarian regimes, the essence of revolutionary reigns of terror lies in summary justice. At its extreme such justice is represented by the officer who has arrested the suspect, being judge, counsel, witness and executioner and all at one time, and the man caught carrying his bag of black-market goods, who is executed by the secret police without opportunity to explain that he is not an intentional counter-revolutionary but has perhaps simply acquired the goods to save the life of a dying child.

Outside of this extreme form, summary justice lies in the conditions of treatment after arrest, prisoners who have never been brought to trial being left to die in over-crowded squalor, often in makeshift prisons (ships, warehouses and the like), insanitary, disease-ridden prisons, where food is inadequate or inedible. Where trials are held, there is no right either to defence or appeal, and execution or imprisonment, saving quirks of fortune, is certainly irrespective of innocence.

With the laws so broad, the definitions of counter-revolutionary acts so wide, the innocent are bound to be brought within this 'revolutionary justice'. Where people are imprisoned, whether with or without trial, sudden and arbitrary executions of prisoners may also take place and, in the worst cases, torture too. Torture is not an essential part of revolutionary reigns of terror but in such extraordinary times such things occur. Both public executions and the use of torture are popular in reigns of terror though neither are essential. It is the number of executions, the sheer size of the operation, the chances of the innocent being drawn in, the absence of proper trials, the makeshift nature of the terror machine and the imprecision of legislation that create a revolutionary reign of terror. Whilst totalitarian regimes rest on secrecy and only at their end reveal the fullness of their horrors, revolutionary reigns of terror involve a degree of openness. This reflects the extraordinary crisis situation in which revolutionary terrors occur, that very absence of the total state organization which characterizes totalitarian regimes.

In revolutionary reigns of terror it is the visible nature of the terror, the arbitrary arrest, bulging gaols, summary justice and mass executions, which creates the conditions under which anarchical terrors grow: hoarders being lynched; people once held in authority, landlords for example, being set upon, publicly humiliated and killed; soldiers surrendering in defeat in civil war being butchered. Such events occur because the state has not achieved the control, the reach, epitomized by the true terror state, the totalitarian regime. Ironically, perhaps, because of this absence of control these reigns cannot strictly be held accountable for such 'anarchical terror', even though it may be characteristic of such regimes. As the case studies will reveal an important task of revolutionary reigns of terror is to bring this anarchical terror under control and it is even more important to bring the arbitrariness of the terror, as reflected in regional differences and the personalities involved, under central control. Power invested in the individual and the locality undermines both the potential and actual power of the central state. Without such central control revolutionary governments cannot become established.

THE PRACTICAL STUDY OF REVOLUTIONARY REIGNS OF TERROR

By their very nature, revolutionary Terrors present problems for their study and this is especially the case for a comparative work. The laws and institutions of Terror are not identical for each case and the details available are mostly patchy. The estimates for victims of revolutionary reigns of terror are also open to dispute. Estimates are likely to vary according to levels of sympathy or lack of sympathy for the regime. Exiles are especially likely to exaggerate. Official estimates, when available, are also questionable, at best providing only the initial basis upon which impressions can be built. Leaving aside the chances that Terror governments are likely to doctor the figures, the problem of gathering accurate evidence stems from the very crisis situation in which Terrors occur. Not only do anarchical terrors run parallel with reigns of terror, they usually coincide with civil wars, foreign wars or both. As a consequence, it becomes important to exclude from the toll of Terror's victims armed soldiers (whether standing or guerrilla) killed in battle against the revolutionary regime. This follows from Townshend's (1986) argument above. It follows also that such soldiers once captured and unarmed, if later summarily executed or deliberately left to die in prison of starvation or torture, would be counted as victims of the Terror.

Geras, in considering the ethics of revolution and concerned with the problem that some violence is bound to occur in revolution, has drawn attention to the critical nature of the use of excess violence. Drawing on just-war theory he has highlighted the importance of directing attack so as to minimize even the unintentional killing of the innocent; the methods used to kill should 'attack the combatant and not the person' (Geras 1989: 200). This is an important consideration if Terrors are to be compared for their relative virulence or mildness.

It must be recognized that in a comparative analysis which stretches from the present back over three and a half centuries, twentieth-century rules for just war could artificially inflate the evidence for terror in the older revolutions and in those countries today least affected by Western ideas. Indeed the problem of generating accurate figures on victims presents a warning against using simple numbers to try to gauge 'excess', though, naturally, examination of the nature of terror must involve consideration of actual deaths and some estimation of their numbers. Clearly such numbers add, each in turn, to the horror felt by the outside observer of the Terror just as much as they add to the terror felt by the population.

The numbers of deaths themselves, even taking into consideration the nature of the deaths and the indiscriminate use of violence that the innocent fall victim too, are not, however, a sufficient means for identifying a revolutionary reign of terror. The identity of revolutionary reigns of terror cannot be separated from consideration of the nature of the laws, and the arbitrariness inherent in their interpretation, the nature of their application and their adjudication. Summary justice: the innocent and the guilty alike arrested and executed; people imprisoned without proper trial (or without any trial) left to die of disease or starvation in squalor and indignity; executions of the innocent as well as the guilty by virtue of the inexactness of the laws and the absence of proper procedures of law to include proper trials with defence counsel, the right to appeal and the real chance of being found not guilty, where, if found guilty, treatment provides for human beings both in body and spirit.

If due attention is given to the nature of the laws against counter-revolution promulgated by the regime, the revolutionary courts, the makeshift prisons, the revolutionary surveillance organizations as well as the number of victims it becomes possible to identify a revolutionary reign of terror including a reasonable means by which its beginning and end can be identified too. If emphasis is put on fear in society, however, this becomes impossible to measure in any objective way. This is not to claim that there are no difficulties in identifying the beginning and end of such Terrors. Terrors are identified by the introduction of the laws on counter-revolution, the construction of the machinery of revolutionary terror – the courts, the trial procedures, the police and secret police systems, the prisons – the toll of victims and suffering; they end with the repeal of those laws, the dissolution of those revolutionary courts and forces and a sharp decline in executions. Revolutions are, however, born of violence and can breed violence. The end of a revolutionary reign of terror need not bring the end of state violence. The example of Stalin's totalitarianism has shown this. The end of Terrors will be heralded by the 'extraordinary' revolutionary courts and organizations being either reformed and given permanence under central control or disbanded. Certainly, the end of a revolutionary reign of terror will correspond with a decline in the frequency of official executions and the anarchistic terror, too, will decline.

Just as at its very end a reign of terror may be brought gradually under control, with no necessary specific single event to herald its end, so too its beginning may grow as each new law increases in its arbitrariness and harshness and the organizations of the Terror grow in size and reach. Revolutionary reigns of terror are, therefore, characterized most easily by their peaks, when the numbers of victims reach their most shocking proportions. At that point, too, legislation is at its most harsh and the instruments and organizations of terror most highly tuned. If an understanding of their causes is to be achieved, however, it is important not to dwell only on these peaks of excess.

CAMBODIA: A PROTO-TOTALITARIAN SYSTEM

The need to distinguish the revolutionary reign of terror from other forms of state terror is particularly crucial in the case of Cambodia, during the years as Democratic Kampuchea, which began with the defeat of General Lon Nol's government and the entry of the Khmer Rouge into the capital, Phnom Penh in April 1975 and ended in January 1979. On entering Phnom Penh, the Khmer Rouge forced the city's population to migrate to the countryside to work on the land. Similar forced evacuations occurred in other towns too. Deaths, of the young, the old and the infirm, were natural consequences of both the long-distance migrations and the hard physical work.

Estimates put on the number of people who died between 17 April 1975 and April 1976 have been between 80,000 – 1,000,000 (Keesing's 1976: 27758), out of a population of only 7.7 million. Vickery (1985: 184–8) estimates the decrease in population between April 1975 and January 1979 to have been 400,000, some of which would have been accounted for by a decrease in the birth rate and others by the war. He argues that it is impossible to know the number of deaths through execution. This is in line with Chomsky and Herman's (1976: ch 6) objections to the misuse of unsubstantiated statistics for the estimation of deaths in Cambodia. Vickery's careful and cautious estimate is made partly in reaction to Barron and Paul's (1977) earlier estimate, which was severely criticized by Chomsky and Herman for its exaggeration. Barron and Paul (p. 206) have argued 1,200,000 to have been the minimum number of deaths between 17 April 1975 and 1 January 1979 as a direct result of government policies. Ponchaud (1978: 92), also criticized by Chomsky and Herman, reported figures of 800,000–

1,400,000. Deaths on this scale, as a proportion of the population even on the lowest estimate of 80,000, go way beyond anything encountered in the following chapters. The highest estimate is above even the most widely exaggerated émigré figures given for the cases of revolutionary reigns of terror.

This case is critical both because it has been described as a revolution (Vickery 1984, Ponchaud 1978) and because the prelude to 'year zero' involved both a civil war and a guerrilla movement, two factors here given special significance in explaining the potential absence of a revolutionary reign of terror. It is fair to point out that in respect of both its civil war and the success of the guerrillas this was an exceptional interlude which differs from the other examples in this study.[5] The civil war took place within a society torn apart by foreign war, the Vietnam War. That war followed a *coup d'état* in 1970 when Prince Sihanouk's government was overthrown and which brought to power a government, under General Lon Nol, more acceptable to the USA. The guerrilla forces which had first appeared in Cambodia in 1946 in the fight for independence from the French had re-emerged in 1958 in a somewhat different guise and had challenged Sihanouk at various times until, in 1967, following a peasant revolt, the new Khmer Rouge had grown to sufficient strength for the 1967 revolt to spread in 1968 to 11 of the 19 provinces in Cambodia (Keesing's 1975: 27154).

Following the 1970 coup, however, Sihanoukist forces joined with the Khmer Rouge to form the National United Front of Cambodia (NUFC) to bring down the Lon Nol government. A government in exile, headed by Prince Sihanouk with a Sihanoukist prime minister, had been set up in Beijing. Khieu Samphan, who was the deputy prime minister and minister of defence in the government in exile and a member of the Khmer Rouge, returned to Cambodia along with the other two Khmer ministers to continue active engagement in the fight. As Sihanouk remarked himself, 'This war is not a civil war, but a war of aggression and colonisation against Cambodia by the United States' (Keesing's 1975: 27149). Whilst the NUFC was supplied by the Vietcong, the Republican Army was supplied by the USA. US air raids ended officially in 1973 but the US continued to play a crucial role in supplying arms and equipment to the republican areas. In June 1974, for example, the US Defense Secretary stated that 690 missions to parachute ammunition and provisions were being carried out each month (ibid). US aircraft also continued flying missions from Thailand.

Between 1970–5 the Khmer Rouge came to dominate the Sihanoukist forces (Keesing's 1975: 27149–54). The establishment of a functioning partial 'government in exile' within Cambodia, in which Khmer Rouge representatives dominated, played an important part in this. Whilst the combined Sihanoukist and Khmer Rouge forces, the NUFC, defeated Lon Nol, it was the Khmer Rouge which in April 1975 took the victory.[6] Pol Pot came to rule over 'Democratic Kampuchea' as prime minister, with Khieu Samphan as president, in April 1976 after a general election was held under a new constitution. There is no denying that the Khmer Rouge brought fundamental change. City populations were forced to migrate to the countryside to work on the land. The sheer scale of deaths wrought inevitably brought dramatic changes. Strictly, though, the defeat of Pol Pot at the hands of the Vietnamese army in early 1979 made it a failed revolution.

Vickery (1985: 253–81), whilst viewing it as a revolution, has argued convincingly that whatever it chose to call itself this was not a 'Marxist communist' regime, as it had no parallel with any communist revolution which had ever previously occurred, either in Asia or in Europe. He also argued that, contrary to claims (see Ponchaud, ch.9), the policies of Democratic Kampuchea under Pol Pot were the reverse of the Chinese Cultural Revolution (ibid: pp. 271–3). In all other cases of communist revolutions the cities, urban workers and technology have been crucial, but in Cambodia they were not. In Cambodia the cities and towns were emptied, and agricultural improvements were made not through improvements in technology but by concentrating all labour on the land (ibid: p. 280). In drawing particular comparison with China he contrasts the importance of workers and soldiers in the Chinese Cultural Revolution and the critical nature of the relationship between rural areas and the cities where workers held power. Commenting on the mobilization against existing organizations in China, Vickery (p. 272) remarks that, 'nothing like this outburst of student and worker rage against bureaucracy and party ever occurred in Cambodia, where the party directed the poorest peasants against everyone else and where students and urban workers were class enemies'.

In seeking a classification for the nature of Pol Pot's regime, he draws first on the vision of Utopia offered by Thomas More. Not surprisingly, given that in More's vision there is missing that very ingredient of terror so clearly present in Democratic Kampuchea, he turns to Bakunin's Anarchist Programme of total transformation and then draws specific parallels with the 'utopianism and violence 'which he finds in Spanish anarchism in the civil war of 1936–9 and the Russian anarchist movements in combination with peasant 'populism' between 1891–1917 (ibid: 281–3). These 'poor peasant excesses', too, he argues characterize the Cambodian Revolution, it was a 'peasantist revolution' (ibid: 287).

Moore (1969: 420) has argued, however, that peasants are attracted not only to reaction but also to communism, and the modernization route which countries take depends on the strength of other social classes and the alignments which develop between them. Wolf (1973) too, through comparison of roles played by the peasantry in twentieth-century revolutionary wars, has drawn attention to the wider social forces which affect peasant movements, such as economic changes, the relationship between town and country and the part played by armies and communist parties. Vickery's comparisons with other violent poor peasant movements clearly represent only a superficial analysis of Democratic Kampuchea and, in drawing parallels with populist and anarchist movements in other than revolutionary situations, in any case beg his claim for classification of Cambodia as a revolution.

In drawing comparisons with anarchist and populist peasant movements, Vickery ignores an aspect of the zero years given emphasis elsewhere, *Angka Loeu*. *Angka Loeu*, ('Higher Organization', but better translated as 'Organization on High' (Barron and Paul 1977: 12) was offered as explanation for coercive orders from day one, 17 April 1975. The organization on high was given as justification to commandeer vehicles, to order people out of hospitals, or later to order people to their death: '*Angka Loeu* wants to re-educate you' (a euphemism for the death sentence) (p.12). As Barron and Paul (1975: 40) explain:

> The Organisation on High was not interested in merely improving or even radically modifying existing Cambodian society. Rather *Angka Loeu* was determined to shatter it to bits and start completely anew. For *Angka Loeu* had resolved to annul the past and obliterate the present so as to fashion a future uncontaminated by the influences of either.

The purpose of this according to Barron and Paul (1975: 41) was to reduce the population to 'one disoriented, malleable mass'. Justification, they report, was offered by officers in terms of *Angka Loeu*'s goal being the ideal communist classless society of genuine equality. Ponchaud (1978: 107), too, draws attention to the significance of the choice of 'organization' over 'party'. '*Angkar*', as Ponchaud prefers, is the object of adoration which organized everything. It is a 'deity',

'the anonymous *Angkar* is the incarnation of the people's will' (ibid:
127). Barron and Paul (1977: 59–60) quote from a report made by
Kenneth M. Quinn in 1974 on the actions taken in the areas occupied
by the Khmer Rouge 'to psychologically reconstruct individual members
of society':

> this process entails stripping away, through terror and other means, the
> traditional bases, structures and forces which have shaped and guided an
> individual's life until he is left as an atomised isolated individual unit: and
> then rebuilding him according to party doctrine by substituting a series of
> new values, organisations and ethical norms for the ones taken away.

As Barron and Paul point out this process was not original to *Angka
Loeu*.[7] They draw comparisons both with Aristotle's analyses of tyranny and with the history of the Soviet Union. Crucially they add 'and
other totalitarian states'. The analogy is then as close to Nazi Germany
as to Stalin's Russia.

Chomsky and Herman have taken great objection to the comparison
of Cambodia with Nazi Germany (1979: 149). They have also questioned the assertion that Cambodia was ruled by *Angka Loeu*, what they
term 'nine men at the centre', without intermediary groups between
the centre and the village-level organizations (ibid: 152). In addition to
the central themes of their book concerning the mis-use and falsifica-
tion of evidence and the failure to keep a proper balance with events
going on elsewhere of similar (sometimes greater) horror, Chomsky
and Herman have made two objections to the view of Cambodia as a
central organization over a mass society: they argue that the accusers
have failed to consider the question of why the people allowed the
organization to take over the country (ibid: 159), 'the standard media
picture: a centrally-controlled genocidal policy of mass execution';
and that commentators have failed to produce a balanced account of
blame for the horrors that occurred in Cambodia.

They argue that the peasantry willingly gave their support to the
regime. 'Evidence suggesting popular support for the regime among
certain strata – particularly the poorer peasants – was ignored or dismissed with revulsion and contempt' (ibid: xi). They argue also that
before the fall of Phnom Penh the war had devastated the country.
Millions of people had left the countryside to escape both the indiscriminate bombing and the starvation which threatened, as a consequence of the destruction of agriculture in the war regions. Linking

these two points, they refer to comments made by Richard Dudman, a US war correspondent captured after the fall of Phnom Penh:

> the constant indiscriminate bombing, an estimated 450,000 dead and wounded civilians to say nothing of military casualties, and the estimated 4,000,000 refugees were almost inevitable results of the short US invasion of Cambodia and the consequent proxy war that ended in defeat for the United States as well as for its client regime in Phnom Penh. (Quoted Chomsky and Herman 1979: 165)

Chomsky and Herman put additional emphasis on the war consequences of these peasant dislocations and devastated agricultural production. The Khmer Rouge had to get the peasants back into the countryside in order to feed the population which otherwise would surely starve. In that light the Khmer Rouge probably saved lives in forcibly moving people out of the towns into the countryside, though they accept that the forced evacuation was 'heavy handed' (ibid: 167).

Certainly the evidence lends support to Chomsky and Herman's stand for balancing exaggerated accounts and mis-apportioned blame. Rice production achieved in November 1975 was reported as exceptionally high, yielding double that needed to feed the population for the year. Lack of transport was given to justify the forced evacuation from the cities, faced otherwise with starvation (Keesing's 1976: 27758). At the same time, however, their two arguments concerning the devastation of society brought by war and the positive support given to the regime by the peasants add to rather than detract from a totalitarian view of Cambodia 1975–9.

For Arendt (1958: chs 10–11), in her detailed analysis of the phenomenon of Nazi Germany, Hitler's totalitarian regime arose out of a mass society, where 'the artificial creation of civil war conditions' (p. 373) had played a part in its development. Crucially, too, for Arendt, popular support and totalitarianism are not incompatible. On the contrary, they are closely intertwined. The very absence of intervening political organizations between the masses and the central state, in conditions of atomization brought by the devastation of society and the consequent destruction of traditional ties, attached the atomized individual directly to the state through the development of a totalitarian movement. There is then no inherent incompatibility in the state actually producing improvements for the masses, support being genuinely given by sections of society, and the state being described as totalitarian. It is the directness of that attachment to the state which is crucial.

The movement towards the domination of *Angka Loeu*, the Organization on High, arose then out of the decimation of society by the war which followed the installation of Lon Nol's government. Vickery (1985: 25) estimates the deaths incurred during that war at between 500,000–1 million. It has been estimated that between March and August 1973 alone 40,000 tons of bombs fell every month (Ponchaud 1978: 191). Bombing and fighting combined to destroy crops, forests, transport systems and factories and led to massive movements of people out of the rural areas into the towns and cities. An estimated 3 million people, mostly refugees from the fighting zones had moved into the towns, the majority of them into the capital Phnom Penh. Of these most were living in the areas controlled by Lon Nol and had been subsisting on rice supplied by the United States (Keesing's 1976: 27758). Thus the basis of a mass society without social ties already existed before April 1975.

Democratic Kampuchea, though it had a mass society ruled over by the Organization on High lacked what Arendt emphasized as the epitome of a totalitarian society, the concentration camp. Democratic Kampuchea never developed a proper secret police force and system of courts either. Perhaps, it did not last long enough to develop fully into a totalitarian regime but at the same time, though the regime with its twentieth-century trappings of war had artillery and radios (especially useful for propaganda) it was not a modern industrialized society such as Nazi Germany and Stalinist Russia had been.[8] Cambodia was a peasant-dominated agricultural society. This does not square with Arendt's view of totalitarianism as a modern phenomenon. Neither does it square with Friedrich and Brzezinski's emphasis that totalitarianism is a new phenomenon of technological society.[9]

Terror in Democratic Kampuchea was perpetrated not through the sophisticated organs of a fully-fledged totalitarian state, but through the army. The army was divided into three sections: the 'regular' army which was used to put down uprisings and protect borders; the 're-gional' troops, which were responsible for security and worked alongside the local political organization, usually itself appointed by *Angka Loeu*; and the 'spy troops' who were unarmed and acted as informers (Ponchaud 1978: 122–3). In essence Ponchaud argues, it was a 'military society' (ibid: 127).

THE PROTO-TOTALITARIAN STATE

In view of the backward nature of the country and the importance of the army, Democratic Kampuchea cannot be properly labelled as a totalitarian regime. There is however a classification which suits it well, the proto-totalitarian system which is the term Walter (1972) applies to the Zulu state under Shaka, 1816–28 and Dingane, 1828–40. 'Without gas chambers, machine guns, or a guillotine, Shaka managed to establish one of the most effective regimes of terror on record' (ibid: 110). His study of Shaka's regime is especially pertinent to the case of Cambodia. Walter continues; 'his regime proves that a system of terror depends not on the instruments of violence, but on the techniques of social control'. The instruments of violence were the Zulu warriors, armed with modified spears, but control came not from the spears themselves. At a flick of Shaka's finger a person could be taken from a peaceful gathering and executed there and then. Violence was not used in irrational anger but as a part of a deliberate policy. For example, massacres when carried out were always total, no child or woman was ever left alive, for they might later produce more children who could later become enemies (ibid: 141). This system of terror achieved total reach and total submission to the state, indeed the state was perceived as being bound together by the process of terror itself (ibid: 177). Terror under Shaka was used as a deliberate means to maintain control, both within the Zulu state and outside. Walter (ibid: 249) describes the state as a 'vast predatory organism directed by a single will' in which 'there was no place for conventional resistance, opposition, or even different identities'.

Nationalism formed a crucial aspect of Shaka's terror just as it had in Hitler's Germany. In Cambodia, too, nationalism, in the form of an anti-Vietnamese campaign, also played an important part. Antipathy to the Vietnamese has been described as 'the Khmer's ancient hatred' (Ponchaud 1978: 188). Like Hitler, Pol Pot was defeated at the hands of a foreign intervention. Communism, whence-so-ever its inspiration, played its part and as such Cambodia shared indeed as much in common with Nazi Germany as with Stalin's Russia. Whether used in the name of nationalism, Communism, populism or anarchism, terror, following Arendt, not just threatened but actually used and in excess, is the essence of both the totalitarian and the proto-totalitarian regime alike, a terror which destroys all attachments, whatever they be (family, village, class, tribe) and creates allegiance totally and directly to the state. The revolutionary reign of terror never reached so far into society, with all forces of opposition and anarchy totally suppressed.

NOTES

1.   There is dispute over the level of control the government has during revolutionary reigns of terror (see Chapter 3). Brinton (1965) is sympathetic with this view. It is a pity that Wilkinson (1974: 50) intent on pursuing his view that 'the idea of a policy of revolutionary terror originated with the Jacobins', fails to draw from his discussion the importance of the arbitrariness inherent in the Law of Suspects (September 1793), in the roles of the Parisian Revolutionary Army and the Representatives on Mission, and in the nature of the executions which took place at Lyon. His whole account attests to the Terror being out of central control. A similar problem arises with Talmon (1955) who, in emphasizing the importance of Jacobin ideology, argues that the Jacobin dictatorship was the first totalitarian democracy. Both because Talmon concentrates the overwhelming proportion of his book on the French case and because his account has serious historical inexactitudes his work is discussed in Chapter 4 but is not included in the general discussion of totalitarianism presented here. Both Arendt (1958) and Friedrich and Brzezinski (1965) argue strongly for totalitarianism being a new phenomenon and as such are at issue with Talmon.

2.   The ideology which is 'elaborate' and 'official' is total in its intention to cover all aspects of each individual's life, in its pursuit of a completely new society, perceived as a perfect state of existence, and in its aim to take over the world. The remaining five characteristics are: 2) a single mass party usually led by a dictator with the party run on bureaucratic lines either over a state bureaucracy or integrated with it; 3) a 'system of terror', physical, mental or both, through a secret police under party control; 4) a monopoly of communications; 5) an approximate monopoly of arms; 6) central bureaucratic control over the economy, previously run on the basis of independent corporations. Under 3, 4 and 5 Friedrich and Brzezinski emphasize that modern technology is essential. 'Modern science' is required in order to be 'exploited' by the terror machine and 'modern technology' is stressed in both communications and arms.

3.   This is why the definition of political terrorism offered by O'Sullivan (1986: 5), which requires ideological objectives and the threat or use of violence to go together, presents problems for state terrors. States can always make pretence at an ideology for justifying the use of violence – democracy (an end to all these insurgents disturbing things then we could have peaceful elections), nationalism (an end to all those foreigners and ethnic minorities who are useful scapegoats to take people's minds off the economic problems), communism (an end to all those people who will not do what they are ordered – they are preventing everyone else getting the fruits of transformation) and so on.

4.   See Gregor (1982: 161) who has argued that, in contrast with Nazi Germany and Stalin's Soviet Union, fascist rule in Mussolini's Italy did not constitute an 'institutionalised terror'. Amongst the reasons he gives is that though the tribunal in Italy 'clearly violated the procedural rules of justice prevalent in liberal democracy', people were often found innocent. He uses Arendt in his support, too, for excluding Italy from classification as a totalitarian state (Arendt 1958: 303 n. 8).

5. In fact the guerrilla movements in Cambodia contrast starkly with the movements in China, Cuba and Nicaragua for lacking a humanitarian emphasis. (See discussion in Vickery 1985: ch.1.) Being caught up in war between 1970–5 can help, in part, to explain this, though Mao's forces, in their battles against the Japanese, had a similar excuse but were not so brutalized.

6. Prince Sihanouk himself was to return to power temporarily (for a few months only) after the victory. He expressed his position on 14 April 1975: 'After victory I will be head of state and there will be an entirely communist government and administration. So either I am a puppet of the Khmer Rouge, or I remain independent and there will be trouble' (Keesing's 1975: 27154).

7. Vickery (1985: 271) seems to misconstrue Barron and Paul's argument. On my reading they do not argue that the zero years were similar to Mao's cultural revolution.

8. This radio system was used regularly to extol the virtues and achievements of *Angkar Loeu* (Ponchaud 1978: 107–8).

9. See 2 above.

3. Reigns of Terror and the Lessons of Comparative History

The classic social science works on the causes of revolutionary reigns of terror are Edwards, *The Natural History of Revolution*, first published in 1927 and Brinton, *The Anatomy of Revolution*, first published in 1938. Both view revolutionary terrors as inevitable stages of revolution. Both delineate them as the 'extreme' (Brinton) or 'radical' (Edwards) stage of revolution which follows the rule of the 'moderates'. The stages of revolution are extracted by both theorists from comparisons drawn from the same four cases: France, Russia, England (Puritan) and America (War of Independence). Essentially they perform exactly what the titles of their books imply, an examination of the necessary component parts of the four revolutions. Drawing generalizations common only to their four selected cases, their propositions stop short of a general theory of revolution. For this they have been criticized (see Skocpol 1979: 37–40). The detail in which the cases are examined, in the case of Brinton most especially, also leaves much to be desired. Nevertheless, they serve together as a stimulating basis for hypotheses on Terrors. In this they stand above all other social science theories, which remain oddly lacking in focus on revolutionary state terror, being concerned rather with the initial revolutionary overthrow and therefore with insurgent violence. Skocpol, *States and Social Revolutions,* has revived the recent literature with her concentration on revolutionary state-building. Whilst not explicitly concerned with reigns of terror, her attention is inevitably drawn to the periods of the Jacobin Dictatorship and the early years of Bolshevik and Chinese Communist rule. Whilst challenging to Brinton and Edwards in emphasis, in broad terms there proves to be an important basis of agreement between these theories.

EDWARDS VERSUS BRINTON: FEAR AND CENTRAL CONTROL

Neither Edwards nor Brinton offers neat definitions of Terrors. Beyond agreeing that it is the rule of the 'extremists' or 'radicals' which follows moderate rule, the two theorists are in sharp disagreement. Edwards is in line with modern writers on terrcrism in emphasizing the importance of fear and follows Kropotkin's line that a reign of terror is essentially a system of government which deliberately uses terror for 'social control': 'It is a reign not an anarchy' (Edwards 1979: 175). The aim is to control society through fear: 'The most important mechanism of a terror is not the killing of people, but the threatening of them' (p.176). In line with Kropotkin, too, Edwards believes that through this expeditious use of violence and the calculated fear which is produced throughout the population, the reign of terror actually saves lives.

> Death and destruction may be necessary to produce the terror, but they are purely incidental. They are the nature of stage technique employed only in so far as is requisite for the required effect. A terror is a scheme for scaring people. (Edwards 1970: 176)

Edwards is quite clear too that it is in the main the noblemen who are executed, plus a few 'clerks and farm hands' who are 'sent to the guillotine along with the marquises and the millionaires in order not to snub the plebeians and in order to convince them that they are in the same danger as the wealthy and the powerful' (Edwards 1970: 177). He offers evidence for this view of revolutionary terrors as a 'scheme for scaring people' which saves lives: Cromwell's two massacres in Ireland which decisively halted further fruitless deaths in war; the clever use of tar and feathering in America; in Russia the printing of the names of the executed in newspapers scared people into submission; and for France the stage-managing of the destruction of Lyon which prevented the outbreak of rebellion elsewhere: 'If it be calculated that the terror did no more than prevent one other revolt such as the Vendée, it saved twenty-five lives for every one it cost' (ibid: 181). This evidence will be challenged in the following chapters, but even if accepted as fact the argument remains open to dispute.

The proposition that Terrors save lives is probably inherently unprovable because of the absence of the counterfactual evidence, but in any case the claim that these Terrors did not produce in reality the loss of life that exaggeration has led us to believe, that far more lives could have been lost and that rumour was rife as some printed documents have recorded does not amount to proof that the reign of terror deliberately engineered that rumour. It cannot prove that had such decisive action not been taken or such rumours not been spread that events would have been substantially altered. After all, news of success in foreign wars would conceivably rally support from some quarters and quieten criticism and reduce actual opposition in others. The bombing of Dresden and the attack on Stalingrad during the Second World War have drawn a contradictory lesson, that direct attacks on citizens lead not to quiescence but renewed vigour for attack. That the tales of Lyon's destruction quelled likely rebellions elsewhere needs proof and alternative explanations compatible with such evidence need to be dispelled, explanations which perhaps draw attention to successes over rebels elsewhere. The superiority of Cromwell's New Model Army might straightforwardly have led the Irish to flee the battlefields. Knowledge of near certain failure usually plays a key role in the decision not to make the attempt. Again, real support, and not only calculated risks of failure in opposition, must also play a part. Edwards ascribes the mildness of the reigns of terror in both England and America to the judicious use of terror, a rather circular proposition in any case. Opposition within France and Russia could simply have been greater from the start.

In fact, Edwards has no need of his argument that in reigns of terror the radicals deliberately engineer fear for the purposes of social control. If rumour abounds, which is reasonable in uncertain times, and those in power manage to turn it to their advantage, then it would be fair to count that achievement as evidence of their capacity to rule. Such practical determination in the taking of decisive action combined crucially with proven capability to succeed (that is, win the battle, put down the riot) constitute straightforward evidence of competence. That those in power took action deliberately to create a condition of fear is superfluous to the point, and because it is impossible to prove on the basis of circumstantial evidence the argument weakens, not strengthens, the case.

Brinton (1965) rejects this view of Terrors as decisive reigns, calculating in their use of terror and effective in social control through fear. For him, they are 'extemporized dictatorships' (ibid: 172). His emphasis is not on fear, but on the mechanisms of dictatorship and the capacity of the extremists to oust opposition from government institutions and so gain complete control over key organizations. Though Brinton em-

phasizes leadership, 'reigns of terror and virtue' are essentially characterized by committee dictatorship. It is a 'rough-and-ready centralization' (ibid: 171). At the top rests a committee of the 'talkative legislative
body' (Rump, Convention, All-Russian Congress of Soviets) – Army
Council or Council of State, Committee of Public Safety, Central
Executive Committee of the All-Russian Congress of Soviets – below
which is an 'extemporized', freshly recruited, bureaucracy, newly appointed law courts, supplementary organizations ('extraordinary courts
and revolutionary tribunals') and last but not least a secret police (the
New Independent parish clergy, plus ad hoc army committees, the
Cheka, the Committee of General Security and the Revolutionary
Committees). In spite of, perhaps because of all these organizations,
Brinton points out that these reigns of terror were inefficient compared
with, for example, Napoleon's France and Brezhnev's Russia:

> Indeed one of the reasons why the governments of Terror seem so tyrannical
> and hard to bear, even retrospectively, is precisely that they were so
> inefficient. They got their big tasks done – saved England, France and
> Russia from dissolution or conquest, but they did it very messily and, in
> detail, very badly ... Nothing is more illuminating in the study of these
> revolutions than the study of local history. Here you see the Terror as it
> really was, no steady and efficient rule from above, as in the army or in
> Sparta, but a state of suspense and fear, a dissolution of the sober little
> uniformities of provincial life. (Brinton 1965: 173)

He comments further on the special inefficiencies of these governments in the success of their economic policies giving as examples the
frequent infringements of the maximum price legislation in the French
Revolution and the development of black markets developed in Russia. In avoiding emphasis on fear and concentrating on the machinery
of Terror, whilst Brinton potentially offers a view of revolutionary
Terror suitable for objective study, in practice such a view proves
lacking for his own devices. He admits that the American case does
not fit (Brinton 1965: 176) and, indeed, America is quietly dropped in
elaboration of several of the 'uniformities' which he offers. Brinton is
not entirely successful in avoiding tautology for in preferring the term
'reign of terror and virtue' part of his explanation for a Terror is bound
up with the definition. This virtue comes from the revolutionaries'
'rigidly deterministic faiths' which do not permit opposition (non-
believers) (ibid: 190–4). Unfortunately, Brinton also includes this 'faith'
as his seventh cause of Terrors (ibid: 202).

THE CAUSES OF TERRORS: NECESSITY IN CRISIS

Edwards views reigns of terror as necessary for two reasons. Radical regimes are needed in order to overcome the problems faced in all revolutions which inevitably build to a crisis:

> When the radicals obtain supreme power they have three main difficulties to face. These difficulties are foreign invasion, domestic insurrection, and their own inexperience in government. (Edwards 1970: 156)

Edwards' second reason for viewing reigns of terror as necessary is a psychological argument:

> The terror furnishes a necessary avenue of release to the overwrought nerves of people in extreme danger. It is at the same time the revenge of a social class for what it regards as a social injustice long endured submissively and in silence. It is the eruption of the volcano. (ibid: 184)

In essence Edwards offers three correlates with reigns of terror – foreign invasion, domestic insurrection and inexperience of office – and two speculative causes, or reasons, for them: aggression resulting from extreme stress and class conflict arising from social injustice. The latter two propositions foreshadow the frustration–aggression theories of both Gurr (1972) and Davies (1962) and Fanon's (1969) Marxist-inspired theory. Edwards (1970: 186) adds, 'a revolutionary terror cannot originate except in a society where popular feeling is wrought up to the highest degree of intensity'. These psychological aspects, furthermore, are given emphasis in explaining how and why reigns of terror come to an end. The end of the reign is due to 'emotional fatigue'. The continuing practical economic problems – the expense of war, the 'paralysis of trade and commerce' and the inexperience of political officials in financial affairs – contribute to the exhaustion of the regime.

Whilst reigns of terror end in mental and physical exhaustion, according to Edwards, they begin with energy as the moderates, too cautious to cope with the crisis situation, are replaced by the radicals, characterized by 'courage, boldness, determination, an absolute faith in the righteousness of their cause and in their own ability to govern' (Edwards 1970: 157). Their enthusiasm draws support, their decisiveness successfully establishes the revolution. Just as the Methodist minister threatens hell-fire and damnation, whipping up emotions, so too,

Edwards argues, the reign of terror exploits and uses stress-induced emotions to produce a catharsis. Only the radicals have the vision and capacity to do this. Without the reign of terror chaos would prevail; without the bold radicals the success of the revolution would ebb away.

To some extent, of course, these views are evocative rather than scientific. The proof of the boldness, ability and determination of the radical leaders is demonstrated tautologically by the fact that they held power at the crucial hour. Edwards' (1970: 157) example of Cromwell replacing Charles I does not represent unquestionable proof of Cromwell's superior ability. At his end Charles I showed tremendous courage. Defined in a non-circular way, perhaps in terms of military prowess, the argument could be made persuasive, though less readily generalized. Similarly the assertion that Marat, Danton, Mirabeau and Robespierre were 'the ablest rulers France had had for many genera-tions' (ibid: 157) is pure speculation. Able ministers such as Necker spring to mind as possible challengers to the generalization. In the light of Miliukov's recent rehabilitation in the Soviet Union, the clear superiority of the Bolsheviks, Trotsky, Stalin and Dzerzhinsky, over the moderates of February–October 1917, Lvov, Miliukov and Kerensky, and the last cabinet of the Tsar can surely be challenged. The specific claim for the superiority of Stalin over Kerensky, for example, would provoke anyone to demand to know on what grounds, and the different grounds would not always produce the same winner. Stolypin like Necker must be complimented too.

In respect of the psychological aspects of Edwards' argument, sup-port is derived from reasoning rather than hard evidence. Lying behind the outburst he discusses the 'economic incentive' which derives from repression and poverty and the development of the 'social myth', that is a kind of religious faith in an ideal future – 'a new heaven on earth' (Edwards 1970: 91) – which asserts both the capacity and right to replace the old regime and to rule in its place (ibid: Chapter 5). As Edwards admits himself such notions are not capable of proof. In fairness though, they are reasonable claims, supported by the consid-eration that people will not risk life, limb and peace of mind to over-throw governments with which they are satisfied. Nevertheless, psy-chological evidence is required for such arguments. Contrary conclu-sions can be drawn from history. The Warsaw Ghetto uprising against the Nazis has demonstrated that if the state military machine is strong then however deeply felt the injustice and however salient the social myth the uprising will be pointless (Moore 1972: 28–9). Without a Marxist-type analysis linking economic and political power the 'economic incentive' would not without further explanation lead logically to a political reaction.

In respect of the 'three difficulties' to be faced by radicals, however, more substance is given by examples. Firstly, foreign invasion: in respect of the Puritan Revolution, Edwards points to the Irish and Scots rallied by the beheaded King's son for invasion of England; for the American Revolution he draws attention to the British government's use of German troops and Red Indians against the revolutionary army; in the French Revolution he emphasizes that France was at war with England, Holland, Prussia, Austria, Spain and Sardinia; for the Russian Revolution the invasions of the American, English, French and Japanese armies are given.

Edwards' argument is two-pronged: foreign invasions rally the people to the revolutionary government's support; at the same time, the need to react to those invasions necessitates that the government transform itself from a legislative body to a war-machine, with full command for the making of quick decisions and the taking of authoritative actions. Command over the army in the face of the enemy brings not only the mechanism for command of people and necessary justification, it also generates patriotism which brings support from the people. As in wartime democracies suspend elections without question, so too in wartime revolutionary governments are bolstered by patriotism which, in combination with the revolutionary 'social myth', proves 'intoxicating' (Edwards 1970: 162).

The second difficulty of 'internal insurrection', Edwards also finds in his four revolutions. Whilst he believes that as a whole the people support the radicals (which he must do in order to be consistent with his claim that patriotism rallies support to them) he argues that the defeated 'conservatives and moderate reformers':

> smarting under their defeat and humiliation and desperately bent upon regaining their former positions of wealth and power by any means whatsoever ... normally arrange to have foreign armies conquer their country, but also organise armed insurrection against the radical government, generally sinking their differences for this purpose. (Edwards 1980: 170–1)

Civil war is not then seen as a spontaneous uprising against the radicals but as a response by those ousted from power whose vested interests, political, social and economic, must be defended by the defeat of the current revolutionary leaders. In essence these internal insurrections represent a form of class conflict, the battle for power between groups representing mutually exclusive economic and status interests.

The evidence mentioned for the English Revolution is that of the Royalist uprising led by the Earl of Derby and the plotted Presbyterian uprising. For the American Revolution, Royalist uprisings are accused of prolonging the war against British forces because of the need to divert troops to deal with them. For the French Revolution, the Vendée is mentioned as the worst of the insurrections, and revolts in Marseilles, Lyon and Toulon are cited. In respect of the Russian Revolution, Edwards argues that communication between the foreign enemies and domestic insurrection made the former especially serious. Four civil wars are picked out as having been started by Tsarist and moderate factions, headed in turn by Kolchak, Dennikin, Yudenich and Wrangel (Edwards 1970: 172). Without that foreign support, Edwards believes these affairs would have been neither so bloody nor so destructive.

Inexperience in government is the third difficulty which Edwards lists, 'troublesome' rather than 'serious' by comparison with the other two. The problem is essentially that the public officials of the old order are unwilling to work for the new revolutionary government, some of them do not simply resign but go on strike, engage in sabotage, and even betray the government to its enemies both at home and abroad. The consequence is economic mismanagement and the growing threat of counter-revolution. The decisiveness of the radicals, Edwards argues, offers the means for bringing the officials to order – some dismissals without pensions, some demotions (if necessary a few executions) are enough – but the problem then lies in not having adequately trained personnel in sufficient numbers to replace the offending officials. Only one supporting example is given, that of an occasion when Trotsky broke a strike of officials in the War Department by giving them notice. Edwards emphasizes that the significance of this inexperience in office is its combination with civil and foreign wars:

> The finances are in desperate shape. Public feeling is strained to the highest point of tension. Some avenue of release for all this accumulated nervousness must be provided. The avenue of release is the reign of terror. (Edwards 1970: 174)

Leaving the empirical evidence to one side to consider in depth in the case studies, there are logical worries about the substantive claims of the general importance of foreign invasion, domestic insurrection and the newness of the revolutionary government. Logically, if at least one of these conditions had not been present in any one of the four revolutions studied, then presumably Edwards' view would be that a reign of terror would not have occurred. There is the practical difficulty that these variables are inter-related but, in any case, Edwards' emphasis on the psychological nature of reigns of terror suggests that pent-up emotions, brought on by the crisis of revolution, would need to find expression in some form of violent outburst. It surely follows that even if one of these difficulties were not present a new revolutionary government would still be obliged to gain control over the remaining problems including those pent-up emotions. If those problems were of sufficient severity, it would seem reasonable to suppose that some coercive measures on the part of the regime would be necessary and would be likely to approximate to Edwards' classification of a revolutionary reign of terror.

Two interesting questions follow which Edwards does not address: could a reign of terror occur in the absence of one, perhaps two, of these difficulties if, say, either the remaining difficulty (or difficulties) were especially grave or some additional problem arose which the government had to tackle? Second, to what extent would the harshness of the reign of terror be associated with the severity of the conditions faced or the policy choices available to the revolutionaries? As a corollary to this, a further question could be asked – might not the revolutionaries' policies themselves add to (or even cause) the crisis situation?

BRINTON: A RE-WORKING OF EDWARDS

It is not surprising that Brinton should, in 1938 when his book was first published, have taken Edwards' explanation for Terrors so to heart, nor that he should have continued to do so in the revised editions, the last in 1965. What is surprising is that he should have added so little. Worryingly, Brinton offers rather less evidence than does Edwards, whose evidence is in any case generally too brief. Following his search for uniformities between the four revolutions, Brinton proposes a seven-part explanation for their 'reigns of terror and virtue'. Crucially, he argues that all seven causes must be present for a reign of terror to occur: the habit of violence; the pressure of a foreign and civil war; the newness of the machinery of government; acute economic crisis; class struggles; extremist leaders; and, 'religious faith' (Brinton 1965: 198–202). All resemble arguments made by Edwards.

'The habit of violence' turns out to refer to the fact that reigns of terror follow earlier outbreaks of violence. Brinton speaks of a 'mood' for violence and gives the examples of the reign of terror in France, which did not start properly until late 1793 but which had been preceded by the Great Fear of 1789 and the September massacres of 1792, and the Terror in Russia which he says did not begin fully until Autumn 1918 but which had been preceded by incidents from February 1917 onwards. Brinton's point is similar to Edwards' argument that 'a revolutionary terror cannot originate except in a society where popular feeling is wrought up to the highest degree of intensity' (Edwards 1970: 186).

Brinton's second variable restates Edwards' central claims about foreign wars and domestic insurrection. It is notable that Brinton refers to the pressure of a foreign and civil war as 'a most important variable'. He groups civil and foreign wars as one variable because he stresses the 'widespread excitement' ('the war psychosis'), which wars of either kind bring and which requires centralization if that crisis is to be overcome: 'War necessities help explain the rapid centralisation of the government of the Terror, the hostility to dissenters within the group – they now seem deserters (Brinton 1970: 199).

The third variable, the newness of the machinery of government again repeats Edwards' argument about 'inexperience in office', though in reflection of their contrasting views over the level of control possessed by the regimes Brinton adds to Edwards' unwilling old administrators the problem of inexperienced new administrators. The fifth and sixth causes are likewise to be found in Edwards' work. 'Class struggles' turns out to be a re-description of civil war enemies, 'the hatred of Puritan for Cavalier, of Jacobin for aristocrats, Federalists and other enemies of the Republic of Virtue, the hatred of Bolsheviks for Whites, Kadets and compromisists, of American Whigs for Tories' (Brinton 1965: 201). The sixth variable, the manipulative extremist revolutionary leaders, restates Edwards' emphasis on leadership in spite of the potential conflict with Brinton's view of Terrors as committee rule.

The seventh factor, 'religious faith' (which explains his preference for the description 'reigns of terror and virtue') is similar to Edwards' 'social myth' in combination with his analogy with a Methodist meeting. Brinton goes beyond Edwards, though, in emphasizing the 'Messianic' aspects of reigns of terror. Brinton's stress is less on the psychological impact than on the nature of the message itself, the promise of an ideal future society, a message to be spread abroad by the chosen people (Brinton 1965: 196):

> Calvinism, Jacobinism, Marxism are all rigidly deterministic. All believe that what happens here below is foreordained, predestined to follow a course which no mere human being can alter, least of all those who oppose respectively Calvinism, Jacobinism or Marxism. (ibid: 191)

Talmon (1955), drawing from the French case and making reference to Russia, has argued that both Jacobinism and Marxism-Leninism led inevitably to Terror because of their totalitarian nature, their ideologies permitting no opposition (see Chapter 4 below). Brinton stops short of suggesting that reigns of terror are ideological movements. Rather, he draws out the 'uniformity' of their being against old forms of Christian religion and, like Edwards on the 'social myth', stresses the bringing of heaven to earth, which explains the preference for the term 'religious faith'.

It is in respect of variable four that Brinton adds most to Edwards. Edwards mentions economic problems caused by unreliable public officials and spends time on the economic incentive as a part of revolution, but by 'acute economic crisis' Brinton focuses on more practical considerations. He remarks on the disruption of production caused by the revolution, the tendency for 'capital to leave the country' and on the increased risk that businessmen face, reducing the chances of either new enterprises being started or old ones being continued. He comments too that 'peasant difficulties lessen agricultural production'. He continues:

> Then comes the war with its demand for men and munitions. The ensuing dictatorship of the victorious extremists is in part an economic dictatorship, a supervision of the whole economic life of the country, controlled currency, price fixing, food rationing, a kind of socialism of the fact long before Marx. (Brinton 1965: 201)

Drawing variables two, three and five together he remarks that:

> The difficulty of distributing inadequate supplies further tries the temper of administrators, adds to the opportunities of denunciators and spies, serves to maintain and sharpen the peculiar excitement, the universal

jumpiness of the Terror. It adds to the tenseness of the class struggles. (ibid)

It is a pity that Brinton does not expand these comments for they offer a pointer to an explanation for reigns of terror which goes beyond the simple proposal of a list of uniformities. If all seven factors must be present, a tall order for any generalization, both their possible interconnections and the possibility that one or more of the proposed factors could be of greater significance than the others need to be investigated.

Brinton does not offer a general explanation for the end of Terrors but uses the analogy of the 'convalesce' following a 'fever' (Brinton 1965: 205). For Edwards (1970: 186–9), the end is due to 'emotional fatigue', an exhausted government finally overwhelmed by all the economic problems consequent upon the cost of the war, the problems of new people in office and 'the paralysis of trade and commerce'. Implicitly, therefore, in spite of his claim that a Terror is a reign not an anarchy, Edwards accepts that reigns of terror never gain full control over the economy. The reign is rather a political reign, decisive and energetic in decision-making and having control over the use of force. In part, therefore, Brinton's and Edwards' disagreement stems from their different perspectives on government and its extension into the economy in particular. It is a difference of view which could reflect political divergence but more probably reflects the earlier, pre-Keynesian, date of Edwards' work. As we shall discover in Chapter 4, Brinton's emphasis on economic problems and the revolutionary government's role in redressing those problems reflects his specialization in the French Revolution.

COUNTER-REVOLUTION

Inherent in Brinton's inclusion of economic scarcities lies a crucial conflict with Edwards' view of 'domestic insurrection'. Brinton accepts Edwards' view of civil war as class conflict. It follows from Brinton's emphasis on economic grievances, however, that rioting, indeed disturbances of any sort, would be likely to arise spontaneously from any or all sections of society. This suggests that it is important to make clear distinctions between different types of counter-revolutionary acts: the sabotage of the civil servant, the émigré seeking help from abroad, the dispossessed aristocrat seeking support at home, the peasant refusing to surrender grain, the producer refusing to surrender his goods, the worker demanding work, higher pay or more and cheaper supplies. It also suggests that the notion of counter-revolution may itself be far more complex than either theorist allows.

The concept of counter-revolution is defined by the revolutionary government and the nature of counter-revolution may differ not simply from one revolution to another but over time. Counter-revolutionaries fall into two categories:

- Those who take up arms against the government or take action enabling others to do so. These are normally identified within a civil war, though assassins fall into this category as would members of the old order who flee the country and raise foreign support for invasion. Conventional descriptions of 'class struggle' could be applied. As a group they can be generalized from one revolution to another.
- Those who do not normally take up arms but simply break the laws introduced by the revolutionary government. These laws are likely to differ across revolutions and might include anything from decrees against hoarding, orders to force acceptance of government bonds in payment for goods, laws against expressing opinions opposed to the revolutionary regime, decrees forbidding the holding of religious ceremonies or orders commanding conscription into the army.

In the same light, a distinction needs also to be drawn between foreign wars and invasions which are inherited from the revolutionary situation before the Terror regime takes over and foreign wars provoked by the extremist revolutionaries once in power. Where choice of policies is involved the necessity for counter-revolution, whether at home or abroad can be questioned.

The differences between problems inherited by the revolutionary government as opposed to those provoked by the revolutionaries' own behaviour once in office and the differences between organized and individual acts of counter-revolution can easily merge in the chaos of civil war. This is crucial, for the art of revolution is to establish a new order out of that chaos, a workable order based either on active support or passive resolution to the impossibility of removal, and mostly some combination of the two. Through force and support combined, the construction of new political organizations and the implementation of new laws, the old order is demolished and rebuilt into the new revolutionary order. There are more lessons than either Brinton or Edwards recognize in the study of counter-revolution under reigns of terror.

The economic problems which Brinton mentions suggest an important inter-relationship of factors which goes beyond a list of variables towards a possible causal explanation. As Brinton intimates, the crisis brought about by civil and foreign wars, the need to conscript troops and to feed and equip them in the face of scarcity (itself a cause of the initial overthrow not yet redressed and made worse by the chaos wrought by the political upheaval) necessitates a government capable of taking command, a government, in other words, that can ensure the surrender of food and equipment needed for troops, one capable of forcing people to become soldiers and to fight for the revolution and of punishing those opposed to the revolution. In times of war, decisive government and patriotism are primary. When battle takes place on the home ground militaristic-style political leadership must be a match for the commands and actions on the battleground. It is an argument also found in Edwards' discussion of the need for a 'war-machine' command government when faced by foreign invasion, a theme similar to Skocpol's thesis on state formation in the revolutionary crisis.

SKOCPOL: STATES AND SOCIAL REVOLUTIONS

Skocpol does not draw attention specifically to the reign of terror as a general stage of revolution. In proposing the importance of factors separate from the causes of the initial revolutionary takeover ('international pressures' most especially) and in focusing on state building, she does, however, offer generalizations for the three revolutions of her study, France, China and Russia, which offer an important contribution to the debate over the causes and demise of reigns of terror:[1]

> In all three revolutionary situations, political leaderships and regimes – the Jacobin and then the Napoleonic in France, the Bolshevik in Russia, and the Communist in China – emerged to re-establish national order, to consolidate the socioeconomic transformations wrought by the class upheavals from below, and to enhance each country's power and autonomy over and against international competitors. (Skocpol 1979: 163–4)

Had they not succeeded, she argues, these three revolutions would have failed, like Germany 1848 and Russia 1905.

For Skocpol, a successful revolutionary state transformation takes the form of a centralized bureaucracy, the 'edifice' of the modern state. Whilst accepting the advantage of Jacobinism and Marxism-Leninism as revolutionary ideologies for the same reasons as Edwards and Brinton – their Messianic, totalitarian nature – she rejects the notion that these ideologies determined the outcome of the revolutions. She is therefore directly opposed to Talmon (1955); she also takes issue with the simple Marxist analysis which focuses on the class origins of new leaders. Concentration on what the new leadership was 'doing' instead of their class composition, she argues, clearly shows that 'they were the people who created administrative and military organisations and political institutions to take the place of the pre-revolutionary monarchies' (Skocpol 1979: 168).

This statement is not incompatible with a more sophisticated Marxist analysis which considers the interests served by all this machinery of state (see Beetham, (1987: 71–80); see also Cammack (1989: 261–80) for a direct attack on Skocpol's (1985) more concentrated work on the state and the rejection of Marxist analysis reiterated within it). From her view of 'doing' Skocpol concentrates on revolutionary state structures. Oddly, given her focus, she does not include an analysis of any government's duties, the policy-making process. That is, not just the construction of organizations and institutions for the implementation of policy but also an analysis of the policies themselves, the responses of those affected by those policies and, in full circle, the government's reactions to those responses. It is here that a Marxist analysis of class interests can prove particularly enlightening.

With respect to the Terror periods of the three revolutions, Skocpol emphasizes, problems faced at home, the importance of mobilization for foreign war as crucial to the development of this centralized modern state bureaucracy. Of France under the Jacobins she remarks:

> under the aegis of mobilisation for war and military intervention in unstable internal politics, a centralised bureaucratic state had been constructed, to be bequeathed to a consolidated French nation. Thus warfare was far from extrinsic to the development and fate of the French Revolution; rather it was central and constitutive. (Skocpol 1979: 186)

Furthermore, war was no accident; events in France must rather be viewed against the balance-of-power politics of Europe at the time.

Skocpol hammers home her claim that the centralized nature of the French state arose mainly from the international pressures of war by drawing a contrast (though to what end is not entirely clear) with England under Cromwell which 'did not face invasions from major military powers' (ibid: 186). The implication is either that English democracy was less bureaucratic or that England avoided a Terror, perhaps both.

With respect to Russia under war communism (1918–21) she quotes Chamberlin: 'no government could have survived in Russia in those years without the use of terrorism ... The national morale was completely shattered by the world war' (Chamberlin 1965: 81, quoted Skocpol 1979: 215). She emphasizes the role especially of the Cheka (the Bolshevik Secret Police) and of other party organizations and Red Army units in using force to extract supplies. The civil war in Russia she depicts in terms of a peasantry drawn into conflict by the problem of extracting supplies for the foreign war (Skocpol 1979: 218). Out of this foreign war crisis which became a civil war a centralized bureaucratic state developed without which the Bolsheviks would not have been victorious.

In China, too, a similar line is taken to explain the development of the modern centralized bureaucratic state which Mao brought to power in 1949 and extended 'step by step, during the 1950s' (Skocpol 1979: 267). Discussing the important land reforms in the Communist areas between 1946–9, which potentially challenge her emphasis on foreign wars, she argues: 'In short, the Chinese Communist Party's quest for rural resources to make possible military victories against Japan, the warlords, and the Nationalists finally resulted in social revolution in the Chinese countryside' (ibid: 262). In similar vein to her discussion of Russia, she puts forward the view that this social revolution furnished both the necessary enthusiasm and supplies to beat the Guomindang in the civil war which ensued after the Japanese departed. Again pre-eminence is given in her explanation for the rise of the modern state to the importance of mobilization for foreign war (which then provokes civil war, civil war therefore being of secondary importance) and the consequent need for coercion and centralization which follows.

In stressing foreign wars as the major propellant of revolutionary regimes through terror to centralization, Skocpol finds sympathy both with Brinton and Edwards. Important areas of disagreement remain, however. In viewing Terrors as temporary forms of government in a

crisis situation, Brinton is at issue with Skocpol's portrayal of centralized bureaucratic state-building. This is especially problematic for the
Jacobin dictatorship which was, of course, overthrown anyway and
Skocpol is obliged to make the link between Robespierre and Napoleon Bonaparte in terms of Napoleon's 'reintroducing administrative
centralization' (Skocpol 1979: 195).

The obvious question arises as to why the Jacobin dictatorship failed
whilst Lenin and the Bolsheviks in Russia and Mao and the Communists
in China succeeded in hanging on to power. This question is bound up with
the issue of the contrasting outcomes of the revolutions. Why, given the
claimed similarity in causes, did the outcome of the French Revolution
differ from the other two revolutions in not being Communist. Skocpol
accepts the more usual explanations for the fall of Robespierre, the fool-
ishness of the festival of the Supreme Being, petty disagreements amongst
the Jacobins, pressure from the *sans-culottes*. These arguments are similar
to those offered by Edwards and Brinton. Skocpol also offers a new
explanation, the condition of the international economy in the 1790s and
the contrasting economic conditions faced at home by the revolutionary
government in France at the time compared with those in Russia and
China in the twentieth century. Given the limited development of industrial
enterprises and the state of the international economy faced by the Jacobins,
no government, she argues, could then have taken full control of the
economy (as the Russians and Chinese were later able to do).[2] She also directs attention to the advantage that China and Russia had in party organization for achieving state control (Skocpol 1979: chs 6 and 7).

By focusing on this international contrast between the three revolutions Skocpol slides neatly out of the obligation to face the obvious
question of whether deliberate choices of policy were made which
were based (at least in the sense of excluding alternatives) on an
ideological commitment. Given that Napoleon, according to Skocpol,
was later to take up that bureaucratic state organization it is reasonable
to question whether or not the Jacobins ever wanted to take state
control of the economy. Only if they had so intended is the potential
for state control of industry relevant to a consideration of either why
the Jacobins fell from power or why the outcome of the French Revolution differed from those of the Russian and Chinese cases. After all,
the outcome of the French Revolution might straightforwardly have
reflected a different ideological perspective with which state economic
control was incompatible, one in favour of private property for example, as the French Revolution was.

In any case, Skocpol's emphasis on these pressures of international trade and foreign wars, what she terms the 'world historic context', is not overly convincing. Taylor (1984: 47–8) has drawn attention to the need for an independent analysis of the workings of the international system, without which reference to it appears 'ad hoc'. Whilst certainly it is true that between 1790 and 1917 both industrialization in the West and international trade had grown apace, China, on Skocpol's own admittance, was hardly industrialized. Furthermore, if the level of international economic development is so relevant then the Mexican Revolution offers a counter-example to Skocpol's argument, for whilst the Russian Revolution ended up with state control of industry, the Mexican Revolution, 1910–20, which happened at the same time and which was both more industrialized and more open to international investment and trade, did not.[3] Indeed it has been argued that in 1910 Mexico showed signs that it could emerge as a modern industrial state (Vernon 1963: 47). The absence of party organization may form part of the answer. Mexico, like France, had no party organization available for the critical post-revolutionary stage. The National Revolutionary Party was not formed until 1929 (Philip 1988: 99). For both Russia and China, though, party organization constituted part of the Communist ideological doctrine.

Emphasis on party organization for the Russian and Chinese revolutions involves a recognition of the importance of Communism in determining policy choices. As such, ideology must form part of the explanation for the differing outcomes of Skocpol's three revolutions. The recognition that ideology can set limits on possible policy choices is a quite different point from the one which Skocpol makes in her attack on ideology as a primary explanatory factor, namely that the outcomes of revolutions do not approximate the ideal societies promised by revolutionaries. Ideologies may nevertheless set limits on the possible policy choices by promoting some whilst ruling others out of consideration.[4] Furthermore, as discussion of Edwards' and Brinton's arguments has shown with respect to counter-revolution at home (for Skocpol mostly amongst the peasantry though for France the Parisian *sans-culottes* too), such policies need not relate only to mobilization for foreign war. In underplaying the importance of the break between the end of the Terror and the Bonapartist outcome of the French Revolution, Skocpol bolsters her conception of Jacobin rule as centralized dictatorship, so crucial to modern state-building. Given Brinton's challenge to this view, it is one which needs careful assessment for it has the potential to undermine her central claim for modern states forming from revolutionary situations through pressure primarily of foreign wars.

The importance of foreign wars as a cause of revolutionary dictator-ships, reigns of terror or reigns of terror and virtue, is then a theme for all three theorists. Each links foreign wars to the crisis of counter-revolution at home. It is the argument of this book that, on balance, it is civil and not foreign wars which play the major part in Terrors and that the ending of civil wars represents the pivotal point of revolutions only after which permanent state-building can begin.

NOTES

1. Skocpol has been criticized for failing to draw attention to 'common features in revolutions such as the Jacobin clubs, Soviets, CCP' as had the natural history theorists (Goldstone 1980: 452). Certainly it is the view of this work that Skocpol should specifically have identified revolutionary reigns of terror. Nevertheless, as the following discussion shows, Goldstone is wrong to criticize Skocpol for failure to draw his proposed comparisons.
2. Taylor (1984: 47–8) has criticized Skocpol for using the international system to fill in where her structural variables do not quite work and is, in particular, critical of her failure to actually explain why industrialization was not a possibility for France in the 1790s and why Chinese Communism differed from Russian Communism. Essentially, he argues, a theory of how the international system works is required.
3. See Vernon (1963: ch.2). Mexico, like France, Russia and China, also had a very large bureaucracy before the revolution (Wolf 1973: 23–4) but the Mexican Revolution is briefly mentioned in Skocpol's final chapter only for not fitting her generalizations drawn from France, Russia and China (1989: 287–9). The Mexi-can case also presents problems for Edwards' and Brinton's generalizations for it was not a revolution involved in foreign wars. The Mexican Revolution is dis-cussed below in Part V, Appendix.
4. Smith (1983: 159) has drawn attention to Skocpol's own emphasis on the Maoist regime's distinctive political capacities developed through the Communists' work amongst the peasantry before coming to power.

PART II
The Classic Reigns of Terror

4. The Archetypal Case: The Reign of Terror in the French Revolution

The most satisfactory way to examine any social science generalization is through the evidence. In as far as the Jacobin dictatorship represents the basis from which all generalizations about reigns of terror derive, the events of the French Revolution are vital for the testing both of existing generalizations and for the generation of new ones. The study of history offers no single narrative, rather a competing set of interpretations of the events and this is nowhere more clearly demonstrated than in the vast literature on the French Revolution. The point here is not to present a straightforward account of the revolutionary reign of terror as if it offered the only possible interpretation but to gain understanding through consideration of the points of contention and so to benefit from the richness afforded both by competing theories and challenging histories. To this end emphasis will be given to important recent works relating to the Jacobin dictatorship.[1]

Progress (such that later publications necessarily represent improvements on earlier ones) cannot automatically be assumed in works on history. Investigations into new evidence and the presentation of new findings are certainly likely to characterize important works and such works become landmarks in discovery if their findings are considered authoritative. This is the case for the classic work on the reign of terror in the French Revolution by Donald Greer, *The Incidence of Terror during the French Revolution: A Statistical Interpretation.* It is a text quoted widely and used extensively in later studies. The book was first published in 1935, just eight years after Edwards' work but three years before Brinton's first edition. This of itself makes it deserving of detailed consideration; indeed, examination of Greer's statistical evidence will be the first step towards the unfurling of the Terror.[2]

SET FOR TERROR

The start of the revolution on 14 July 1789 had been a spontaneous uprising and it had led to the establishment of a constitutional monarchy. Riots re-emerged in the autumn of 1791, in reaction to the drop in the value of the *assignats* (the paper currency secured not by gold but by the church lands sold off by the Decree of 19 December 1789) and the inflation which followed (Soboul 1974: 233). The *assignat*, at 82 per cent of its nominal value in November 1791, fell to 57 per cent by June 1792 and grain prices rose by 25–50 per cent as peasants refused to exchange their grain for the devaluing currency (Sutherland 1985: 139–40). Incidents of pilfering from grain carts and thefts from markets soon swept through every region of France (Soboul 1974: 233). In the towns grocery price increases led to riots which demanded that hoarders be punished and prices fixed. Such riots were particularly bad in Paris and the north. In the rural areas of the south, widespread rioting also broke out though the protests took a different form – the rising corn prices led the poor to demand a complete end to feudal dues. By the spring of 1792, France was again submerged by the scale of insurrection which had heralded the revolution in 1789 and the riots carried on into August (Sutherland 1985: 140–1). As disorder within France grew, the émigrés published their intention to invade France and gathered troops at Coblenz. On 20 April 1792, the Constituent Assembly voted to declare war on the King of Bohemia and Hungary (ibid: 144).

The war, or rather the failure to achieve quick victory, led to the end of the monarchy and at the same time opened the way for the fall of the Girondins. The king and his supporters had hoped the war would lead quickly to foreign armies restoring him fully to the throne, whilst his opponents in the Assembly had hoped that victory would rally support around the majority Brissotins (later Girondins) (Soboul 1974: 236). In practice, the escalating war was to draw power towards the Jacobins, around the opponents of both the king and the war.

In a crisis of escalating foreign war and riots at home the atmosphere hung heavy with counter-revolution. The king was overthrown in August 1792 and the Constituent Assembly was reformed as 'the National Convention' and elected by male suffrage (excepting some royalist and moderate groups) (Wright 1974: 59). These elections took place on 20 September 1792. The first act of the Convention was to declare France a republic. In the charged atmosphere of counter-revolution, legislation, the forerunner of terror, was introduced in August 1792 to set up an extraordinary criminal tribunal to try those suspected of counter-revolutionary crimes. This was followed by legislation enabling home searches for suspects and weapons, providing an 'oath of allegiance', to be sworn by priests and officials and for émigrés' lands to be broken up and sold. Priests refusing to sign the oath were given 15 days to leave the country and the penalty for failure to do so was transportation to French Guiana (ibid: 56).

Summary justice was not introduced at this stage; defence counsel, witnesses and a right to appeal remained. In September, however, an anarchistic Terror broke out. The Paris Commune, not the Convention, armed the people of Paris on hearing the news of worsening fortunes in the war (Langwy was lost) and that an uprising, which turned out to be short-lived, was taking place in the Vendée. From 2–7 September, prisons and monasteries came under violent mass attacks. National guards and surveillance officers of the Paris Commune joined in and massacres resulted. Around 1,300 prisoners were killed, one-third of whom had been imprisoned for political offences (Wright 1974: 57).

The election of the National Convention in September 1792 restored order, but order was to prove temporary for no agreed policies emerged. Though the splits were not always Girondins (majority) versus Jacobins (minority), on the issue of the monarch and the necessity for his execution, however, the Jacobins were bound tightly together whilst the Girondins were split (Wright 1974: 60). After a debate lasting two months, the vote finally went against the king. He was executed on 21 January 1793. At the same time, the Girondins had received a decisive blow and power had moved to those Jacobin deputies and their most eloquent leader, Robespierre, who sat in the upper seats in the Chamber of the Convention. This gained for them the collective name of 'the Mountain' (*Montagnards*).

THE LAWS AND INSTITUTIONS OF THE TERROR, MARCH 1793–AUGUST 1794

The reign of terror began on 29 March 1793 with the creation of the Committee of General Security. Its role was to take charge of internal security and the police. On 6 April, a second committee was established, the Committee of Public Safety. This was to prove the more famous of the two not least because in July 1793 Robespierre was to become its head; it also had responsibility for both internal and external affairs. In essence it was given power to take quick action in response to crisis. From the start there was a degree of overlap of responsibilities for internal affairs between the two committees.

Between the setting up of these two committees other terror organizations were also introduced. On 10 March the Paris Revolutionary Tribunal was set up and on 21 March a law was introduced to begin the organization of surveillance committees, or revolutionary committees, in the French communes (local districts) to take measures necessary in the defence of the nation and, therefore, of the revolution (Lucas 1973: 126). The creation of the Committee of General Security heralded the initiation of the Representatives on Mission under which 82 deputies of the Convention (which had replaced the National Assembly) were sent to the departments (the French counties). Their job was to ensure both the recruitment of 300,000 new soldiers and the loyalty of the old; many high-ranking officers were to be sacked in consequence (Wright 1974: 65).

The Revolutionary Tribunal, established first in Paris to try counter-revolutionaries, was composed initially of five judges and had a jury of twelve. In September, however, it was reorganized for speed and at the end of October trials were limited to three days. Total suppression of legal counsel and witnesses for defence was not officially withdrawn until 10 June 1794 by the notorious law of 22 Priarial though, as St Just remarked, by then defence counsel and witnesses were mere 'phantoms' anyway (Greer 1966: 20). During the winter of 1793–94 revolutionary tribunals similar to the Paris Revolutionary Tribunal were established at Arras, Cambrai, Brest, Rochefort and Toulouse. In practice, though, the majority of Terror victims were sentenced by civil or military commissions, set up by the Representatives on Mission in the main regions of civil war and rebellion (ibid: 21).

The military commissions consisted of five judges (officers and soldiers), a prosecutor and a clerk. There was no appeal. At first restricted to the trial of people captured while bearing arms or émigrés and clergy who had refused to sign allegiance to the new regime, most military commissions began to try all kinds of people accused of political crimes and in two instances, at Granville and Angers, the Representatives on Mission explicitly extended the powers of the commissions to all counter-revolutionary crimes (Greer 1966: 21). The civil commissions (variously termed revolutionary, popular or extraordinary commissions) closely resembled the military commissions. The most famous became known by their most notorious member. In Lyon, for example, the commission was known as the Commission Parien (ibid: 21–2).

Along with the revolutionary tribunals and commissions specially set up for the purpose, revolutionary justice was also administered by the existing department criminal courts. These courts operated as they had under the *ancien régime* with neither juries nor appeal. It was the nature of the laws instituted during the reign of terror which turned them into instruments of the Terror. Where the judges showed reluctance to act in line with new expectations, deliberating over law, applying too much leniency, the Representatives on Mission often sent important cases for trial to Paris (Greer 1966: 22).[3] Those courts which succeeded in circumventing the obligations of the new laws avoided transformation into the equivalents of revolutionary tribunals.

Just as the institutions of the Terror expanded, so the laws under which victims of the Terror were arrested, imprisoned and executed extended their reach. The first law of Terror, opening the way to both indiscriminate arrest and summary justice, was introduced on 19 March 1793.[4] Under this law the penalty of death was to be imposed on all those carrying arms in rebellion or caught in possession of evidence of royalist support. Refractory clergy, that is those who refused to declare allegiance to the republic by taking the oath, were to be given the death penalty. Anyone found to have assisted such clergy was deported. This was summary justice. Under the March 1793 law those arrested were to be tried and executed within 24 hours, without either jury or right to appeal (Sutherland 1985: 171). The accused were assumed guilty and had to prove their innocence against the odds of technicalities and time. On July 26 1793 hoarding of food and staple goods was made a capital offence, though in April 1794 deliberate counter-revolutionary intent had to be proved. Infringement of the Maximum (the law introduced in September 1793 which put maximum levels on both prices and wages) was never made a capital offence (Greer 1966: 17–18).

On 17 September 1793 the law of 19 March was greatly extended. Under this Law of Suspects suspicion of counter-revolution was sufficient justification for arrest. It was no longer necessary actually to be found carrying arms in a counter-revolutionary gathering, bearing evidence of royalist support or expressing opinions against the regime in public places. Reported expression and behaviour were enough. Under this law the surveillance committees' powers were also expanded (see

Wright 1973: 120–1, Document 13). By the law of April 1794, suspects were transferred from the provinces to Paris, though discretion
permitted a few departmental tribunals to continue executions, a discretion which was ended in June. On 10 June 1794, the legislation
reached its height. The Law of 22 Prairial ended the (meaningless)
right to defence counsel and witnesses and made death the sole penalty
of appearing before the Tribunal (Greer 1966: 20).

From April 1793, too, pressure had begun to mount for the formation
of *armées revolutionarie*, people's armies, to fight not external war but
internal uprisings. A decree to establish these people's armies was
proclaimed on 4 June 1793 though they were not formally set up until
a law was introduced in September 1793 (Cobb 1987: 49). People's
armies were intended to control counter-revolutionaries, to defend the
revolutionary laws and to protect public safety and supplies. The most
important and also the most notorious was the Paris People's Army
formed on 5 September 1793 under Ronsin. These armies were set up
under the Committee of Public Safety but in practice generally took
their orders from the Committee of General Security and surveillance
committees (ibid: 339). Orders could also be issued by the Representatives on Mission and other revolutionary organizations. Membership
of these armies was voluntary, well paid and top heavy with officers
(ibid: 195).[5]

THE VICTIMS OF THE TERROR

Greer puts the start of the Terror as March 1793 and its end as August
1794, marked by the fall of Robespierre in Paris in July but adjusted
for the delays for news and consequences of Robespierre's fall to
reach the provinces. The statistics which Greer analyses are the official
records of the number of death sentences passed by the courts during
the Terror. Some were guillotined and others were shot. The incidence
of the official victims of the Terror rose dramatically towards the end
of November 1793, hitting their peak in December 1793–January 1794
(Greer 1966: 165). During these two months very nearly half of all the
official executions occurred. During the month of December, 3,350
victims met their death. In January, a further 3,500 executions took
place. In February the figure was back down to 792, comparable to the
500 victims for the month of November. Before November, the highest
figure had been 210 for April; after February the figures remained

high, 589 for March, 1,000 for April, 800 for May, 1,150 for June and 1,400 for July, falling dramatically in August after Robespierre's execution (ibid: 113–15). The official toll amounted to 17,000.

Though lacking complete information on imprisonment Greer estimates that probably more than half a million people were held prisoner between March 1793 and August 1794. On the basis of this, he estimates that only 3.33 per cent of those imprisoned were actually executed. Many of these prisoners were transported and many more died of disease whilst in prison. Dysentery, typhus and cholera wreaked their toll, especially where conditions were most crowded. In order to accommodate such huge numbers, all sorts of unsuitable buildings had to be used, the most notorious of which, a large warehouse at Nantes, at one time held 10,000 Vendéans. Old ships were also used (Greer 1966: 28). Many of those prisoners who died of disease did so before they came to trial and Greer argues therefore that disease, whilst reducing the official numbers of executions, actually increased the true death toll of the Terror. In addition (mainly from the West), captured rebels were shot without trial and others were drowned in the shivering waters of the Loire. Estimates for these drownings have ranged widely but 2,000 is given as a reasonable figure. A figure of not less than 12,000 is estimated for those executed without trial (ibid: 36).[6] Overall Greer estimates the total toll of the Terror to have been 35–40,000 people, more than twice as many as the 17,000 officially recorded. Out of a total population in the 1790s of 25,200,000, such deaths hang heavily on Edwards' claim that fear saved lives.

GREER'S ANALYSIS OF THE DATA: THE PRIME IMPORTANCE OF CIVIL WAR

The availability of this data on suspects is unique for a reign of terror and it facilitates a detailed statistical analysis which cannot be made for any other Terror. Its findings are, therefore, specially significant and deserving of attention. Greer investigates the nature of the crimes for which the victims met their death, the areas from which they came, their social class and the month of their execution. His findings offer qualified support for the importance of foreign war, economic problems and class conflict as causes of the Terror. Greer's evidence, however, points overwhelmingly to the importance of civil war as a cause of the

Terror and the punishment of rebels at home as the factor which pushed the Terror to its peak.

In addition to estimating a figure for terror victims at more than double Edwards' total, Greer presents evidence which refutes Edwards' claim that it was mainly aristocrats who were executed; this undermines his suggestion that executions were used for dramatic purposes to quell opposition through fear. Greer finds that on the basis of the divisions of eighteenth-century France, 84 per cent of the official victims were from the Third Estate (Greer 1966: 98, Table IV). He emphasizes that in proportion to their number the clergy, nobles and the rich suffered far more than the lower classes, at a ratio of 8:1. Nevertheless he finds the class with the largest proportion of executions in relation to its size to have been the upper middle class. These non-noble high-ranking administrators, professionals and top businessmen belonged not to the top rungs of society (aristocrats and clergy) but to the Third Estate (see Table 4.1).[7] (Table 4.1 is extracted from Greer's discussion, pp. 106–7.)

Table 4.1   Official Terror Victims as a Proportion of Each Class

Estimates of class composition France towards end of 18th century		No. of executions	Executions as a proportion of each class
Class	Approx. Numbers		
Nobles (including *noblesse de robe*)	400,000	1,362	0.341
Clergy	300,000	1,082	0.361
Third Estate			
Upper middle class	500,000	2,310	0.462
Lower middle class	1,000,000	1,750	0.175
Working class	3,000,000	5,163	0.172
Peasants	20,000,000	4,660	0.233
Total population:	25,200,000		

Edwards' mistaken view was most probably drawn from the events in Paris itself where 62 per cent of the total executed were indeed from the upper classes (including the nobility at 25 per cent and the upper middle class at 28 per cent). In practice, however, cases involving important people, nobles, local notables and officers from the provinces were often sent to Paris for trial (Greer 1966: 104–5). This was obligatory for every region from 4 June 1794, under the law of 22 Priarial. The artisans executed in Paris were all Parisians (19 per cent of total) with only 4 per cent of those executed being peasants (ibid: 144, Table I; 164, Table VII).

Greer's social class statistics do not however, as is usually assumed, lead him to reject class analysis outright (see for example Moore 1966: 518 and Louie 1966: 385).[8] Greer demonstrates through analysis of the social class composition of victims in areas of full-scale civil war that the nature of class conflict differed from area to area. It is a view which Lyons (1978: ch.4) shares. Civil war broke out in the west in March 1793 and was in full swing by April. From May anti-Jacobin rebellions (the Federalist Revolts) began to break out elsewhere, first in Lyon and then in Marseilles and Bordeaux. It has been claimed that by the summer 60 departments were embroiled in civil war, though this has been dismissed as exaggeration – outside of the west, full-scale rebellion was essentially concentrated in these three towns (ibid: 41).

In the west, where feudalism remained relatively intact (Moore 1969: 93) peasants retained affection for the local gentry and clergy and were strongly opposed to Jacobin rule so when civil war came to the region following the call for conscription it turned into a pro-royalist counter-revolution (Greer 1966: 61). Not surprisingly, peasants formed over half of the number of the official executions recorded. A clear contrast can be drawn with the class conflict in Bordeaux and Lyon: in Bordeaux, where civil war broke out on 6 June 1793, battle was drawn between pro-royalist forces (nobles, clergy and upper middle class) and the (pro-revolutionary government) lower middle class, and the victims came overwhelmingly from the middle and upper classes with just 2 per cent peasants and only 9 per cent of those executed being working class, in spite of 'a large working class population' (ibid: 104); in the silk-weaving town of Lyon, on the Rhône, however, 25 per cent of those executed were workers and the number of executions at 1,880 was far higher than the 501 total for the southern federalist centres (ibid: 103). In industrializing Lyon, hit by crisis in the silk industry, the once independent artisans, 'now turned wage earner', faced unemployment, inadequate food supplies and the threat of starvation. Under these pressing economic conditions, the Jacobins, with proletarian support, fought for and gained effective power in the commune (city council). The response was an insurrection by anti-Jacobin forces which resulted in the execution of the Jacobin leader, Chalier on 29 May 1793. This signalled the start of Jacobin terror in Lyon.

It can, of course, be argued that despite whatever these groups thought they were fighting for – the restoration of the monarchy, the victory of the Girondists, for employment, better working conditions and food or in protest against conscription – the real interests being served by insurgency and civil war were the class interests of either the bourgeoisie or the aristocrats. In the long view of history this analysis seems valid. Greer's argument, which seems generally to have been misunderstood, is that faced with an immediate crisis situation the Jacobins used the Terror against whosoever opposed the regime and wheresoever opposition was found. The aristocracy and the rich, he argues, were not attacked because they were 'class enemies' but because they were striking out against the regime. Likewise peasants objecting to conscription and Girondists (as in Lyon) opposed to Jacobin policies were attacked because they rose against the regime: 'Obliged to fend against multiple attack they had unleashed the Terror as a means of defence. They believed that the Republic's survival was the Terror's justification' (Greer 1966: 123).

This 'multiple attack' on the regime's survival came not only from full-scale civil wars but also from the foreign wars and economic problems too:

> The mechanism and the policies of the regime grew out of the surcharged atmosphere of a great national crisis, out of the hysteria induced by the lurking menace of famine, out of defeat and treason on the frontiers, and out of sporadic civil war within the country. (Greer 1966: 127).

Greer re-affirms the prime importance of counter-revolution at home through analysis of the crimes for which the official victims met their death, through examination of the geographical incidence of executions and through a consideration of events surrounding the Terror's peak. The crime for which most of those victims met their death was sedition. The substantial majority was convicted under the laws of March and September 1793, the law of suspects; fully 72.25 per cent of all victims met their death for expression of opinion or performance of an act construed as being against the regime.

Examining the geographical incidence of the Terror, Greer finds a strong association between the most intense civil-war areas and the numbers of executions: 52 per cent in the west (the areas around the Vendée) – Loire-Inférieure (3,548), Maine-et-Loire (1,886), Vendée (1,616); and 19 per cent in the Rhône valley (where Lyon is situated) – Rhône (1,880) (Greer 1966: 40 and 147, Table III). In total, 76 per cent of all executions occurred in the departments where insurrections involving a thousand or more people occurred (ibid: 70), Seine (Paris) with 2,639 executions being the fifth and only other centre where official executions reached totals over 509 (ibid: 147, Table III). With two maps, the one for the number of executions in each region, the other classified for level of disturbance (down to 'no dangerous disturbances'), the fit is almost exact with only the two northern regions, Pas de Calais and Nord, having a high level of executions correlated with foreign war (ibid: maps + Table III). Greer concludes that 'it is an inescapable fact that the Terror struck hardest in the regions of civil war' (ibid: 40).

Greer further supports his emphasis on civil war through consideration of the peak of the Terror. The steep rise in victims in December and January, Greer (1966: 115) claims, 'represents the punishment of rebels'. Victory in the civil wars had begun back in October when Lyon was taken. A few days later the first major victory occurred in the Vendée and by 23 December the civil war in the west was effectively at an end, though outbreaks of rebellion continued in the Vendée into the spring. In December Toulon was taken (ibid: 114–15). The continuation of executions through into the spring of 1794 Greer puts down mainly to the delays in capturing and trying rebels involved in these civil wars. Most of the victims for February and March were from the Vendée region, Lyon and nearby Feurs (ibid: 115).

On Greer's evidence civil war constituted the major factor which pushed the Terror to its peak. Louie (1964) has confirmed on reworking Greer's statistics that when divided by the population for each area the official victims of the Terror remain highest in the areas of civil war. Sutherland too (1985) has endorsed this emphasis. Looking beyond the period of the Terror at the wider context of the revolution in which the reign of terror occurred he has argued, 'the Terror as repression was thus an episode of the dialectic of revolution – counterrevolution which was a theme of the whole period' (ibid: 219).

INSURRECTION AT HOME AND FOREIGN WAR

Whilst civil war was the prime cause of the Terror, economic problems and foreign wars are recognized by Greer as having contributed to the crisis of revolution. Though less than 1 per cent of all executions were recorded for violations of economic legislation (Greer 1966: 82), Greer draws attention to the problem of famine as a contributor to civil war, most especially in Lyon. The failure of economic policies is brought in to explain the rise in executions from the spring (after 22 Prairial) into the summer of 1794, that is after the end of full-scale civil war, the punishment of rebels and when the threat of foreign invasion had been reversed (ibid: 116–17).

For the importance of foreign wars Greer's evidence offers greater support. For the frontier zones some 22 per cent of all crimes recorded were for 'intelligence with the enemy' (Greer 1966: 153, Table IV) and Pas de Calais, with 392 executions, and Nord with 157 are among the 19 departments where more than 100 executions occurred. These figures are a long way off the top five departments (see p. 67).

The conscription in March 1793 of 300,000 young men to fight foreign wars had played a part in domestic disturbance throughout France (Greer 1966: 49). In the Vendée, the major centre of counter-revolution, resentment over conscription had triggered the spontane-ous rebellion on 10 March 1793 which within a month had turned into full-scale civil war (ibid: 61). The city councils in both Toulon and Marseille had engaged in negotiations with the English and Spanish, and in Toulon English forces had actually entered the city (ibid: 57). The peak of the Terror and the punishment of rebels coincided with a reversal in foreign war fortunes. By December, victory had been gained against both British and Austrian troops in the north and the Spanish and Piedmontese in the south, and the English had been driven from Toulon by Napoleon Bonaparte's artillery (ibid: 114–15; see also Suth-erland 1985: 217–19).

Civil war had, in addition to the threat of famine at home, been affected by conscription to fight foreign war, and some of the victims of the Terror had been connected directly with these wars. At the same time, as both Soboul (1966) and Sutherland (1985) argue, the decision to go to war in April 1792 had been made in order to divert attention from the political disturbances at home which had themselves been provoked by the devaluation of currency at a time of scarcity and rising prices.[9] From the autumn of 1791 France had been hit by a new wave of rioting and by the spring of 1792 insurrection in some areas matched the scale which had swept France to revolution in 1789 (ibid: 140–1). These riots had been spawned by the problems of food supply (in the north and around Paris) and the question of land and the remaining feudal laws (in the South) (ibid: 144).

Soboul (1974: 236) quotes Louis XVI, who welcomed war as a means to restore his own power:

> In place of civil war there would be a political war in Europe and this change would greatly improve the situation. The physical and moral condition of France is such as to make it impossible for her to resist even a partial campaign.

Whilst the king believed engagement in foreign war would restore him to power, the Brissotin (Girondin) majority in the Assembly believed that quick victory against the enemy would rally support to its side. Robespierre stood out as the prime opponent of the war and his cause found support with Danton and in some of the press (ibid: 236) (in the end there were only ten votes against the decision to declare war). The war chosen was not a naval war against England but a land war, and then not against the formidable German princes first suggested as targets but against a weaker opponent with expectation of quick victory (Sutherland 1985: 144).

Hampson has argued that the decision to go to war in April 1792 grew from within the revolution rather than being enforced from outside: 'The war was not the inevitable response of the European powers to a threat that their rules dared not tolerate; it was begun by France, as a matter of internal politics' (Hampson 1988: 186). Without engaging in class analysis, Hampson then challenges Skocpol's emphasis on international pressures. Essentially he argues that the revolutionaries pushed themselves into war through the logic of their own revolutionary 'moral absolutism' which ruled out compromise and asserted their own superiority over other nations, conferring 'ideological respectability on old xenophobia' (ibid: 138).

CONFLICTING EXPLANATIONS: IDEOLOGY AND ECONOMIC DETERMINISM

Whilst the reign of terror grew from the crises of foreign war, economic problems and most especially civil war, correlations alone cannot prove the case for the Terror's necessity.[10] Whilst these crises had to be faced and emergency measures were certainly needed, there remains open the question of the extent to which these crises, rather than being forced upon the revolutionary government from outside of its control, were in fact brought upon it by its own policies. The question of 'excess' also remains. Whilst Terror may have been necessary if the revolutionaries were to retain their hold on power – the suppression of counter-revolution both at home and abroad – the possibility remains that more terror was applied than was necessary. In this case the issue of the rise in executions from spring/summer 1794, which occurred after the end of full-scale civil war and the turn in fortunes of foreign war, is especially pertinent, though the nature of the punishment of rebels at the peak of the Terror (Dec 1793–Jan 1794) is also an issue. In both cases consideration of policy choice and related ideology is crucial.

In as far as the decision to go to war went against Robespierre's view, the crisis of foreign war must obviously be viewed as a condition thrust upon the Jacobin regime and not one resulting from policy. The 'moral absolutism' to which Hampson refers surely ruled out compromise and peace and encouraged revolutionary war abroad long after defeats had been turned into victories and foreign troops had been expelled from French soil. These are issues related to the revolution as a whole, however, rather than the reign of terror in particular, and Robespierre's fall from power came too soon after the fortunes of war began to turn for these issues to be central to an analysis of Jacobin rule.

The issue of the *assignats* also fails to illuminate the narrower period of March 1793–August 1794. Feher (1987) goes so far as to argue that the decision to print the new paper money led inevitably to the need for force to control the economy and so led naturally to the development of the Jacobin Terror. Again, the introduction of *assignats* pre-dated the establishment of the Committees of Public Safety and General Security by over three years. Certainly economic problems, from monetary policy and the resulting economically provoked disturbances, contributed to the crisis situation of March 1793. Whilst the need for force may well logically have followed, that this should have developed into terror does not. It is clear from Greer's statistical analysis that the peak of the Terror was itself largely associated with full-scale civil war fought against armed counter-revolutionaries.

The earlier work of Talmon (1955) combined both Jacobin economic policy and revolutionary 'absolutism' into both an explanation for the Jacobin dictatorship and a justification for terming it the first form of 'totalitarian democracy', the second being the Soviet Union – 'Democracy' because of the Jacobins' ideology of equality of both social status and economic distribution; 'totalitarian' because the Jacobins offered a single order political system: 'An exclusive creed cannot admit opposition. It is bound to feel itself surrounded by innumerable enemies...From this sense of peril arise their continual demands for the protection of orthodoxy by recourse to terror' (ibid: 253). For Talmon the imposition of economic and social democracy through a political system is incompatible with political democracy which must respect 'human freedom' and permit opposition. Whilst Talmon's plea for human freedom may be entirely praiseworthy, his conjectures concerning the French revolution are entirely misplaced. Opposition over policies did exist within the Committee of Public Safety (and indeed between the two Committees of Public Safety and General Security) and the policies which prevailed aimed at equality of neither economic distribution nor social status. It is policies adopted by the Jacobins once in power to which investigation must, then, turn.

BUREAUCRATIC CENTRALIZATION: MOBILIZATION FOR WAR AND THE ECONOMY

Quick victory did not follow on the decision to go to war in April 1792 and by March 1793, when the Terror began, the revolution seemed threatened on all sides by foreign wars, widespread disorder and the outbreak of civil war in the west. By May civil war had broken out in Lyon and by the summer civil war or its threat, in rioting and disorder, was widespread. Skocpol (1979: 189) argues that the bureaucratic centralization, characteristic of the modern state began to develop in the 'Montagnard Government' partly in response to pressure from the *sans-culottes* but crucially in response to the war effort, raising and feeding soldiers, requisitioning materials, regulating prices and labour. She draws attention to the *levée en masse* of August 1793. Under this mobilization for war all married men under 25 were conscripted and all others, older and married men, women and children, were mobilized in the war effort, manufacturing goods, nursing, generating propaganda and the like (Sutherland 1985: 201). In support of her argument that the development of a centralized state was the consequence of the war effort she quotes Sydenham (Skocpol 1979: 189):

the 'regulation of the economy was soon as extensive as the bureau-cracy of the day and the power of coercion could make it' (Sydenham 1965: 167). The extent to which this bureaucracy developed in response to the war effort or economic problems at home which pre-dated the outbreak of war remains an important debate. This is especially the case given Soboul's and Sutherland's claim that foreign war was chosen as a screen for domestic economic problems.

The economic problems faced by France were not related simply to the war effort but to the inefficient pre-revolutionary economy. The greatest problem, one which had bothered the French economy throughout the eighteenth century, was that of supply (*arrivages*), of grain in particular, to towns (Cobb 1987: 254). The transport system was the major cause of the underdevelopment of the French economy (Price 1975: 1). Roads were in a poor condition and mule, cattle and horse carts were unsuitable for transporting heavy goods. The toll system made the roads expensive to use. Heavy goods were mainly carried on the rivers but an incomplete system of waterways necessi-tated a large amount of unloading and loading for carriage by road at various points. For transportation between Lyons and Roanne, for example (that is the rivers Loire to Rhône), 400–500 ox-teams were regularly employed (Braudel 1985: 352) – the water levels of the Rhône made it unusable for three months of the year in any case (Price 1975: 16). These loadings and unloadings and delays at locks gave ample opportunity for theft of goods (Cobb 1987: 255). The war simply added to these supply problems.

It was this problem of distribution and the consequent threat of famine which lay behind the domestic insurrection and problems of war mobilization which thrust the Jacobin regime into crisis. Through-out 1793–4 large towns in particular and Paris most especially were on the edge of starvation (Sydenham 1974: 20–1). Laws against hoarding to back up requisitioning for the war effort were introduced in July 1793. In September 1793, its complement, the General Maximum, was introduced. The fixing of a maximum on prices was to be decided by the districts and on wages by the town councils:

> Need for popular support in the critical months of 1793–4 had probably more to do with the adoption of the famous Law of the Maximum than any chain of economic reasoning. The immediate need was to check the rise in prices and speculation and ensure a supply of basic foods and other essen-tials for the civilian population. (Kemp 1971: 94)

In October, a Subsistance Commission headed by Lindet and answerable to the Committee of Public Safety was set up to prepare lists of maximum prices (Soboul 1974: 390). State-owned factories were established to manufacture ammunition and foreign trade was controlled by the state between November 1793 and March 1794. The civilian supply (food rationing and control and regulation of food production) remained the responsibility of the districts and not that of the Subsistence Commission (ibid: 390–1; Sydenham 1974: 187). After the law against hoarding was abolished in April 1794 Soboul argues that the role of the Subsistence Commission (from April 1974 renamed the *Commission du Commerce et des Approvisionnements*) went no further than the publishing of price lists and that, though the commission took a special interest in soap and sugar prices, in the end the only real attempt to control prices was for bread (Soboul 1974: 391–2).

Though a state bureaucracy had developed to co-ordinate the war effort, control over the Maximum had been given to the districts, decentralized authorities, and it was from these districts that demands for a force to ensure supplies had come.

THE PEOPLE'S ARMIES: THE 'TERROR ON THE MOVE'

The setting up of the revolutionary armies had come as the result not of imposition by the Convention but of demands for them in various parts of France (Cobb 1987: 43). These civil armies were first thought of in April 1793 as a response to fears of counter-revolution. By 4 June the Convention had agreed to the idea, though it took until September to get around to setting them up formally (ibid: 49). Cobb mentions reports of an army being recruited as early as 12–13 May in Lyon and he speculates that perhaps 'the advanced state of preparation may even have precipitated the crisis of 29 May' (ibid: 34). He reports too that demands for the setting up of a revolutionary army came from Toulon and was not imposed by the Convention (ibid: 41). The motives for those demands for revolutionary armies differed over time but: 'Almost all these armées, with the exception of those recruited in a group of departments, originated in towns which were having difficulty supplying their markets...areas poor in grain but with large populations to support' (ibid: 42).

The job of the people's armies, set up formally in September 1793 under the Committee of Public Safety, was to control counter-revolution, to defend the revolutionary laws and public safety and to 'supply the urban markets and to ensure the circulation of provisions, merchandise and people' (Cobb 1987: 160). The task of the Parisian Revolutionary Army was partly to play its part in the war effort, requisitioning foodstuffs, metals and materials from churches, but its major task was to protect the passage and ensure the supply of food (grain in particular) to Paris and, following the introduction of the law of the Maximum, to 'lend force' to the control of prices (ibid: 276–83): 'In the final analysis a controlled economy necessitated a resort to force' (ibid: 288).

Cobb (1987: 323–7) shows that the majority of arrests made by the Paris army were within the zone which supplied the city. Permanent garrisons of these civil soldiers were stationed at more than two-thirds of the grain stores, positioned on major rivers and roads (ibid: 255). For the local revolutionary armies (at departmental and communal level) the war effort was their prime purpose with the supply of towns of secondary importance (ibid: 289). Grain supplies were on the whole a less acute problem in the provinces, though this was not everywhere the case. For Toulouse, Lyons (1978: 122–3) emphasizes the role of the people's army as the 'coercive weapon' for requisitioning supplies for the town. In general, Cobb concludes that the creation of the armies of revolution, 'like the Maximum itself', 'set most of the rural population against the towns' (Cobb, 1987: 307). In turning the rural population against the Jacobin regime, it was the role played by the people's armies in the dechristianization movement which had the most damaging effect (ibid: 283).

DECHRISTIANIZATION

Dechristianization, the ransacking of churches, monasteries and other religious buildings, had started before Robespierre came to power. Churches had been stripped of valuables and materials useful for the war effort and they had been used for storage of weapons, as barracks or as stables. Sometimes religious relics, statues, crosses and the like were ceremonially destroyed and Sutherland (1985: 208) remarks that in such cases 'it is clear that dechristianization went beyond the war effort'. Dechristianization started because the constitutional church run by clergy who had signed the revolutionary oath of allegiance had failed (ibid: 210). Many constitutional priests had been involved in counter-revolution but the dechristianization movement itself stirred up widespread resistance. Whilst the Terror showed its ugliest face in the areas of civil war, in the more peaceful areas of France terror identified itself in the form of dechristianization:

> Hiding a few sacks of grain or disguising one's wealth from the sporadic control of amateurs in the towns was comparatively easy for a peasantry that had defrauded tax collectors for centuries. With the complicity of neighbours, it was even possible to avoid conscription. But it was impossible to avoid dechristianization and many people resented it. (ibid: 217).

Cobb emphasizes the bad image of the Terror produced by dechristianization at the hands of the disorderly people's armies (Cobb 1987: 511). They were, he argues, 'anarchical forces in both the best and worse senses of the word'. Many of the soldiers were 'true democrats', intent on destroying the old inegalitarian order, but others were involved in a different sort of anarchy made up of 'blind violence and sometimes cruelty' (ibid: 512). The people's armies were 'the terror on the move' (ibid: 2). It was these armies which represented the visible terror and it was a Terror essentially out of control. These revolutionary armies had arisen out of crisis, mostly in response to the problems of supply, many arising before official sanction, taking the law into their own hands; and in their hands the law became force. They used that force against any act of counter-revolution, which the revolutionary soldiers saw in a whole host of economic and religious conduct: 'Born in anarchy, many of these *armées* remained anarchical' (ibid: 160).

On 4 December (14 Frimaire) the Committee of Public Safety began its battle to gain control of the Terror.

THE LAW OF 14TH FRIMAIRE

Under Article 1 of the law of 14 Frimaire the National Convention was declared to be the centre of government. Article 2, however, established the Committee of Public Safety as the true centre of power, with the Committee of General Security given powers over the police only. It read:

> All constituted bodies and public officials are placed under the immediate supervision of the Committee of Public Safety, in accordance with the decree of 10 October 1793, and for all those officials concerned in the

general and domestic police forces, this supervision is the particular responsibility of the Committee of General Security, in accordance with the decree of 17 September 1793. (Soboul 1974: 356).

The impact of the law was to remove power from the departments and to give it to the districts which were, in turn, put under the control of national agents appointed by and responsible to the government and therefore, in effect, to the Committee of Public Safety (Sutherland 1985: 235). Most importantly, under Section 18, the law disbanded all of the departmental and local people's armies, with the exception only of the Paris army, and also ended the collection of taxes which had been levied to pay for them (Cobb 1987: 524). At the same time and in consequence of the measures taken under Section 18 the powers of the Representatives on Mission were greatly reduced (Sutherland 1985: 236).

Before the law of 14 Frimaire, the Jacobin government had had full control neither over the forces of coercion nor over supply. Power had been devolved to the districts and local councils. The law of 14 Frimaire (4 December 1793) was introduced not at the height of the crisis of civil and foreign wars but as the civil wars were ended and defeats in foreign wars turned to victories. The war economy had been run by an emergency government and the law of 14 Frimaire marked the beginning of the Jacobin government's attempt to gain control over the unruly terror. According to Cobb (1987: 523):

> The law of 14 Frimaire was the result of the collective decision of the Committee of Public Safety. The origins of the law can be traced to Carnot's hostility in principle to armies of the interior, the unshakeable opposition of Lindet and the Prieur de le Côte d'Or to the use of force against the peasants, and above all to the examples of forced dechristianization which ran counter to Robespierre's metaphysical ideas.

Sydenham (1974: 22) argues that the aim of the law of 14 Frimaire was to control the Terror, though not to end it. The Paris Army, which still needed to operate and enforce the supply of Paris, remained, though it too was to go at the end of March. All other local and departmental armies, running essentially out of control, were at an end from December 1793 and restraint had been imposed on the local powers of the Representatives on Mission. In disbanding the people's armies, however, the force to uphold the Maximum had also disappeared.

THE LAWS OF VENTÔSE

Whilst Cobb views the law of 14 Frimaire as the establishment of the 'dictatorship of the Committee of Public Safety' (Cobb 1987: 526), Sutherland stresses that the Law of 14 Frimaire had only begun a process of centralization. Lucas (1973: 388), in a detailed local study, offers support; the law did little to change the Terror in the departments of the Loire. From the case of Javogues, Lucas argues that the Representatives on Mission were especially opposed to the centralization of the Terror and the law of 14 Frimaire therefore in practice produced little effect over the anarchy of the Terror in the departments. In late February and early March 1794 the laws of 8 and 13 Ventôse set up a bureaucracy for the organization of punishment and arrest. The Committee of General Security was given the power to arrest suspects on information given by local revolutionary committees (Sutherland 1985: 236). Regional revolutionary committees had been suppressed under the law of 14 Frimaire and the anarchic powers of local revolutionary committees were brought into line by the Ventôse laws. These laws, Sutherland (ibid: 236) argues, turned the two committees into a 'genuine dictatorship'.

Central state control over the coercive forces was not, however, completed by these Ventôse laws. Though the revolutionary tribunals had been made aware that they were under observation by the law of 14 Frimaire their centralization was yet to come. Furthermore, the strengthening of the police powers of the Committee of General Security by the laws of Ventôse created a problem which was to prove fatal to the Jacobin dictatorship. In order to achieve complete control over the forces of terror the Committee of Public Safety had also to gain control over the Committee of General Security whose police methods, in practice, went against its own intentions. This split between the two committees proved highly damaging to the Committee of Public Safety's attempt to gain control over the Terror itself. It becomes clear that Skocpol's preferred term 'Montagnard Government' in fact conceals not only the conflict between central and local authority but also that between the two Committees.

CONTROL OVER THE COERCIVE FORCES AND THE END OF THE TERROR

The rise in executions which occurred in June/July 1794 before the fall of Robespierre on 9 Thermidor (27 July) has generally been put down to in-fighting and the 'psychology of terrorism'. Once started, terror is hard to stop (Greer 1966: 116–17). This is the view taken by both Edwards and Brinton (see Chapter 3). Edwards and Greer also draw attention to the importance of the disaffection of the Paris workers as a consequence of a failure in economic policies. Skocpol agrees that these factors combined to produce the downfall of Robespierre, adding the proviso 'in the world-historical context of late 18th century France' (Skocpol 1979: 192–3); she also mentions Robespierre's attempt to enforce the Republic of Virtue and the failure of the Committee of Public Safety to remain united (ibid: 193). This split had not developed suddenly; differing views over policy had been important, none more so than over the policy of terror itself.

The split had begun back in November 1793 in response to the atrocities and destruction unleashed by the fall of Lyon. On the 5 Frimaire (25 November) Ronsin and the Parisian Revolutionary Army had entered the city and dealt out summary justice. At one point, over a third of Ronsin's Parisian Army was fighting in Lyon (Cobb 1987: 554). Writing about the executions, Ronsin commented: 'It is time to cut down the procedure!' (Wright 1974: Document 16). Soldiers of the Paris army were also those mainly, possibly exclusively, involved in the massacres which took place in addition to the official executions (Cobb 1987: 368). Danton, along with other 'indulgents' had led a campaign against the Terror. This 'indulgent' view had met strong opposition from the *Héberistes* (led by Hérbert and including Ronsin, the head of the Parisian army). The law of 14 Frimaire had addressed criticisms of terror to some degree. Robespierre, opposed to the anarchy of the dechristianization campaign and a supporter of religious toleration, attempted to achieve a compromise between the opposed positions (Wright 1974: 89). On 5 February, he launched a campaign for the building of 'private and public morals' (Sutherland 1985: 243). Through an appeal to morality, Virtue, Robespierre aimed to reduce the Terror (Wright 1974: Document 24, Soboul 1974: 397).

Robespierre's vision, heavily inspired by Rousseau's ideas of the general will and the social contract, was for a fundamental change in the way that people thought, towards the public good (Hampson 1986: 62–3). The worship of the Supreme Being was to replace the old hierarchical Catholic religion. The new civil religion with faith in human nature was to retain its spiritual and ethical content but to lose all the divisive aspects of Catholicism which made it a source of power separate and therefore in revolutionaries' eyes in opposition to the state. In reflection of this appeal to Virtue, the Committee of Public Safety clamped down on dishonesty amongst revolutionaries and 're-called terrorists who showed themselves to be lusting after blood' (Soboul 1974: 397). The Representatives on Mission were accountable to the Committee of General Security. Fouché was recalled from Lyon on 21 March (Sutherland 1985: 240). The *Héberistes* were arrested on 13–14 March and executed on the 24th. By 5 April, the Dantonists had been arrested and executed. Danton who had been corruptly making money out of the revolution was considered to have no place in a government setting itself above society as the epitome of public morality (ibid: 232).

With Ronsin gone, the Parisian army was disbanded on 28 March. These developments have been linked to a military plot to remove Robespierre from power. Cobb (1987: 567–617) takes the view that rumour of a plot was in fact used by the government to get rid of the Paris army whilst at the same time maintaining its image of revolutionary zeal. By March, in any case, the revolutionary army seemed to have run its natural course and pressure from soldiers as much as anyone else was towards a return to normality (ibid: 616–17).

Further central control over the forces of the Terror was introduced on 8 May when the provincial revolutionary tribunals were suppressed and all counter-revolutionary crimes were from then on to be tried by the Paris Revolutionary Tribunal. On 10 June the law of 22 Prairial was passed. This law officially deprived the accused of the right to defence and, however vague the crime, gave the Paris Tribunal only one punishment, death. The chances of acquittal were remote; dossiers on these 'suspects' were processed by special commissions (Sutherland 1985: 242).

THE LAW OF 22 PRAIRIAL

The law of 22 Prairial (10 June) had been introduced after assassination attempts had been made on both Robespierre and Collot d'Herbois. The aim of the law was to complete central control over the forces of terror. Representatives on Mission with continuing records of excessive use of terror were to return to Paris. All suspects were from then on to be tried in Paris, so fully ending the decentralized system of revolutionary tribunals. In April 1794 the Committee of Public Safety had set up its own special police (*Bureau de Surveillance*) (Sutherland

1985: 242, Schama 1989: 839). This new police bureau directly threatened the power of the Committee of General Security. Retention of power for the committee rested on the continuation of the Terror and not its end (Soboul 1974: 409).

The law of 22 Prairial was never allowed to operate properly. The Committee of General Security, in charge of gathering information on suspects, chose to bring large groups of people under a whole range of different charges from the relatively minor to the highly serious, and condemn them as a group rather than trying them each in turn. Prison conspiracies were used as an excuse (Soboul 1974: 406). The effect was highly damaging for Robespierre's government, made worse by the committee's ridiculing of Robespierre's Fête of the Supreme Being on 20 Prairial (8 June) (Sutherland 1985: 242).

THE FAILURE OF POLICY

Soboul (1974: 391–2) argues that had the Committee of Public Safety not been split over social and economic policies – Carnot, in particular, was opposed to building state-owned factories other than for munitions and Saint-Just's promises in Feb–March 1794 to distribute confiscated properties to the poor came to nothing (p.396) – and had it not sided with the bourgeoisie in making wage maximums a central plank of policy from April 1794 (workers wanted low prices and the bourgeoisie wanted low wages) then it would have had a chance of winning against the Committee of General Security. On 23 July 1794, five days before Robespierre went to the guillotine, the list of maximum wage rates was published by the Paris Commune. They represented a substantial wage cut for workers. The anger these cuts produced amongst the workers led to the uprising which opened the way for Thermidor. On the night of 9 Thermidor (27–8 July) Robespierre, Saint-Just, Couthon and 19 of their close allies were captured and sent to the guillotine (ibid: 393).

Soboul perhaps pays too little attention to the implications of disbanding the people's armies, the Paris army in particular. Without the Paris army, disbanded at the end of March, there would no longer have been an organization capable of ensuring the arrival of supplies to Paris, and without either price maximums would have been impossible to enforce. The inherent conflict of interests over price fixing and wage restraint was therefore bound to sharpen. The Committee of Public

Safety was caught in a catch 22 situation. Without the justification for terror which the crisis of foreign and civil wars had brought, the continuation of the Terror sapped support. To gain control over the Terror it was necessary to suppress the violent people's armies which also provided the organization for feeding the towns, and Paris in particular. Failure to supply the towns also led to a withdrawal of support.[11] To stop the Terror or to retain it, to increase central economic control or relax it – either way led to crucial support being lost for the government and the government was split (Soboul 1974: 410). Whether or not, as Skocpol debates, the nature of industrial enterprises in France in 1794 offered the potential for central economic control, the decision to try to gain control over the Terror took away the practical force which guarded against hoarding and price excesses and which ensured the safe transport of supplies. Robespierre had opted for a spiritual solution, the Republic of Virtue. This emphasis on virtue in practice grated on the failure of the Committee of Public Safety actually to gain control over the Terror.

Robespierre's fall from power came for essentially two reasons:

- He had failed fully to centralize the means of coercion. The Committee of General Security and its policing activities had remained beyond the control of the Committee of Public Safety. The Jacobin government had, therefore, proved unable to gain control over the Terror. Indeed, the combination of emphasizing Virtue – 'we desire to see an order of things where all base and cruel feelings are suppressed, and where the law encourages beneficent and generous feelings' (Robespierre, 5 February 1795, in Wright 1974: Document 24) – whilst the Terror continued had proved disastrous.
- He had failed to adopt a practical economic policy capable of satisfying material demands, feeding the towns, and Paris in particular.

Lindet and Carnot who had been opposed to the excesses of the Terror were not executed and remained in the Committee of Public Safety though, in August, its dictatorial powers were ended and its responsibilities split between 16 committees (Sydenham 1974: 28). On 1 August the law of 22 Prairial was repealed and on 10 August the Revolutionary Tribunal was reorganized and was to consider in evidence the issue of intention to commit a crime as well as the nature of the criminal act (ibid: 29). Lindet retired from the Committee of Public Safety in October 1794 and was appointed President of the Committee of Commerce, Agriculture and the Arts (Soboul 1974: 434). Violence and famine continued, but the reign of terror was at an end.

PARTY, POLICY AND CENTRALIZATION

The establishment of the revolutionary state began only after the fall of Robespierre. Under the conditions of war, both civil and foreign, the committees of Public Safety and of General Security had formed only an emergency government, which the Committee of Public Safety had in practice failed to establish as permanent. The view of this period as temporary government was frequently declared by the revolutionaries themselves (see Carter 1981: 146–7). It is, then, Brinton's portrayal of the reign of terror as a temporary government which is supported.

The issue of whether the outcome for Robespierre could have been different had the Jacobins constituted a political party with organization and an agreed policy comparable to that of the Bolshevik Party, turns out to be a relevant point but for reasons other than those posed by Skocpol. Party discipline over the members of the Committee of General Security and the members of the Constituent Assembly sent to the regions and particularly associated with Terror – Le Bon (north), Carrier (Nantes, west), Fouché and Collot d'Herbois (Lyon) and Ronsin – might have provided a means for the control of excess. A party would have required an agreed view, but policy agreements amongst the Jacobins, over economic control, the use of terror and dechristianization, did not exist. Talmon's (1955) portrayal of the Jacobin Terror was, then, historically inaccurate. The evidence of Robespierre's fall has shown in any case that a spiritual ideology, even had it been unanimously accepted, would have been unlikely to have saved the regime.[12]

The survival of the Jacobin regime through the adoption of practical policies involving state control along the lines adopted by the Bolsheviks is ruled out by Skocpol for lack of industry in eighteenth-century France sufficiently developed to offer potential for state control. There is some evidence against this view in the development of state-owned armament industries and the potential for nationalization of mines which was avoided (Soboul 1965: 390–1). But practical policies did not rest solely on the potential for state control of industry. It was the problem of supplying the towns which lay behind the attempt to control prices and wages through the Law of Maximum. This law compounded the conflict of interests between town and country. As the people's armies showed, one form of practical response was to use force. An alternative would have been to have encouraged peasants to increase production and to sell their surplus more readily through perhaps redistributing the land in favour of the peasants who worked on it. Such ideas were not, however, compatible with the Committee of Public Safety's thinking for it did not square with revolutionary rights of private property (ibid 1974: 394–6). Whilst promises of sorts were made in Feb–March 1794, no significant redistribution of land took place and lands confiscated under the laws of 1789 (church lands) and 1792 (emigrés' and suspects' lands) were in practice sold to the highest bidder. By way of speculation, the land was often bought by rich townspeople and rented back to the peasants. Indeed anyone advocating radical 'agrarian law' ran the risk of execution (Kemp 1971: 88).

Policies adopted by the Jacobin regime reflected not only the constraints on the economically possible in 1793–4 but also the politically desired. Ideology had played a part, ruling out some policies, encouraging others. In practice, neither able to gain central control over the Terror nor capable of offering practical solutions to economic problems, Robespierre's regime was doomed. Of course, there was excess terror used in the French Revolution and in part the use of terror reflected ideology. As Hampson (1986: 64) remarks:

> If none of them had ever heard of Rousseau, there would have been a bloody business, but it would have been different. Ideology played its part in suggesting extreme solutions, in making compromise more difficult and in emboldening men to pursue fearful goals with easy consciences.

The evidence has clearly shown that some at least of that excess terror came not from Robespierre's insistence nor even from the collective decision of the Committee of Public Safety. It was failure to gain control over the Committee of General Security and therefore the Terror itself which caused the escalation of executions towards the end. Without gaining central control over the forces of coercion a revolutionary regime cannot transform itself from an emergency government into a permanent one.

NOTES

1. Skocpol (1979: 333, fn. 38) has noted that Cobb (1987), in the earlier French
    edition, was one of the three works (the other two being Palmer 1941 and Soboul
    1974) from which she draws her discussion of the Jacobin dictatorship. In fact
    Cobb's work (which is not specifically referred to again anyway) includes mate-
    rial which suggests a rather different emphasis from the one which she takes.
    Sutherland (1985) gains particular significance not only because it was published
    after 1979 but because it engages directly with the debate dominated by Soboul
    (1974) with which work Skocpol too takes issue.
2. Greer's (1966) work is itself a debate with the contentious French histories of his
    day (the élite/mass analysis of Taine; the necessity, 'a dictatorship of national
    defence', of Aulard; and an economic explanation, Mathiez). Such debates re-
    main as fresh today as then and are relevant to more modern revolutions too.
3. In his study of Marseilles (where 289 people were officially executed), Scott
    (1973: 336–7) has shown that the Revolutionary Tribunal, 'a regular court given
    revolutionary powers', conducted itself according to the law and all accused
    were given the opportunity to defend themselves. By contrast Sydenham (1974:
    22), has drawn attention to 'the firing squads by which Barras and Freron supple-
    mented the work of the guillotine at Marseilles and Toulon'.
4. It is interesting to note that this law was first proposed by a Girondin, Lanjuinais
    (Sutherland 1985: 172). Lanjuinais was made a peer by Louis XVIII (ibid: 219).
5. It is a common error to suppose (see, for example, Adelman 1985: 4) that the
    conventional army was used to suppress counter-revolution in the major areas of
    civil war. Though this was sometimes the case, in Toulon for example, in fact it
    was usually the Paris People's Army which was used (Cobb 1987: ch.3, espe-
    cially section IV on Lyon). The Paris army also played an important part in the
    west (Loire–Inférieure) and also in Britanny (Finistére, ibid: 323).
6. Greer accepts that whilst the prison deaths from disease and overcrowding repre-
    sent a crucial aspect of the nature of the Terror, as unintentional deaths their
    analysis would be unlikely to contribute to an understanding of the motivations
    behind the Terror. He greatly regrets the need to drop from his analysis, for lack
    of equivalent records in individual cases, the cases of prisoners killed before trial
    (Greer 1966: 33).
7. For full descriptions of the composition of each social class listed in Table 1,
    column 1, below, see Greer (1966: Table V). The Upper Middle Class consists
    more fully of: non-noble high-ranking administrators, professionals (lawyers,
    architects, doctors and the like), top businessmen (bankers, manufacturers, pub-
    lishers, merchants and the like). The Lower Middle Class was mainly shop-
    keepers and trades people plus the lower ranks of public employees (clerks,
    police and so on) plus salesmen, nurses, millers, actors and the like.
8. Louie (1964: 384–7), in a re-working of Greer's statistics, has taken issue with
    Greer's class analysis. To some extent, his argument is odd, for he disregards
    Greer's own attempt to examine the proportions of victims within each class
    (reproduced in column 4 in Table 1 above). Re-doing the calculation for himself,
    Louie confirms Greer's finding. Taking Greer's statement that 'the Terror was an
    intra-class, not an inter-class, war' (Greer 1966: 98) out of context (for it comes
    before Greer goes on to examine the social incidence of victims as a proportion
    for each class) Louie mistakenly goes on to criticize Greer. He rightly points out
    that it would be useful to know the sizes of social classes within each depart-
    ment, though he remarks that such data are simply not available. Even so, as will
    be explained, Greer does make some attempt to consider this for the important
    areas, Bordeaux, Lyon and the Vendée.

Moore (1966: 518) takes issue with Greer and his statistic that 84 per cent of all victims were from the Third Estate: 'it seems impossible to deny that the Terror was an instrument of class warfare at least in its essential outlines'. Like Louie (1966: 385), Moore takes Greer's statement that 'the Terror was an intra-class, not interclass, war' out of context. This phrase often appears in works as if it were Greer's final word.

9. Skocpol (1979: 187) stresses only the effect of the foreign war in causing inflation and ignores the inflation which was its precursor in spite of seeming to accept Soboul's account of the Brissotins engineering war to draw patriotic support in the expectation of quick victory.

10. Louie (1966) expresses concern over the validity of the correlations with respect to the recordings of charges made against each victim. He draws attention to the difficulty 'in the feverish heat of the Terror' (p.384) of being sure of the meaningfulness of each recording. This is a rather less important criticism, though, than Louie implies. Indeed, 'sedition' may have been the easiest and quickest catch-all phrase. It is the nature of revolutionary reigns of terror, after all, that the innocent as well as the guilty fall victim.

11. In his study of Marseilles, Scott offers support to Soboul's view that the Jacobins were unconcerned with the social distress faced by ordinary people: 'distress affecting the lower classes was blamed by the Jacobins on the machinations of their political enemies and so the need for radical social reform was obviated' (Scott 1973: 344).

12. Whilst accepting that a case can be made for observation of the structure of the Jacobin Clubs, Feher (1987: 67), in considering it an early political party, argues that the Jacobin idea of a general will prevent it acting as a party because it ruled out factions. The argument presented has suggested that disagreements amongst Jacobins were very important, but it is notable that viewed from either direction the Jacobins fail in practice to fit the idea of a political party. In elections candidates were always obliged to stand as individuals.

5. Revolutionary Terror in the Russian Revolution: The Second Classic Case

One of the problems in seeking generalizations is the interdependence of events. Dramatic events, such as the French Terror, are especially likely to provoke reaction from others in similar situations. At the very least it would be expected that rather than ignoring one of the most startling episodes of history, some attempt to draw lessons might be made, with the intention either to avoid similar outcomes or to emulate them, and in practice probably a combination of the two. The extent to which such intention proves feasible is of the essence, for if the political actors of history cannot benefit from the lessons of history it follows that the discovery of reigns of terror in each revolution would indicate the unearthing of a law-like generalization; if not, the common occurrence of revolutionary reigns of terror leaves scope for the politicians involved to make choices but under commonly encountered circumstances.

There is no doubt that the Bolsheviks pondered at length the lessons of Robespierre (Carr 1966, Vol.1: 160–7). Carr quotes Lenin: 'the great bourgeois revolution of France 125 years ago made their revolution great by means of the terror' (ibid: 165). In *Terrorism and Communism*, written in 1920, Trotsky makes comparison with the French Revolution:

'The iron dictatorship of the Jacobins was evoked by the monstrously difficult position of revolutionary French. Here is what the bourgeois historian says of this period: 'Foreign troops had entered French territory from four sides. In the north, the British and the Austrians, in Alsace, the Prussians, in Dauphine and up to Lyons, the Piedmontese, in Roussillon the Spaniards. And this at a time when civil war was raging at four different points: in Normandy, in the Vendée, at Lyons, and at Toulon.' (page 176). To this we must add internal enemies in the form of numerous secret supporters of the old regime, ready by all methods to assist the enemy.

The severity of the proletarian dictatorship in Russia, let us point out here, was conditioned by no less difficult circumstances. There was one continuous front, on the north and south, in the east and west. Besides the Russian White Guard armies of Kolchak, Deniken and others, there are attacking Soviet Russia, simultaneously or in turn: Germans, Austrians, Czecho-Slovaks, Serbs, Poles, Ukranians, Roumanians, French, British, Americans, Japanese, Finns, Esthonians, Lithuanians... In a country throttled by a blockade and strangled by hunger, there are conspiracies, risings, terrorist acts, and destruction of roads and bridges. (Trotsky 1963: 50)

Trotsky goes on to throw the mantle of reflected glory over the Bolsheviks' shoulders by quoting Plekanhov who in an article on 'The Centenary of the Great Revolution' published in 1890, wrote of the Jacobins' 'gigantic courage to take all measures necessary for the safety of the country, however arbitrary and severe they were'. Clearly Trotsky predates Edwards in drawing causal generalizations about reigns of terror – wars with foreign countries, civil wars at home and counter-revolutionary plots – and supports Brinton in stressing hunger. The nationalities prove a new factor.

Trotsky's analysis comes in the form of a defence against accusations of the terrorism inherent in the Marxist notion of 'the dictatorship of the proletariat' made by Kautsky in 1918 in a publication of the same name. Ideology versus pragmatism remains the crux of the debate over the revolutionary reign of terror in Russia 1918–22. In essence the debate over the Bolshevik Terror revolves around the question of whether the use of coercion amounted to a necessary expediency in the face of mounting economic, political, social and international pressures or whether, rather, the terror was the essential means by which a pre-conceived ideology of class conflict, involving the suppression of the bourgeoisie and rich peasants in favour of the proletariat, and therefore the establishment of the communist state, could be turned into reality. Whilst the evidence of the importance of the civil war in inflaming the terror is generally accepted, that evidence alone is unable to settle the disagreement over whether or not Bolshevik ideology, in the guise of war communism, provoked the civil war or whether, in turn, use of terror was itself a necessary action taken to redress counter-revolution.

THE EARLY DAYS OF REVOLUTION

Like the French Revolution in July 1789 overthrow of the old order in Russia began with a spontaneous uprising. After February 1917, in

Russia, though, events moved more quickly than in France. By October 1917 (November 7 on the new calendar) the Bolsheviks were installed in power and they, unlike the Jacobins, kept power in their grasp. Events between February and October 1917 developed in ways similar to those in the French Revolution after the outbreak of war in April 1792. Worsening war fortunes drained support from the Provisional Government, set up in February, and protests against the war took place in Moscow and Petrograd. Economic problems contributed to disorder at home – The problems of food supply, inflation, decreasing wages (money as well as real income), and unemployment were especially grave. In Petrograd and Moscow bread rations were cut by half and distribution problems grew worse as the railway system fell apart. Without grain coming from the Ukraine, by the summer of 1917 Moscow and Petrograd faced starvation. The amount of money in circulation more than doubled between January and October 1917 and workers' pay fell from around 19.3 roubles per month at the start of the February Revolution to only 13.8 by the summer of 1917. Whilst wages were falling for those in work the numbers out of work were growing equally sharply as industries closed down production and workers were dismissed. Strikes were the inevitable consequence (Liebman 1972: 139–40). In June the Provisional Government embarked on an offensive in Galicia, which failed to bring victory. Violent workers' demonstrations broke out and peasant conscripts in the army began to desert from the war front to claim their land. Land seizures escalated between July and October (ibid: 141, Wolf 1973: 88–9).[1]

In this combination of unfavourable war fortunes and domestic insurrection the situation which opened the way to Bolshevik rule was similar to that which had brought the Jacobins to power. In practice, however, political events were very different. On the night of 24–5 October (7–8 November) the Military Revolutionary Committee of the Bolshevik Petrograd Soviet took power by force, overthrowing Kerensky's Provisional Government. A situation of dual power had existed between the Provisional Government and the Soviets (local councils of workers and soldiers) from the start (see Carr 1966, Vol.1: 92–3). The Petrograd Soviet, under Order Number 1 which ordered the formation of soldiers' courts, had control over the army (Ulam 1969: 419). Alone in their opposition to the war, and offering a combined policy of economic reform, peace and political change outlined in Lenin's 1917 'April Theses', the Bolsheviks gained support and membership of the party organization grew. At around 23,600 just before the February Revolution, membership was approximately 115,000 soon after the October Revolution (Carr 1966, Vol.1: 210). In August the Bolsheviks scored a notable success in the city elections in Petrograd where they gained a third of the votes cast and ran the Socialist Revolutionaries (at 37 per cent) a very close race. Following a failed coup by the commander-in-chief of the Russian Army, General Kornilov, the Bolshevik ranks were further swelled by crucial changes in party allegiances amongst the leaders of the soviets. In September the Bolsheviks gained a victory in the Moscow elections, this time with an overall majority of 51 per cent of the seats (Liebman 1972: 231). The power of the Provisional Government had ebbed away on the tides of war, economic hardship and peasant demands for land reforms.

Already set in motion, elections to the Constituent Assembly were held on 12–14 November, less than two and a half weeks after the October coup. The outcome was a victory neither for the Bolsheviks nor the Mensheviks but for the Social Revolutionaries, the party most favoured by the peasants. The Constituent Assembly met on 18 January (31 on the western calendar) and was dissolved the next day.

SOVNARKOM AND VTsIK

With the fall of the Provisional Government a temporary central government was set up, the Council of People's Commissars, Sovnarkom, with Lenin as Chairman. Local government continued under the workers', peasants' and soldiers' councils (soviets) with a new kind of double power retained within the All-Russian Central Executive Committee (VTsIK) of the Congress of Soviets which had first met in June 1917. Whilst Bolsheviks were now present on both VTsIK and Sovnarkom, which had not been the case under the dual power of the Provisional Government and Soviets, rivalry between the two central organizations continued, 'a time of very noticeable friction' (Carr 1966, Vol.1: 156, quoting a commentator of the day). Five days after the overthrow of the Provisional Government, Sovnarkom decreed itself powers of legislation (for the interim until the Constituent Assembly could be formed) with VTsIK given the right to 'defer, modify or annul that legislation' (ibid).

The Socialist Revolutionaries in VTsIK were soon objecting to Sovnarkom issuing decrees without consulting them. The result of the ensuing debate went against the Soviet Revolutionaries and Sovnarkom won the vote to issue urgent decrees without consulting VTsIK, and this power was retained within the draft of a new constitution for the Russian Socialist Federal Soviet Republic (Carr 1966, Vol.1: 157). The new constitution was approved by the All-Russian Congress of Soviets when it met for the fifth time in July 1918. The important clause for the development of Sovnarkom's power read: 'measures of extreme urgency may be put into force on the sole authority of Sovnarkom' (ibid: 222). As Carr goes on to remark, under conditions of civil war, when all measures were likely to count as urgent and with Lenin, whose revolutionary prestige counted for so much, at its head Sovnarkom was bound to evolve as the government of the RSFSR. Between 1917–21, Sovnarkom issued 1,615 decrees and VTsIK only 375 (ibid: 222, fn.1). Neither VTsIK nor the local soviets were able under pressure of civil war to provide the central organization required (Rigby 1979: 169).[2]

On coming to power, the new Bolshevik-dominated government, Sovnarkom, faced two immediate problems: the conduct of the war and the supplying of the capital city. Stocks of grain in Petrograd, on the day after the October Revolution, were down to starvation levels, less than sufficient rations to supply the population of Petrograd with half a pound of bread (Rigby 1979: 16). (Moscow became the capital city on 10 March 1918 when the government moved there under threat of German invasion (ibid: 30).) Trotsky's Military Revolutionary Committee of the Petrograd Soviet, which had led the Bolshevik takeover, took on the task of obtaining supplies through force, requisitioning food, penalizing speculators and sending troops to obtain supplies from the provinces (ibid: 16).[3] Provisional Military Revolutionary Committees were soon set up under the authority of VTsIK.

Exactly one calendar month after the Bolshevik takeover, Sovnarkom issued a decree to abolish the existing judicial structure and replace it with both new legal institutions and procedures. Promising democratic reforms, election of judges, a system of appeal, it decreed the setting up of revolutionary tribunals made up of peasants and workers. Their job was to 'fight counter-revolution ... as well as to try cases against profiteering, speculation, sabotage, and other abuses of merchants, manufacturers, officials and other persons' (Bunyan and Fisher 1965: 292). On 1 January 1918 (new calendar) the operation of the revolutionary tribunals was clearly laid out. The tribunals were to be elected by the soviets, all trials were to be by jury (between 6–8 elected jurors for each trial), were to last no more than a week and were to be open to the public. All suspects were to be brought to trial within 48 hours or released, were to have the right to defence counsel and to appeal via the People's Commissar of Justice to the Soviet (ibid: 293–5).

THE CHEKA: SECRET POLICE TO 'TERROR MACHINE'

On 20 December 1917 (7 on the old calendar) the All-Russian Extraordinary Commission for Combatting Counter-revolution and Sabotage was set up under Sovnarkom. This Cheka or Vecheka, the acronym for its full Russian title, was a secret police system. The Cheka was to become the instrument of the Terror; as an 'extraordinary' organization it was not intended to be permanent (Leggett 1981: 129).[4] The job of the Cheka was to bring counter-revolutionaries and saboteurs before the Revolutionary Tribunal, to work towards a plan for fighting counter-revolution and to make investigations into counter-revolutionary acts in order to break them up (Bunyan and Fisher 1965: 297). The police functions of the Military Revolutionary Committees (MRCs) were taken over by the Cheka, leaving the MRCs with control only over military operations (Rigby 1979: 60). With negotiations for peace under way, the MRCs soon effectively lost all of their functions. Truly effective soviet-based people's militias never developed and over time the Cheka took on ordinary police duties too (Leggett 1981: 122–3).

From the start, partly as a consequence of their secretness, the Cheka's powers were in contest with other revolutionary organs and nowhere more so than with the soviets and their revolutionary tribunals (see Gerson 1976: 189–209). With the setting up of the Red Army the soviets were further to lose power. The MRCs were replaced by the Worker–Peasant Red Army following a decree of the Sovnarkom on 28 January 1918 (Bunyan and Fisher 1965: 568–9). Whereas the MRCs had been accountable to the soviets, the Red Army was under the authority of Sovnarkom.[5] On 22 February 1918 a proclamation was issued declaring 'The Socialist Fatherland in Danger' (Carr 1966, Vol.1: 168). Straight away the Cheka issued instructions to local soviets which amounted to summary justice. Spies, organizers and agitators of counter-revolution, speculators, those buying and selling arms for use by 'the counter-revolutionary bourgeoisie' or leaving for the Don to join in counter-revolution were all 'to be shot on the spot ... when caught red-handed in the Act' (Bunyan and Fisher 1965: 576). The first such execution took place on 24 February, it represented the point from which the revolutionary tribunals began to lose power.

By February 1918 the full staff at the Cheka headquarters was 120 (Carr 1966, Vol.1: 169), by 10 June 1918 they numbered 1,000 (Leggett 1981: 34). An armed combat detachment of the Cheka had also been formed at the end of March. By the end of April it alone numbered 1,000 (750 of them riflemen) (ibid: 36). From April onwards local chekas were set up, 43 by June 1918, though atrocities on their part led to their abolition in January 1919 (ibid: 37 and 137). By January 1919, in addition to the Petrograd and Moscow chekas, there were 40 provincial, 365 district and 34 frontier chekas and the Cheka troop corps had grown to 20,000, making a total of 37,000 personnel under the Cheka establishment (ibid: 100). By December 1921, Cheka numbers had reached their peak of 143,000 (ibid: 346). Essentially the organization grew with the civil war. In February 1919 the Cheka's right to shoot without trial was restricted to the areas under martial law. By June, though officially still restricted to areas of civil war (a restriction regularly disregarded), the role of the Cheka was expanded from mainly military into more economic concerns – keeping transport moving, the railways especially, and seeking out deserters from industry as well as from the army.

THE VICTIMS

For Russia, there is no equivalent to Greer's statistical analysis of the French terror; similarly detailed evidence is simply not available. George Leggett, *The Cheka: Lenin's Political Police* (1981), offers the most thorough and the most recent work. As Leggett (ibid: 463) clearly establishes, the difficulty of generating a reasonable estimate of the number of Cheka executions is compounded by the nature of the available sources. Emigré works generally exaggerate whilst the Soviet press of the time (from September 1918, the names and crimes of those executed were supposed to be published) were underestimated by failure to report executions (ibid). This lack of evidence naturally prevents any systematic analysis of either the social origins of victims or their crimes.

The most frequently quoted estimate of the numbers who died as a direct consequence of the Terror is Chamberlin's figure of 50,000 (Liebman 1972: 338, Hingley 1970: 126), which does not include those killed bearing arms. As Hingley contrasts nicely estimates have ranged from 12,733, given by Latsis, the chairman of the Ukraine Cheka, to 1,700,000 for 1918–19 alone given by Deniken, the White Russian General. On considered estimation Leggett (1981: 467) puts the number of deaths during the Terror of December 1917 – February 1922 at around 280,000. Of these he deduces that around half died through execution and the remainder in insurrection. This figure he compares with Conquest's estimate for 1917–23 of a minimum 200,000 executions expanding to a maximum 500,000 if those killed in insurrections and those dying as a direct result of treatment in prisons or concentration camps are included. As Leggett points out, however, Conquest's figures include deaths not at the direct hand of the Cheka and extend beyond the end of the Cheka's existence. Leggett takes as his cut-off points the dates on which the Cheka was set up, 7 (20) December 1917, and replaced, 6 February 1922. Gerson (1976: 188) too takes the replacement of the Cheka as the end of the revolutionary terror (astonishingly Edwards (1970: 182) puts the Red Terror as 'lasting [only] into 1919').

As Greer had for France, Leggett for Russia had the problem of separating out the direct from the indirect victims. In addition to the 17,000 official executions Greer reached the estimate of 35–40,000 by the inclusion of those who had died in the prisons as a direct result of their appalling conditions and captured rebels, shot without trial. Leggett has only Latsis' official figure of 12,755 (1918–20) to build upon. This figure he expanded by consideration of prisoners summarily executed (perhaps as many as 1,000 of whom were shot in order to counteract the effects of an (unfulfilled) end to capital punishment in January 1920) in order to pre-empt the periodic amnesties or when 'evacuating prisons in the face of approaching White forces', or 'regular mass exterminations by shooting or by drowning in barges' (Leggett 1981: 464 – a chilling reminder of the drowning in the Loire in Jacobin France). Leggett, unlike Greer, does not, however, appear to take into consideration deaths caused by prison conditions. The figures on forced labour camps (run jointly by chekas and the Commissariat for Internal Affairs) such as are available – between 34–120 camps and 8,660–60,457 inmates between 1 January 1920 and 1 December 1921 (ibid: 178) suggest that prison numbers were not great, though as Leggett points out this may have been due to the Cheka's habit of mass extermination. If so then their numbers are largely already taken account of in the figure of 140,000 executions. Evidence on concentration camps (solely maintained by chekas) suggest that at the dissolution of the Cheka, in February 1922, there were 56 camps with a 'holding capacity' of 24,750 (ibid: 180).

Comparison between French and Russian figures is not, then, straightforward but Greer's estimates of 40,000 victims bears comparison with Leggett's 140,000. With the population of France in 1793 at around 25 million and Russia in 1917 at around 103 million the victims of the Terror turn out to be remarkably similar as a proportion of population size. It would be wrong to read any particular significance into this but the advantage of suggested equivalence which is comforting for a comparative study.

Just as Greer's estimate expanded the official figures and so undermined Edwards' assertion that dramatic executions actually save lives, so does Leggett's expansion of Latsis' official figures. The printing in the press of the names of those executed by the Cheka may have had the effect of creating fear in the hearts of the potential counter-revolutionary and no doubt in the innocent too, but rather than the ten lives saved by this exploitation of fear, the estimates suggest that more than ten times the number listed were in fact being killed. Nevertheless, Edwards' claim cannot be held to be totally without foundation in the initial period. Between January and July 1918, Latsis records only 22 deaths as compared to 12,733 from July 1918–December 1920 (Leggett 1981: 464). Carr (1966, Vol.1: 171, fn.3), whilst accepting that the number of victims was comparatively low in the first half of 1918, argues that the figure of 22 is far too low and many have referred only to Moscow's total.

As did Greer for France, Leggett finds the toll of victims most highly correlated with the areas of civil war. He (1981: Appendix C) offers the following set of figures: June 1919, 5,000 people executed in Tsaritsy following the defeat of the White Army; between 1,300–2,000 shot in Odessa before the White Army captured it on 23 August 1919; upwards of 3,000 prisoners executed in Kiev, before the end of August 1919; 1,500 executed in Saratov, 1919–20; following the defeat of Wrangel in November 1920, total executions in Balaklava and Sebastopol perhaps as high as 29,000 with estimates for the Crimea as a whole put at 50,000–150,000. The reprisals following the end of the civil war have been given an outside estimate of 100,000 (40,000 being the lowest estimate) for the Tambov provinces, the Ukraine and Siberia together.

The evidence, such as it is, does not permit the careful breakdown of social statistics in which Greer engages. In the Tambov provinces and the Ukraine especially peasants overwhelmingly formed the victims. During the year from mid-1920 to mid-1921 peasant rebellions were particularly rife especially in the Ukraine, the Kuban Cossack region and the Tambov provinces (where between 40,000–50,000 peasants were involved in the Tambov revolt at one point). In the anarchist Makhno's rebellion, 1918–21, Leggett reports estimates of 200,000 peasants being killed, though these would have included Reds as well as Whites, and of the Whites only a proportion would have been at the direct hands of the Cheka. There were reports too of the bourgeoisie being singled out for execution, in Adzerbaijan for example (Leggett 1981: Appendix C).

Some exact statistical information does exist for 17,000 inmates of forced labour camps of whom, on 1 November 1920, just under a half were Cheka prisoners: 39 per cent were peasants, 34 per cent workers. Their crimes were as follows: 4,500 counter revolution; 3,500 'crime'; 3,000 speculation; 3,000 military desertion; and 2,000 'mis-use of authority' (Leggett 1981: 178). No similar statistics are available for the concentration camps. It is impossible to be sure of the extent to which these analyses parallel the statistics for the executed. Sakwa (1988: 62) offers a more detailed breakdown for the arrests and execution by the Cheka in Moscow between December 1918 and November 1920: 67 per cent (26,700) of those arrested were accused of speculation of whom 53 were shot; 13 per cent (5,250) were arrested for 'labour offences' (taking bribes, desertion from work, theft from work and the like) of whom 102 were shot. Most of the 'speculators' – bagmen – were arrested in raids on the markets and 70 per cent of these were listed as unemployed.

Clearly the fact that reigns of terror occurred in both the French and Russian cases of itself represents support for Edwards' and Brinton's claim for terror as a necessary stage of revolution. In respect of these revolutions' common causes, the breakdown of figures offers support for the crucial association with civil war, for the importance of economic crimes and for class conflict in some areas.

EXPLAINING THE TERROR: EXPEDIENCE OR IDEOLOGY?

In respect of foreign wars, certainly both Russia and France were at war when the Bolsheviks and Jacobins came to power but important differences between the two cases existed. In France, where revolution had broken out in 1789, war had developed in 1792 as a reaction to the revolution. By contrast the February 1917 revolution in Russia had occurred, at least in part, because of the devastation already brought by the country's involvement in World War I. The failure of the Provisional Government to end the war, or even turn its fortunes in Russia's favour, had opened the way for the October Revolution (Ulam 1969: 448). The intention to end Russia's involvement in the war was a crucial plank of Bolshevik policy and indeed the one clear issue on which the Bolsheviks were divided from all other parties at the time. This anti-war stand was an important difference between Bolsheviks and Jacobins.

After protracted negotiations which broke down in February 1918 (and which produced Sovnarkom's proclamation 'Socialist Fatherland in Danger' and prompted the move from Petrograd to Moscow), Lenin succeeded in negotiating a peace with the Germans. The Brest–Litovsk Treaty was signed in March 1918. The treaty secured neither the end to foreign invasion nor the removal of its threat but it did remove the immediate prospect of the defeat of the revolution through German occupation of Petrograd. (For a full account of events leading to Brest–Litovsk see Ulam 1969: 511–42.)

The repercussions of Brest–Litovsk were serious:

- The Ukraine, the major wheat-growing area, was sacrificed to the Germans, seriously exacerbating the grain shortage already wrought by the years of war and the revolution itself. The need to feed the cities, Moscow and Petrograd most especially, became immediately more critical.
- The sacrifice of the rich industrial areas of the Baltic further threatened economic collapse and made future battle, requiring an increase in the production of armaments, a potential Achilles heel.
- Parts of the Caucuses were conceded to Turkey (Ulam 1969: 532).
- Finland and the Polish territories were surrendered to the Germans.
- In total 27 per cent of arable land, 33 per cent of manufacturing industries and 26 per cent of the population went to Germany (Bradley 1975: 46).

It was the nationalities who were most affected by the changes and their differences were to play a part in the developments of the civil war which lay ahead.

The most immediate problem facing Lenin was that of political opposition. Before Brest–Litovsk the Left Socialist Revolutionaries (Left SRs) had shared power with the Bolshevik Party on Sovnarkom. Having voted against the treaty in the All-Russian Congress of Soviets and lost, the Left SR members withdrew. The Sovnarkom thus became a single-party government, though Left SRs remained in both the local soviets and the Soviet Central Committee, VTsIK, and continued to do so after 14 June 1918 when the Right SRs and Mensheviks were banned for being counter-revolutionary. The All-Russian Congress of Soviets which met in Moscow in July 1918 had 745 Bolsheviks and 352 Left SRs, leaving just 35 other delegates (Carr 1966, Vol.1: 169–72).

Lenin's insistence on ending the war, even at such heavy cost, in the eyes of Menshevik and Left and Right SRs alike had cast him and the Bolsheviks in the mould of German spies whilst the parties opposing the treaty were viewed in Bolshevik eyes as counter-revolutionary supporters of the Allies. When the Japanese landed in Vladivostok in April 1918 opposition was galvanized into action:

'In the spring and summer of 1918 Moscow became a focus round which Allied and German agents, fragmentary groups of the Right and Centre, and the surviving parties of the Left all wove their several, or sometimes joint, plots and intrigues against the Soviet Government. (Carr 1966, Vol.1: 169).

This culminated in a series of assassinations and revolts. On 6 July, two SR members of the Cheka assassinated the German Ambassador and revolts followed in Moscow and the provinces. The Moscow insurrection was repressed and 13 Left SRs were shot (including members of the Cheka and delegates to the All-Russian Congress of Soviets). Assassinations continued and in August Uritsky (second-in-command of the Petrograd Soviet and head of the Petrograd Cheka) was killed in Petrograd; on the same day Lenin was badly wounded in an assassination attempt (Leggett 1981: 105). The result was the adoption by the VTsIK of the following resolution (quoted in Carr 1966, Vol.1: 176):

All counter-revolutionaries and all who inspired them will be held responsible for every attempt on workers of the Soviet Government and upholders of the ideals of the socialist revolution. To the white terror of the enemies of the Workers' and Peasants' Government the workers and peasants will reply by a mass red terror against the bourgeoisie and its agents. (VTsIK Resolution, 2 September 1918)

As Carr points out, the resolution bears ominous comparison with the Law of Suspects of the same day and same month in France, 1793. According to Carr (1966, Vol.1: 176) 2 September 1918

marked the turning-point after which the terror, hitherto sporadic and unorganized, became a deliberate instrument of policy... Faced with treason on this large scale at a moment when allied forces were landing in Murmansk and Vladivostock, when the Czech legions had begun open hostilities against the Bolsheviks and when the threat of war was looming on all sides the Soviet Government was under no temptation to resort to half measures. (ibid: 173).

THE EFFECTS OF POLICIES

Leggett opposes the view of the Terror as a necessary reaction to crisis; he argues that terror was inherent in both Lenin's theory and practice of revolution: 'The Red Terror undoubtedly sprang from Lenin's doctrine of terror, preached and practised since October as an integral part of his unrelenting pursuit of power' (Leggett 1981: 102), the terror 'stemmed logically from Lenin's doctrine of class conflict, which postulated the dictatorship of the proletariat imposing its will on the bourgeoisie by a reign of terror' (ibid: 113).

Trotsky's defence, in terms of the pressure of circumstances threatening the revolution, and Lenin's that 'Terror was forced upon us by the terrorism of the Entente, when the hordes of the Great Powers of the world fell upon us, stopping at nothing' (quoted by Leggett 1981: 102) are rejected by Leggett for the very reason that foreign intervention only began in August 1918 (with the occupation of Archangel by Anglo-American troops, a Japanese landing in Vladivostok and the Allied forces' advance on Baku). He dismisses earlier foreign threats and encroachment and argues that in practice it had been Bolshevik policy which had sparked Allied aggression following Trotsky's decision in mid-May to disarm the Czech legion by force (ibid: 102). Whilst squarely blaming Lenin's doctrine and practice of terror, Leggett does allow that the civil war made the terror more ferocious (ibid); atrocities occurred on all sides (see Hingley 1970: 129–30). Crucially, though, Leggett argues that the civil war itself began as a peasant reaction to Lenin's provocative policy of food requisitioning, a deliberate policy of terror directed against rich and middle peasants (ibid: 103).

Opinions clearly contrast on the period between the setting up of the Cheka and the events of Summer 1918: for Carr, the use of coercion is viewed as the necessary reaction of any new revolutionary government faced with a similar counter-revolutionary situation; whilst Carr draws attention to the Left SRs' role in assassinations, Leggett claims that it was only the restraint imposed on Lenin by the Left SRs in Sovnarkom (until March 1918) and VTsIK which ensured that the terror remained mild. Carr would not deny Lenin's many utterances on the need for terror, as discussion of Lenin's references to the Terror of the French Revolution has shown, but he notes behaviour as well as statements. Relatively few executions took place in the first six months (which Leggett also allows) and Carr views Lenin's opposition to those who wished to abolish the death penalty as realistic.[6] It was abolished the very day after the Bolshevik takeover and debated and withdrawn and re-established at various times.

CIVIL WAR, FOREIGN WAR AND THE NATIONALITIES

Leggett's claim that Trotsky provoked allied aggression and support for the civil war by ordering the Czech Legion, on its way back to Vladivostok following the Brest–Litovsk Treaty, to be disarmed, by force if necessary, is not without foundation. It was an incident, however, which arose from the Allied powers' inability to take the decisive action necessary to extricate the Czech Legion from Russian soil, an inactivity which was itself provocative (Bradley 1975: ch.3). A series of incidents between Czech and Soviet troops reached a climax when a group of Czech soldiers lynched a Hungarian prisoner of war and having been arrested by Soviet troops were sprung from captivity by some Czech soldiers whilst others took arms from the arsenal (ibid: 88–9). In this light, though Trotsky's reaction was heavy handed it proves an unacceptable example of terror used for purely ideological reasons.

Both Bradley (1975) and Mawdsley (1987) agree with Leggett in dismissing Lenin's and Trotsky's claims that Allied intervention was a coordinated move to overthrow the Bolsheviks. Though the Allied forces (Britain, France, USA, Japan) did not like the Bolshevik government, and additionally so after the treaty of Brest–Litovsk, their prime concern in 1918 was to win the war (Bradley 1975: 55). After the Armistice in November 1918, the Allies were unable to agree a coordinated plan. The best they achieved was reached on 22 January 1919. From then on Bradley characterizes the action of the Allies as 'uninformed, impulsive and fraught with disagreement' (ibid: 68). Mawdsley (1975: 283–4) argues that 'The "fourteen-power" anti-Bolshevik Allied alliance that was featured in Soviet propaganda was a myth' and goes on to dismiss the importance of each in turn in no uncertain terms. Elsewhere he remarks, 'Allied commitments to Russia were tiny and confined to distant outlands' (quoted in Sakwa 1988: 22).

The threat of foreign invasion in August 1918 was not then a serious threat to the revolution and whilst the Allies played some part in territories on the edges of Soviet territory (such as Murmansk and Vladivostok in the North) and offered some financial organizational help, the war which threw the RSFSR into crisis was above all a civil war. It was a civil war, furthermore, in which the nationalities played a crucial part. The Bolshevik forces, the Reds, were essentially encircled by forces opposed to the revolutionary government. The Whites consisted of separate regional armies, occupying territories of the various nationalities not all of whom supported the White armies. In brief the civil war consisted of three White army advances led by Admiral Kolchak in Siberia (defeated July 1919), General Denikin in the south (from July 1919, reversed November 1920), General Yudenich in the north west (May 1919, peace December 1919) and a fourth attack led by Marshal Pilsudski in Poland (April 1920, armistice October 1920), strictly a foreign war (Bradley 1975: 55).[7]

In the south the Whites were looked upon by the Georgians, Adzerbaijanis and Armenians, who sought independence and resisted White incursions, as enemies for claiming the Caucases part of Russia. Lack of willing support for the Whites from the Crimeans and Tartars, who wanted only autonomy not independence, also proved damaging in battles against the Reds (Bradley 1975: 163). A similar problem was present in the Cossack territories where Don and Kuban cossack support proved an uneasy alliance. In the Ukraine, released by Germany after the armistice, local forces resisted both Red and White armies and Makhno's anarchist forces, eventually defeated by the Reds, were in alliance with the Bolsheviks from 1918–20. (For a full account of Makno's forces and their relationship with the Bolsheviks see Footman 1962: ch.6.) In the north west, White army fortunes were weakened by the independence hopes of the Lithuanians, Latvians and Estonians; in the east, Siberia contained 'hundreds of nationalities, which though insufficiently powerful to obtain independence were sufficiently powerful to subvert any power they disliked'; and the cossacks in the Urals 'jealously guarded their autonomies' (Bradley 1975: 164). In essence the local forces were divided, sometimes hostile to each other, often hostile to the Whites.

It was the Reds who offered hope to these nationalist dreams, promising and then granting forms of self-government (if often less than perfect) and in some states even granting forms of independence. These states were finally incorporated into the USSR some twenty years later but the Bolsheviks' lack of Russian chauvinism and nationalist policies proved astute (Mawdsley 1987: 282).[8]

POLAND: THE REVOLUTIONARY WAR

The Red Army engaged in only one strictly foreign war, in spite of the Bolsheviks' proclaimed ideology of world revolution. The war against Poland began when the Polish Army invaded the Ukraine in May 1920. Neither economically nor militarily strong enough to offer practical support to the Soviet Republics in Hungary (March–August 1919) and Bavaria (April–May 1919), Lenin was unable to resist the temptation offered by the Polish advance. War with revolutionary Poland had been wanted for some time (Davies 1975: 179, Bradley 1975: 173). Having achieved initial success in driving the Polish Army out of the Ukraine, Lenin urged that the Red Army march on Warsaw in the first step towards world communism, with Germany the glittering prize (Ulam 1969: 58). By 1920, following the Kapp Putsch in March, the German workers were in open rebellion in the Ruhr (see Moore 1978: 328–53). Germany was a prize in not only political ideological terms, for Germany's economy offered the prospect of the highly developed capitalist base which communism required and was nowhere more urgently needed than in economically backward Russia. Meeting defeat in Poland, however, the Red Army was forced to retreat in October 1920, leaving Poland its independence.[9]

NECESSITY AND CHOICE: ECONOMIC PROBLEMS AND CLASS CONFLICT

Leggett's other claim for the Bolsheviks' ideological use of terror was levelled in terms of their deliberate provocation of the peasants. He draws attention to the decree of 9 May 1918 which called 'all working and propertyless peasants to unite immediately for a merciless war on the Kulaks' and a further decree of 27 May which enabled the 'forcible collection of food supplies in grain-producing provinces in order to feed the starving cities' (quoted in Leggett 1981: 63 and 64). For this purpose, special groups of reliable workers were organized by local food committees under the authority of Narkomprod, the People's Commissariat for Food Supply (or procurement). The decree stated specifically that the purpose of these 'food detachments' was 'to organize the labouring peasantry against the Kulaks' (ibid: 64). On the 11 June, committees were set up all over Russia to help these food organizations. By a decree of 4 August 1918 the Food Commissariat set up guarding posts at critical points on the rail, road and waterway networks, where foodstuffs could be confiscated and those suspected of profiteering placed in the hands of the Cheka. For Leggett, the Bolsheviks cast poor peasant against rich peasant and cities against the countryside and so provoked the outbreak of peasant insurrections in July–September 1918.

Whether cast in class terms or not, the similarity between the role played by the people's armies stationed along the roads, and the waterways ensuring supplies to the towns, and to Paris in particular, in 1793–4 cannot pass without remark. Requisitioning in Russia, just as in France, was a part of warfare. As Carr argues (1966, Vol.2: 229): 'The requisitioning of essential supplies – meaning, at this time, food and equipment for the Red Army and food for the urban population – was rendered imperative by the civil war and could be justified on grounds of military necessity'.

Malle is in sympathy with Leggett's argument:

> The policy of food procurement was carried out with harshness and contempt for peasants' needs both because the Bolshevik leadership adopted a moralistic attitude to speculation, the economic reasons for which were disregarded, and because the economic interests and needs of the peasantry did not find any legitimation in Marxist ideology. (Malle 1985: 497)

Adding further support to Leggett, she continues: 'this policy was the greatest impediment to political support in the countryside and a decisive incitement to the organization of counter-revolution and the radicalization of opposition'. Malle's argument is that the reality of the situation demanded that the price of grain should have been increased (ibid: 346–7). In contrast to Leggett, she allows that in the face of the peasant revolts in the summer of 1918 Lenin spoke against the harassment of middle peasants and the price of grain was increased (ibid: 500). In the grip of civil war, however, policy was again hardened in January 1919 and coercion, not the incentive of profits, was used once more to secure surplus for fighting the war and for feeding the cities.

The need to feed the cities had been pressing from the start and the urgency was made greater by the Bolsheviks' decision to end the war with Germany. Unemployment grew as the armaments factories and industries geared up to war production were run down (see Smith 1983: 242–3). In Petrograd the number of people working in factories in April 1918 was only around 40 per cent of what it had been in January 1917, and the figure continued to fall. Many of the unemployed left the city for the countryside, but of those remaining there were 60,000 registered as unemployed in May 1918, with the total number of factory workers in Petrograd on 1 April 1918 only 148,710. The unemployed faced starvation and caused disturbances, protesting through picketing and demonstrations. The threat of starvation caused problems amongst the employed too. As hunger grew, productivity fell and where factories were unable to keep workers occupied, absenteeism became rife. (For figures above see ibid: 243–8; see also McAuley 1989.)

WAR COMMUNISM MID-1918–MARCH 1921

The policies introduced by the Bolsheviks from the summer of 1918 are known as 'war communism'. Their interpretation is vigorously disputed within the literature (see Sakwa 1988: 20, Roberts 1970, Malle 1985: ch.1). At an extreme, the view is held that the policies of war communism were either designed to turn the country into a true communist state or were the pragmatic response to the problems of economic scarcity and the urgent needs of civil war.

The policy package which comprised war communism is hard to pin down. Malle (1985), in a work of some 548 pages, refuses to define the term on the grounds that it was itself a dynamic system within a revolutionary change, and therefore encompasses the destruction of the old and facilitates the construction of the new, with itself a 'substantially incoherent phase' (p.25). Even so (p.373) she offers a neat description: 'that period which was characterized by a set of institutions aiming at central control over production and distribution, according to criteria and principles inspired by the nature of the class struggle and the ideology supporting it'. For Malle (ibid) it was the policy of food procurement which began the period of war communism. On 13 May 1918, by a decree of VTsIK and Sovnarkom, Narkomprod, the Commissariat for Food Supply was given extraordinary powers, in particular for the requisitioning of grain. (Medvedev 1979: 143).

Carr (1966, Vol.2: 152), along with most writers, puts the start of war communism not as May but as early August 1918 after a decree which significantly intensified the requisitioning of the grain. Under the decree the groups of workers and rural-based local food committees, 'committees of the poor' set up in May, were greatly expanded. Soviets, trade unions and factory committees were given powers to organize food detachments of 'workers and poorest peasants' to go to the grain-growing areas 'to obtain grain at fixed prices or requisition it from Kulaks' (quoted in ibid). Similar detachments were also organized to gather in the harvest. Not surprisingly the rich peasants, and some middle peasants, too, resisted. From the end of 1918 to early 1919 the committees of poor peasants were disbanded and collective farms began to be set up, and in February 1919 factories, trade unions and urban soviets were permitted to acquire land and organize their own collective farms (ibid: 159–65). Farms were also allotted to specific factories.

Industrial war communism began in June 1918 with nationalization. By the end of 1918 all areas of industry had been nationalized (banks had been nationalized after the October takeover.) Vesenkha, the Council of National Economy, which had been set up within weeks of the October Revolution, became the state organization for the central planning of industry, fixing prices, setting targets for export production and home consumption. By early 1919 the far smaller rural industries had been drawn in, while industries producing similar goods were collected together to form 'trusts' (Carr 1966, Vol.1: 179). In the end one-man management took over the organization of each enterprise, thereby reducing the importance of the trade unions. Vesenkha's importance declined in 1919 as its powers became overshadowed by the Council of Labour and Defence (STO) (ibid: 198). With the state as the major employer, control over labour was a natural step. In September 1918 the unemployed were forbidden to refuse work (Carr 1966, Vol.2: 202). In April 1919 labour was mobilized to work extra hours (ibid: 210). Initially this conscription was directed at absentee industrial workers, the bourgeoisie and peasants directed to do special duties (like cutting wood for fuel) but from March 1920 labour conscription was stepped up under STO and fell more heavily on industrial workers (Malle 1985: 479 and 502). Wage fixing began to be introduced from February 1919 (Carr 1966, Vol.2: 205).

From December 1918 a revolutionary tax (first tried in October 1918) began to be levied initially in money and later in kind from those owning property and earning more than 1,500 roubles a month. It was designed to 'fall with its full weight on the rich part of the urban population and the rich peasants' (quoted in Carr 1966, Vol.2: 248). This 'tax in kind' is taken as the policy which gave war communism its special distinction. It was calculated on the basis of supposed family need and anything above that was requisitioned (ibid: 250). The fixing of prices gave rise to rationing (with discrimination in favour of Red Army families, manual workers and some others) (ibid: 233). From May 1919 food rations for children under 14 were given free of charge and free distribution of state services and food rations were generally introduced. By 1920 rationing gave way to wages in kind and a money economy effectively ceased to exist as inflation drove it out of existence – the purchasing price of money in circulation at 1 July 1921 was worth little over 1 per cent of what it had been worth at 1 November 1917 (ibid: 259). Though not a policy as such, an illegal black market grew up which became an essential part of the economy. Eighty-five per cent of the workers in Moscow were using it to buy bread (Sakwa 1988: 60) and between 65–70 per cent of food needed for subsistence in the RSFSR as a whole was supplied in this way (Malle 1985: 504).

The extent to which these policies were forced upon the Bolshevik government hangs essentially on whether or not alternatives existed. Malle (1985: 49) points out that the alternative means for obtaining grain supplies were available through the inducement of increased grain prices. Though Lenin softened the policy for middle peasants in the autumn of 1918, to increase payment to the kulaks was not an ideologically acceptable alternative for the Bolsheviks who, as Marxists, rejected the anarchy of the market and held speculators and rich peasants in contempt. Panic had also played a part following Brest–

Litovsk, as had fear of losing the support of the industrial workers in the cities (ibid: 497–8). Essentially, though, communism had set boundaries on options.

By contrast, Malle argues that the nationalization of industry was not ideologically motivated but a reaction to worker demands, coming mostly from those employed in factories which would otherwise be shut down. Furthermore, she argues, payment in kind developed in response to workers seizing factory goods and exchanging them for food on the black market, whilst labour conscription developed because of worker-absenteeism (Malle 1985: 498). (For a discussion of the flight from cities during the civil war and the conditions faced by those remaining, see Brower 1989.) Whilst constrained by ideology, policies were reactions to circumstances directly encountered.

THE END OF WAR COMMUNISM AND THE INTRODUCTION OF NEP

War communism as a reflection of Marxist ideology is in any case undermined by its reversal in March 1921 when, at the Tenth Party Conference, Lenin introduced NEP, the New Economic Policy.[10] The introduction of NEP amounted to the reintroduction of the market. Its most important measure was the replacement of the 'tax in kind' with a new tax calculated as a percentage of crop production. The tax was to be graduated, falling most heavily on the rich, but it did permit peasants to retain a surplus above family needs which could be sold on the market (Carr 1966, Vol.2: 282). To facilitate this sale of surplus, restrictions on movement of goods for trade were removed in May. In effect, the black market became legal. Drought brought the horror of famine to the Volga basin in the summer and, in a turnaround, foreign aid was accepted through an agreement with Hoover's American Relief Fund (ibid: 285). The incentives offered by NEP for peasant production began to reap rewards in the spring of 1922, and the favourable weather of that summer brought the best harvest since the outbreak of the revolution. In March 1922 the new tax in kind was reduced to a standard 10 per cent (ibid: 294), and the decree of May 1922 made peasants' tenure of their land secure.

NEP, directed essentially at agriculture, had a bearing on industry too. In the summer of 1921 a series of measures effected a Bolshevik form of privatization as state control gave way to commercialism in the form of leases and trusts. Leasing was designed for small rural industries and non-profitable nationalized concerns whilst trusts were formed to gather small enterprises producing the same goods into large concentrations, with proper book-keeping and the purchasing of supplies on the market rather than exclusively from the state. State subsidies were in some cases withdrawn, and in those cases all goods produced could be sold on the open market; for trusts receiving state subsidies (all essential heavy industries), up to half of their products could be sold on the market. By 21 March 1922 the fuel industry became fully commercial (Carr 1966, Vol.2: 298–309). Alongside this increased commercialization a free labour market was reintroduced (compulsory labour being gradually abandoned) and a money wage system re-emerged with wages related to productivity (ibid: 318–22). In contrast with agricultural policies, on the whole the measures introduced brought little improvement in industrial production (ibid: 310). NEP did, however, bring a change from wage fixing to the establishment of a minimum wage.

NEP was not to last long and Lenin's early death, in January 1924, was to deny certainty over the long-term intentions following its introduction. For the short term, however, there seems no doubt that NEP was a central factor in the ability of the Communists to hold on to power after the civil war ceased to offer justification for coercion. This economic realism contrasts starkly with the metaphysics which Robespierre had offered in similar circumstances.

THE END OF THE CIVIL WAR AND THE CRISIS OF COERCION

Lenin's introduction of NEP at the Tenth Party Conference in March 1921 had occurred at the end of the civil war, when the country was faced with the worst worker and peasant disturbances since the summer of 1918 and, most critically, the Kronstadt Rebellion,.

In the summer of 1920 peace seemed to have returned as the Bolsheviks gained control in the civil war, but soon peasant uprisings started to increase and worker rebellions began to break out in the Red areas. Peasant rebellions against food requisitioning had been common from 1918 but in the late summer of 1920 they had escalated. The Tambov Rebellion broke out in August 1920 when 'the starving peasants of Kirsanov District rebelled against the oppressive extortion of grain' (Leggett 1981: 330). The revolt soon spread and a form of guerrilla warfare broke out led by the outlaw and ex-Left SR, Anatov. Coinciding with the Polish war and revived civil war action in the Don and Ukraine (Wrangel's and Makhno's forces) the Tambov Rebellion was not suppressed until April 1921, though by September 3,500 Cheka troops had been sent in to fight the rebels (ibid: 331).

Sakwa (1988: 240) argues that under these pressures the war communist economy 'collapsed'. Food shortages were the major factor. Compared with January–March 1920, grain procured from the provinces had fallen to less than half and grain from Siberia failed to reach the central, Bolshevik, areas because of transport disruptions, peasant riots and banditry (Malle 1985: 513). Moscow itself faced acute crisis. There were food shortages, chaos on the railways, drought which ruined not only the harvests but also the drinking water, and fires swept through the dry lands destroying peat and forests, creating fuel shortages and covering Moscow with smoke and soot. Before long not only Moscow workers but the soldiers also became rebellious. Indeed, between late 1920 and March 1921 2,000–3,000 soldiers of the Moscow garrison were shot. By January 1921 bread rations in Moscow, Petrograd, Kronstadt and Ivanovo–Voznesensk were reduced by over one-third and growing social disorder was the inevitable consequence (Sakwa 1988: 241). Factory workers and miners met in their workplaces criticizing the government and demanding better food supplies. These disputes soon grew into demands for freedom, freedom both to trade and to work and freedom from repression.

The use of force was the initial response but the Cheka thereby only made matters worse: 'The Cheka's heavy-handedness was itself a cause of the disturbances' (Sakwa 1988: 242). In Moscow the Metalworkers Union Conference of 2–4 February 1921 passed a resolution demanding free trade and a 'fixed tax in kind' to replace forced requisitioning. Workers were soon on the streets and when, on 20 or 21 February, a strike broke out at the money-printing factory soldiers called to suppress the strike refused to shoot. Replacements were brought in, resulting in several deaths and injuries; strikes and demonstrations then erupted and, on 23 February, 10,000 workers took part in a demonstration. Martial law was imposed. The workers responded by operating a go-slow in the factories and as a consequence the trade union leaders (Mensheviks) were arrested (ibid: 243–5).

During the month of February 1921, throughout Russia 118 independent risings were reported by the Cheka (Leggett 1981: 325). These rebellions culminated in March 1921 in the most famous one of all, the rebellion in Kronstadt, stronghold of the Bolshevik Revolution. As elsewhere, food shortages, resentment over food requisitioning and labour compulsion led to the Kronstadt Rebellion and anger was whipped up by disgust of the Cheka's reactions. On 17 March the Bolsheviks defeated the Kronstadt rebels with an estimated 1,000 Communists dead, wounded and missing; on the rebel side 600 were dead, 1,000 wounded, around 2,500 taken prisoner and 8,000 fled to Finland (ibid: 327). These then were the realities faced by Lenin at the Tenth Party Conference when NEP, which amounted to a reversal of war communism, was first introduced by Lenin.

On the one hand the introduction of NEP undermined any claim for war communism being determined purely by Marxist-Leninist ideology; some at least of the policies introduced under war communism had been responses to circumstances directly encountered, the civil war and the need to feed the cities in particular. On the other hand, the need to introduce NEP as a replacement for war communism shows that some at least of those policies had directly exacerbated the crisis. The development of the terror cannot be put down to necessity alone. As Sakwa (1988: 268) concludes: 'the economic policies of war communism were justified by ideology but often provoked by necessity'. War cannot, as Skocpol suggests, alone explain the development of central state organization during the period of the Red Terror. Ideology played its part in the choice of policies and whilst coercion (the Cheka, food requisitioning, labour conscription) developed in part at least to fight the civil war it developed also in response to the problems of supplying the towns. Unarmed domestic insurrection close at home and not only more distant full-scale civil war threatened the Communist government.

Significantly, the change in policy from war communism to NEP had had to await the end of the civil war when, as in France, the instruments of terror had lost their emergency justification. The Tenth Party Congress marked the point at which Lenin began both to bring the Cheka under central state control and to build the new permanent state under which the power of Sovnarkom was to give way to Communist single-party rule.

THE COMMUNISTS HOLD ON: CONTROL OVER THE COERCIVE FORCES

Under the conditions of civil war, the Cheka, the Extraordinary Commission, had perfected its arbitrary powers into a form of summary justice. As Leggett (1981: 202) remarks, the Cheka 'acted as policeman, gaoler, investigator, prosecutor, judge, and executioner, all in one'. The provincial chekas, too, were the instruments of surveillance; they made searches and arrests, carried out investigations and passed sentence, 'guided by Soviet decrees, by expedience and by revolutionary conscience'! (quoted in ibid from Latsis). Punishments ranged from fines to imprisonment without time limit and from punishment in concentration camps to execution. In areas under martial law the chekas could shoot on the spot, and it was the chekas which made application for areas to be put under martial law; mass executions were common (ibid: 199–203). The chekas, in the very summary nature of their powers, operated outside of the law.

Sakwa (1988: 271) emphasizes the independence of the Cheka: 'the secret police machinery, with its arbitrary executions sometimes taking place directly contrary to the party directives ... emerged as an almost autonomous fiefdom despite several attempts by the Moscow party organization and the national leadership to bring it under control'. In Moscow, where party control ought to have been feasible, certainly in relation to areas more distant from the capital, between 18 January, when the death penalty was officially abolished, and 24 May 1920 the Cheka shot 345 people; on the night before abolition (17 January) in defiance of the spirit of the law, 2,000–3,000 prisoners were alleged to have been shot (ibid: 242–3).[11]

With the introduction of NEP the importance of the Cheka in obtaining supplies was reduced. Following debates in the press over the Cheka excesses, in June 1921 its powers were cut (Leggett 1981: 343, Carr 1966, Vol.1: 187). The GPU replaced the Cheka in February 1922. Dzerzhinsky, its head, had been out of the way in Siberia from the beginning of 1921 and remained so to the end of March 1922. The Cheka ceased to be an 'Extraordinary Commission', and became instead subordinate to the Department of Internal Affairs. Prisoners had from then on to be sent to trial in the courts within two months of arrest (Carr 1966, Vol.1: 188). The leather jackets of the Cheka gave way to the bright blue uniforms of the GPU (Levytsky 1972: 47).[12]

The Tenth Party Congress had set in motion two crucial policy changes demanded by the people: changes in economic policy away from compulsion to the elasticity of the market, and curbs on the Cheka. As repression within the economic sphere was being wound down, however, centralization of the party-state was stepped up. At the Tenth Party Congress party discipline was the order.

THE ESTABLISHMENT OF SINGLE-PARTY CONTROL

There were three aspects to the development of central party control in Russia: the removal of political opposition in the form of parties and trade unions; the construction of discipline within the Communist Party; and the decline of Sovnarkom. By the summer of 1918, the opposition parties, the Anarchists, Mensheviks and Socialist Revolutionaries (Right then Left) had been suppressed, though throughout the civil war they (Left SRs mainly) had remained in the Congress of Soviets (the December 1920 All-Russian Congress of Soviets was the last to admit members from those parties). Within the trade unions opposition had played a crucial and visible role in the crisis which had broken out in the summer of 1920, reaching its peak in February 1921. It had given rise to heated debates within the Bolshevik Party (see Sakwa 1988: 247–64). Lenin's decision to liberalize the economy whilst strengthening the party at the expense of external political opposition was crucial to central party–state control.

From March 1921 opposition within the Communist Party, permitted by a statute of 1919, was banned, too, and party discipline made compulsory (Carr 1966, Vol.2: 208). The first purge started in October 1921; overall, 24 per cent of party members were expelled, the percentage being slightly higher for intellectuals (Carr 1966, Vol.1: 211–13). In differentiating the GPU from the Cheka, Carr (ibid: 218) remarks that:

> It is not unfair to say that the main ultimate difference between the Cheka and the GPU was that, whereas the former directed its activities exclusively against enemies outside the party, the GPU acted impartially against all enemies of the regime, among whom dissident party members were now commonly the most important.

Sovnarkom's legitimacy had been undermined by the violence of the civil war and the terrorism of the Cheka in particular (Rigby 1979: 173–4). It had been an emergency government under crisis. The importance of the party had grown gradually through the civil war. From early 1919 the Politburo, the Political Bureau of the Communist Party Central Committee, had begun to develop as a sort of 'court of appeal' against Sovnarkom decisions (ibid: 183). Lenin, along with Trotsky and Stalin, were amongst its five members. As local soviets had been weakened by the pressures of the civil war and the Cheka, local party committees had grown to play an important role in the provinces. From 1919 onwards, the strength of Communist Party organization had increased. Given the still relatively small membership of the party, the vast size of the RSFSR and the problems of communications, party control was far from total but it was relatively effective (Mawdsley 1987: 274). From mid-1921 onwards party organization began to displace the importance of Sovnarkom, which had presided over the period of civil war as the centre of government.[13] The RSFSR adopted its modern title of the Union of Soviet Socialist Republics in December 1922.

Lenin's imposition of iron discipline at the Tenth Party Conference has been seen as the fulfilment of his vision of the Communist state as theorized in *The State and Revolution* of 1917. Carr has defended the move against the accusation that it was purely ideological by arguing, with Michels' iron law of oligarchy in support, that all modern mass political parties (whether Communist or not) must demand loyalty (unity and discipline) and that the monolithic party machine is, therefore, an inevitable development.[14] At a time when economic policy was to be so dramatically changed, a policy likely to provoke yet further fractionalism – insistence on party discipline – was the logical political partner for NEP (Carr 1966, Vol.1: 184). It was not party political dogma which had led to the monolithic party – dogmatic Marxists would not have introduced NEP – but 'the flexibility of Soviet policy, and of its empiricism in the choice of means' (ibid: 185). As further evidence of this flexibility the agreements made for American aid and the setting up in July 1921 of a (bourgeois) aid committee to deal with the famine are also cited (ibid: 185–6).[15]

Harding, through an analysis of Lenin's written works, has argued that Lenin's political actions as a good Marxist followed from the objective analysis of economic conditions. In late 1920–early 1921 Lenin had accepted that the economic forces had actually declined and that neither the forces of production nor the productive relations were sufficiently developed to sustain Communism (Harding 1981: 324). Production levels were now lower than they had been in the 1890s (ibid). The avenue to world revolution through Poland had also been closed. Without international support and a national proletariat actually reduced in size, Lenin changed to a policy designed not for 'the building of socialism but preparing the path towards socialism' (ibid: 325). This programme required a strong central state to hold out against rich capitalist countries and also (in reflection of the weak and demoralized soviet proletariat) to develop policies aimed at the complete destruction of the forces and relations of the feudal mode of production. Brower's (1989:76) empirical analysis supports this view; through the absence of a money economy and the development of a black market, in the towns war communism had not weakened but strengthened 'the operations of a petty capitalist economy'.

Lenin had succeeded where Robespierre had failed. At the end of the civil war, a flexible material response to demands had restored an important level of support. In directing policy away from peasant requisitioning and forced labour to the market, the gaining of control over the coercive forces, (the Cheka) so necessary for the construction of the permanent state had been eased.

COMPARISONS BETWEEN FRANCE AND RUSSIA

There is no disputing that in the Russian case it was civil war above all which stimulated the revolutionary reign of terror. This had also been the case for France, but in Russia the case is more glaring. Whilst Russia had begun the October Revolution embroiled in war with Germany, a peace had soon been negotiated, and though the Allied forces had aided the civil war they had been kept to the edges of the RSFSR. The Polish war, the only truly foreign war, had begun with an advance from Poland which had been quickly reversed by the Red Army; the war which had then been unsuccessfully pursued had been a counter-offensive revolutionary war. National, not international war, constituted the major problem to be faced by the Bolsheviks between 1918–21. There may be a lesson here, that with foreign war ended the Bolsheviks from 1921 were the more able to get on with the jobs both of state re-construction and of responding to the political, economic and social crises at home. If so then the very reverse of Skocpol's claim is true – international wars undermine state-building rather than encourage it. As the French Revolution stands alone in having fought so many countries on so many fronts for so long (1792–9) it is perhaps best not to make generalizations on this point. As in France too, policies introduced by the Bolshevik government had themselves contributed to the counter-revolution: Brest–Litovsk, the tax in kind, labour conscription and food procurement . The crisis of civil war and domestic disorder had necessitated coercion, but not all the terror could be counted as necessary. Excess terror had developed partly in response to policies chosen (when choice was available policies adopted reflected ideological repulsion of capitalism and capitalistic behaviour) and partly in reflection of the uncontrolled powers of the Cheka.

As in France too, in Russia during the civil war a temporary government had ruled and at the end of the civil war it had failed to establish itself as the executive of central government. The Sovnarkom had given way to party organization, the organization which had itself proved at an advantage in gaining control over arbitrary terror. There is no disputing that international conditions in respect of world trade and inter-state relations differed at the times of the Russian and French revolutions. Over 128 years it would be odd had they not. But political ideologies had also developed in reflection of those economic and international changes. After all, the ideology of Communism had itself taken form as a reaction against capitalism. With the introduction of NEP, from March 1921, the Soviet Union had re-introduced the market and the contrast between the revolutionary outcome in Russia ('party-state devoted to state-controlled nationalized industries') and that in France ('centralized, bureaucratic state with a private-propertied society and market economy') was not so stark in the early days (Skocpol 1979: 234). The party-state 'as dictator and overseer of the mode of production' had yet to await the rise of Stalin (Harding 1984: 43). The single-party state, however, was a model destined to be taken up by future revolutionary governments.

NOTES

1. For a particularly lively account of Russia 1917 see Ulam (1969: ch.7) and Liebman (1972: chs 4–8).
2. Though an argument not emphasized elsewhere, Rigby (1979: 87–8) claims that the Defence Council set up under Sovnarkom to mobilize the country for the war effort became in effect the Sovnarkom's 'alter ego'. It consisted of Lenin as chairman (as chairman of Sovnarkom itself and, Rigby points out, the only other formal position held by Lenin), Stalin (representing VTsIK), Trotsky (as chairman of the Revolutionary Military Council), Nevsky (Minister of Railways) Bryukhanov (Minister of Food Supplies), Krasin (Chairman of the Extraordinary

Commission, the Cheka). It became the Labour and Defence Council (STO) on 31 March 1920 (Rigby 1979: 91).

3. The problem of supplies was made worse by the railway strike aimed at bringing pressure on the government to introduce a multi-party system (Rigby 1979: 16).

4. Leggett (1981: 129) claims that it was an 'ad hoc committee which claimed affiliation to Sovnarkom but was never established by it', but Carr (1966, Vol.1: 167) simply points out that the decree seems to have been kept secret and was not published until December 1927. For the text of the decree see Bunyan and Fisher (1965: 297–8). Rigby (1979: 243) claims Dzerzhinsky was not a member of Sovnarkom until the end of December 1922 whereas Leggett (1981: 151) says he became a member on 16 March 1919.

5. Old army ranks had been abolished at the end of December 1817. Initially the Red Army was built from volunteers and incorporated many units of the imperial army which had shown themselves loyal to the Bolsheviks, for example 'the 5th Zaamur Division, 12th Finnish Rifle Division, the Latvian Rifle Division and the 45th Infantry Division' (Bradley 1975: 50). Following initial defeat on the Eastern Front, the Red Army was brought under top political leadership with Trotsky as Minister of War, 'Commissar for War'. Officers ceased to be elected, gaining position by achievement and many former Tsarist officers were employed as military experts. As the war progressed so ex-Tsarist officers grew, outweighing the rest (ibid: 168).

6. Amazingly, Dzerzhinsky was himself opposed to the death penalty. There was a tradition amongst Russian revolutionaries to be against the death penalty in theory. As noted above, no executions took place in the first three months of the revolution. For a discussion of death penalty see Carr 1966, Vol.1: 162–3 and 172–3.

7. For a detailed history of the civil war see also Footman (1961). For the best map available see Malle 1985: 436.

8. For a full discussion of the nationalities see Carr (1966 Vol.1: ch.11). According to Bradley, in addition to their better handling of the nationalities (the Reds took care, for example, not to send local Reds into battles in their own regions where defeat threatened) and the strength of coordination which the Bolsheviks faced in their stronger defensive position (four separate armies fighting in often hostile territory against an encircled Bolshevik territory), the Bolsheviks also had the advantage of controlling the more industrial regions where armaments were produced. The Donets and Ekaterinberg in the Urals, held for a time by the Whites, were 'devastated and disorganized' and 'controlled for too short a time to have brought advantage' (Bradley 1975: 165–6). Mawdsley (1987: 274–5) too emphasizes the rich industrial regions around Moscow. Footman (1961: 305), who essentially offers an account of the civil war rather than an analysis, concludes that Reds and Whites were evenly balanced but Communist Party organization probably tipped the balance. Mawdsley (1987: 274) emphasizing the limitations on Communist Party control adds, too, that Bolshevik programmes were also relatively popular and the Terror, on balance, also contributed to Red success.

9. Davies (1975) has argued that the Polish war has not been given the significance which it deserves. It played a crucial part in the increased use of coercion by the Cheka and in the later coercive stages of War Communism too, the militarization of the railways and forced labour in particular (Davies 1975: 187). He points out that over half of the resources of the Red Army and eight out of its sixteen armies were in operation against Poland. It should be noted, however, that on Leggett's evidence given above, most of the victims of the terror came from the civil wars (see Leggett 1981: Appendix C. The defeat of the Red Army in the Polish war no doubt, as Davies argues (pp.191–4) played a part in the decision to

introduce NEP, in March 1921, as indeed did the excess of terror itself. These arguments are developed below.

10. Roberts (1970), in defiance of the weight of historical opinion, argues through concentration on Lenin's writings, that Lenin's 'retreat' to NEP does not undermine the claim that War Communism was a deliberate set of policies (nationalization, the end of a money economy and so on) to introduce socialism. He argues that no-one, no more outside than inside Russia, knew how to set about state planning and the haphazard appearance of policies is not therefore inconsistent with an ideologically motivated plan. Whilst no doubt Roberts' argument about the difficulties of planning is fair, it's an odd view which fails to take into account the actual changes in circumstances faced by the Bolshevik government. This is especially problematic given Harding's (1981) later and far lengthier analysis of Lenin's writings from which he reaches the conclusion that Lenin did indeed reassess his economic policy in the light of his analysis of the changed economic forces at the end of the civil war.

11. Leggett (1981: 464) puts the figure at only 300 prisoners shot. If the higher figure is an exaggeration it indicates, even so, how popular feeling was running against the Cheka. Between December 1918–November 1920 the Cheka had arrested nearly 6 per cent of the adult population of Moscow (Sakwa 1988: 242).

12. Carr (1966, Vol.1: 189) argues that over political offences the GPU retained 'arbitrary powers'. According to Conquest (1968) the evidence is unclear as to whether the GPU could any longer execute people. In decrees of August 1922 and January 1923, however, the GPU was given powers to banish and exile people for up to three years. Certainly the GPU conducted investigations for political crimes and continued to have 'wide powers of search and arrest'.

13. Rigby (1979: 191–213) argues that Lenin (and Trotsky too) was against the dominance of the party organs (politburo and the central committee) over Sovnarkom. Lenin's failure to get his way he puts down to Lenin's illness, especially critical when Sovnarkom organization revolved around Lenin, and Trotsky's unwillingness to become the deputy leader of Sovnarkom. Kamenev who accepted the post was simply not of equivalent stature and capability.

14. See Michels (1962). For a particularly clear and concise exposition of Lenin's *The State and Revolution* see Polan (1984: 14). It is a work best examined in relation to his other writings (Harding 1981).

15. As a consequence of drought in the Volga basin, the southern Urals and areas of the Ukraine, 27 million people faced starvation by the end of 1921. Consequent deaths are estimated at nearly 5 million (Levytsky 1972: 43).

6. Old Revolutions, New Lessons: The American War of Independence and the Puritan Revolution

The English and American revolutions are the two remaining of the four cases from which both Edwards and Brinton draw their generalizations about the reign of terror as a necessary stage of revolution. Neither case fits indisputably into the classification of revolution: the American case was a colonial war of independence which had to wait until after the civil war, 1861, for wide-reaching social and economic transformations (Moore 1966: 112–13); the English case, too, has been criticized for insufficient social and economic change to justify classification as a revolution (for a summary of the debate see Aylmer 1983: 1.) In England, the restoration of the monarchy a few years after Cromwell's death posed further problems for its revolutionary claims. The comparative method requires that cases be included not only when events are similar but also when they are different but with good reasons for expecting them to have been the same (de Felice 1980). Inclusion of these two cases is justified theoretically because they are included by both Edwards and Brinton. In respect of the American case especially, however, comparisons of difference rather than similarity prove the more instructive and serve as a warning against the inclusion of other wars of independence. Both cases pose practical problems because of the difficulty of obtaining accurate information on victims, a particular problem for the case of England which took place over 350 years ago. Even so, each seems to provide useful points of comparison and offers support for the value of comparative history, even when stretched over centuries.

THE AMERICAN REVOLUTION

The American Revolution has long been praised for its democratic nature. Arendt, drawing comparison with the case of France (and Russia, too, in part), has singled out its lack of violence, holding the American Revolution as historical proof against the 'age-old and still current notions of the dictating violence, necessary for all foundations and hence supposedly unavoidable in all revolutions' (Arendt 1973: 213). Her point is that in the American case people met together, communicated with each other and through agreement constructed a constitution for the 'foundation of freedom' (ibid: 139). She dismisses the notion found in Marxist theory that violence is a determining force in history with revolution at the end of each epoch necessary for the destruction of the old order before the construction of the new. It is odd then to find the American Revolution amongst Edwards' and Brinton's generalizations about reigns of terror being necessary in revolutions.

Both Edwards and Brinton agree in placing the Terror from the declaration of independence (1776) for the duration of the war, the peace treaty being signed in 1783. As was noted, in Chapter 3, Brinton quickly began to drop America from his generalizations openly admitting 'that the final victory of the extremists did not quite follow the pattern of our other three revolutions' (Brinton 1965: 176). There was, he claims, a radical stage but no terror on a scale equal to those in France, Russia and England. Specifically, he drops America from inclusion in his seventh causal variable, 'religious faith'. The American case is not accused of having had a 'reign of virtue'; the Whigs had no deterministic ideology. Given that Brinton requires all of his seven causes to be present for a reign of terror, it is odd that he makes this exception for America without drawing the logical conclusion that a reign of terror is either not a necessary stage of revolution or that the nature of the radicals' ideology is decisive.

Edwards is less charitable and makes quite explicit his intention to include the American revolution on equal terms with the other three. Washington was made 'a military dictator in the full sense of the term' (Edwards 1970: 165) by the grant of power which enabled him to conscript troops, arrest, raise armies and obtain supplies. Edwards' emphasis on the particular importance of the war is clear. Whilst he allows that America's terror was mild, pursuing his claim that terror in spreading fear actually saves lives, Edwards explains this mildness in terms of its particularly astute use. On Edwards' account the American terror comprised some executions in Kingston, New York, after Burgoyne's invasion, a hundred or so Tories executed after the battle of Cowpens in South Carolina on 8 October 1780 (10 of them hanged from a Tulip tree), and he remarks that generally tar and feathering was used rather than executions: 'Spying and fearful threats proved the most efficient means of terrorization' (ibid: 180). He gives the example of Pennsylvania, where 500 were proclaimed traitors of whom only two were executed. Pressing home the clever use of terrorization to prevent counter-revolutionary action and so save lives, he emphasizes that only around 20,000 men (loyalists) actually took up arms in support of the British against the American revolutionaries (patriots).

Now, there are a number of important issues which are glossed over by both Brinton and Edwards. As America engaged in a war of independence against Britain, the stages of America's revolution cannot be given equivalence with those of France and Russia. By the time the Jacobins and Bolsheviks came to power the old order had been overthrown. In France, King Louis XVI had already been guillotined; in Russia, Tsar Nicholas II had been banished to Ekaterinburg. Since the outbreak of those revolutions, July 1789 and February 1917 respectively, a readily discernible and genuine period of revolutionary government had occurred which, in relation to the 'radical' or 'extremist' phase, could fairly be termed 'moderate' – the rule of the Provisional Government in Russia and of the Girondins in France. The same is not true of America. The outbreak of a war of independence from the British by the 13 colonies (states) of America was not and could not be decisive in the same way. As Ferguson (1979: 156) explains:

> The outbreak of war [April 1775] brought about the dissolution of legal governments and the transfer of power to patriot organizations. As the existing colonial legislatures responded to Massachusett's appeal for aid, endorsed the resolutions of Congress, or undertook military preparations, British governors dissolved them.

The result was that revolutionary power devolved to local committees. 'Extra-legal' provincial congresses were elected which introduced laws, took control over the militia and its supplies and set up 'committees of safety' to take charge of military operations. In this piecemeal way Congress took on the role of revolutionary government classifiable neither as a moderate nor an extremist stage of revolution and power remained devolved to the provincial congresses.

Whilst Edwards refers only to groups of leaders in the reigns of terror (Franklin, Washington, Jefferson, Adams), Brinton names Jefferson as leader of the American reign of terror along with Cromwell, Robespierre and Lenin as leaders of theirs. This is odd given that it is

Edwards, not Brinton, who views the radical phase, the reign of terror, as dictatorship. For both, the declaration of independence marks the beginning of the extremist stage. On 4 July 1776 Congress reached agreement and the Declaration of Independence, drafted by Jefferson, was signed.

There is no doubt that the situation in America after the declaration bore resemblance to the conditions faced by Jacobins and Bolsheviks in respect of foreign war and economic shortage, though in both respects the similarities are superficial. The wider economy in America was very different from the economic chaos faced by France and Russia and foreign troops joined in to support, not destroy, the revolution.

War Abroad and at Home

The revolution began in April 1775 with fighting against British troops in New England. Shortly afterwards the American Continental Army was recruited to support these local troops and Congress appointed Washington its head. Following the Declaration of Independence, Americans loyal to Britain soon joined the British against the 'patriot troops'. It has been estimated that just under 20 per cent of the population actively supported the British army with the number of loyalists serving in it reaching around 10,000 in 1780, approximately 16 per cent of the adult male population (Ferguson 1979: 173–4). British occupation of Long Island, New York, met with American support but this was not the pattern elsewhere. Loyalists first fought patriots openly in Delaware, Maryland and Virginia and the British invasion in 1778 first of Georgia and then of Carolina turned events clearly into civil war. Georgia fell easily into British hands, Carolina held out longer and was taken in 1780.

As a war of independence, it would be inaccurate to count the American case similar to either France or Russia in terms of generalizations about foreign wars; the loyalists joined the British forces and not vice versa. The foreign dimension was expanded in 1777 when France began to provide support, at first passive, in the form of material aid and then active, in the form of fighting troops, though again it was the reverse of the French and Russian experiences, for the French aided the (American) patriots not the (pro-British) loyalists. In 1778 France declared war against Britain and in 1779 Spain joined France. Then in 1780 Britain declared war on Holland and, embroiled in international war, was no longer able to concentrate all her energies into fighting in America. Again what is odd is that rather than the 'reign of terror' under Jefferson being encircled by threatening foreign powers it was the British government which found itself in the position of Robespierre and Lenin. British defeats started with the battle of Cowpens in 1781 and ended in March 1782 with a resounding defeat both on land and at sea at Yorktown. Britain gave in; the peace treaty was signed on 30 September 1782.

The Economy: Government Scarcity and Economic Boom

Throughout the war Congress faced economic crisis. Resources were inadequate to equip, pay or even sometimes feed the army. As in France and Russia, inflation was rife. To finance the war, in a way similar to the *assignats* in France, Congress printed its own continental currency. By January 1780 these dollars had fallen to only one-tenth of their worth compared to January 1778 and one old dollar exchanged for 40 continental dollars. At this point Congress stopped printing the new currency in recognition that it would soon become worthless. It must be noted that Congress also shared with the rule of the Jacobins and Bolsheviks the problem of profiteering on the part of merchants and farmers. Though Congress suffered economic problems, the country did not, and this differs significantly from the conditions faced by France and Russia. Congress could not rely on taxes (the war was, after all, being fought over British taxes) but the country itself was benefiting from a booming economy.[1]

The multiplier effect was at work in America from before and right through the war. Britain had to spend money on her troops in America and they in turn spent their wages on American goods. The arrival of French troops added to the effect. Demand pushed up prices, which stimulated production. Though individual fortunes won could also be lost, the only social group which did not benefit were the urban workers whose wages failed to grow as fast as food and housing costs increased (Ferguson 1979: 213–14). Inflation is a natural response to too many people chasing too few goods. Both state and local governments took action both to keep prices down and get supplies for the army. Laws were introduced to make people accept paper currency and the prices of both wages and commodities were fixed by law (the double maximum demanded by the *sans culottes!*). Regulations were introduced to control monopolies and other means for keeping prices high, and firms were not permitted to export goods needed for the army. These regulations were enforced by local citizens' committees which, according to Ferguson (ibid: 215), 'kept merchants and their activities under surveillance and investigated complaints against them'.

This control of prices and wages began in the New England states at the end of 1776. Following their initiative, in February 1777, Congress urged all other states to follow suit, but by 1778 only New York, New Jersey and Pennsylvania had fallen into line (Alden 1969: 449). As in France and Russia a black market developed, and as merchants could sell their goods, they demanded higher prices from the army than the government considered either fair or affordable. In June 1978, Congress recommended that attempts to control rising prices be abandoned (ibid: 449).

A Reign of Terror during the War of Independence?

Sometimes feelings of anger against loyalists led to mob violence, mostly tarring, feathering, beating and forced marches, and some suicides resulted (Alden 1969: 451–2). Anger against those held responsible for high prices also resulted in mob violence against pacifist Quakers as well as active loyalists.[2] When paper money became so devalued as to be nearly worthless, the army began taking supplies by force: 'By 1779 impressments were one of the ways that the army was kept in the field; within another year they were the only way' (Ferguson 1979: 219). Requisitioning of grain and other supplies occurred; goods were taken for impossibly low prices and worthless government certificates. Such impressments, requisitioning by another name, were sometimes exacted by the use of force, though on the whole demands met little resistance. Even so some farmers simply ceased to produce any surplus above their families' needs.

In 1777, Congress asked the states to confiscate loyalist property to help the war effort further (Alden 1969: 454). By 1778, laws had been enacted by the states which confiscated the property (land was of course included) of all those who aided the British. An oath of allegiance was introduced and failure to sign it resulted in withdrawal of citizenship (ibid: 454–5). As a consequence over 100,000 people left America, most of them crossing the border to Canada (Ferguson 1979: 229–230) As a proportion of their populations (around 2.5 million Americans and 25 million French at the time) this meant that five times as many Americans left America as French émigrés left France during their respective revolutions. Unlike the French exiles, few of these Americans returned. In fact, Greer (1966b: 111) estimates the actual number of emigrants at 129,099, which makes the figure for American exiles as a proportion of population size actually eight times greater than that of France. Alden (1969: 493) estimates the number of loyalists who left America to have been in the region of 50,000. On balance, the estimate of emigration per head of population as five times greater for America than for France is probably about right. It has been suggested that by 1790 a further 100,000 people had migrated away from the east (Ferguson 1979: 232). Tensions stirred by war, patriot versus loyalist, would surely have been greatly eased by such movements.

There was also an astonishing amount of violence in the war period and stories enough to suggest that behaviour towards victims bears comparison with some of the horrors in both France and Russia. In the south, the death penalty was imposed on slaves who tried to reach loyalists in order to support the British cause. To this end African Americans were evacuated from war zones and patrols in these areas were increased. There is no doubt that fear, indeed terror, was being used in the south where, spurred by the British inducement of freedom, around 5,000 slaves managed nevertheless to get through (Ferguson 1979: 172–33). With respect to treatment of prisoners, Ferguson (ibid: 201–2) draws attention to the American seamen captured aboard American privateers and held in New York harbour on British prison ships, where they suffered disease, hunger and squalor. Under the military conventions as they then existed, Congress had to pay the prisoners' upkeep. As it could not afford to do so and having no equivalent prisoners for an exchange, the prisoners were left to suffer and usually to die.

The war itself was extremely violent. Peckham has calculated the deaths of patriot troops during the revolution. Usually put at 4,435 killed and 6,188 wounded, his findings suggest a far higher figure. The total of those who 'died in service', those killed in battle, dying afterwards of wounds or dying in prisons he puts at 25,324, 0.9 per cent of the 2,781,000 American population (black and white) in 1780 (Peckham 1974: 132). Taking 200,000 as the approximate number of men in service he calculates that 12.5 per cent of the soldiers engaged in the war died. These figures do not reveal the number of loyalist Americans who died fighting for the British. Lop-sided though the figures are, they show clearly that the American War of Independence was a very bloody affair.[3]

In line with treatment of the French and Russian Terrors, troops shot in battle would not count as victims, though people left to die in prison could. The problem is that if the war era was a reign of terror then it would not be the patriots who counted as victims but the loyalists. Peckham's tables of military engagement (many of which were just skirmishes and incidents) do reveal some incidents of patriots terrorizing loyalists and as we have already discovered some at least of these prisoners who died in prison ships score against Congress.

Peckham makes no mention of the executions, used by Edwards (1970) as examples of Terror in Kingston, New York and the Battle of Cowpens. Careful reading of the list of battles and incidents nevertheless reveals some terrorizing, of Indian towns and villages in particular. Recorded for April 1779 are the Indian towns of Chickamuagu Tenu and Onondagany being burnt and their inhabitants slaughtered (ibid: 59). In line with Ferguson's (1979) comments, things seemed to get more out of hand towards the end of the war. In March 1782, Andrew Pickens and Colonel Elijah Clarke along with 300 militia, set out to stop Indian raids, burnt 13 towns and killed 40 Cherokees (ibid: 94). Whether or not the Cherokees were armed when attacked is unclear. For 7 March 1782, Peckham records 'Gnadenhutten, Muskingum River, O.Pa. militia under Colonel David Williamson massacred 96 Christian Delawares' (ibid) and for 10 November 1782, 'Chillicothe, O. Colonel John Floyd with 300 of General George Rogers Clark's force destroyed this Shawnee town, killing 10 and capturing 10' (ibid: 97). Of course, examples can be found for both sides. In reprisal for Gnadenhutten, patriot Colonel William Crawford was burned at the stake at Sandusky, O. on 4–5 June 1782 (ibid: 96). Between 14–18 September 1780 at Augusta, Georgia having captured 29 patriots at a trading post loyalist forces hanged 13 of them on the spot (ibid: 75).

There is no doubt that incidents such as these must have struck terror in the hearts of those under close threat and shocked those at a distance. They do not, however, amount to evidence for a reign of terror; these were not actions ordered and organized by central government. America lacked the machinery of a reign of terror, a proper secret police system and revolutionary courts exercising summary justice.

A Reign of Terror after the Peace?

Edwards and Brinton have been led by the indication of a similarity of causes, war and economic problems, to the proposition that a reign of terror occurred in America during the civil war years. It did not. Once the peace treaty had been signed with Britain scope for a reign of terror opened in the newly independent country in the form of reprisals against the loyalists who had supported Britain and had acted or actually fought against the patriots. After the British departed, loyalists were financially penalized, heavily taxed and fined. Some were imprisoned, some banished and some fled to Britain where their property was confiscated:

> But there was no slaughter of loyalists; few reprisals occurred when American forces reoccupied areas after British evacuation, nor were there even many instances of individual murder, except in parts of the country where loyalists were strong enough to fight. Ferguson 1979: 200

Between the period of British withdrawal and beyond the peace, anarchistic battles between the two sides broke out, especially around New York which had been occupied by British forces and where the people had collaborated, and in the Carolinas, where civil war had raged most actively. Loyalists together with Indians massacred people living on the edges of the New York frontier and patriot forces responded like with like. This unbridled hatred was matched in the Carolinas as 'the war in the south degenerated into plunder and murder by both sides' (ibid: 201). These killings were meted out by bandit forces, not regular troops which, on the whole, acted within a code of decent behaviour, exchanging and treating prisoners correctly (ibid).

Alden (1969: 493–4) is a little less charitable than Ferguson about the patriots. He emphasizes in particular the oath of allegiance (clearly anti-monarchist in tone); failure to sign branded people as enemies and cost them all rights of speech, the right to carry out their professions and the like. He emphasizes too that if traitors (those who had borne arms against the patriots or encouraged others to do so) failed to leave after being expelled, or then returned, they were faced with the possibility of execution, often without the right of defence.

Elements of a reign of terror are clearly present in these accounts, in the absence of proper defence in particular, suggesting as it does that the innocent may have fallen victim. Even so, whilst the evidence signals the threat of terror posed by the ending of civil wars, these events cannot be classified as a revolutionary reign of terror.

General Lessons

The interesting question to be answered, then, is not what America had in common with Russia and France but why America did not have a reign of terror whilst Russia and France did. One possible explanation stands out, the potential for safe flight. Whether to Canada, to Britain or out into the vast areas of western America itself, flight must have relieved the pressure on a reign of terror; such release could even have been enough to contain the explosion. Overwhelming support for the patriots may also have been important. Ferguson (1979: 220–1) considers that latent loyalist support may well have added greatly to the estimated active support at just under 20 per cent of the population. Even so Ferguson emphasizes the patriots' unity. Georgia, he argues, was the only area where the British invaded and succeeded in establishing a 'civil government'. He also points out that there were 'almost no outstanding traitors':

> The unity, moreover, was voluntary and not coerced by overwhelming power at the center. Congress would have had the greatest difficulty in repressing defections if they had been supported by state governments; without even the constitutional authority to compel obedience among the states, Congress relied upon their free acceptance of its decisions. (ibid: 221)

The one weak spot of support was the economy. Profiteering and resistance to taxation for war held the potential for class conflict to develop its uglier aspects but, together with the avenues of escape, the absence of hunger and famine relieved the tension. A country without the threat of starvation ('without misery and want' as Arendt 1973: 68 puts it) can avoid terror. Whilst the need to feed, clothe and equip soldiers was pressing, the need to feed the cities in America found no equivalence with the French and Russian revolutions and the problems faced by Paris, Moscow and Petrograd in particular.

Unity of support for the patriots was, then, crucial in reducing the level of counter-revolution opposition to which necessitates terror. The constitutional weakness of the central power, Congress, over the 13 state governments was surely also important, as was the consequent decentralization of the local citizens' committees. Neither bore comparison with the level of central control over profiteering achieved by the revolutionary organizations of the Russian and French revolutions. There is circularity in this argument. The American case lacked the laws and organizations of Terror and therefore it did not have a reign of terror. This point is not empty of explanation, however, once the limited role of Congress is understood. As a war of independence against the British colonial power this case could not follow the pattern of a revolution against an established order in an independent nation.

The Constitutional Army

The Constitutional Army justifies particular consideration as a revolutionary organisation. Washington won the argument (against a background of defeats and a prospect of more to come) to establish his 'respectable army' in late 1776. Its total standing force was to be 75,000 soldiers serving a minimum of three years (Martin and Lender 1982: 76). Crimes committed by the soldiers (looting, desertion and the like) could result in death or up to 100 (later 500) lashes. Soldiers who had faced the reality of battle rarely chose to re-enlist (Ferguson 1979: 205 and 133). Strong inducements to join were offered; $20 (the sum grew as the war went on) on enlisting, clothing and 100 acres of land for those who served for the duration of the war. Congress could only ask the states to provide the required numbers of men; the states relied on the inducements, though by no means all were successful in this (ibid: 204). The consequence was an army made up of those in most need of such incentives: the poorest, the indebted, the unemployed, indentured servants, slaves and captured soldiers, both British and German (Martin and Lender 1982: 90).

There was then no equivalent of the *levée en masse*, for the continental army, nor was it a professional army in line with the European armies of the day. Officers and men often came from the same social class and captains and lieutenants were elected by the men who served under them (Bonwick 1986: 369). Though it grew more professional, it remained amateurish, fighting in any case alongside the local militias. In its manner of battle, too, pitched battles on open terrain were avoided; it preferred to surprise and harass enemy troops (Peckham 1974: 133). These tactics have been compared with guerrilla warfare. Though penalties in the army were harsh, punishment was applied not only for organizational considerations; ideas about society and property were also important. Martin and Lender (1982: 134) give the example of General Nathanial Greene who:

fully appreciated the sensitive task of establishing legitimacy. He rigorously insisted that his small army not plunder the countryside or take advantage of civilians in other ways, no matter how poorly treated or supplied ... Like Washington, Greene comprehended that restraint toward civilians, regardless of the enormity of army grievances, was essential to having the war effort serve as a mainspring of national legitimacy and resultant nationhood.

Such considerations contrasted starkly with the behaviour of British (and German) troops, who left 'the whole country struck with terror' (comment made by an inhabitant of North Carolina quoted in ibid: 173). Ferguson (1979: 177) is more measured, emphasizing the American soldiers' insanitary behaviour. He acknowledges that the British 'insulted, abused, and pillaged Americans, regardless of whether they were loyalists or patriots' and unfavourably contrasts British and American practices: 'The British, however, often just seized what they wanted, whereas American impressments were conducted most of the time with a show of legal process and at least the promise of repayment' (ibid).

The lessons to be drawn from such comparisons are not fundamentally different from comparing Castro's guerrillas and Batista's regular army, Mao's guerrilla army with the Guomindang and the Japanese armies, and the FSLN with Somoza's troops. It is notable that the American army did not pursue a revolutionary war as had France and Russia in Poland. Like Russia it lacked the finances and, unlike Russia, it lacked the ideology. A revolution fought against taxes could not reasonably expect to raise more taxes to support an army, in order to continue a war once the British had been defeated.[4]

Conclusion

There seems to be an additional lesson to be drawn from the American case. The civil war took place *before* the government which was to establish stable legitimate constitutional rule (under Washington) came to power. As such, violent opposition had been defeated; there were not only avenues for escape, but also time to prepare for flight. The civil war had provided the opportunity (to a limited extent) for the new regime to show itself in operation. The decision to enter into the process of careful construction of a constitution and the election of the first president are important, but these events could not have taken place within a civil war. Perhaps a foreign war would equally have hampered the developments, but it was not a problem which America was obliged to face.

THE ENGLISH REVOLUTION, 1649

In the Puritan Revolution, too, civil war had been fought and won in England before the execution of King Charles I and the consequent establishment of the new revolutionary government, the Rump parliament. Battles on English soil re-emerged only briefly, in 1651, though wars in both Ireland and Scotland were a critical feature of the new government's problems in the years 1649–51.

Civil war between the monarchy and parliament had broken out in England in 1642. Charles I was taken prisoner by the Scots in 1646 and handed over to the English in 1647. He escaped in November 1647, civil war re-erupted in 1648 and the victory of the parliamentarians culminated with the beheading of the king on 30 January 1649. England became a republic, 'the Commonwealth' as it was to be known. Along with the monarchy, the House of Lords was also abolished and the Rump parliament, a purged House of Commons, ruled. The executive of the Rump was the Council of State, a selected group of MPs with Oliver Cromwell as its first temporary president. On 15 March 1649, Cromwell was appointed Lord-Lieutenant and Commander-in-Chief of Ireland. On 20 April 1653, he dissolved the Rump parliament and in December of the same year the short-lived 'Barebones Parliament', which had replaced the Rump, was itself dissolved. Cromwell accepted the title of Protector and 'the Protectorate', as it then became known, lasted until May 1660 when Charles II, Charles I's son, was restored to the throne. Cromwell had died, of natural causes, in September 1658.

There is some confusion over when the reign of terror occurred. Both Brinton and Edwards agree that it began with the opening of the Rump in 1649. Brinton has it ending with the Rump, in April 1653, whilst Edwards is unclear and perhaps extends the period to the end of the Barebones Parliament in December 1653. In as far as Cromwell's rule clearly breaks with the old order, following as it does the execution of the king, the English example of a revolutionary stage of terror fits more easily with the Russian and French cases than does the American Revolution. There are serious problems, however, in establishing clear evidence, complete statistics certainly, of the nature of the terror and the number of its victims. The revolution happened too long ago. Not all parliamentary documents have survived, not even the crucial 'Instrument' under which the Barebones Parliament was to act (Aylmer 1983: 18). There is no reason even to suppose that accurate accounts of victims in Ireland would ever have been kept. The English case appears, at first, unlikely to generate any special pointers towards a better understanding of modern revolutions; it turns out, however, to provide rich ground.

Foreign Wars, Domestic Insurrection and Sabotage

On coming to power, Edwards argues, Cromwell faced the same three conditions met in America, Russia and France. The Scottish and Irish armies raised by Charles' son (the future Charles II) represented the foreign wars, though worryingly for a generalization those same 'Scots and Irish wars' also counted as evidence for the domestic insurrection (Edwards 1970: 159 and 171) (the royalist uprising under the Earl of Derby is also mentioned under this latter heading). Though no evidence is offered to support the problems presented by inexperience in government (the unsupportive officials of the old administration), Edwards does make reference to Cromwell's 'spy system', an efficient and effective user of threats (ibid: 179). Brinton (1965: 199) too mentions the Irish and Scots rebellions in support of the generalization about 'the pressure of foreign and civil wars'; likewise he fails to give any supporting examples of conflict with administrators, nor can he substantiate the claims for either 'acute economic crisis' or his sixth abstract variable about the struggle for power. With respect to class struggles the 'hatred of Puritan for Cavalier' is simply stated. (In view of the unlikelihood of civil war where each side loved each other clearly more evidence is needed to support a class analysis!) With respect to the 'element of religious faith' (the 'reign of virtue'), however, Brinton spends some time on the Puritan aspect of the revolution. This is the one point of clear difference between the two views and will be returned to.

Essentially Edwards, and possibly Brinton (he does not go into sufficient details to be sure), lays emphasis on the Irish war as the cause of the reign of terror and the treatment of the Irish as evidence. He labours the point that the Terror was used to save life through its expeditious use of generating fear. He claims that Cromwell's whole campaign in Ireland was designed to minimize loss of life. The argument goes that Cromwell ordered two massacres combined with 'the most dreadful threats' which had the desired effect of spreading fear and rumour to prevent further rebellion: 'The deliberate massacre of forty-two hundred men, two-thirds of them English, was his solution to the problem. By that action he subdued the island in less than nine months' (Edwards 1970: 178). The result, he argues, was beneficial in England and Scotland. Lives were saved in the English army which enabled success in the Scottish war; in England further civil war was avoided. The spy system kept threats to the Commonwealth to a minimum and the victims of the Terror in England to 'about twenty-five men and the imprisonment (never long imprisonment) of a few hundred' (ibid: 179).

This is an odd account of the years 1649–53. Edwards' (1970: 179) claims (supported by Cromwell's own account) that Cromwell's policy in Ireland 'resulted in a great saving of life' and the assertion that 'the statistical evidence shows beyond doubt that Cromwell's conquest of Ireland was the least bloody of any in all its long history' (ibid: 177) naturally invite dispute. What is perhaps more odd for a proposed generalization is that no mention is made (by Brinton either) of the foreign wars fought with the Dutch 1952–4, nor is there any reference to the demands made and actions taken by the Levellers and Diggers as evidence of 'domestic insurrection'.

It is best to be clear as to the nature of the Scottish and Irish wars – were they civil or foreign? They were civil wars. England and Scotland were united in 1603 when King James VI of Scotland succeeded Elizabeth I to the English throne as King James I. Ireland had been at various times conquered and colonized from 1172, though it was not until the fifteenth century, under the Tudors, that a full attempt was made to impose the English language, customs and so on. English settlement of Irish lands began fully under James I. Irish rebellion against these English settlements, which drove the Irish off their land, broke out in 1641 and precipitated the English civil war (Hill 1969: 19–23; Berresford Ellis 1975: 8–20). Foreign war, though threatened, did not pose an actual threat to the Rump in 1649. France and Spain were at war with each other at the time and Charles' son, with a court in exile and laying claim to the title of Charles II from the moment of his father's execution, was unable to raise any practical foreign support. It was to be from bases in Ireland and Scotland that the future Charles II was to launch his campaign for the restoration of the monarchy. Once launched into the civil war, Charles I, badly in need of the troops otherwise occupied in Ireland, had entered into negotiations with the Irish on the promise of religious freedom and self-government; consequently, by the second civil war of 1648, the Irish were against parliament (ibid: 12–17).

The Rump Parliament: Problems and Policies

The Rump Parliament in 1649 faced a threat of foreign invasion which did not materialize. Royalist forces grouping in Ireland and Scotland concentrated their attention first in Ireland and brought further civil war by the summer. The immediate problems faced by the Rump were economic. These were in many respects similar to those found in the American Revolution, a lack of government revenues but a basically sound economy. For the first year of the Rump economic problems followed from the destabilization of production brought by the civil war. Poverty was a serious problem in the wake of a series of bad harvests, made worse by the civil wars of 1642–6 and 1648. In the north of England, starvation was a serious threat (Worden 1974: 166). Aylmer (1983: 12) argues that food rioting itself was serious though only between the years 1647–9, covering then only the first year of the Rump. The Levellers and Diggers, popular movements for greater political, economic and social democracy and wider religious toleration, which had played an important part in the civil war, came to particular prominence at this time. Their threat to the Rump parliament was made especially serious at this point by strong Leveller support within the army. For future years, however, general economic improvements most probably (for precise figures on GNP per capita were not then available) weakened the movement's potential threat to the new regime. During the 1650s, real wages have been estimated as pretty stable and population growth seems to have steadied (ibid: 12): 'In fact, the poor seem to have been better off in the 1650s than in any preceding decade' (Hill 1969:136 and Appendix C).

Soldiers seem to have been well paid but in 1649 grievances arose over failure to pay army wages at all. The parliamentary army (Cromwell's New Model Army) had defeated the Royalists in 1648. In peacetime it had become a financial burden – in March 1649 it numbered 47,000 (Worden 1974: 165). Arrears of pay were a pressing problem and by the spring of 1649 army discontent posed a serious threat to the survival of the new government (ibid: 166). The naval budget, too, posed an additional heavy burden on government finances (ibid: 167). (Oddly, Edwards (1970: 188) claims that England faced no debts.)

The Rump set about solving the debt crisis and took three lines of action: it increased taxes on property and excise, raised a loan from the City of London and sold off lands confiscated in the civil war, those belonging to crown and church estates from 1649 and royalist estates from 1651 (Worden 1974: 167–8, Hill 1969: 143–4). The printing of a new currency was not an option open to Cromwell in an England too long ago for paper money to have been introduced. In contrast with America, then, the Rump raised taxes, and in so doing it stirred up resentment amongst both the landed property-holders and ordinary people whose burden was increased by the excise duties. Pressure to reduce the size of the army and its budget persisted throughout the Interregnum, 1649–60 (Hill 1969: 144). The sale of Crown lands eventually proved particularly valuable in resolving the problem of army pay (Worden 1974: 169).

In 1649 this resolution of army pay was urgent not only because of army discontent and Leveller–supported mutinies within the army during the spring but also because of Charles II's strengthening campaign for restoration in Ireland. The Levellers were opposed to war against the Irish (Brockway 1980: 85). They rejected the popular conception of the Irish as vermin, strengthened by the rumours of butchery and even cannibalism which had followed the Irish massacre of English settlers in 1641–2. In May, a serious Leveller army mutiny was suppressed; loyal regiments under Cromwell and Fairfax pursued and caught the mutineers and 'coldly and cruelly broke the back of the movement' (Roots 1966: 145). Civilian unrest continued but Levellerism in the army was essentially at an end and the movement as a whole never recovered.[5] A further mutiny in September 1649 was easily suppressed though the Levellers kept up their popular opposition into 1650. Suppression of Levellers within the army, in reducing radical pressures, strengthened both the army and the Rump (Worden 1974: 196–200).

In July 1649, the army left for Ireland. Cromwell departed for Ireland in August and in so doing left the centre of politics, parliament itself. Of course he kept contact, but his absence from London restricted his control over events back home. In this Cromwell contrasts with Robespierre and Lenin who remained in their capitals.[6] Cromwell arrived in Ireland shortly after an English victory at Dublin and he proceeded quickly to launch the sieges at Wexford and Drogheda of which Edwards makes so much. These were 'cruel but crucial victories', as Worden confirms Edwards' view, adding by way perhaps of excusing his own conclusion, 'All historians mourn these dreadful massacres' (Worden 1074: 216).

Ireland: Drogheda, Wexford and Beyond

Cromwell's campaign in Ireland began on 10 September 1649 with the siege of Drogheda, a town north of Dublin, situated on the River Boyne. The town fell very quickly. Cromwell ordered all those found carrying arms and every tenth soldier surrendering to be killed, the rest to be sent to Barbados; Catholic priests were to be sought out for execution. Some 3,500 men, women and children met their deaths. Cromwell went south along the east coast to Wexford, where 1,500 soldiers and civilians were 'slaughtered' (Berresford Ellis 1975: 21–2). In the early spring of 1650, he successfully fought a campaign in the south west of Ireland and returned to England in May. Contrary to Edwards' claims, Drogheda and Wexford did not halt the Irish troubles and therefore save lives (Roots 1966: 155–6). A further big battle took place in June 1650 in the north which again the English Army (now under Lieutenant-General Ireton) won. Ireton next moved south to Waterford, along the coast from Wexford. At the end of July the town surrendered. Ireton moved up to Limerick on the west coast and attacked the town. More English troops arrived in the country following 'The Act for the impressment of soldiers for the service of the Commonwealth in Ireland' on 18 April 1651 (Berresford Ellis 1975: 24). Under it, 10,000 men were conscripted, failure to comply being punishable by three months in prison. In October Limerick fell, reduced as much by plague and hunger as by battle. Ireton had ordered a few who had tried to leave the sieged town to be hanged as examples to the rest (ibid: 24). The English army then moved to County Clare in the west of Ireland, where Ireton died of the plague in November 1651.

The Scottish War

Forced to abandon Ireland as a base for the restoration, Charles II's campaign switched to Scotland. In defiance of the English Parliament, Charles II had been proclaimed King of Scotland in February 1650 (he was crowned in January 1651). Royalist military actions began in March 1650 and by June it became clear that an invasion of England was intended (Young and Holmes 1974: 299). With Ireland left in Ireton's hands, on 20 June parliament made public its decision to invade Scotland. Having returned from Ireland in June, Cromwell and his troops left for Scotland in July and on 3 September 1650 they fought the Battle of Dunbar. It proved critical, for the Scottish army was defeated by an army only half its size, demonstrating the clear superiority of the New Model (ibid: 307). Charles had crossed the border in August 1650 and marched south into England. Illness delayed Cromwell in Scotland and the decisive battle finally took place at Worcester, exactly one year after Dunbar, on 3 September 1651. Charles escaped to France and General Monck set about consolidating control over Scotland.

Legislation for Terror and Counter-revolution in England

The combination of Leveller disturbances between September 1649 and January 1650 and the threat of the English Presbyterians siding with the Scots led the Council of State, the executive of the Rump parliament, to draw up the Engagement Act. It was introduced in January 1650 and amounted to a requirement of a declaration of loyalty to the government. It was regarded as essential for security (Worden 1974: 227–9). Under the act people who were unwilling to declare their loyalty were forbidden to hold office, to take legal proceedings or to receive tithes (ibid: 231–2). For their various reasons most of the expected opponents felt able to take the oath. The one group which made outward objection were members of the Presbyterian clergy who denounced the government from their pulpits.

As a consequence of this public act of counter-revolution, from February the Rump turned its attention to religion, introducing through the summer a series of puritanical acts against swearing, adultery and the like. As Worden (1974: 235) comments: 'such enthusiasm as the Rump did display for the spreading of the Word was almost invariably linked with political considerations'. The banning of race meetings, for example, arose not because of puritanical reaction to the fun of horse racing but because Royalist love of horses made these meetings ideal places for Royalist intrigues. The threatened war with Scotland represented the major political consideration of the time. In the event Cromwell gained victory at Dunbar and after the Scottish Presbyterians had been defeated greater religious toleration was allowed through the Toleration Act of September 1650, though it was not to last long.

In February 1651, John Fry was dismissed from the Rump on the grounds of Presbyterian sympathies and by March the Rump had made clear its opposition to sects and stated a preference for religious conformity. Again this coincided with increased threat to the Rump (ibid: 236–42).

In December 1650 an insurrection had been attempted in Norfolk which had led to the unearthing of an extensive Royalist organization in England (Worden 1974: 243). As a consequence, in March 1651 two important executions took place, those of Sir Henry Hyde and Browne Bushell. In the same month the intelligence system (run by Thomas Scot and George Bishop) arrested Thomas Cope, a Royalist, whose interrogation unearthed a larger Royalist conspiracy involving prominent Presbyterian ministers. Many were arrested, the most famous being Christopher Love (ibid: 243–8). He was executed after considerable petitioning and indecision at the crucial point when Charles II's army, having marched down from Scotland, through England, reached Worcester. When in September 1651, Cromwell's army defeated the Royalists and Charles took flight, counter-revolution too was effectively at an end. Cromwell returned to London triumphant.

Up to this point, it is clear that a persuasive argument can be made in terms of the problems faced by the new revolutionary government necessitating a reign of terror in order to deal with counter-revolutionaries in England. From September 1651 to April 1653 (or possibly December 1653) the wrangling Rumpers are blamed for Cromwell's eventual need to dissolve the parliament (Edwards 1970: 191). Just as for Thermidor in France, this is far too simple an argument.

The Rump and Barebones Parliament: September 1651– December 1653

From Worcester onwards relations between the Rump and the army went from bad to worse. For the army, the Rump was too slow in its reforms, too disorderly in its behaviour and it seemed to threaten the army's survival (Worden 1974: 285). For the Rump, the army was neither dispassionate enough about politics nor subservient enough to parliament. Over the issue of elections, Cromwell dissolved the Rump in April 1653.[7] Between Dunbar and the coup, which had been predicted since January, a number of important pressures had developed. Of particular significance was the growth of religious zealousness. In a pattern not entirely dissimilar to the impact of dechristianization in the French Revolution, missionaries took off to villages and small towns:

> The roaming missionary, offending settled congregations, became a disturbingly common feature of religious life in the provinces. Soldiers, too, often interfered with established patterns of worship. The celebration of Christmas...was attacked in 1652 with an unprecedented bitterness, until the Rump was driven to take fearful measures to ensure that the London shops remained shut and that the feast was not observed. (Worden 1974: 293)

Demands for the end of tithes mounted (ibid: 294).

Having first been predicted in November 1651, in May 1652 war broke out against the United Provinces, over the Navigation Act passed by the Rump in October 1651, which restricted the carriage of goods to England in a way highly detrimental to Dutch trade (Worden 1974: 299).[8] The war lasted into 1654. To finance it (it proved to be a very expensive enterprise) taxes were increased further and Royalist estates began to be confiscated (ibid: 305). The war and the problems of raising money to pay for it took up a great deal of the Rump's time and left too little for the issues which the army considered important to be debated and enacted (ibid: 306–9 and ch.15). Hill argues that revenues remained inadequate and the problem of taxes lingered long after the war was won in 1654 (Hill 1969: 144). It was Ireland which bore the brunt of the actions which resulted from these problems; there terror continued to reign throughout this period, after Worcester and on into 1654.

Terror in Ireland

Terror was without doubt abroad in Ireland in 1649.[9] In addition to the massacres of Drogheda and Wexford, a kind of 'burnt earth' policy was employed. Woods were chopped down and crops were cut and burnt (Berresford Ellis 1975: 26). Cromwell's calculated policy of destroying agriculture had devastating effects on Ireland's economy. On Dr William Petty's, the physician-general of the army, account people barely subsisted. The extent to which massacres after battles and sieges and the devastation of lands count as a reign of terror in the sense of an organized terror beyond the atrocities of war can be debated. In the realm of religion, however, there is no room for dispute. Catholicism had originally been banned in the English dominions in

Ireland in 1641 (ibid: 29). In 1650, on Christmas Day, all the statutes against Roman Catholicism were brought into force. Five pounds per priest was offered as a reward. Fifteen were recorded executed in 1651 (ibid: 29) and a further 15 in 1653 (ibid: 39). Presbyterian ministers were also hounded. Those caught were first imprisoned and then transported to Scotland (ibid: 31).

Contrary to Edwards' argument about saving lives, the suppression of the Royalist forces in Ireland did not end the Irish rebellion. Opposition went underground and a kind of guerrilla campaign began. This opposition became known as the 'Tories'. Ludlow, who replaced Ireton on the latter's death, continued the campaign against the Irish rebels. In the counties of Wicklow, Kildare, Carlow and areas of Dublin where Tories were especially active, from 28 February 1652 anyone found carrying arms was ordered to be killed. Attention was then turned to Galway which held out until 5 April 1652, meanwhile other towns fell. This time Ludlow permitted 40,000 Irish soldiers to leave Ireland and join foreign European armies (Berresford Ellis 1975: 43). On 12 August 1652 the Rump passed legislation for the confiscation of Irish lands, the redistribution of the land to be used to settle debts with those who had financed the English Army and to give soldiers in lieu of arrears of pay (ibid: 47–8).

The Act for the Settling of Ireland enabled not just property confiscation but also the hanging of those who had 'contrived, advised, counselled, promoted and acted in the rebellion, murders or massacres' or had aided or abetted 'by bearing arms or contributing men, arms, horses, plate, money, victuals or other furniture or habiliments of war' (Berresford Ellis 1975: 51). The estimate of those who could be included within the categories of those to be hanged was put at 100,000, or around 12–13 per cent of the population at the time. Other categories of crimes were included in the act for which the penalty was property confiscation but not the death penalty. Even Protestants, just failing to show 'constant good affection', were to have their estates taken but were to receive varying proportions of their value. Perhaps most chilling of all, the act gave the commissioners the power to re-situate people 'to any such place in Ireland as should be judged most consistent with public safety' (ibid: 52).

On 24 September 1652, the Irish rebellion was officially declared ended. A large number of trials of the Irish then took place concerned with the Irish massacre of 1641–2. Whilst the trials were conducted in a procedurally correct manner, the evidence appears to have been based on gross exaggerations. The estimate put on the number of colonists killed in the 1641–2 massacre was 300,000. Berresford Ellis (1975: 54) suggests a figure of 5,000 as a more likely one! In short, trials returning a guilty verdict were carried out for crimes which had not been committed. The trials continued and by Autumn 1653 nearly 200 executions had taken place (ibid: 78).

Cromwell dissolved the Rump parliament in the first half of 1653 and the 'Barebones parliament' opened on 4 July. The new parliament introduced legislation to settle the lots of Irish land. Only Connaught and County Clare were to be exempt; there all the Irish were to be transferred on penalty of death by May 1654. The remaining three-quarters of Irish land was to be distributed to English soldiers and financiers of the war. For those Irish considered likely criminals or political opponents it was decided to send them not to Connaught but to the plantations, to Barbados in particular. It had been a solution first experimented with by Cromwell after Drogheda in 1651. By the autumn of 1653 transportation of men, women and children had begun, some going to new England and Virginia (Berresford Ellis 1975: 87). The 'Act for the speedy and effectual satisfaction of the Adventurers for lands in Ireland, and of the Arrears due to the soldiery there and of other public debts and for the Encouragement of Protestants to Plant and Inhabit Ireland' was approved on 26 September 1653.

By 1654 removal to Connaught was well under way with some executions or transportations to Barbados for those who refused to go. This provided the solution for military units to be disbanded. Ten thousand soldiers left for Ireland to become farmers in 1653, a further 1,000 in 1654. Later other English soldiers were given the opportunity to settle as colonizers in the West Indies. To this end it was decided to transport Irish women and young girls and boys of around 12–14 years of age to act as their servants; accounts of the lives they encountered make bitter reading (see Berresford Ellis 1975: 148–54). The exact number of Irish 'Barbadosed', as the curse became known, or sent elsewhere in the New World can only be estimated. About 50,000 seems probable (ibid: 154).

The Establishment of Revolutionary Government

During 1653 a variety of different governments existed: the Rump until April, when it was dissolved by Cromwell who then oversaw the establishment of the Barebones parliament; the Barebones parliament until Cromwell's second coup in December; and the Protectorate which followed. Cromwell held the elective office of Protector, later to be made Lord Protector. There is no denying the importance of the army and of Cromwell in particular in these events and superficially the argument holds that a militaristic organization was necessary whilst the new revolutionary regime raised the means for fighting the wars in Ireland and Scotland and, indeed, fighting counter-revolution at home. Both the temporary nature of the Rump and these changes in government in 1653 count, however, against generalized claims that the necessities of war lead to the establishment of a modern centralized state.

The Rump and Barebones parliaments were essentially (to use an expression found in both Roots 1966 and Woolrych 1982) 'expedients', 'each rather hastily cobbled up to fill a hiatus in legitimate government or to avert a threatened breakdown of it' (Woolrych 1982: 391). Worden agrees in his summary of the Rump as rarely having had 'preconceived or clearly defined programmes' He adds: 'It was also a government which much of the time did not know whether it was coming or going' (ibid: 185). Edwards' notion that the Rump parliament represented a dictatorship under Cromwell is clearly disputed. The setting up of the Barebones parliament itself was testimony to Cromwell's limited 'political movement' (Woolrych 1982: 392).

Woolrych (1982: 393) argues that the downfall of the Barebones parliament lay in its religious fanaticism and the cleft which the zealots drove between themselves and the moderates. Of Cromwell and those who sought to set up the Protectorate, he comments: 'They had simply discovered how much they differed from the zealots over how such a reformation should be achieved, and over the priorities between the kingdom within and the kingdom without' (ibid). For Woolrych, it is the Protectorate which establishes a proper state structure: 'a balanced polity, with distinct powers corresponding very loosely to those of king, council, and parliament' (ibid). Woolrych (ibid: 394) quotes G.E. Aylmer in support: 'It can also be thought of as the long-delayed and grossly overdue return to normality after the protracted but essentially temporary expedients of a wartime and then post-war regime'. As for France and Russia the establishment of permanent state structure had to await the end of civil war and the peak of terror which ensues.

In England Cromwell, whose base of power lay in the army rather than a party (like Lenin's) or even parliament, was obliged to use the military twice to dissolve parliament before the Protectorate was established with himself as its undisputed head. Threat of insurrection in

England and a plot to assassinate Cromwell persisted through 1654 into March 1955 but Colonel Ruddock's rising in May 1654 was easily suppressed with an ease which demonstrated Cromwell's hold on power (Young and Holmes 1974: 323). Royalist outbursts did not re-erupt until after Cromwell's death.

The Comparative Lessons of the Puritan Revolution: Policies and Necessity

It is impossible to produce a figure for the victims of Cromwell's reign of terror, but there is no denying that one occurred and that Ireland bore the brunt. Ireland's lands helped to finance the Dutch war, settled debts to the financiers of the civil wars of 1642–6 and 1648, funded payment of arrears in soldiers' pay and provided them with farms on their disbandment; Ireland's people, those who survived that is, provided labour for the colonies of the West Indies and North America. Compared with events in Ireland, however, religious persecution and victims of the Terror in England were few. This difference within the one revolution proves useful for drawing comparative lessons. With respect to America, a number of possible explanations for the lack of a Terror were considered: the existence of an avenue of escape, the absence of a need to feed the towns, the absence of a foreign war, the nature of the army (both its organization and the behaviour of its troops), the absence of a machinery of terror, the nature of the ideology and success in civil war before the new revolutionary regime was installed.

Certainly in the Puritan Revolution there were no avenues of escape equivalent to Canada and Britain for the American Revolution, though 4,000 Irish soldiers were permitted to leave to join European armies and Presbyterians in Ireland were sent to Scotland. Possibilities for escape cannot, though, account for the concentration of terror in Ireland. Both England and America had relatively sound economies, the problems of feeding the towns after 1649 bore equivalence neither with France nor Russia, though Ireland's economy was certainly more backward than was England's in 1649. In the Dutch war, England had the foreign war which America had lacked, but it was a naval war which broke out only after the Terror had been underway for some time. With respect to the machinery of terror, the centralized state organization contrasted with America's sovereign states and local citizens' committees though, again, such considerations cannot explain Ireland.

In respect of army organization, there were clear differences. The American army had deliberately avoided the establishment of a permanent professional army like the New Model Army on the grounds that it had led to militaristic government in England. 'Constant pay' was one of the major inducements offered for enlistment (Young and Holmes 1974: 52). The cavalry was particularly well paid, had a ready supply of recruits and was largely made up of men who were literate and even within the ranks there were men of some property. By contrast, however, the foot soldiers were neither well paid nor literate and the problem of desertion necessitated conscription, 'impressment' (Woolrych 1961: 97–9). Even so the army was well trained, well equipped, wore a uniform and pioneered modern methods of battle. Contrary to the myth of the time and in contrast to the American case, however, officers were not from humble origins and as Woolrych puts it, 'large-scale promotion from the ranks still lay in the future' (ibid: 104).[10] The behaviour of soldiers is nowhere especially remarked upon, though there was great resentment against their enforced billeting. It is fair to allow that such a professional army could, under orders, be especially effective in carrying out policies of terror.

It is civil-war differences and the ideology governing policies which seem to offer greatest insight into the relative mildness of the Terror in England and Scotland as compared with Ireland. In England, Cromwell gained the benefits of having fought and won civil wars (1642–6 and 1948) before coming to power. The Royalists had been defeated and so the threat of counter-revolution weakened. Civil war only encroached onto English soil at the end of the Scottish war (Aug–Sept 1651). Whilst the Scots were themselves divided over support for the Commonwealth, Irish Catholics represented a united threat. The Irish rebellion of 1641–2 had demonstrated this in English eyes even before Charles II chose to launch his campaign for restoration from Ireland. The treatment of the Irish cannot, though, be ascribed solely to necessity without need to consider the role of ideology in directing and shaping policy choices. The argument (which is not especially persuasive) that the massacres of Drogheda and Wexford were needed to end the Irish Civil War cannot alone explain the black earth policy, the redistribution of Irish lands and the transportation of Irish people to Connaught and the Colonies.

Cromwell needed to pay the debts incurred in fighting the civil wars and to find a means to pay his soldiers and settle them on their disbandment at the end of the wars. Certainly it was necessary to do something in the face of inadequate government revenues. The alternative policies of further increasing taxes and excise were available and reluctance could have been met by force in England rather than in Ireland. A proportion of the army could have been disbanded without reward; after all, loyal soldiers had been used against Leveller mutineers in 1649. The breaking up of English estates (which the Levellers had demanded) might otherwise have been used to satisfy the troops and others, the City of London in particular, to whom the government was indebted. Avoidance of these alternatives reflected favourable attitudes towards the English propertied classes but it was directed towards the troops as well. Equally, the policies that were chosen reflected negative attitudes towards the Irish and the Catholic religion and to a lesser extent Presbyterianism and other minority religious groups such as the Ranters and Quakers. The extent to which these attitudes reflected religious ideology as opposed to nationalistic loathing of the Irish is impossible to say. Worden's (1974) emphasis on political expediency over religious ideology for England, suggests perhaps that hatred of the Irish as Irish rather than as Catholics was probably the more important factor.

Brinton made much of the 'religious faith' aspect of revolutionary 'reigns of terror and virtue'. His emphasis was not on religion itself (he notes Jacobinism and Communism both to be anti-religion) but on its fervour. The use of the term 'religious faith' is intended as an analogy. Though he does make mention of the puritanical aspects of revolutionary regimes (Russia aside) his stress is on the deterministic nature of Puritanism, Jacobinism and Communism. Whilst certainly the religious legislation introduced by the Rump and Barebones parliaments reduced toleration, for the Rump at least, important legislation had also been introduced at one time which had increased toleration. Treatment of Scottish Presbyterians hardly compared with the treatment meted out to Irish Catholics either.

Consideration of the policies avoided by the Rump and Barebones parliaments proves particularly instructive and the debate over the extent to which the English Revolution counts as a revolution proves relevant in this. The objection to the English case being called a revolution has rested on the claim that the events, whilst definitely a political revolution – the Star Chamber and High Commission went for ever, parliament from there on controlled taxation, bishops never regained control over parliament and the House of Commons and those it represented had from then on to be considered (Hill 1969: 165)

– did not achieve a social transformation. Skocpol has accepted this argument on the grounds that no peasant revolts occurred (though in fact this was untrue for Ireland) and landlords continued to hold onto power instead of being replaced by a new class (Skocpol 1979: 141).

Aylmer (1983: 26) challenges the claim that this was a purely political revolution and points out the effect that it had in producing a movement away from the aristocracy and greater gentry at all levels towards the lesser gentry and the middle classes:

> Whether these men were necessarily more capitalist than those whom they replaced seems to me an unanswerable question, but not decisive in this context. For if we think more in terms of social status, that is in the way more familiar to people in the mid-seventeenth century, then it was – by any standards – a momentous change, and one to which only a verbal pedant would deny the word revolutionary. (Aylmer 1983: 26).

Hill accepts the absence of social-class change and terms the English revolution an 'incomplete revolution':

> The army was not used, as Hugh Peter (a Preacher from New England) wished, 'to teach peasants to understand liberty'. A society of the career open to the talents was not established. There was no lasting extension of redistribution of the franchise, no substantial legal reform. The transfers of property did not benefit the smaller men, and movements to defend their economic position all came to nothing'. (Hill 1969: 165)

Here lies an important lesson. The absence of wide-reaching social transformation in England reduced the necessity for violence to be used against landowners. The argument is simple, and surely obvious: increased counter-revolution is the result of far-reaching social and economic policies and given that counter-revolution contributes to the development of reigns of terror, then Terrors are likely to be the more striking where the policies of social change entered into by the revolutionary government are the more radical. In as far as counter-revolution is in part at least stirred by government policies, as the examples of France and Russia have demonstrated, revolutionary ideologies which aim at wide trans-formation are bound to increase Terrors. The reverse is equally true: the lack of social revolutionary zeal in both the American and the English revolutions played a part in the relative lack of terror in America and England compared with France and Russia most especially.

In the English Revolution, Ireland paid the price for peace in England. Irish lands had been divided to settle soldiers' pay arrears and government debts, some of which had been incurred through policies which brought war with the Dutch (the United Provinces), and its people had been terrorized. Reduced in size and many of its soldiers re-settled in Ireland, the army proved unable to prevent the restoration of Charles II. Different policies, involving fundamental re-distribution of English land, could have produced a very different outcome. Entertainment of such policies would, though, have required failure in the suppression of the Leveller army mutinies of spring 1649. Without radical pressure, policies pursued in the English Revolution remained conservative, anti-Irish and sympathetic to those who had served loyally in the New Model Army.

NOTES

1. For the above paragraph see Ferguson (1979: 179–80). Ferguson is used throughout this chapter and is not greatly supplemented by other sources. This reflects a lack of sources on the American Terror which is not surprising given the conclusions drawn here.
2. See Ferguson (1979: 216–18) for an account of one such case in Philadelphia 1779 where mob violence erupted. Such incidents were the exception rather than the rule.
3. Amazingly Peckham (1974) only uses the term 'Americans' for patriots. Loyalists are described as 'the enemy'.
4. The history of the western expansion of the American Republic in the first half of the nineteenth century seems to suggest that finances were probably more important than ideology. Florida was taken by force in 1812, Texas annexed in 1845 and California was gained as a consequence of war with Mexico. American history written from the perspective of the Red Indians could make a case for revolutionary war too.
5. A important source of support for the Levellers' causes came from the troops and Aylmer (1983: 12) speculates that the success in securing payment to meet soldiers' back pay was also highly material to the Levellers' decline.
6. Worden argues that in separating himself from the Rump, Cromwell had the advantage of being viewed as a 'potential saviour' (Worden 1974: 209). Perhaps this helps to explain Robespierre's downfall; Lenin, who spent all his time in the capital, counts against the point, for he alone amongst the three established a revolutionary system of power which avoided any restoration of the monarchy.
7. Worden (1974: 373–4) takes issue with the generally held view that the Rump was angling to hold on to power whilst the army pressed for elections. Rather, he argues that it was parliament which intended to hold elections and the army which prevented them being held.
8. That England provoked war with the Dutch deserves emphasis. As Worden (1974: 199) remarks: 'the growing diplomatic confidence, commercial assertiveness and naval strength of the Commonwealth encouraged its leaders to challenge Dutch supremacy'.
9. This section, for absence of alterative sources, is entirely reliant on Berresford Ellis (1975). This is by no means ideal but the dearth of studies on this period is

because the records kept of the period 1650–60 were destroyed in 1922, all 56 volumes! Only some extracts of the manuscripts have survived. Berresford Ellis also makes use of material in Irish, usually ignored by other historians of the period and pays particular homage to M.A. Hickson, *Ireland in the Seventeenth Century – the Irish Massacres of 1641–42* (2 vols), Longmans Green, London 1884, which contains documents of the trials held from 1652 onwards (Berresford Ellis 1975: 250–2).

10. It should be noted that this challenges Adelman's argument. Adelman (1985: 23–50) emphasizes the meritocratic nature of the New Model Army but in fact allows that the officers were mainly from the lower gentry, and propertied.

PART III
Guerrilla Movements and Civil War to Revolution

Introduction

Necessity alone, the pressure of circumstances generally and unavoidably encountered in revolutions, cannot explain revolutionary reigns of terror. The absence of a Terror in the American Revolution has shown us that. Examination of terrors in France, Russia and England has also shown how revolutionary terrors differ both in their intensity and their levels of anarchy. To an extent, a positive relationship seemed to hold between the toll of victims, the duration of Terrors and the multiple pressures faced by the new revolutionary regimes – foreign wars, civil wars, domestic insurrection and economic problems. A generalization appeared to emerge above the rest, however, in respect of civil wars, their timing and severity in particular. Where civil wars had been won before the new regime had come to power then a reign of terror might be avoided, as in America, or minimalized, as in England. The greater the intensity with which civil war raged after the fall of the old regime, the more severe the Terror and more shocking the number of its victims. France, Russia and Ireland seemed each clearly to highlight the special importance of civil war.

Full blown civil war had not been the only form of domestic rebellion which Terror regimes had faced. The problem of feeding the cities, a problem inherited from before the revolution and made worse by the revolutionary upheaval itself had also brought rebellion at home. This disorder had combined with the armed civil war to pose the crucial domestic threat to the revolution. The problems of foreign war had played their part but in a lesser role. As the armed civil war began to be contained it had been this domestic rebellion which had challenged the revolutionaries' capacity to hold on to power. Whilst force had been justified by armed rebellion, once ended widespread rejection of coercion had added to the domestic insurrection.

The evidence also suggested that policies enacted by these revolutionary governments reflected more than expedience and that policies chosen exacerbated the crisis. In France, the dechristianization movement and the metaphysical appeal to virtue added to the terror. In

Russia, the Bolsheviks' attitudes to the peasantry, their views on free market economies and their desire to spread international revolution through the Polish war also played their part in heightening the reign of terror. In England, Terror was stoked both by hatred of Roman Catholicism and of the Irish race. Even in the American Revolution those of African origin and Quakers had suffered greatest from the anarchic terror. Whilst in the long view of history revolutions can be seen as the break between the old mode of production and the new, with the implications for class analysis which follow, in the shorter run of Terrors class analysis remains limited. Greer demonstrated this clearly for France. At base, revolutionary reigns of terror are the fight for the survival of the revolution in the face of opposition and the most critical opposition is to be found at home, not abroad. Terrors occur during crisis at the critical point of change from the old order to the new. Naturally, those who lose out form the core of the counter-revolution. Though losing-out usually implies both an economic and political loss (power flows from property ownership) this is not exclusively the case. As the revolution proceeds, grievances of all descriptions form against the new regime and this adds quickly to the band of counter-revolutionaries.

Reigns of terror play their part in the destruction of the old order certainly, and to a lesser or greater extent to the establishment of the foundations for the building of the new. The chaotic disruption of revolution and the horrors of the Terror themselves are decisive in making that break with the old ways. In establishing new ways, reigns of terror do not always succeed. As Robespierre showed clearly, those presiding over Terrors do not always hold on to power. The contrast between France and Russia suggested, furthermore, the temporary nature of the military-type organization of reigns of terror, formed in crisis, while the establishment of permanent government rests on gaining control over those newly formed forces of coercion. Retention of power does not imply that success has been achieved in carrying through a particular revolutionary vision. Survival, as the example of Russia and Lenin's introduction of NEP has shown, required more than just determination to hold on; it demanded flexibility of policy and practicality in approach. If policies in reigns of terror reflect ideological perspectives, this is to imply only that policy choices are limited by those perspectives, not determined by them. For Russia the point of Marxist-Leninist ideology was that it gave primacy to economic change and a Communist Party organization, once centralized after the end of the civil war, capable both of smoothing NEP through into practice and gaining control over the Cheka, and therefore over the Terror itself. The less practical, more metaphysical aspects of both the puritanism of the English Revolution and the 'virtue' of the French Revolution, made these revolutions less well equipped to cope with the establishment of the new order. For that to have happened, a base of support needed to be cultured and the revolutionary forces of coercion centrally controlled.

It is time to turn away from the cases included by Edwards and Brinton to new ones, and whilst keeping in mind these authors' contending propositions to pursue the likely significance of these new findings. In order to examine the relevance of civil war breaking out before the revolutionary government takes power, attention must move on to revolutions of a more modern kind.

The three revolutions considered here – Cuba, which brought Castro to power in 1959, Nicaragua which brought the Sandinistas to power in 1979 and China which brought Mao to power in 1949 – all share a common feature. Each involved a period of guerrilla struggle and civil war before the revolutionary takeover and was not obliged to contend with the outbreak of full-scale civil war as they set about establishing their new orders. Whilst sharing some similarities their differing revolutionary perspectives prove useful for the further consideration of the importance of policy choice.

7. Cuba 1959: A Different Type of Revolution

Pre-revolutionary Cuba was politically unlike England, France or Russia. The country had no monarch, no *ancien régime*. General Batista had installed himself in power after a *coup d'état* in 1952. His action had been taken in order to pre-empt elections in which his candidacy for the presidency appeared unlikely to be successful. In those elections, Fidel Castro had sought to be elected as a representative for the Orthodoxo Party, a broadly democratic socialist party. In Cuba, repugnance for Batista's undemocratic act was hardened by his incapacity to tackle the stagnant economy and its concomitant social ills.[1]

In a very short time, the use of force replaced Batista's hoped-for legitimacy based on economic success. Brutality increased. In 1953 Castro and followers made their first attack, on the Moncada Barracks. The date, 26 July, was to give the revolutionary movement its name. The attack was unsuccessful, many were killed and Castro himself was captured and sentenced, but released in a general amnesty in May 1955. In December 1956 a band of guerrillas sailed from Mexico and arrived in the southern part of Cuba, in the furthest region from the capital Havana, and took refuge in the Sierra Maestra, the mountainous region of Oriente province. Estimates vary, but after some guerrillas were killed in battles with Batista's troops, survivors numbered 10–19 (Fairbairn, 1974: 266). This was the core of a revolution which was to sweep Batista from power in two years.

THE GUERRILLA MOVEMENT

Based in the Sierra Maestra, the least developed area of Cuba, the guerrilla movement was rural and gained support from peasants; but this was not a peasant revolution (Wolf 1973: ch.6). The majority of Cubans lived either in towns or in the capital and of the rural population most were rural proletariat employed in sugar mills and on cattle ranches, or seasonally employed in cutting cane. The peasantry formed only around 10 per cent of the potential work-force (Blackburn 1963: 84). Passive support for the guerrillas was soon gained from the peasants of Oriente but their active support began only some nine months befor. the revolution (Guevara, 1969b: 186). The revolution gained support from all social classes and the initial core of revolutionaries had consisted of a cross-section of workers and professionals (O'Connor, 1972; Thomas 1967: 259–60). Over the two years, December 1956 to 1 January 1959 when Batista was overthrown, the guerrillas' numbers were swollen by mostly young people fleeing Batista's repression. In the cities and towns urban resistance movements proved vulnerable to the violent Batistiano police. By the time of Batista's flight, the small band of guerrillas had grown to an estimated 4,000–5,000 (Keesing's 1959: 16631).[2]

Whilst the guerrilla campaign was fought essentially in Oriente province, and later extended to the neighbouring Camagüey province, the 26 July Movement kept links with the towns. Contact was also maintained with the Revolutionary Directory founded by a student in opposition to Batista in December 1956 and centred on Havana University. A pact between Castro and the Revolutionary Directory had been made in Mexico in July 1956 (see Thomas 1971: 771 and 888). A general strike was organized for April 1958 and, whilst impressive in the support it received, the strike failed to remove Batista. The 26 July Movement returned to its base in the Sierra Maestra.

The advantage of the Sierra Maestra was its impenetrability. Tanks could not be used there and the effect even of aircraft bombs was muted by the dense undergrowth. On the ground, the army could be taken by surprise with the guerrillas choosing the odds. Such tactics not only demoralized Batista's army, they enabled the guerrillas to take the soldiers' weapons and ammunition for use in future attacks. Such battle tactics, however, were not the only important feature of the 26 July Movement. The guerrillas' conduct towards both soldiers and peasants was important. Their message of a better society came essentially, and certainly initially, through their practice. Captured soldiers were set free, an excellent contrast with the behaviour of Batista's troops who always killed captives (Thomas 1971: 998):

> We do not wish to deprive these Cubans of the company of their loving families. Nor, for practical reasons, can we keep them, as our food, cigarettes, and other commodities are in short supply. We hope the people of

Cuba will understand our position in this respect. (Castro, explaining the policy of releasing soldiers on Radio Rebelde, quoted in Fairbairn 1974: 271)

Peasants were treated with consideration: 'The first task is to gain the absolute confidence of the inhabitants of the zone; and this confidence is won by a positive attitude toward their problems' (Guevara 1969a: 87). Food was always to be paid for in some way (ibid: 46) and the guerrillas were never to compromise peasant communities by staying more than one night, an expedient against betrayal in any case. Fairness was equally important for the guerrillas themselves in matters of distribution of supplies (ibid: 61).

As territory was won and numbers grew, the guerrillas' Robin Hood existence had given way to a more permanent form of organization. By the beginning of 1958 the guerrillas had established a liberated zone over a large area (nearly 2,000 square miles of Oriente (Thomas 1971: 974). Supplies and food became organized. Hospitals, a radio station, a council to administer justice and small factories were established and on the land their own agricultural production was begun with surplus recruits being put to work alongside peasants. It was, to use Sinclair's (1970: 25) term, a 'government in miniature'. Inside the liberated zone the task was also begun of explaining and teaching the revolutionary message, a message which dwelt on legal, social and economic justice. It promised improvements in health, education and social conditions (such as housing), fairer economic distribution (in agriculture and industry) and a return to the 1940 Constitution.[3]

In the encampments, the guerrillas organized themselves into groups capable of fighting soldiers outside the favourable terrain of the Sierra (Guevara 1969a: 33). In the winter of 1957–8 they made hit-and-run attacks on sugar crops and related production machinery and buildings in order to undermine the Batista economy. They attacked roads, destroyed bridges and disrupted telecommunications. Batista reacted with greater violence. In revulsion of Batista's repression the US stopped shipments of arms to Cuba on 13 March 1958 and from then on no more arms were sent to the regime (Thomas 1971: 985). The Roman Catholic churches appealed to Batista for restraint but the appeal went unheeded. After Castro's attempt to combine an urban and rural attack in the general strike in April 1958 had failed to defeat Batista, the Cuban people were further repulsed by the treatment of captured rebels, mainly young men in their teens. Hatred of Batista's regime grew yet more. Batista's 'Big Push' against the guerrillas in May 1958 failed and from then on the Sierra Maestra was virtually left alone by his troops. A new tactic was now tried. In order to gain international attention, foreign nationals were kidnapped and then released unharmed.

In September 1958 Castro launched his final attack on the Batista regime. The guerrillas, now highly trained, moved out of the Oriente base into the Camagüey province and fought the troops head on. By the middle of December, they had taken the whole of Camagüey and their march had moved them on into the Las Villas province, more than half way up the island. Batista's troops had begun to change sides. By late 1958 even officers were deserting (Thomas 1971: 1040). On 23 December, using tanks, aircraft and bombs, Batista launched a full-scale attack on Castro's forces. Casualties were estimated at 3,000 (Keesing's 1959: 16632) but the forces of the 26 July Movement gained control of Santa Clara. Meanwhile, ten miles from Havana, Castro's supporters exploded an ammunition dump; elsewhere, in areas supposedly under Batista's control, others came out openly in Castro's support. On the morning of 1 January 1959, Batista fled to the Dominican Republic and along with his family went some 50 aides. Another 500 or so people, with close connections with the regime, fled to the United States. Hundreds more took refuge in embassies in Havana (Keesing's 1959: 16632–3). Castro arrived in Havana a week later, on 8 January 1959.

REVOLUTIONARY GOVERNMENT: WAR TRIALS

The revolutionary government was at first a combination of middle-class opponents of Batista, politicians, lawyers, journalists, and Fidelistas, that is members either of the guerrilla army or of the urban resistance movement. Dr Urrutia was president, Dr Cardona, prime minister and Dr Castro, commander-in-chief of the armed forces. In practice, however, Castro acted as a 'kind of extra chairman', unofficially holding meetings in the Havana Hilton with close allies in the cabinet (Thomas 1971: 1065–8). Immediate government business included arresting and punishing those members of Batista's police force and army accused of torture and unlawful killings, and also purging the system of those, such as judges, who had served Batista's regime and benefited from its corruption. Thirty-six of the 40 Supreme Court judges were dismissed and 20 per cent of the lower-ranking judges (Thomas 1971: 1069). In order to destroy the past and root out corruption the criminal tribunals were dissolved, as were political parties (ibid: 1085). The police force, its torturers arrested, was re-organized, with many of those who had occupied the police stations during the revolution taking charge (ibid: 1071). The old army was replaced (some officers and a few soldiers were integrated into the new army) by the guerrilla army. The military commands of the provinces were given to guerrillas, Raul Castro in Oriente, Matos in Camagüey, Morales in Las Villas, Escalona in Pinar de Río and Gálvez in Matanzas. Thomas (1971: 1072) remarks that 'this new army soon appeared to be essentially the executive of the regime'. Organized as part of this army was G2, the section in charge of military intelligence. Under the leadership of G2 Ramiro Valdés was to become the principal organization against counter-revolution, evolving into a secret police force (Thomas 1971: 1321).

With the departure of Batista, the nature of his regime was revealed: 'The extent and horror of the Batista era became apparent only after it had ended. Bodies and skeletons, torture chambers and tortures were discovered and photographed in the press' (Thomas 1971:1073). The alleged perpetrators were brought to trial: police officials, soldiers, spies and informers. By the middle of January, 150 had been executed. Executions continued and by the beginning of July the total had reached 500 (Keesing's 1959: 16633–4).

Between 1–10 January 'justice' was despatched by military courts and those found guilty were executed on the spot. From 10 January until the end of June (when trials were transferred from military to civilian courts) war criminals were tried by tribunals made up of two or three from the rebel army, a legal adviser and sometimes a local citizen. There was counsel both for the prosecution and the defence. The laws under which these people were tried were the decrees which had been issued in the Sierra Maestra in February 1958. These had required military officers to resign, politicians to cease collaboration with Batista and warned of intention to punish those who committed crimes under government orders. In essence, men were on trial for crimes against humanity: 'Those who applauded the Nuremburg tribunals cannot oppose our courts martial' (quote from the newspaper, *Revolución*, 13 January, Thomas 1971: 1073). 'From then on [10 January], as seems clear from the press accounts, the trials were fair in the sense that a genuine effort was made to establish the guilt or the innocence of the accused' (Thomas 1971:1074). Not all were shot; some were imprisoned and others let go after initial examination. By

20 January about 207 had been shot, each having been found guilty of the murder or torture of prisoners.

Thomas accepts that these trials were fair, even commenting on the unfairness of those who got away, mostly those at the top. Matthews (1969: 127), too, emphasizes that Urrutia, the then president and a former judge, when writing later as a strong critic of Castro, still considered the trials fair. The number of victims of Batista's regime have been put as high as 20,000 and though undoubtedly an exaggeration, (see ibid: 127) as a reporter in the *New York Times* put it at the time (12 January): 'No figures can be given as yet, since the work of exhuming bodies is going on all over the island ... The public evidently supports the executions now being carried out. Hardly a Cuban does not have some relative who was killed during the Batista terror' (Keesing's 1959: 16634). Severe criticism over the trials was voiced in the United States, and the public trial of Major Blanco, accused of torturing and killing 108 people, backfired. The trial was held in a sports stadium so that everyone (including Americans) could see its fairness. Though carried out with full defence procedures it brought bad publicity; it was accompanied by a crowd yelling and shouting for Blanco's execution. As a consequence, the trial was transferred quickly from the sports stadium to a courtroom and Blanco was retried (Keesing's 1959: 16901). Prime Minister Cardona resigned and was later to play an important part in organizing resistance to Castro from the USA.

GOVERNMENT CHANGES: ECONOMIC REFORMS, COUNTER-REVOLUTION, AND FOREIGN INVASION

Castro, hitherto the commander-in-chief of the armed forces, became prime minister on 16 February; his brother Raul replaced him as head of the army. Whilst Castro's new position was popular, Raul's was not and within the 26 July Movement itself it caused dissension. The new revolutionary government set up in the spring of 1959 consisted of a coalition of representatives of the movements which had played their part in the revolution: the 26 July Movement itself, the Students' Revolutionary Directorate and the Popular Socialist Party which was the re-shaped Cuban Communist Party divested of the old elements which had opposed Castro's guerrilla revolution (Azicri 1988: 27–8). In March, legislation was introduced confiscating the property of all those, ministers, officials and the like, who were closely associated with the Batista regime. On 18 May 1959 agrarian reform was introduced (see Scheer and Zeitlin 1964: ch.5; Dumont 1970: 28–9). Large estates (of 402 hectares and above) were to be expropriated, being 'paid' for by state bonds. This was similar to the practice of the American Revolution, the difference being that expropriated farmlands (though not cattlelands) were to be turned wholly into cooperatives. These lands included those owned by American sugar companies, amongst them the United Fruit Company. In addition all rented land was expropriated with plots under 27 hectares being given free of charge to the tenant-farmers. Expropriation of land was to be done by the National Institute of Agrarian Reform (INRA) in coordination with the rebel army; Castro was president of INRA.

These agrarian reforms led to a number of defections in the summer of 1959. The air force commander went into exile, President Urrutia resigned, the leader of the Orthodoxo Party asked for asylum, and diplomats resigned while abroad. Cubans in their thousands began leaving the island, claiming fear of Communism (Fagg 1965: 104). In October 1959, Hubert Matos, a close associate of Castro in the Sierra Maestra, resigned as military governor of Camagüey in protest at Communist Party infiltration into the government and against Raul Castro's appointment as head of the army, in particular. Matos was arrested. The next day the entire executive of the 26 July Movement in Camagüey resigned. More arrests followed in the province (Thomas 1971: 1244–7). Further recriminations over Communists in the government broke out within the cabinet.

From July 1959, Castro's personalized power became more directly linked to the people. Thomas (1971: 1235) has described it as 'direct democracy', 'the immediate communion between the "maximum" leader and the people'. Gonzales (1974: 92–6) has emphasized Castro's charismatic authority and both have likened his appeal to the people with that of Jesus Christ. Following Urrutia's public condemnation of Communists in the government, on 17 July, Castro resigned. Castro appealed directly to the people through the medium of television and Urrutia was obliged to resign. Public protests ensued and Castro was persuaded to resume his position as prime minister. Urrutia was replaced by the moderate Dorticos (Thomas 1971: 1232–5). During the counter-revolutionary crises which followed, with further resignations within the cabinet, Castro held the revolution together.

In the month leading up to Matos' arrest a plot to set up a provisional government had been unearthed in Las Villas which had implicated the cattle farmers of adjoining Camagüey and had revealed links with Trujillo in the Dominican Republic. Ranch owners had special objections to the breaking up of large estates under the agrarian reform law. An estimated 2,000 people were arrested (Thomas 1971: 1238). Guerrilla movements operating in the Escambray mountains in Las Villas and the Sierra Maestra were, on their capture in October, found to include US citizens and to have been supplied with US weapons. Some of these Americans were executed along with Cuban rebels (Keesing's 1959–60:17788). From October 1959 flights over Cuba from Florida began; some of these were American planes dropping bombs on sugar mills. Coinciding with one of these incidents a drunkard made an attempt on Castro's life (Thomas 1971: 1243).

After the agrarian reforms came nationalization of properties owned by US corporations. In the summer of 1960, Texaco, Shell and Esso refineries refused to handle Soviet crude oil which had been exchanged for sugar. In June these refineries were seized. On 6 July, Eisenhower cancelled 700,000 tons of sugar. On 7 July, American properties worth 800 million dollars were confiscated. In October more or less every other American enterprise – banks, hotels, theatres and the like – were nationalized (Dumont 1970: 34). By the end of October the total value of assets seized had reached nearly US$1,000 million (Keesing's 1959–60: 17787). Though compensation was offered in bonds redeemable after 20 years, the dispute had begun with the American government which was to lead eventually to the new regime entering the Soviet camp (Lévesque 1978: 20).

In January 1961 relations between the United States and Cuba were broken by President Eisenhower and attention became focused on exiles in Florida determined to overthrow Castro. By the beginning of 1961 the number of exiles who had left since January 1959 was reported in the US as having reached 100,000 (Keesing's 1961: 17911).[4] Ex-prime minister Miró Cardona formed the Cuban National Revolutionary Council on 21 March (with temporary headquarters in New York and rumoured to be financed by the CIA) which brought together a variety of groups that had been formed by exiles to overthrow Castro (Keesing's 1961–2: 18151). On 7 April 1961, 1,200 Cuban exiles, trained, armed and transported by the US, landed in the Bay of Pigs. It was a complete failure. On 8 April, Cardona had called on the Cuban people to overthrow Castro and to install 'a democratic regime based on liberty and social justice' (ibid). A popular uprising failed to coincide with the landing and the invaders were quickly overpowered and disarmed (Matthews 1969: 180–6; Fagg 1965: 106–80).

TERROR RE-AWAKENS: THE REORGANIZATION OF THE ARMY

In October 1959, to try those arrested, following the Matos crisis and capture of rebels in Camagüey and Las Villas, the government brought back the military courts of the early days of the revolution. Habeas corpus was suspended. Matos and his officers were tried in December 1959 by a tribunal weighted in favour of the prosecution (Thomas 1971: 1255). He was sentenced to 20 years; his officers were given sentences of between two and seven years. The trials continued through to the middle of 1960, with sentences of up to 30 years being handed out, though few received the death penalty. In a mass trial, on 10 February 1960, 104 people received from 3 to 30 years with 30 people found not guilty. (Keesing's 1960: 17538–40).

After the Matos crisis, the new army was run down and reorganized into a volunteer army. This militia, made up of 150,000 women and men serving as soldiers for eight hours a week after their regular jobs, was organized and officered by the army. It was formed to guard against counter-revolution and members of G2 sometimes headed these local militias as well as conducting military intelligence in the provinces (Thomas 1971: 1321). From 1960 onwards a civilian branch of the militia developed made up of Committees for the Defence of the Revolution (CDR). These were basically networks of informers against local people though they were also used for carrying through the vaccination programmes and literacy campaigns. The main activity in 1960 was to inform on anyone selling their furniture, which signalled illegal emigration. Safe emigration was bought at a price, the gift to the state of all possessions (ibid: 1322).

Thomas (1971: 1238–9) remarks that from this point:

> The social benefits conferred by the revolution upon the poor and the landless were accompanied by imprisonments, delayed trials, occasional executions, more and more arbitrary seizures of land and overcrowded prisons. Castro's prisons were no doubt to begin with an improvement on those of Batista. Torture was unusual, but thoughtlessness, overcrowding and humiliations frequent. The numbers in prison were also already higher than under Batista.

He puts the figures for 1960 as high as 10,000 political prisoners (ibid). Some of these, he suggests, had had 'something of a trial, some had not', though for non-political prisoners Thomas reports trials were both carried out and properly so. With such large numbers of prisoners makeshift prisons had to supplement overcrowding and old fortresses were used (ibid: 1351).[5]

There is disagreement over the numbers executed and imprisoned. Thomas (1971: 1460) has put an estimate on the period 1959–'early 1961' at nearly 2,000 executed, adding, 'But who can be certain of figures in this realm?' Cuba has never provided complete statistics. Goldenberg (1965: 209) supports Thomas' estimate though elsewhere the figures reported are lower, at over 600 by the end of March 1961 and 650 by the end of 1962 (Keesing's 1962: 19098–9). Five of the Bay of Pigs invasion force and five accused of sabotage and plotting to assassinate Castro were executed in September 1961. The remaining trials of those captured and involved in the April 1961 Bay of Pigs invasion took place in March–April 1962. All 1,179 prisoners pleaded guilty and received sentences of up to 30 years. There were no executions resulting from these trials. The émigré paper *Avance* reported the number of political prisoners at between 15,000–20,000 (Goldenberg 1965: 209).[6]

POLICY CHOICE AND NECESSITY: ECONOMIC PROBLEMS AND COMMUNISM

The agrarian reform laws introduced in May 1959 had provoked counter-revolution, amongst cattle farmers of the Camagüey most especially. The growing strength of Communists (PSP members) within both INRA and the cabinet had angered both Liberals at home and the American government and had driven increasing numbers of exiles abroad. Relations between the US government and Cuba had gone from bad to worse and the economy had been further undermined as a consequence. By March 1961, Cuba had moved into the Soviet camp. The extent to which the Communist route taken by Cuba constituted a chosen policy becomes a crucial question in reaching an understanding of the Terror. In the literature, support can be found both for the view that the move to Communism was chosen (for example, Gonzales 1974) and that the path taken by Cuba was not deliberate (for example, Matthews 1969).

The 'necessary' conditions for a reign of terror, counter-revolution from within and invasion from without, had been experienced by the new Cuban regime and economic problems had also been pressing, but these conditions were different from those found in either France or Russia. The revolutionary government had inherited a stagnant economy, highly specialized in sugar production for export to the USA. American-owned sugar mills and plantations produced 40 per cent of Cuba's sugar and this represented an investment by American-owned companies (Atlantica del Golfo, Rionda, Cuban–American sugar and the largest, the United Fruit Company) of US$275,000, covering 1,666,000 acres of land (Keesing's 1959–60: 16902). Any economic reforms undertaken by the new government were bound to affect US interests.

If promised social reforms – land re-distribution, health, literacy, employment programmes – were to be paid for, the options available were few. Diversification of production, which would reduce dependency on imports and at the same time cushion the effects of the vagaries of the sugar harvest, could not offer a quick solution. The only real short-term option available to the revolutionary government would be to increase export revenues by increasing sugar production and to receive large amounts of aid.[7] The commercial treaty of reciprocation agreed between the USA and Cuba in 1903 made the USA the major purchaser of Cuban sugar. Under it a negotiated increase in prices paid was an option, but in practice not a real option when world market prices were low, as they were in 1959. Castro had gone in person to America to ask for help but the levels of aid required were above what the USA considered reasonable (Thomas 1971: 1213). As a consequence, Castro sought aid and alternative markets elsewhere.

In February 1960 the USSR agreed to buy 425,000 tons of sugar during 1960 and one million tons a year for the following four years. Cuba was also credited with US$100 dollars for the purchase of Soviet industrial equipment (Lévesque 1978: 14). Help from the Soviet Union had actually come rather late and only after the USA had been approached. The first economic agreement made with the USSR back in April 1959 had been for the purchase of 170,000 tons of sugar, less than the amount sold by Batista in 1958. Indeed the Soviet commitment to spend US$31.3 million on Cuban exports for 1959 and 1960 was considerably lower than the sum spent, at US$47.1 million, during 1957 alone (ibid: 13).

Cuba's economic problems were made worse in May 1960 when the USA cut off aid to Cuba and then worse still, in July 1960, when

Eisenhower slashed the permitted import of Cuban sugar by nearly 20 per cent (Keesing's 1960: 17542). The US action in May had reflected the growing friendliness between the USSR and Cuba over the previous three months though diplomatic relations had not been established until 8 May (Lévesque 1978: 15). In July US action had been taken in retaliation for the nationalization of the American oil refineries and in return, between August and October, the Cuban government had nationalized virtually all the remaining American enterprises. The USSR agreed to buy the cut of 700,000 tons of sugar from the quota to be purchased by the US (ibid: 16). In November 1960, China agreed to buy one million tons of sugar in 1961 and to provide technical aid and help with equipment; in December the Soviet Union agreed to buy, for the year 1961, not the one million tons promised in February but 2.7 million tons of sugar at very favourable prices.

Cuba's trade relations with the USSR had developed from necessity. A small country specializing in the production of sugar and highly dependent on its export revenues was obliged to sell to the highest bidder and accept aid from whence-so-ever it came. The nationalization of American-owned properties had been carried out essentially in retaliation to US actions. Castro had described the 20 per cent US cut in the sugar quota in July as a 'blind stupid act' and had threatened that as the Americans 'take pound by pound of sugar away from Cuba, we will take sugar mill by sugar mill and cent by cent until the last US investment in Cuba disappears' (quoted in Keesing's 1959–60:17542). Eisenhower in return, in direct response to a speech made by Khrushchev, had declared that he would not allow Cuba to be controlled by 'international communism' (Lévesque 1978: 19). Cuba had, then, effectively found itself caught up in an international cold-war dispute. Squeezed from outside, the revolution became directed towards Communism. With the Bay of Pigs invasion all other options were ended (Thomas 1971: 1372).

US reaction to Cuba had itself been provoked by the Cuban government's conduct before the summer of 1960. The agrarian reforms in 1959 had nationalized American land and companies, ever-growing numbers of exiles were seeking refuge in the United States and there was evidence of Communists gaining prominence in the government. These developments had led to protests, resignations and finally the Matos trial. Suspicion had been aroused over the war trials, too, and the exiles had inflamed suspicion. In themselves, the agrarian reforms were not Communist. According to Dumont (1970: 28) the reforms were 'much more mindful of the Italian laws of 1949–50 inspired by Christian Democratic principles, than of the popular democracies of Eastern Europe passed around 1945'. Only estates over 402 hectares were expropriated. (In Poland and Bulgaria they had been 20–50 hectares and above.) Furthermore, cattle ranches and farms with production of 50 per cent above the regional average were permitted to remain as large as 1,342 hectares. All rented lands were expropriated and tenant farmers of small plots were given the land; large farms were not divided but taken over wholly as cooperatives. In essence the Agrarian Reform Law was moderate. It was INRA put in charge of administering and requisitioning estates which caused trouble and it was in INRA that the Communists were mainly to be found.

The Cuban Communist Party, loyal to proletarian party-led revolution, had originally opposed the 26 July Movement for being a rural guerrilla organization. Some of the Communist Party members had, however, later changed their view and supported the guerrillas' push to overthrow Batista. These had formed the Popular Socialist Party. Their growing influence and importance within the government developed through their understanding of economic organization. A member of INRA remarked: 'These Fidelistas are excellent when it comes to stirring up people politically or creating militias, but they are less well prepared to organize the economy' (Dumont 1970: 31). The Communists in the Popular Socialist Party had a better understanding of how to organize production. Thomas (1971: 1313), drawing attention to the fact that Communists had been used by Batista for their bureaucratic skills, argues that Castro wanted Communists in the government and in INRA especially because of their capacity for organization, so essential in a revolutionary economy. Friction between the Communists and the guerrillas had provoked the Matos crisis. The heavy-handed behaviour of INRA had stirred the anger of the cattle-ranchers of Camagüey and support amongst the propertied classes had been eroded even amongst those who had given their every support to the revolution, some of whom had not only financed the revolution but had handed over requisitioned lands with 'good grace' (Dumont 1970: 30).

Because the revolution held together around him Castro managed to deal with these frictions, though one of the consequences had been that the Cabinet met less often (for example only twice between November 1959 and March 1960) and the new revolutionary army (essentially based on the 26 July Movement) needed to be reorganized into a volunteer army (Thomas 1971: 1247 and 1321). His third response had been increased reliance on coercion, coercion which had, through the development of G2 and CDR and the large numbers of arrests and increased executions, become a reign of terror.

ASSESSMENT OF THE TERROR

It seems that different considerations need to be applied to the three sets of trials, those between 1–10 January, those between January – July 1959 and those after October 1959 when habeas corpus was suspended, up to and shortly after the Bay of Pigs invasion in April 1961.

The first ten days amounted to a short-lived reign of terror, a period of summary justice though it is doubtful that innocent people were executed. For the subsequent run of executions the comparison made with Nuremburg and the plea that these trials were for crimes against humanity seem appropriate. The evidence supports the claim that those executed and imprisoned were indeed murderers and torturers. Strictly there was the problem of retrospective legislation, which had bothered Cardona. The laws under which the trials were carried out had been introduced in the Sierra Maestra in February 1958 but in a debate focusing on political legitimacy it should not be forgotten that Batista had come to power illegally by a *coup d'état* . Such arguments are not cut and dried, but on balance those trials seem ill-fitting under the heading of a reign of terror.

Of the October trials, which followed the resignations in Camagüey and rebellions in Las Villas, different considerations need to be introduced. Some at least of this counter-revolutionary activity was provoked by the government's policies, the agrarian reform legislation and the conduct of INRA in particular. Whilst a genuine and very serious plot was unearthed, it is hard to accept, with between 1,000–2,000 people arrested, that other than injustices were done. The evidence given to the International Commission of Jurists (1962) confirms this, as do the reports of over-crowded conditions where some prisoners were held without trial. Thomas recounts examples where defence witnesses and lawyers were themselves arrested after trials and where the defence could not be heard for noise. 'It is true', says Thomas (1971: 1459), 'that most accounts of inhumanity date back to 1960–1, when invasion was daily expected, but no good regime should be capable even under provocation of such malign behaviour to its opponents'.

Executions were carried out on political prisoners and prison conditions were appalling, but there is no evidence of summary executions.
Such as it was, by comparison with France and Russia, the surveillance apparatus was unobnoxious. Of course G2 and the Committees
for the Defence of the Revolution struck fear in the hearts of those
whose only crime was to own property but the Terror's reach was not
generally capricious. The clash came between those

> who had authority on their side in the old regime and those who had it in
> the new: the property owners who did not suffer under Batista's repression
> but were picked on by the G2 and the CDR; and the ordinary people
> without property who suffered under Batista's repression and torture but
> for whom under Castro authority seemed now 'on their side'. (Thomas
> 1971: 1353)

It is fair to say that events in Cuba do not match the events of either
the Russian Red Terror or the Jacobin dictatorship. Compared with
these it was a mild terror, not simply because its executions, taking the
higher figure of 2,000 as a proportion of Cuba's 7 million population
(1 in 3,500), represents a far smaller ratio than the 1 in 735 for Russia
and 1 in 625 for France. Even if all those who died in Cuban prisons
could be added to this figure it could not adjust the ratio near to those
proportions. The Terror seems mild because in addition to the absence
of a policy of summary execution, the possibility of release and the
absence of routine summary justice, there is scant evidence of brutal
tortures. Inhumanity lay essentially in prison conditions.

There are a number of possible explanations for why Cuba's terror
was mild, two of which held for the American Revolution, also. The
vast borders to the west and Canada had offered escape routes in the
American case; though financial penalties were imposed in the case of
Cuba, people were permitted to leave. This reflected both the revolutionaries' attitudes and the strength of support, which the Bay of Pigs
failure had clearly shown. As for America, support had been the result
of the civil war having taken place before the revolutionary government had come to power. In Cuba the contrasting behaviour of the
Batistianos and the guerrillas had played a major role in casting Castro
in the role of saviour.

Unlike Washington, Castro had faced the threat of foreign invasion,
renewed counter-revolutionary activity at home and serious economic
problems. Unlike the buoyant American economy, Cuba's economy
was stagnant and highly specialized in sugar production, 40 per cent of

which was produced on American-owned lands (Keesing's 1959–60: 16902). In a country so dependent on the US the social democratic policies introduced logically amounted to a highly transformatory ideology. The American Revolution had not been fought for similar social and economic changes but by comparison with the material changes envisaged in the Russian Revolution, the Cuban revolutionary programme was moderate. Furthermore, though the agrarian reforms created opposition within the propertied classes, Cuban revolutionary policies did not set town against country. The guerrillas had gained an understanding of rural life and a sympathy for the peasantry. Whilst in Russia war communism had led to underpayment of peasants and then forced extraction of goods and in France force had been used against the peasantry for the supply of towns, Castro's government was generous with the peasants, indeed more so than could be afforded (Dumont 1970: 38).

The relative mildness of the Cuban terror reflected the high level of support given to the revolutionaries. This had been gained through the nature of the policies chosen as well as the passage to power through a guerrilla movement to civil war. The moderate Terror also reflected Castro's capacity to gain control over the coercive forces. Control over G2 had followed from the rise to power itself. G2 had been formed within the guerrilla army, later transformed into the national army in January 1959. The Matos crisis had revealed the lack of central control over the new guerrilla-based armed force. As a consequence, Castro had dissolved the army and replaced it with a volunteer force which drew strength not from the guerrillas but from the people and G2 was developed from a military intelligence organization into a broader institution of surveillance extended through the CDR. Over G2 Castro had kept control. When counter-revolutionaries captured in the Escambray mountains in the winter of 1960–1 were mistreated by G2 in order to extract information, once brought to Castro's attention, he stopped it immediately (Thomas 1972: 1322).

THE ESTABLISHMENT OF A SINGLE-PARTY STATE

Castro held the revolution together but by 1961, with the US-backed Bay of Pigs invasion defeated, export markets secured with the USSR, and the army, police and judiciary under state control, Castro began the process which followed from his alliance with the Soviet Union of developing a single-party structure.[8] The intention to form a single-party state was first announced in July 1961. At the end of 1961 the three revolutionary organizations within Castro's coalition were unified to form the Integrated Revolutionary Organization which in 1965 became the Cuban Communist Party (Azicri 1988: 27–8).

NOTES

1. For a concise general introduction to the background to the Cuban Revolution see Goldenberg (1965, Part 2: chs 1–3); Blackburn (1963) and Wolf (1973: ch.6). See also O'Connor (1972) who, in offering an analysis of Cuba's political economy, emphasizes its high level of stagnation. Azicri (1988: 36) lists the main social and economic problems facing Cuba in 1957–8 as the following: low economic growth; over-specialization in sugar for exports and over-dependence on sugar revenues for national income; 'extreme dependence' on the USA for trade and investment; a high rate of both unemployment and underemployment; and a highly unequal distribution of income between urban and rural areas.

2. The idea that only 300 guerrillas defeated 30,000 of Batista's troops (see Fairbairn 1974: 267) is a myth which seems to have developed from a remark made by Guevara (see Blackburn 1963: 76, fn. 57) but Guevara's comment referred to May 1958 before the guerrilla movement transformed itself into a combat army.

3. See Castro's *History Will Absolve Me* speech made at his Moncada Barracks trial and later released as an underground pamphlet (Castro 1968) and the Manifesto of the 26 July Movement issued in November 1956 (Bonachea and Valdes 1972: ch. 5). For the promise turned to practice see Huberman and Sweezy (1969).

4. At first, few obstacles had been placed in the way of those choosing to leave Cuba, but at the end of 1960 it became more difficult. Police permission was required from then on, money was not to be taken out of the country unless a return was booked (air tickets had to be paid for from abroad) and émigré property was to be confiscated. In spite of these restrictions emigration increased (Goldenberg 1965: 209–10).

5. The International Commission of Jurists (1962) which carried out interviews in Cuba at the end of 1961 provides numerous accounts of appalling prison conditions (see Part 4, Section VI). See also Goldenberg (1964: 179) on the conduct of trials.

6. As Goldenberg cautions, 'but naturally nothing definite is known'. Thomas (1971: 460, fn 29) draws attention to the problem of using émigré sources, giving as an example an estimate of nearly 7,000 executions published in 1963 in an exile newsheet. He rejects this as exaggeration and draws attention to even wilder estimates made later.

7. For a general consideration of the problems faced by countries dependent on exports for growth and specialized in the production of primary goods for the export market see O'Kane 1987: ch.7. Huberman and Sweezy (1969) argue that socialism, a planned economy, was the only solution to Cuba's economic ills.

8. A further law against counter-revolutionary activities was introduced in November 1961 but executions in practice became less frequent (Keesing's 1962: 19099).

8. Nicaragua 1979: Resisting Terror

Like the revolution in Cuba the revolution which overthrew the Somoza dictatorship in Nicaragua in 1979 began with a guerrilla movement which developed into a civil war, success in which brought the revolutionary Sandinista regime to power. Proximity to revolutionary Cuba, both in distance and time, was to bring to the Nicaraguan revolutionaries advantages and one serious disadvantage. The Communist outcome of the Cuban Revolution was to distort US relations with Nicaragua.[1]

GUERRILLA MOVEMENT TO CIVIL WAR AND VICTORY

Whilst Nicaragua lacked an *ancien régime*, the Somoza dictatorship, at the end of a 43-year long dynasty, was more entrenched than Batista's after just six years in power. The Nicaraguan guerrilla movement had been inspired by the Cuban victory, an inspiration enhanced by Nicaragua's own guerrilla hero, Sandino, who had opposed Somoza back in the early 1930s. The FSLN, the Sandinista Front for National Liberation, was founded in 1961 (FLN in its first year) and an attempt was made in 1963 to adapt the guerrilla pattern of the Sierra Maestra to the hills along the border with Honduras. It ended in failure. In 1967, a second attempt to adopt this rural, peasant-based strategy for revolution had again ended in failure. The movement withdrew to the cities where underground organizations were developed and sporadic armed attacks on banks and the like were carried out to finance the movement.

In December 1972 an earthquake devastated the capital, Managua, and when the National Guard used the opportunity for looting and international relief funds were channelled into Somoza's and friends' pockets rather than into emergency aid and city reconstruction, public opposition to Somoza was pushed into action (Walker 1982b: 17; Black 1986: 189). The failure of the rural guerrilla strategy in the mid-sixties, the later experiences in the towns and then the events in Managua led the FSLN to embark on a strategy in many ways more in tune with the combined urban–rural reality of the Cuban experience than the myth of a purely rural movement. At the end of 1974 the FSLN attacked the home of one of Somoza's leading administrators and kidnapped a number of the regime's top people. In retaliation, Somoza's National Guard stepped up repression under a 'strategy of siege' which was not lifted until September 1977 after US President Carter's threat to remove US\$3.1 million in US aid (Chavarría 1982: 29). The FSLN collapsed under the pressure of the National Guard onslaught but, as in Cuba, the repression brought increasing middle-class support to the revolutionary movement.

Unlike the Cuban case, however, the FSLN was not simply a guerrilla movement, it was also a party. In 1972 membership was down to only a few members (Gilbert 1988: 41) and after the 1975 collapse factionalism ('tendencies') developed within the party over strategy and class allegiance within the FSLN. Through recruitment, the FSLN had changed both its social composition and ideological complexion. The original GPP (Prolonged Popular War) had favoured rural guerrilla warfare; influenced initially by Guevara it had later taken up more Maoist strategies and become heavily influenced by Giap and the Vietnamese struggle. The TP (Proletarian Tendency) favoured urban guerrilla warfare; the Terceristas (the Third Way) preferred allegiance with the 'bourgeois' opposition and was essentially pluralist in its ideology. Its leadership included Eden Pastora (Commander Zero) and the Ortega brothers, Daniel and Humberto. In a resolution of these tendencies the FSLN developed a combination of military and political strategies which directed it towards urban warfare and a unity of all groups opposed to Somoza (Booth 1985a: 143–4; Skidmore and Smith 1984: 366). In May 1977 the Terceristas produced 'The General Political–Military Platform' which gave details of its plan for a broad opposition movement; later in the year it formed the 'Group of Twelve', a group of prominent and highly respectable business, professional and church figures who called for a provisional government to include FSLN representation (Gilbert 1988: 9).

In January 1978, Pedro Joaquin Chamorro, the editor of *La Prensa* who had regularly published material in condemnation of the Somoza regime's repression and brutality, was assassinated. In protest, Somoza's business properties were attacked, street barricades were erected and a general strike, organized by the business community, lasted for two weeks. This assassination led to the development of the FAO (Broad Opposition Front), made up of mainly business groups, among them COSEP (High Council of Foreign Enterprise). Opposition groups elsewhere began to form. Following celebrations in February to commemorate the forty-fourth anniversary of Sandino's death, the National Guard opened fire on a religious gathering in Monimbo. A rebellion erupted amongst the local Indians which lasted six days during which 200 people were killed. In April, a student strike broke out, then a strike of hospital workers and these were followed by women's protests.

In July 1978 the FSLN again engaged in military action when 25 guerrillas attacked the national palace and took hostage almost the entire membership of the Chamber of Deputies plus around 2,000 employees. With church help in negotiations Somoza gave in to the guerrillas' demands for the safe release of 59 political prisoners, money and the resolution of the hospital workers' strike. In August the FAO organized a further general strike. In the same month another spontaneous uprising, like that in Monimbo, broke out in Matagalpa. In September, others occurred in four more cities; Leon, Masaya, Chinandega and Managua. Somoza reinstated the state of siege, bombed the towns and then ordered troops to retake each of the towns in turn. The FSLN, along with thousands of others, took to the hills and the National Guard began 'Operation Clean Up', the capture and punishment of opposition (Chavarría 1982: 27–33).[2]

In November 1978 the Inter-American Commission on Human Rights published a report on the September 1977 massacre, filed by six members of the commission who had visited Nicaragua in October. The report, one of the most damning ever published, referred to the indiscriminate bombing of civilians, the carrying out of 'summary and mass executions' of adults, youths and 'defenceless children', of excessive torture, of arbitrary arrests and the use of 'generalized repression against all young men between the ages of 14 and 21' (Keesing's 1979: 29805). The death toll was estimated at 5,000, the injured at 10,000 and 60,000 sought asylum abroad, mainly in Costa Rica (Chavarría 1982: 33). In November, Costa Rica itself was drawn into the fight against Somoza when the National Guard began attacking across the border.

The United States attempted to negotiate a peaceful solution which broke down absolutely in January 1979, and in February the US ended military aid which had been under suspension since September 1978.

Meantime a system of local organization, the United Peoples Movement (MPU), set about organizing the resistance (Chavarría 1982: 33). In January 1979 a general strike broke out and in March the FSLN, its troops by then numbering 5,000, launched into full military action. A set-back occurred at Esteli, under occupation by the FSLN, when the guerrillas were routed and massacred, leaving 1,000 dead or captured. Other setbacks followed. On 5 June, however, the FSLN took Leon and held it. Again the president declared a state of siege but the National Guard failed to regain the city. The FSLN also held Matagalpa. In the capital Managua, the MPU played a decisive role in helping the Sandinista guerrillas, and by 12 June the FSLN held the slum areas of Managua, which Somoza's troops therefore began to bomb (Keesing's 1979: 29807).

On June 16 the FSLN announced from Costa Rica that it had formed a 'provisional junta of national reconstruction' whose aim was to overthrow the Somoza regime, hold elections and install a government of 'national unity' (Keesing's 1979: 29808–9). Meantime bombings continued in Managua, with an estimated 10,000–20,000 civilian casualties. By the end of June most of the major cities were either wholly or partly in FSLN hands. To avoid further civilian casualties in the capital the FSLN forces withdrew and increased their attacks on other towns. By 6 July they had cut off the National Guard's supplies. They then regrouped to renew their attack on Managua. On 17 July, Somoza resigned and was replaced by the FSLN provisional government as part of the deal to an agreed settlement to the war between the FSLN and the USA. Red Cross estimates put the number killed after January 1978 (Chamorro's murder) at 40,000–50,000. Figures released by the UN High Commissioner for refugees reported 110,000 Nicaraguans out of a total population of 2.5 million having fled the country after September 1978. Of these 50,000 were in Honduras.[3]

The Sandinista government had emerged through a bloodbath in which the FSLN had been kept afloat by the active support of all levels of the Nicaraguan population, but it had been the towns where support had been most important. The FAO, the MPU resistance movement, the workers' strikes and demonstrations had all played a vital part. In Cuba the failure of the general strike in July 1958 had produced a triumphal civil war like Garibaldi's unification of Italy. As the Cuban guerrilla army fought its way up the island from the Sierra Maestra, and rebellion erupted in Havana in support, Batista had fled. In Nicaragua, the guerrilla army and people's movements had fought side-by-side and the comradeship of action had nurtured cooperation and compassion.

THE NEW REGIME: BARRIERS TO TERROR

The provisional government had agreed three things from the start: that reprisals would not be taken against members of Somoza's regime; that the Archbishop of Managua, Mgr Miguel Obando y Bravo, would give sanctuary to those wanting to leave Nicaragua; and that human rights would be upheld (Keesing's 1979: 29810).[4] Once in office the new government announced the restoration of all political, religious and human rights, the dissolution of the old National Guard, the creation of both a new national army and a separate police force and the abolition of the death penalty and of military courts. On 21 August a 'Statute on Rights and Guarantees for the Citizens of Nicaragua' was issued, with immediate effect (see Keesing's 1980: 30025–6). The statute stated that 'the right to life is inviolable and inherent to a human being'. Torture was prohibited, slavery too. The abolition of the death penalty was confirmed and prison sentences were put at a maximum of 30 years. Justice was to be administered according to strict guidelines: detention without a warrant 'except in cases of flagrant crimes' was forbidden; those arrested were to appear in court within 24 hours or otherwise released; the purpose of imprisonment was stated to be for improvement with a view to release; and court proceedings were to be open other than for 'moral, public order or national security considerations' (ibid). Freedom of expression and information were also guaranteed, as was the right to strike and the right to hold private property. In short, the most determined efforts to avoid a reign of terror were immediately brought to bear.

In July a 'Basic Statute' had been introduced which dissolved the Congress and created a Council of State to draft a new constitution and take on the role of government until elections could be held under the new constitution. The Statute on Rights and Guarantees included the promise of democratic freedoms, including the rights of political organization, to vote and to stand for election. The new government estimated that it would take three to four years before elections could be held. In accordance with the promise made by the FSLN in June, the membership of the Council of State was to constitute a government of 'national unity'. The Council included 13 moderates (seven from the FAO and six

from the employers' organizations), 12 members of the National Patriotic Alliance (which included the MPU, the Group of Twelve and the
Independent Liberal Party) and six members of the FSLN. Only Somoza's
National Liberal Party lacked members in the government. The leadership
of the Council of State, the junta, was made up of representatives from
these various groups, Ramirez (Group of 12), Robelo (FAO; Robelo was
also head of his own political party the National Democratic Movement,
MDN), Daniel Ortega (FSLN–Terceristas), Hassan (MPU), plus
Chamorro's widow, Violeta (Keesing's 1980: 30025).

THE WAR TRIALS

The trials of those accused of crimes under the Somoza regime, mainly
members of the National Guard, opened in December 1979; the Statute on Rights and Guarantees for the Citizens of Nicaragua applied
(Keesing's 1980: 30317). There were eight special tribunals and three
appeal courts. Of the 7,000 originally arrested many had been released
after initial investigation. Given the large number which remained,
however, trials had to be restricted to one week and judges were
sometimes law students or leading Sandinistas, the professional judges
being viewed as having been part of Somoza's system. On Christmas
Eve 70 prisoners were released and a few days later 180 people who
had taken refuge in embassies were allowed to go free. The trials
dragged slowly on, however, and by mid-1980 thousands of National
Guards were still awaiting trial (ibid 1981: 30660). By February 1981,
these trials had been completed and on 20 February the special tribunals were dissolved.

The official toll was 4,331 people who had been given prison sentences of between 1–30 years, 1,000 had been let free, having been
found not guilty or pardoned, and a further 979 had been released for
lack of evidence (Keesing's 1981: 30976). Contrary to the claims of
abolition, however, several people were reported executed and an Inter-American Human Rights Commission Report in 1981 complained
of irregularities in the conduct of these special tribunals, and criticized
the conditions under which prisoners were kept (ibid 1982: 31291).
The Commission also reported the 'virtual elimination in Nicaragua of
the use of torture and summary executions' (ibid: 31407). This presented a stark contrast, not only with Somoza's regime but with the
other countries included within the report, Guatemala and El Salvador

in particular. These same two countries were also highlighted for their human rights violations by the 1981 report of the US Council on Hemispheric Affairs.[5]

The institution of summary justice had been avoided in Nicaragua. The special tribunals had permitted all accused to have legal representation, the media had access to the trials, and the law applied had existed before the crimes had been committed (Booth 1985b: 40–4). The conduct of trials, given the problems created by such large numbers, had been conducted fairly according to the due process of law (see Gorman and Walker 1985). Prison conditions, if not ideal, had resisted abuses of torture and deliberate maltreatment normally associated with reigns of terror, nor had a secret police force been created.

THE FSLN AND CONTROL OVER THE FORCES OF DEFENCE AND SECURITY

Whilst no secret police force equivalent even to Cuba's G2 had developed, the Sandinista Defence Committees (CDS), the neighbourhood-based mass organizations, could be compared with the Cuban CDR (Committees for the Defence of the Revolution). The CDS had proved crucial in the overthrow of Somoza:

> Sandinistas characterise the committees as grassroots popular democracy, an institution designed to empower the masses and allow them to participate actively in reshaping their communities. Enemies of the revolution, especially those outside the country, see the CDS as an instrument of totalitarianism, a national network of spies and political enforcers. Gilbert (1988:69)

In practice members of the CDS were all along permitted to belong to any political party, church or other organization. Membership was voluntary and continued to be so and recruits were not armed. Their role was mainly that of consciousness-raising and implementing reforms such as building roads, schools and improving sanitation (ibid: 64–72). Where 'abuses of authority' did occur (such as the intimidation of Sandinista opposition or the refusal to give ration cards to those who would not participate in the night watch), Gilbert (ibid 69–70) reports that the FSLN was quick to criticize, emphasizing the voluntary nature of the CDS activities and insisting on 'persuasion' not repression for building support. The CDS were also only one of a number of grass-roots organizations, including workers and farmers unions, women's associations and youth organizations (the youth organization is the only group for which FSLN membership is required).

Similar to both the Cuban and American cases, Nicaragua also had militias. These 'popular militias' were essentially neighbourhood-based reserve forces for the Sandinista Popular Army (EPS) and sometimes for the police, and they acted in alliance with the defence committees. In contrast with both America and Cuba, however, the FSLN's aim was always to turn the army into a wholly professional force and from the beginning the EPS was a career army. In this respect, its closest comparison was with the New Model Army of the English Revolution. In 1979 in the '72 hours document' confirming an FSLN promise made in 1960, the FSLN published plans for replacing the National Guard with a national army built from the guerrilla movement committed to the revolution and the FSLN, 'its historic vanguard' (Gilbert 1988: 62). The Sandinista Popular Army was formed around the original FSLN guerrilla movement but included members of the National Guard who had defected to the Sandinistas, plus members of the popular militias. It was trained with help from Cuba and by mid-1980 numbered between 13,000–18,000 (Gorman and Walker 1985: 100). This professional army was developed for the defence of the country against possible counter-revolution but, along with the popular militias, it was used to help re-build the country after the civil war.

Whilst the new National Unity government of revolutionary Nicaragua was pluralist, this new national army, EPS, was put under the direct authority of the National Directorate of the FSLN rather than under the control of the junta or the Council of State. The police force was also placed under the National Directorate, which coordinated policy for the police and army under the Defence and Security Committee. Members of the National Directorate were ministers of defence and of the interior (police) (Gilbert 1988: 62–3). Within eighteen months of coming to power the FSLN had established control over the coercive forces of the revolutionary state.

JULY 1979 TO FEBRUARY 1981: ECONOMIC RECONSTRUCTION AND THE MAINTENANCE OF SUPPORT

The trials initiated after the Sandinista revolution in 1979 had not then turned into a revolutionary reign of terror by 1981 and in February the tribunals had been disbanded. The new regime had set out to avoid a Terror as its statutes had shown and it had succeeded. In spite of the appalling devastation caused by the civil war this success in avoiding a reign of terror had been assisted by economic and international advantages not shared by Cuba.

War damage was estimated by the Red Cross at US$5,000 million and out of the 2.5 million population the UN High Commission for Refugees estimated 600,000 people as homeless and 900,000 illiterate. Thirty-two per cent of the population was unemployed.[6] Damage to harvests had severely reduced exports and the fall in coffee prices added to the government's economic problems, with exports down 25 per cent on the previous year. The new government possessed a trump card: Somoza's assets included ownership of some 20 per cent of Nicaragua's cultivatable land (Skidmore and Smith 1984: 307). These assets and his family's properties were immediately expropriated and up to a point, with Somoza gone, land reforms, nationalization and redistribution, could be implemented without the need to displace existing landowners. Other private landholdings were not touched. In addition to this trump card the government was fortunate in the foreign goodwill it received, from both North and South America, both Eastern and Western Europe and from North African countries. US President Jimmy Carter's making Human Rights a priority was a good thing, too, for the Sandinistas came in on a wave of anti-Somoza publicity. Luck also played a part. At the time of the Nicaraguan Revolution, America had its attention fixed on a far richer revolutionary investment, Iran.

In the short term the Sandinista government declared a state of emergency (which did not violate its own statute on human rights) to tackle recovery from the war. It lasted 90 days and in January 1980 an economic plan was introduced to increase exports, to tackle inflation (running at 40 per cent) and to encourage investment and so provide jobs for the unemployed. National banks, though not foreign ones, were nationalized, with compensation payments of six and a half per cent in five-year bonds. Insurance companies were similarly treated and plans released to nationalize the mining, fishing and forestry industries. The state became the major purchaser of export crops (mainly coffee, sugar and cotton) at fixed prices. Unexploited natural resources were decreed state property and, to frustrate rich exiles, high level banknotes were withdrawn and exchanged for government bonds. The bonds were not payable for six months, giving the government a short-term financial benefit. The national debt was put at US$1,600 million but loans were forthcoming from both the IMF (US$22 million) and the Inter-American Development Bank (US$500 million). The USA provided emergency aid and drew up an offer for the long term as well. Large loans and emergency aid soon followed from Venezuela, Mexico, West Germany, France, Sweden, the Netherlands, the USSR, Algeria, Libya and Cuba. The Food and Agricultural Organization approved a grant for the emergency aid of small cotton growers of US$2.9 million. In February the national literacy campaign was launched and again financial help was forthcoming. Cuba sent 1,200 people to help with the campaign, 1,000 doctors, nurses and technicians to help in the reconstruction, and in February 1980 offered US$50 million in aid (for the above figures see Keesing's 1980: 30317).

Nicaragua's economic relationship with the USA contrasted with Cuba's. The latter's economy was highly specialized (in sugar production for export) and trade was overwhelmingly the preserve of the USA. In Cuba, once the United States had turned against the revolutionary regime it had become essential to find new trading partners, a gap which the USSR came to fill. Nicaragua's economy, however, was both more diversified and less dependent on the USA. Between 1950–78 exports to the United States had dropped from 75 to 25 per cent of total export revenues (Maxfield and Stahler-Sholk 1985: 246). By the time the revolution occurred, exports were going largely to the Central American Common Market and Western Europe. The potential for alternative sources for both financial assistance and additional trade was therefore far greater than for Cuba.

Nicaragua had four main exports (coffee, cotton, beef and sugar) and this diversification, though limited, lent flexibility to foreign trade and home consumption. In short, both the structure of Nicaragua's economy and trade potential reduced the possible effect of US economic action and at the same time provided the basis for non-alignment, rather than the Communist bloc alternative which had, in effect, been Cuba's future. As had post-revolutionary Cuba, Nicaragua sought further diversification. Restrictions were put on imports, luxury goods in particular, to redress the problems of declining terms of trade (ibid: 252–3). War was to come to add greatly to these difficulties.[7]

The passage to revolution through civil war, a virulent civil war fought at great sacrifice in towns and cities throughout the country, had defeated opposition and had won the Sandinistas strong support. Popular support had been won from a broad spectrum of society and it had been active and organized support, made strong by repulsion of National

Guard behaviour. Interestingly, though, the FSLN guerrillas, unlike the 26 July Movement in the Oriente, had not established liberated zones of sufficient duration to establish a 'government in miniature'. In the end, the civil war had been in practice an urban guerrilla movement; it was this factor which had drawn the multiple movements together in action and which had driven home most starkly the contrasting behaviour between the forces of the old regime and the new. This wide support had been tapped by the government of national unity and pluralist organizations were encouraged. (For a full discussion of pluralism in Nicaragua, see Coraggio 1986.)

In Cuba revolutionary government had soon given way to the personalized power of Castro. In Nicaragua there was no such development. The FSLN was a party organization. In Cuba the 26 July Movement had, in government, been found lacking in the necessary administrative skills and the Popular Socialist Party (the reformed Community Party) had been drawn in to help. Crucially too, the FSLN had learned the lessons of Cuba and had begun straight away to establish a professional army under the National Directorate of the FSLN; the police had been placed under the control of the FSLN. With Sandinista control of the defence and security forces a revolutionary government of national unity was possible and was compatible with the goals of the revolution, a united economy, democracy and social reforms such as literacy, better housing and employment. The lessons of history had been learned from Cuba. In addition to the advice on building a strong army against counter-revolution Castro's advice to the FSLN was not to go for full nationalization but to preserve responsible private businesses. The disadvantages of having close political and economic ties with the USSR were also made clear (Walker 1982b: 8).

The revolutionary government had nevertheless faced some counter-revolution. It had initially come from the National Guard. At the end of 1979 incidents had occurred along the border with Honduras, where some of the National Guard had fled, forming the anti-Sandinista Nicaraguan Democratic Force (FDN) (Keesing's 1980: 30318). By February 1980 many of these had been captured by the Honduran army, though isolated incidents continued and in September 1980 anti-Sandinista forces formed in Guatemala too (ibid 1981: 30660). Towards the end of 1980 another anti-Sandinista force also grouped in Honduras, though this group was also opposed to Somoza. This Nicaraguan Democratic Union (UDN) and its armed wing (FARN) developed around a group of conservative businessmen.

The first threat to stability from inside the country had come in April 1980 when the two moderates, Sr Robelo and Sra Chamorro had resigned from the junta (Keesing's 1981: 30660). Their resignation had been prompted by worries about the economic policies combined with earlier changes within the cabinet and the Council of State which gave greater representation to the mass organizations, thereby under-mining the power of the business groups and increasing the powers of the National Directorate (Gilbert 1988: 110–13). COSEP was particu-larly worried by economic reforms affecting private enterprise but a compromise was reached through guarantees in law and Robelo and Chamorro were replaced by other businessmen Cruz and Córdova. Further resignations began to occur in August, and in September and November assassination plots were unearthed. In the latter case the vice-president of COSEP, who happened also to be Robelo's brother-in-law, was killed (ibid 1981: 30660 and 30976). In November 11 representatives of conservative organizations on the Council of State resigned in protest over the banning of an MDN rally (Robelo's party) (ibid: 30976). In late 1980–early 1981 violence had also erupted in the Zelaya region where Miskito Indians had tried to gain local self-government and special seats on the junta (in the eighteenth century there had been a separate Miskito Kingdom which had stretched across into Honduras).

BARRIERS TO TERROR COME DOWN: POLICIES AND COVERT WAR

From the moment President Reagan replaced President Carter in Janu-ary 1981 things began to get worse for the Nicaraguan government (Walker 1985b: 23). In October 1980 the USA had signed a $75 million aid agreement but, on 1 April 1981, all economic aid to Nica-ragua was suspended (Keesing's 1981: 30977). It was alleged that the Sandinistas were supplying arms to guerrillas in El Salvador, an accu-sation which they denied. Other countries stepped in with aid, West Germany, Sweden, Spain, the EEC, Venezuela, Costa Rica, Mexico, Brazil, the Soviet Union, Bulgaria, Libya and Cuba, the latter two offering US$100 million and 64 million respectively. These increased associations with Communist countries and Libya ensured that rela-tions with the USA went from bad to worse. In November 1981 and September 1982 the USA, along with Chile and Argentina, stopped loans from the Inter-American Development Bank and the United States stopped a further loan in June 1983. In February 1983 under pressure from the USA the World Bank had refused a large loan and by May 1983 Nicaragua's total foreign debt had reached $2,800 million (ibid 1983: 32304).

From May 1981 a 'covert war' against Nicaragua began to be funded by the USA through the CIA based on the FDN, the Honduran-based anti-Sandinista group formed from former members of the National Guard. The CIA also recruited civilians as the FDN's political front, though they had little real control over the military forces, paying both military and civilian leaders salaries of up to US$7,000 a month (Gilbert 1988: 164–5). In response to the threatened invasion, the Nicaraguan government began training 200,000 people's militia to supplement the then 40,000 regular army (Keesing's 1981: 30976). Ordinary recruits came mainly from the sparsely populated northern borders. Though some were ex-National Guard, many were drawn to the FDN in reaction to Sandinista policies in the area.

The Sandinistas first used force against the Miskitos on 20 February 1981, following a ceremony celebrating the end of the loathed literacy campaign. Four Indians and four soldiers were killed (Rooper and Smith 1986: 12). Some Miskitos left for Honduras and joined the anti-Sandinista forces. As a policy against counter-revolution the Indians were moved out of the war zone, partly under suspicion and partly as a safety operation. The Sandinistas burnt crops behind them and the affair gave rise to tales of genocide. The findings of the investigation into these incidents by the Inter-American Commission of Human Rights, however, rejected these claims though some isolated incidents of Miskito murder by Sandinistas, and evidence of brutality, were uncovered (ibid: 12).[8] In the case of murder the soldiers were punished and generally the affair was handled diplomatically (see ibid; Bourgois, 1986). Even so many more Miskito Indians were reported to be leaving for Honduras. By August 1982 about 20,000 were reported living on the Honduran side of the border (Keesing's 1985: 32305).

Under threat, in March 1981 the Nicaraguan government had reduced the ruling junta from five men to three leaving Daniel Ortega, Ramirez and the lawyer-businessman Córdova (Keesing's 1981: 30976–7); in July 1981 further economic policies were introduced which angered the business groups. 'Idle land', land left unworked, was to be confiscated and redistributed and properties (both land and factories) left vacant for more than six months by owners living abroad were also to be seized. Fourteen companies were immediately affected. At the same time, further intended policies were announced: the nationalization of the sugar distribution industry; the institution of close checks on those holding profits outside of Nicaragua; state-control of farm co-operatives; and the confiscation of property from those found guilty of 'counter-revolutionary activity'. In September the Sandinista government introduced a state of 'economic and social emergency' designed to prevent the occupation of land outside of the agrarian reform programme, to stop strikes, factory takeovers or obstruction of production. These measures accompanied the cuts in government expenditure which the Sandinistas made at the same time: subsidies were reduced on food, transport and services and heavy duties were imposed on luxury goods imported from outside Central America. The publication of false information about the economy, the destruction of production materials and equipment, the stoppage of public transport, the unofficial raising of prices and the incitement of foreign government to inflict damage on the national economy were all made crimes. All were measures familiar in reigns of terror, reminiscent especially of Russia. In Nicaragua, however, the penalties laid down had a maximum of three years imprisonment. (For the above see Keesing's 1982: 31290–1.)

These agrarian reforms remained limited in their aims, touching only large estates with the purpose of relieving peasant needs for land and redressing the problem of idle, unproductive resources. As Close remarks, 'The reform gave no incentives for peasant land seizure; neither did it promote class confrontation or attack large capitalist land-holders as a class' (1988: 90). (In 1982–3 the private sector produced 60 per cent of GNP and around 80 per cent of agricultural output – Keesing's 1983: 32303.) Gilbert (1988: 116) points out, however, that anti-bourgeois statements were made by some members of the National Directorate. Certainly these measures provoked reaction. In early July 1981, Eden Pastora, the deputy minister of defence and head of the militias, and Jose Valdivia, the deputy interior minister, both resigned and joined guerrilla movements in Costa Rica. Humberto Ortega, the minister of defence, took on the additional role of head of the militias. Reaction was especially strong within the business sector, from COSEP in particular, and in October four of COSEP's leaders were arrested. At the same time, and perhaps more surprisingly, the general secretary of the Communist Party (PCN), plus 23 of its radical union CAUS (Labour Action and Unity Confederation) members, were also arrested. They had published a document criticizing the economy and accusing the government of 'organised and systematic sabotage' (Keesing's 1982: 31291). Three of the members of COSEP and four of the PCN were given seven months' imprisonment and in December a further member was put under house arrest (the three COSEP members were released after only four months). Also in October, US and Honduran navies began manoeuvres in the Caribbean off the Honduran and Nicaraguan coasts and whilst clashes continued along the Honduran–Nicaraguan border, in November reports were heard of a counter-revolutionary force actually inside Nicaragua (ibid).

The *Washington Post* reported in February 1982 that the CIA had been given a budget of US$19 million to undertake covert action against Nicaragua. To deal with the increased forces making incursions from their bases in Honduras, in March a state of emergency was declared, later extended to May 1984; the press and broadcasting were brought under government control, with two newspapers, *El Nuevo Diario* and *La Prensa* being temporarily closed. Preparations for the elections were postponed. In May 1982, under the July 81 Agrarian Reforms, the house of Robelo, president of the MDN, was possessed. This was especially provocative to government officials who openly opposed the government, for some of their properties were confiscated too. In combination with the postponement of elections and the state of emergency these reforms led to a number of important defections, including that of the Nicaraguan US ambassador. Capital flowed out of the country, estimated for 1982 at US$112,900,000 (Keesing's, 1983: 323023).

Battles between the Sandinista Peoples Army (EPS) and the FDN began in earnest in March 1982 on the Honduran–Nicaraguan border. In April, in Costa Rica, Eden Pastora's FRS (Sandinista Revolutionary Front), Misurasata (Sr Rivera), the MDN (Robelo) and UDN/FARN combined to form the Democratic Revolutionary Alliance (ARDE) and were later joined by the ex-ambassador to the US. ARDE refused to join with the FDN, and in 1985 Robelo was to lead the MDN out of ARDE into the FDN. In spite of important differences between them these various anti-Sandinista guerrilla groups came generally to be termed 'the contras'. Entry to Nicaragua was sought initially through the Miskito territories. The contras included two Miskito Indian groups, Misura in Honduras (led by a former Somoza security agent) and Misurasata, in Costa Rica, which was separate from the FDN and restricted itself to working for Miskito autonomy rather than the overthrow of the Sandinista government (Rossett and Vandermeer 1986: 255–6). In response, these north eastern territories were declared a military emergency zone. The first serious attempt to invade Nicaragua was made in March 1983.[9]

THE PEOPLE'S TRIBUNALS AND ELECTIONS IN WARTIME

On 11 April 1983, 'anti-Somozista people's tribunals' were established in Nicaragua to 'try crimes against humanity' and attempts to 're-establish Somozism in Nicaragua' (Keesing's 1983: 32304). These tribunals were each made up of three people with a lawyer in control. The sessions were to be open and, in line with the Statute of Rights and Guarantees, they were not permitted to impose the death penalty, 30 years being the maximum sentence with any sentence above five years bringing with it the confiscation of property. These courts were set up in response to growing opposition forces in Honduras and Costa Rica, each receiving aid from the USA (ibid: 32305). The FDN received the bulk of the aid but the FRS received some CIA funding too (Gilbert 1988: 165). The first major encounter with opposition guerrilla forces in Honduras occurred in March 1982 and by the beginning of 1983 invasion into Nicaragua had increased dramatically. Several thousand Nicaraguans fled to Honduras. In February–March around 2,000 contras entered the northern areas of Nicaragua but were beaten back. War with Honduras threatened. In May incursions began from Costa Rica in the south, under the leadership of Eden Pastora. From 1984 the number of attacks mounted, by land, sea and air and by 1985 contra forces in Honduras had grown to over 16,000 (Keesing's, 1984: 33271). In August 1985 a bill was passed in Nicaragua to introduce compulsory conscription to the army.

Against this background of war, the promised elections went ahead, not in 1985 but in November 1984, potentially coinciding with the presidential elections in the USA. The results were an impressive victory for the FSLN with 66.9 per cent of votes cast for its presidential candidate, Daniel Ortega, and winning 61 out of the 96 seats in the National Assembly. With the US government the one dissenter, these elections have generally been accepted as fair (see Close 1988: 135–8; Americas Watch Committee 1985: 128).[10] After the elections increasing emphasis was put on pluralist organizations. Revolutionary mobilization and experience in participation were increasingly developed into the social bases for participatory democracy (Gilbert 1988: 76; Coraggio 1986: ch.3; Downs 1985). In the same month, November 1984, however, Ronald Reagan was re-elected president and a further US\$100 million was voted in aid for the contras in June 1986 (Keesing's, 1984: 34548).

Whilst both the Central and South American states worked towards a negotiated peace settlement, 1986 proved the decisive year for Nicaragua. In the face of the escalating war, the state of emergency was reintroduced in October 1985 and 134 people were arrested for aiding the contras. More people were arrested later and interrogated. In the interests of security, censorship was stepped up and in June 1986 *La Prensa* was again closed. The war reached its peak at the end of 1985, when a sustained contra attack at the end of October and beginning of November was repulsed; 30,000 reservists were in the ranks. By March 1986 the contras were in retreat and, in May, Eden Pastora and 450 of his troops surrendered their arms and sought political asylum in Costa Rica (Keesing's 1986: 34542–4).

INTERNATIONAL PRESSURES FOR PEACE

In June 1986 the International Court of Justice at the Hague ruled that the USA had been in breach of international law in interfering in the internal affairs of Nicaragua (Keesing's 1986: 34548). In March 1987, the Costa Rican government expelled contras from its territories and President Arias pressed forward with a Central American peace plan for a negotiated settlement to the Contra–Nicaragua war. By 7 August 1987 an agreement was signed (for which President Arias of Costa Rica was awarded the Nobel Peace Prize in October). In accordance with the peace plan, *La Prensa* was re-opened, the 1981 exile property seizure law was revoked and some prisoners on each side were freed. In November, preparations began for negotiations for a ceasefire with the contra leadership and the release of 985 prisoners was announced, including 200 National Guards. A temporary ceasefire began on Christmas Eve. On 19 January 1988, the Anti-Somocista popular tribunals were disbanded (ibid 1988: 35892).

At the end of February the US Congress rejected Reagan's request for more funds for the contras. Further prisoners were released and exiles began to return. Throughout 1988 the government extended the ceasefire month by month, though some contra attacks continued. In November 1989 the Nicaraguans suspended the truce. The UN responded immediately by sending in a peace-keeping force. At the end of 1988, the official casualty figures since the war began in January 1981 were put at 29,113 deaths and 28,244 injured. In March 1989 the new US president, George Bush, requested only humanitarian aid to the contras. Then in February 1990 the FSLN government again held elections which this time they lost. Violeta Chamorro, widow of the assassinated *La Prensa* editor and a leading member of the first Sandinista government, was elected president. Just as Churchill had been rejected in Britain at the end of the Second World War, it was time for change.[11]

INTERNATIONAL REPORTS

An Amnesty International report published on 12 February 1986 and later criticized for being biased in paying too little attention to contra abuses (Keesing's 1987: 35446) was summarized as follows:

> The report stated that abuses by Sandinista officials consisted mainly of frequent short-term imprisonment of prisoners of conscience; prolonged pre-trial incommunicado detention of political prisoners and restrictions on their right to fair trial; and poor prison conditions. Amnesty also said that it had received reports of torture and arbitrary killings by military personnel in remote areas, but that in many cases those responsible had been tried and punished. (Keesing's 1986: 34545)

In response to a request from the National Commission for the Promotion and Protection of Human Rights, of the 300 releases requested 108 prisoners were freed in June 1986 (ibid 1987: 35446). In April 1987 a movement was formed to protest against prison conditions, claiming that there were 10,000 political prisoners in a prison system that was 'unjust and cruel'. The New York-based Lawyers Committee for Human Rights published a report in November 1987 in which it criticized the popular tribunals (abolished in January 1988) for acting outside the regular court system. At the same time the contras were accused of 'continuing gross human rights violations' including 'political killings, disappearances and other serious mistreatment of civilian non-combatants' (ibid 1988: 35949).

The condition of the Miskito Indians in the territories bordering Honduras provoked particular concern. The Inter-American Commission on Human Rights had in December 1984 reported on 'forced relocation, arbitrary detention, and in a few cases of torture and killings in reprisal for the killing of soldiers by the contras' (Keesing's, 1984: 33274). America's Watch Committee (1985: 127) requested a ful! account of 70 Miskito Indians who were missing in 1982–3 and 21 deaths in 1981–2. A report published a few months earlier by the Spanish Human Rights Association, whilst also expressing concern over the treatment of the Indians, added that 'there was greater respect for human rights in Nicaragua than in many other Central American countries, and that Nicaragua had neither death penalty nor disappeared persons' (Keesing's 1984: 33274).

THE AVOIDANCE OF A REIGN OF TERROR

Even in the face of war Nicaragua had avoided descent into a reign of terror. As in any war there had been cases of abuse, but the government had neither installed organizations of Terror nor introduced laws to institute Terror. According to their Statute on Human Rights and Guarantees the avoidance of Terror had been the Sandinistas' aim. Pressure of circumstances can, however, as study of reigns of terror have clearly shown, push revolutionary governments into actions which run counter to ideological intention. In Nicaragua conditions which helped the government to avoid a revolutionary reign of terror had existed. By the time the Contra–Nicaragua war had erupted, the Nicaraguan government had had almost two years in which to establish not only new political and legal institutions but a newly formed loyal army. Both the police and army had been placed under the control of the National Directorate of the FSLN.

The passage of the FSLN to power through civil war had played the major part in avoiding further insurrection and this was especially the case when the civil war had been fought so bitterly and had drawn in active support from all socio-economic groups and organizations. It is not insignificant that the one area in which the clearest potential for a reign of terror had existed, the Miskito Indian territories bordering Honduras, should have been the area where the native population had given some support to the contras. The possibility of the Indians escaping over the border into Honduras had perhaps acted as a safety valve on terror in a similar way that flight to Canada had during the American Revolution, though in practice escape seemed to have fuelled the war.[12] Sensitive handling of the area by the Sandinistas and the capacity to bring anarchistic terror under control were surely important too. Whilst willingness to respond with care, recognizing ethnic prejudice for what it was and adjusting policies accordingly (Rooper and Smith 1986), clearly reflected the Sandinistas' humanitarian stance, their control over the coercive forces, with their capacity to punish soldiers guilty of murder and abuse, should not be ignored.

The government's policies, political, economic and social, also played their part in maintaining support. In time of war it is normal to curtail some aspects of democracy – suspending elections, withdrawing the freedom to criticize the government and reducing freedom of movement, for foreign nationals especially. In holding elections Nicaragua compares well, though elections have been held in other revolutions. In Russia elections to the Constituent Assembly in January 1918 demonstrated that the Bolsheviks lacked majority support. In the French Revolution, in the elections held during the Terror, only one in five of those eligible to vote had bothered to do so. In Nicaragua the FSLN had gained over 60 per cent of the votes cast in 1984 on a 75.4 per cent turnout (Coraggio 1986: 86). The staging of the elections in 1984 had soothed swelling political opposition to undemocratic procedures and reaffirmed the Sandinistas' support which victory had brought in the civil war. The government had also retained a loyal opposition, choosing not to establish a single-party state (Close 1988: 127–8). Even after the FSLN victory in 1984 members of other parties were included in the cabinet (Coraggio 1986: 98). As Coraggio has argued, the Nicaraguan Revolution broke the mould and produced a revolution which was both socialist and democratic.[13]

The economic programme pursued by the revolution had been restrained. The possibility of redistributing vacant Somoza lands reduced the potential numbers of counter-revolutionaries angered by dispossession whilst providing the government with sufficient leverage to introduce some agrarian reforms which could appease poorer sections of society. The government had sought a mixed economy rather than total state ownership, reducing potential opposition from the business community. In 1986 over 54 per cent of farms and 60 per cent of businesses were privately owned (Close 1988: 98).

The international situation in which the Nicaraguan Revolution unfolded cannot pass without comment. The greatest threat to the new regime came not from the existence of organized opposition in Honduras and Costa Rica *per se*, but from the availability of resources from the USA to aid this opposition. (For a full discussion of CIA funding and the Iran–Contra Affair see Gilbert 1988: ch.7.) Without US assistance, the contra war could not have attained the proportions it did. The failure of counter-revolution from abroad to combine with civil war at home, or even widespread insurrection in the cities, is not therefore surprising.

This, nevertheless, serves as a warning to the drawing of generalizations from cases across time and place. As a small country in a modern world the revolution in Nicaragua developed within international constraints, though these international pressures were not restricted within Skocpol's categories of trade and war; the availability of US aid to the new regime and its withdrawal; the provision of aid from elsewhere, including countries such as Cuba which had itself had a revolution only 20 years before; the level of assistance given by the USA to forces opposed to the Sandinistas; the capacity for the surrounding Central American countries and South American ones, too, to negotiate a peace all played their part in constraining the Nicaraguan government's behaviour. The International Court of Justice ruling that the US had been in breach of international law had an impact, and international organizations concerned with human rights also played a role. Investigations into abuses of human rights by Amnesty International, the National Commission for the Promotion and Protection of Human Rights, the Lawyers' Committee on Human Rights helped keep Nicaragua on the human rights path which it had promised on coming to power in 1979. For a country dependent on foreign aid, bad publicity for human rights abuses would have proved a risk to future help.

Nicaragua had had the opportunity to learn the lessons of history, of Cuban history in particular, though the revolutionaries' capacity to learn and use advice reflected the advantages which Nicaragua in 1979 had over Cuba in 1959. The economy was less specialized in production, less dependent on one trading partner and the government had the Somoza family lands and properties at their disposal. Against the odds of war, policies chosen with care, balancing support with control over coercion, had kept the FSLN in power without recourse to Terror.

NOTES

1. In order to attempt to overcome the political biases in the literature, see, for example, Valenta 1985; as too short a time has elapsed since 1979 for a definitive study such as Thomas' on Cuba to have emerged for Nicaragua, this chapter

relies heavily on Keesing's Contemporary Archives. These archives are especially comprehensive for this case and take care objectively to reproduce the findings of various reports. Whilst following the logic of previous revolutions, the election of 1984 could have been an appropriate place to stop, the continuing and escalating Contra war required that the study be brought as up-to-date as possible. Whilst the war continued, the threat of a reign of terror remained a theoretical possibility and one which could seriously threaten, indeed potentially destroy, the emphasis of this work.

2. For a detailed account of these events see Keesing's 1978: 29020–1 and 29373–6.

3. For statistics in this paragraph see, in order, Keesing's Archives 1979: 29809, 1980: 30025 and 1979: 29810.

4. As evidence of their good intentions the Sandinistas actually directed surrendering National Guardsmen to churches under guarantee of safety (Keesing's 1980: 30025).

5. By comparison, 'violent deaths' for El Salvador during 1981 were given as 16,276 (Salvadorean Human Rights Commission), 13,353 (Judicial Aid Organization, corroborated by the University of Central America) and 6,116 by the US Embassy in San Salvador. Judicial Aid estimated 60 per cent of deaths were at the hands of the security forces and 20 per cent killed by the left (Keesing's 1982: 31616).

6. For the statistics above see, respectively, Keesing's Archives 1979: 29810 and 1980: 30026 and 30317.

7. The costs of war (40 per cent of the 1985 budget), war damage (70 per cent of 1984 export revenues) and disruption to harvests, especially bad in 1984, all combined to undermine the economy (Central American Historical Institute 1986: 266–7).

8. Rooper and Smith (1986) point out that the Sandinistas diagnosed their own racist attitudes in their behaviour towards the Indians (5 per cent of the population) and sought to rectify their prejudice from 1982 and have since sought to accommodate these historical desires for autonomy. Bourgois (1986: 469) argues that without US intervention conflicts in this area would have remained non-violent.

9. For the above section, see Keesing's Archives 1982: 31616, and 1983: 32303–6.

10. US objections to the 1984 election focused around the non-participation of the Democratic Coordinator, a group formed from COSEP, four conservative parties and two Unions. The parties were weak and the decision not to participate seemed to be based on a recognition that success in the elections would be impossible. The coordinator became the political arm of the FDN, encouraged to participate by the Nicaraguan government, and the left-centre and ultra-left parties, each highly critical of the revolution, managed to gain considerable concessions in the campaign and win one-third of the National Assembly seats (Gilbert 1988: 121–3). For a favourable analysis of the democratic importance of the 1984 elections, see Coraggio 1986: ch.4.

11. For this paragraph see the *Economist* 5 September 1987: 53–4, the *Guardian* 2 and 8 November 1989 and February 1990. Should anyone be wondering whether this perhaps removes the events in Nicaragua from classification as a revolution the answer is definitely not, for two reasons: as a member of the first Sandinista government, the election of Violeta Chamorro to the presidency in no sense represents a return of the Somoza order – this is confirmed by the wide coalition which she represents; secondly, what better demonstration of the total change from the old Somoza political system could there be than the election of the opposition (and what better practical proof that Nicaragua is a democracy)? Clapham (1985: 67) has found only five countries in the whole of the Third World where an opposition has been elected to power.

12. 10,000 refugees returned from Honduras in March 1986–7 (Keesing's 1987: 35447–8). There were 19,000 Nicaraguan refugees in Costa Rica in mid 1985 (Keesing's, 1985: 34036).

13. Gilbert (1988), through an analysis of FSLN documents and statements, has shown that the party views itself as a Marxist-Leninist vanguard party. Through an examination of the FSLN 'in action', however, he demonstrates that the FSLN is socialist, not Communist (like the 'Moscow-line' Nicaraguan Socialist Party (PSN), from which the early 1960s revolutionaries broke). Gilbert draws attention to the conflict between their supposed theoretical position and their practice: 'Socialists, they promote petty capitalism in the countryside and preside over a mixed economy in which about half of production remains in private hands. Marxist materialists, they accept believers into their ranks, even into the leadership of the party and preside over a national religious revival. Anti-Yankee nationalists, they seek accommodation with Washington and negotiate with people whom they previously described as Washington's mercenaries' (Gilbert 1988: 178). In the tradition of Western European socialist parties, what the FSLN really wants is to improve the quality of life for ordinary people: 'so many children without shoes, children who have to quit school to work on farms' (Daniel Ortega commenting in the midst of the contra war, quoted in ibid: 181). As the 1990 election showed, like Western European socialist parties, the FSLN was willing to be voted out of office.

9. China 1949: A Counter-Case?

If Nicaragua managed to avoid a reign of terror and Cuba escaped with a relatively mild one because in these revolutions guerrilla movements came to power through victory in civil war then Mao Zedong's victory in China in 1949 appears to present a counter-example. There a communist guerrilla army had defeated the Guomindang in a civil war before taking power in 1949, yet a revolutionary reign of terror had then developed from 1950. Furthermore, the civil war in China had been both especially drawn out and hard fought. For lack of available detailed evidence this is not a case which permits deep analysis, but consideration of the Chinese case nevertheless proves both instructive and constructive.

THE GUERRILLA MOVEMENT, CIVIL WAR AND FOREIGN WAR

The guerrilla movement in China had grown out of the Communist Party, founded in 1921, a decade after the 1911 revolution which had overthrown the Manchu dynasty. The 1911 revolution had failed to establish a new central authority. Following the Soviet doctrine of the day, the Chinese Communist Party (CCP) had gone into alliance with the bourgeois Nationalist Party, the Guomindang, and sought revolution through proletarian uprisings in the towns. The alliance proved fatal and in 1927, having together taken Shanghai, the Guomindang turned on the CCP and killed an estimated 5,000 Communists (Wolf 1973: 145). In retreat, the Communists were obliged to withdraw into the countryside and to turn from a proletarian-city movement into a peasant-rural movement. In doing so they developed a theme first suggested by Mao after an investigation in 1926 into the peasant movement in Hunan (Schram 1971: 250). At the same time, Mao redefined the revolutionary peasant strata as semi-proletariat (those who owned part and rented part of their land) and proletariat (the poor peasants who owned no land and laboured on the land) (ibid: 211). In this scheme the 'big landowners' were the 'big bourgeoisie', with gradations of revolutionary opposition according to land-holdings, through 'middle bourgeoisie' and 'petty bourgeoisie'. In parallel, within the cities these categories were applied to owners of large capital, (banks, industries, enterprises) down to shopkeepers and the like as petty bourgeoisie; the revolutionary classes were the semi-proletariat (service industries) and the proletariat (the factory workers and coolies). Mao also emphasized the need to create the Red Army. His vision was of a regular force and not of small bands of guerrillas, the *foco*-type movement which provided the motor for the Cuban Revolution or which first developed in Nicaragua in the early 1960s. For Mao, 'the dispersion of forces has almost always led to defeat' (Mao 1928, quoted in Fairbairn 1974: 92). The Red Army was to use the mountains for protection but was to have proper machine-gun, rifle and trench-mortar companies (Fairbairn 1974: 92). It was to be a democratic army where treatment of men and officers was equal, and it was this democracy, with its stark contrast with the Guomindang army, which was to play the crucial role in winning over the captured soldiers to the new force (ibid). Land reforms were to play the central role in winning over the peasants.

By 1931 the Red Army had grown to over 300,000 soldiers and the Communists had control over an area in south central China of around 50 million people. This area became known as the Jiangxi Soviet. Before the end of 1930, however, Tchiang Kai-chek the leader of the Guomindang, began an offensive against the Communist-controlled area. Civil war between the Communist forces and the Guomindang broke out in full force and the onslaught continued in a series of campaigns until 1933. In 1934, the Communists, again in retreat, embarked on the Long March which took them 6,000 miles north, first to Shaanxi, later Shanxi and Hebei, where in more protected and more sympathetic circumstances they set up new bases and embarked on land reforms (Wolf 1973: 147–9). In 1935, Mao Zedong became head of the Communist Party.

In 1931, a new threat to both the Guomindang and the Communists had developed in the form of Japanese aggression in Manchuria. By 1936 the Communists again joined forces with the Guomindang to form a united defence against the Japanese. Tchiang Kai-chek was accepted as the head of the government, the Communists dropping their claim to separate government, and the Red Army became the

Eighth Route Army under Tchiang's command (Fairbairn 1974: 96–7). The Japanese invaded in 1937. There is agreement that the invasion and its development played a decisive role in establishing the Communists, not the Guomindang, as the rightful heirs to government. It happened in three ways: The Japanese pattern of advance put the Communist army in the direct path of defence which cast it in the role of the true defenders of China whilst the Guomindang spent time fighting the Chinese population itself; the appalling behaviour of the Japanese troops rallied the people to opposition; and the Japanese, concentrating on taking the cities, failed to pursue the guerrilla movements which again began to form in the Communist areas (Wolf 1973: 153; McAleavy 1972: 297–308). The international situation, the outbreak of war in Europe in 1939 followed by the bombing of Pearl Harbor in 1941, brought the Americans in to defeat Japan. The Americans too, General Stilwell most especially, were shocked by the Guomindang's attack in the Communist-held liberated areas against Chinese forces which were considered much needed in the fight against the Japanese (McAleavy 1972: 310–13).

The end of the war in the Pacific and consequent Japanese withdrawal from China in 1945 left the Communists in control of the largest proportion of China. In March 1945, of the 914 counties 'theoretically under Japanese occupation', 678 were under Communist control and the 19 Communist-held 'liberated areas' included over 100 million people (McAleavy 1972: 317). The Red Army continued to grow. The Eighth Route army had 338,000 troops in Central China. In addition the new Fourth Army, now Communist, which had defected from the Guomindang in 1941, had 150,000 soldiers and some 27,000 more were in the south (ibid: 318). The Guomindang forces, though, were four times greater than the Communist forces (ibid: 323). An attempt by the Americans to achieve a truce in the form of a coalition government broke down and by the end of 1946 civil war was again raging. Meantime the Russians had taken Manchuria. On the withdrawal of American troops, the nationalist forces (Guomindang) took victory after victory. The tide began to turn, however, in mid-1947 when the Communist guerrillas started to restore liberated areas recently defeated by the Guomindang. The war had left the Communists better equipped. By mid-1948 the Communist Liberation Army, expanded both by new recruits and deserters from the Nationalist forces had grown to 2,800,000; the Nationalists numbered 3,650,000 (ibid: 324). In January 1948 cracks were appearing at the top of the Guomindang, too; the Democratic League, formed in opposition to Tchiang Kai-chek, now sided with the Communists. From November 1948, through a series of victories in great battles, the Communist takeover began, eventually bringing the party to power in 1949 over China as one nation. The Nationalist forces were finally driven from the mainland in March 1950.

THE BASIS FOR VICTORY

Mao had learned from the defence of the Jiangxi Soviet in the earlier civil war. Ironically, this was to lead him towards a greater emphasis on guerrilla forces than on a regular army. The emphasis was put on the peasants' active contribution to the revolution and the 'mass line' became an important development in Mao's thought: 'All correct leadership is necessarily from the masses, to the masses' (Mao 1943, quoted in Schram 1971: 70). The masses were – as an analogy much used by the Communists at the time had it – the water for the Red Army's fish. Without them the army could neither survive nor move around. Treatment of peasants by the army, as in Cuba and Nicaragua, became an important tactical element. Soldiers were obliged to treat the peasantry with every consideration, being courteous and polite, always paying for things and replacing accidental damages (Fairbairn 1974: 99–100). The contrast with the behaviour of first Japanese and later Nationalist soldiers was dramatic.

Victory had also been cultured in the practice of agrarian and political reforms within the liberated areas. In 1940, Mao had published *On New Democracy*, which was intended as a first stage of revolution; the second was socialism (Smart 1974: ch.6). In it he put forward his programme for the new revolutionary society. He envisaged the Communist Party in power over a state-run economy with a widescale redistribution of land but where rich peasants would, initially at least, retain a place, full collectivization being part of the long-term but not the short-term goal. These reforms had been put into practice in the Communist areas after the Long March where they had been tested and perfected. Before the Long March, collectivization had been Communist policy, but in pursuit of wider class support Mao had adopted the 'rich peasant line'. This line, too, had been improved and extended through practice. In recognition of the problems it had brought (rich peasants keeping the best land) progressive taxation had been introduced and an emphasis put on village cooperatives, political control of villages as well as land redistribution (Wolf 1973: 147–50). These village organizations were to prove crucial for Communist support in the post-World War II civil war. Communist Party support had also been canvassed directly; membership had reached nearly 5 million by 1949 (Meisner 1977: 71). In contrast to Guevara's advice on avoiding propaganda in guerrilla war, the party had launched a 'rectification of conduct' campaign in 1942. Party members were re-educated through party texts to replace individual with party interests (McAleavy 1972: 314; Brugger 1981: 29–38).

COMMUNISTS IN POWER: THE TERROR 1950–3

After the Communist victory in 1949 China was divided into six military areas (in a way similar to the post-revolutionary arrangement in Cuba 1959). Military administration dominated civilian administration until 1954. In September the Chinese People's Political Consultative Conference, under Mao's chairmanship, enacted the Organic Law, under which the civilian administration was established for the new People's Republic. Mao was Chairman of the People's Republic as well as being Chairman of the CCP and Chou En-lai became Premier of the new Government Administrative Council. This new government had 24 ministries, 11 of which were headed by non-Communist Party members and three of the six vice-chairmen of the republic were also not Communists (see Meisner 1977: 70–2.) This was the period of 'New Democracy'.

'High on the list of priorities' of the new Communist government was the punishment of Tchiang and other war criminals (McAleavy 1972: 32). In view of what had happened in the dying months of the Nationalist government this desire for retribution is understandable. From August 1948, the Nationalists had introduced a system of terror. It had begun with the summary execution of those people accused of infringing the new law, brought in to curb inflation, which demanded that all gold, silver and US dollars be exchanged for a new currency. After these executions there followed the executions of those accused of conspiracy or under suspicion of being Communists. These victims were 'dragged before drum-head courts and then out to some public place to be shot through the back of the head' (ibid: 325). McAleavy adds, 'Scenes of this kind were of daily occurrence in Shanghai, the busiest street-corners were invariably chosen for the execution of the victims, who were nearly all young men'. On occupying territories vacated by the Eighth Route (Communist) Army in 1945 the Guomindang had buried peasants alive in mass graves (Belden 1973: 299–311). Disgust further eroded US support, and in this Tchiang Kai-chek produced a reaction similar to those later evoked by Batista and Somoza.

The Communists' reign of terror when it came, however, went beyond a system of war trials and was directed rather to the wider issue of counter-revolutionaries. With the Guomindang left in control of the islands of Formosa, Quemoy and Matsu, counter revolution remained a serious threat (Chesneaux 1979: 34). With the outbreak of the Korean War in late June 1950, the United States had made Taiwan a military protectorate. The threat of counter-revolution in combination with foreign intervention raised the serious possibility of a renewed civil war backed by a powerful foreign state (Meisner 1977: 80). Guomindang air raids into China continued well into 1950, the first enemy plane being shot down in March 1950 (Brugger 1981: 63). In the large cities, secret drug dealing and gambling organizations were operated through connections with the old Guomindang secret police.

Under the auspices of the Ministry of Security (Gonganqu) which was headed by General Luo Rui-qing, a secret police force was established to hunt out these gangsters and political opponents. Often they were tried publicly (Chesneaux 1979 40–1). From Taiwan, the Guomindang continued to direct counter-revolutionary activities, through secret agents and radio transmitters. These spies and saboteurs worked alongside and within the secret societies. In 1950 the secret police force began to destroy these societies too. The police network was wide. In the cities each local committee (each one governing around 100 households) and in the countryside each local administration unit (*xiang*) had a public security section (Meisner 1977: 77).

On 6 June 1950, along with his programme for land, taxation and education reforms, Mao had referred to the need to defend against counter-revolution and had called for 'bandits, spies, despots, and other counter-revolutionary elements' to be suppressed through a combination of 'severity towards the principal offenders with leniency towards the rest' (quoted Keesing's 1950: 10855). In February 1951 an official decree was made concerning 'Regulations regarding the Punishment of Counter-revolutionaries' (Meisner 1977: 80). It heralded greater secret-police repression of ever more widely defined counter-revolutionary activities; as a result mass meetings were held where public denouncements of accused counter-revolutionaries were made, many resulting in the death penalty (ibid: 81). These 'offences against the state' included 'working for imperialism', incitement of armed forces to rebellion, being actively engaged in rebellion, espionage, sabotage or aiding enemy aircraft and warships, supplying military equipment, being members of secret societies, being former National-ists who 'failed to atone for their crimes' or were actively engaged in counter-revolution, and resisting or encouraging others to resist grain requisitioning, the collection of taxes and other 'administrative orders' (Keesing's 1950–2: 11419).

In 1951–2, with public cooperation, the police set up mass move-ments to eliminate counter-revolutionaries. These movements (*Yundong*) were mobilizations towards the re-enforcement of new values through discussion, posters and marches. These *Yundong* received both training and advice from Soviet technicians and an organized system of repres-sion developed with special prisons and camps. 'This apparatus was solid and durable, even if it did not attain the size and harshness of the Soviet Gulag' (Chesneaux 1979:41).

Estimates on the number of executions have ranged as high as 15 million, though this figure, a Nationalist estimate, is considered by McAleavy to have been greatly exaggerated; he estimates the figure as 'unlikely to have been much lower than one million' (McAleavy 1972: 340). Brugger (1981: 73) reports that in the Guandong province alone 28,332 people (one in every thousand of the population) were ex-ecuted in early 1951. Meisner remarks pointedly that China has never published comprehensive figures and expresses doubt that full records even exist. Piecing together the 'fragmentary official reports' he esti-mates ('as accurate a guess as one can make') a figure of 2 million (this includes an estimate for 'the considerable number of executions that took place outside of formal judicial procedures'). Many more, he adds, were imprisoned or were sent to forced labour camps (Meisner 1977: 81). It is impossible to know what proportion of deaths were the result of the anarchical terror, the breaking out of long-repressed hatred amongst the people, rather than the officially sanctioned Terror. The New China News Agency reports of the day referred to executions as simply 'large groups', though specific numbers were given for particular cases, each less than 100 (Keesing's 1951: 11419). Chesneaux is cau-tious, referring to 'some sympathetic observers' who estimate that there were 800,000 victims, a figure which includes not only executions but also arrests, imprisonments and re-education. With a population of 600 million in 1950, an estimate of 1 million deaths would certainly put the horrors of this period of China's history on a scale nearly equal to that of both the Russian and French reigns of terror. In any event the proportion seems unlikely to have been as low as for Cuba.

THE CAUSES OF THE REIGN OF TERROR: COUNTER-REVOLUTIONARIES, WAR AND LAND REFORM

Both Chesneaux (1979: 40) and Meisner (1977: 78–80) argue that the repression was essentially defensive; the threat from the Guomindang was real, civil war a genuine possibility. In addition, in 1950 the Korean war had erupted, unexpectedly, and by the autumn of that year China had sent volunteer army divisions to fight in Korea. The USA had immediately made moves to protect Tchiang's government in Taiwan (old Formosa) and by May 1951 had stopped all trade between the US and mainland China.

China, unlike Nicaragua (and Cuba before the Bay of Pigs) had no breathing space for reconstruction; economic devastation had been wrought not only by civil war but also by foreign war against the Japanese. The Korean war further exacted a heavy toll of both men and resources that might otherwise have been available for rebuilding the economy and in addition debts were incurred to the Soviet Union (Chesneaux 1979: 33).

The reconstruction of China was certainly made all the more difficult by the outbreak of the Korean war and it is extremely unlikely that China actively sought to be drawn into a full-scale war at such a time (Brugger 1981: 64). Even so, the nature of the reconstruction itself seems independently to have played a part in the Terror. The programme for reform was developed in accordance with the ideas of New Democracy: private enterprises were permitted though they were to be under the control of the state to the extent that a state plan for economic reconstruction and social reforms (health, education, marriage laws, better standards of living and of decency) could be co-ordinated. Land reforms were central to this. The Agrarian Reform Law was introduced in June 1950. It was designed to apply to the newly liberated areas recently brought under Communist control and aimed to end 'feudal exploitation by the landlord class' (Keesing's 1950: 10855).

The reforms included the confiscation of landlord properties and the requisitioning of supplies; compensation was to be given. The confiscated land was redistributed to the poor peasants. The village community politics established in the liberated areas before 1949 were used to enforce the law. People's Tribunals were set up for the purpose. Once the accused had been described as a 'class enemy' these tribunals allowed no right of appeal (McAleavy 1972: 339).

Things began to get out of hand. 'A great orgy of hatred' according to McAleavy, was unleashed when poor peasants saw the splendour and abundance of the landlords' wealth. In some villages public confession was enough but in others landlords were shot and even lynched. In 1951–2 the People's Tribunals moved to the cities, and corrupt government officials and capitalists, involved in tax evasion for example, were brought to trial. Soon employees were denouncing their employers just as peasants had denounced landlords. The accused were made to confess and pay heavy fines; many suicides resulted.

These fines and properties were much needed for the war effort and it is difficult to separate out the natural consequences of the land reforms from the demands of war. Mass mobilization through the village political structure, the foundation of the New Democracy and of reconstruction cannot though be ignored. The mass mobilization campaigns began in 1950 with the land reforms and an appeal for funds for the Korean war, and continued through into 1951 with 'Increasing Production and Being More Economical' (Chesneaux 1979: 36). The new Land Reform Law came into effect at the end of June 1950.[1] With China fully engaged in the Korean war, by November agrarian policy became tougher, especially in the central south area (Wuhan) where land reforms met resistance (Brugger 1981: 72).

From June 1950 onwards, 'thought reform' for the educated was introduced. In the summer of 1951 this ideological reform movement began in earnest within the universities, first amongst the professors, then other intellectuals and then across the education system as a whole (Goldman 1967: ch. 5). In May 1951 mobilization of trade unions began and the 'three antis' movement (against graft, waste and bureaucracy) was launched in August. This encouraged industrial workers to detect the misuse of property, theft, waste of time, over-bureaucratization, illicit practices and, later, forms of nepotism (Brugger 1981: 80–3). In January 1952 the 'five antis movement' began in the private sector. 'Speak bitterness' and confrontation meetings were organized, and sometimes the mobilization campaign got out of hand (ibid: 83–5). Whilst the landlords brought to trial always lost their land and sometimes their life, the urban businessmen brought before the People's Tribunals were mostly fined (ibid: 84).

THE END OF THE TERROR

The Terror ended at the beginning of 1953, when the People's Tribunals were disbanded. There are competing explanations as to why. Threat from the Korean war was diminishing, though was not past until the middle of 1953, after the Terror had been brought to an end. Initial Chinese successes in the Korean war and the stalemate achieved from mid-1951 onwards sapped the threat of US-backed invasion from Taiwan (Meisner 1977: 82). The Korean war in combination with the mobilization campaigns had strengthened central control. The people's militia had expanded from 5 million to 12.8 million between 1950–1 which had in turn produced recruits for the People's Liberation Army in Korea (Brugger 1981: 75). As Meisner (1977: 92) remarks: 'Three years after the establishment of the People's Republic the goal of a strong state had been realized – and it was a state (like all states) which rested on a powerful army and an extensive police apparatus as well as on a broad base of popular support'.

This support had been gained through real achievements. The mobilization campaign had pushed changes on at so rapid a pace that industrial production had nearly trebled between 1949 and 1952 (Chesneaux 1979: 47). In agriculture cereal production had risen from 113 million tons in 1949 to 164 million in 1952, an especially impressive figure given that 150 million tons had been the best pre-war figure (ibid: 44–5). Politically, too, the local party organization had been strengthened within the villages and state control over the economy had been expanded significantly (Brugger 1981: 84–5). Only after the revolutionary Terror had come to an end and Stalin had died (March 1953), however, did China begin clearly to develop its political and economic system according to the Soviet model. The Five Year Plan of 'transition to socialism', essentially favouring heavy industry, was adopted in 1953 and a new constitution was introduced in 1954 (Chesneaux 1979: 56–68) under which the Government Administrative Council gained the new name of State Council and ruled as a central organization over a county (*xien*) and village (*xiang*) local government network. The regional military control established in 1949 was combined within the civilian administration (Meisner 1977: 71). This had been made possible through the growth of the Communist Party between 1949–52 both within the civilian administration and the army: 'Between 1949 and 1952 the organizational web of the CCP was extended throughout the fabric of Chinese society and this was to be the basis for the radical re-weaving of that fabric' (ibid: 72).

COMPARATIVE OBSERVATIONS

The extent to which the terror had been anarchic, in the sense of getting out of hand as opposed to being centrally controlled, is impossible to assess in the absence of a breakdown of accurate figures. The latest assessment, (Gray 1990: 291–2) has emphasized that though the agrarian reforms were intended to be introduced without violence they were bound to get out of hand: 'There was an inevitable ambiguity between the desire to conduct land reform justly and peacefully and the desire to terrify the rural upper classes in order to neutralize them politically'. There is no doubt that the potential for anarchic terror had been greater in China than in either Nicaragua or Cuba. The injustices in Chinese society were more deeply rooted, more complex and more widely felt. In Cuba and Nicaragua, repression was most keenly felt at the direct hands of Batista's and Somoza's military forces, forces which mostly came from outside local communities. Social and economic problems could not readily be blamed on local people, either. Foreign ownership was important, especially in Cuba, and in Nicaragua the Somoza family combined political with economic power in the form of large land-holdings. Social and economic injustices were perceived to be related more directly to government, a focus sharpened by Batista's coup in 1952 and Somoza's callousness over the 1972 earthquake. In China, social and economic ills were identified with oppressive landlords. Once the revolution had taken place in the newly liberated areas (those occupied by Nationalist forces in 1946), the landlords were sitting targets.

It seems impossible to deny that the mobilization movements, which themselves arose from the ideology of the revolution, played a significant part in explaining the Terror. The Chinese Revolution aimed at fundamental transformation. As the comparisons between revolutions have surely shown so far, the more far-reaching the aims of the revolution the bigger the pool of potential counter-revolutionaries. It is, of course, impossible to know for certain what effects the outbreak of actual rather than threatened civil war would have had on the Terror. Compared with both Russia and France, a reasonable expectation would be for a Terror to have occurred on a far greater scale than actually occurred in China between 1950–3. The Chinese revolution combined the aims of the Russian Revolution, fundamental socio-economic reconstruction, with those of the French Revolution, metaphysical transformation (see Hinton 1968 which captures the completeness of this change in the documentary study of a Chinese village in Communist-controlled North China in 1948.[2]) The internal evidence showed that there had been clear advantages in having had a civil war before coming to power. It had given the Communists the opportunity to introduce land reforms, to try them out, change their ideas and develop schemes for political organization and mobilization. These successes in agricultural production and organization had brought them reward in peasant support, as had a comparison both with the Guomindang's behaviour in the civil and foreign wars and the behaviour of Japanese soldiers. The mass mobilization campaigns were later able to tap this support.

Chesneaux (1973: 148) has drawn attention to the problems created by the speed with which the Guomindang was routed in 1948–9 and draws an important comparison between the old liberated areas of rural north China and the newly liberated areas of the rural south together with other liberated cities and towns. In the northern areas occupied by the Communists after the Long March he comments on the solid basis of mass support built up over 10–15 years of 'bitter struggle' conducted by the poor peasants against Japan, the Guomindang and the landlords. This was not so in the newly liberated areas, where Communist power had begun in 1949, 'as the fruit of a sudden victory that was almost premature ... and not as a result of a prolonged political and military struggle at village level' (ibid). As we have seen, it was in the southern areas that the agrarian reforms met with most resistance and where they were most likely to get out of hand. Ironically, in view of the problem China has presented in the overall virulence of its revolutionary reign of terror, the differences between the old and newly liberated areas confirm the general hypothesis presented here that civil wars before revolutions lessen reigns of terror.

Comparison with both Nicaragua and Cuba suggests that a delay in the outbreak of the Korean war might have opened the way for a more moderate terror. Unlike Nicaragua, where legislation (the statutes) had played an important part in avoiding terror, it is clear that in the Chinese case there had been no expressed intention actively to avoid a reign of terror,[3] nor had there been the same kinds of international pressures. Ironically, international considerations seem to lead to the opposite of Skocpol's conclusions. By virtue of China's size the country was able to shut itself off from the rest of the world and make its revolution without interference from outside, much as Russia had done once the civil war had been brought to an end. This is the reason why figures needed for an examination of the reign of terror are unavailable.

Skocpol (1979: 266) argues that there were 'two sets of world-historical and international contextual factors: (1) political influence upon China from previously revolutionized Soviet Russia; and (2) enhanced possibilities in the twentieth century for state-propelled national industrialization'. She admits that this was essentially an agricultural rather than an industrial-based revolution, and that China and Russia had fallen out by 1957 and parted company by 1958. She argues further that the outcome of the Chinese Revolution differed from that of the Russian Revolution in being far more egalitarian and successful in its agricultural policies (ibid: 259–81). The importance of Soviet influence on China in the early 50s (1953–7), is undeniable but after Stalin's death the nature of Chinese revolutionary ideology seems both to have been a more direct influence and of greater importance. China chose to 'lean to one side' (McAleavy 1972: 331) because the revolution had been made by a Communist Party and a Communist army where Marxism-Leninism, adapted by Mao to an agrarian society, had been an essential stimulant to Mao's thought and action. The mass mobilization character of Maoism was central not only to the development of the peasant egalitarianism which Skocpol argues characterizes modern China but also, as we have seen, to the development of a reign of terror between 1950–3.[4]

CONCLUSION

In the absence of the necessary figures, China remains a potential counter-example to the general thesis proposed here – that the timing and intensity of civil wars is of greatest significance for the occurrence and virulence of reigns of terror. Discussion such as has been possible has, though, made a case for the terror having been milder than it would otherwise have been if civil war had broken out after rather than before 1949. This argument has been drawn from comparisons not only with other revolutions but also between the pre- and post-revolutionary experiences of the old and newly liberated areas. Consideration of the Chinese case has reaffirmed the need to consider both the policies chosen by revolutionary governments and the underlying ideology. Reigns of terror cannot be explained only in terms of necessity in the face of unavoidable conditions directly encountered. Their severity has the greatest chance of being contained if civil wars do not break out once a revolutionary government has taken power and where guerrilla movements have been victors in civil war before the transfer of power. Such revolutionary governments come to power with both high levels of support and the potential for gaining and maintaining central control over the forces of coercion. The more total the transformation envisaged, the more enemies the revolution will make, however, and the more likely that reigns of terror will develop. Even then, the support won through victory in civil war before coming to power will dilute a Terror.

NOTES

1. Oddly, Skocpol (1979: 262) quotes Schurmann (1968: 431–2) on the effects of land reform, and the slide into terror for lack of party control at village level. Yet, she draws no special attention to the years 1950–3 and emphasizes only the growth of the bureaucracy and party membership of the new revolutionary state making no mention of the growth of coercive forces (263–4).

2. Hinton defines the word 'Fanshen': 'Literally, it means "to turn the body" or to "turn over". To China's millions of landless and land-poor peasants it meant to stand up, to throw off the landlord yoke, to gain land, stock, implements, and houses. But it meant much more than this. It meant to throw off superstition and study science, to abolish "word blindness" and learn to read, to cease considering women as chattels and establish equality between the sexes, to do away with appointed village magistrates and replace them with elected councils. It meant to enter a new world.'

3. In March 1951 Mao had ordered that the mass movement 'be carried out precisely, cautiously and in a planned and methodical way controlled from above' (Mao, quoted by Brugger 1981: 73–4).

4. It should perhaps also be added that concentration on the ideology behind these mass mobilization campaigns within the Terror and the perspective on coercion which it provides also adds to our understanding of the nature of the later Cultural Revolution and events in Tianamen Square in 1989 too.

PART IV
Classic Revolutions in Modern Times

Introduction

The three revolutions, China, Cuba and Nicaragua, borne on guerrilla movements through civil war have broadly supported the claim that it is essentially full-scale civil war occurring after gaining power which drives revolutions into full-blown reigns of terror. The cases have confirmed that the relationship is not simple, policies chosen from the options available to the revolutionary government must also be taken into account. The more fundamental the transformation envisaged and the more hampered the task by economic conditions, the greater the chance that the new government would resort to terror. Nicaragua, like America before, has shown that a revolution can avoid a reign of terror. In a sense, though, the example of the three guerrilla revolutions has suggested that this work began from a position of some naivety. Though policies adopted by guerrillas in rebellion compared well with those adopted by the states' armed forces, only in Nicaragua had a determined effort to avoid terror followed through to the establishment of the revolutionary regime. Whilst a case could be made for Cuba having avoided excess, a similar case could not be made for China.

The initial view of the aims and methods of guerrilla movements grew from a focus on support. The three cases also directed attention to an additional advantage of the civil war path to revolution. On gaining power all three revolutionary regimes brought with them the means to establish and maintain control over the coercive forces of the revolutionary state. Guerrilla forces could be used to form the basis of a new army, a new police force, if needed even a (new) secret police force, and experience gained in military courts could also be drawn on in replacing the old judiciary. This path to revolution eased the establishment of central control over the coercive forces of the revolutionary state. In France and Russia the problem of gaining control over the coercive forces, new as well as old, had played an important part in pushing those Terrors to excess, threatening the very survival, and in the case of France, the establishment of the revolutionary regimes.

Modern revolutions seem to have differed from old ones – guerrilla movements have replaced spontaneous revolutions. The cases also seem to have supported an impression that revolutionary reigns of terror are dying out; Cuba's terror was mild, Nicaragua's non-existent. These impressions are wrong. Two revolutions have occurred in recent times which fit the classic mould. It is time then to turn to these in order to consider further the general lessons which can be drawn for reigns of terror.

In 1974 a revolution broke out in Ethiopia and by the end of 1978 a revolution was in progress in Iran. Both revolutions occurred on the rise of spontaneous mass movements. In neither instance was the revolutionary government brought to power through victory in civil war and each revolution passed through the stage of a reign of terror. These Terrors were both surrounded by the classic conditions of civil war, foreign war and domestic insurrection stirred by economic problems. The problem of nationalities and of religious differences was also present. In each case too, the policy decisions of the revolutionary governments played their part in heightening the Terrors. In spite of special features, the two cases demonstrate clearly the possibilities for and the advantages to be gained from making comparisons across continents and centuries.

10. The Ethiopian Revolution: The Military Institute Terror

The Ethiopian Revolution began in February 1974 with an army revolt. Privates and NCOs arrested their top officers and mass demonstrations broke out in Addis Ababa. The grievances were essentially economic, inflation having been especially high in 1973. These economic grievances combined with direct resentment of the regime for there were close links between the royal family and the military élite. Top officers were all from the nobility and there were large discrepancies between the officers' and NCOs' pay. The wealth of government ministers (every one of them aristocratic) was even more glaring. Compensation for inflation inflamed the resentment when NCOs were given an extra US$7, taxed, whilst the commissioned officers were given US$200–300, tax-free, and government ministers a staggering US$700 (Erlich 1986: 232–3).

In the capital, Addis Ababa, these perceived and actual injustices of an uncaring and corrupt regime were driven home by the revelation that a disaster in Wollo Province had been covered up. As a consequence of a famine in 1973, 100,000 people had starved to death (Erlich 1986: 232). Like the Somoza regime after the Nicaraguan earthquake in 1972, the government had stood by and done nothing to help the victims. Clapham (1988: 37) argues that there was an even greater significance to the disaster: the political infrastructure had collapsed. Whilst in Nicaragua, Somoza's inaction had demonstrated callous indifference and selfish corruption, in Ethiopia the inaction was symptomatic of the political system's general decay. Just as for the French Revolution and the February Revolution in Russia, this was a true *ancien régime*, a feudal system which had collapsed from within.

In response to the army mutinies, the prime minister was replaced; it was not enough. Further mass demonstrations and strikes erupted, in the towns and the capital in particular. Between March–June 1974 strikes broke out amongst workers, government workers especially, demanding improvements in pay and conditions of work, the setting up of trades unions and changes in government and administrative personnel (Ottaway 1976: 477). Peasants seized land and destroyed property and young people, students and schoolchildren began to demonstrate in favour of land reforms and against the government. In Eritrea, the Eritrean Liberation Front (ELF) stepped up its attack and the police, army and air force also began to revolt, demanding that those responsible for the 'genocide of famine' in Wollo be put on trial; demands were made for constitutional change and fundamental land reform. These revolts began on 4–5 March among the police in Asmara and airmen at Debre Zeit air base; by April the revolts had spread. In Addis Ababa police and NCO-led army units began arresting former ministers, military officers and government officials (Keesing's 1974: 26637–8).

Since February, soldiers' committees had begun to form; now similar committees were developed within the police and military, leading to the formation of the delegate-based Co-ordinating Committee of the Ethiopian Armed Forces, Police and Territorial Army. It was to be known as the Derg. The exact membership was kept secret but the number was estimated at around 108, possibly up to 140. On 26 June, the Derg took power. At first, working in co-ordination with the official regime, it continued to arrest leading figures and by 13 July, 82 were under arrest (Keesing's 1974: 26639). On 22 July the government, under Endalkachew who had been installed in February, resigned. The Derg continued its arrests and in so doing undermined Emperor Haile Selassie's position. Those close to him were arrested, 160 aristocrats in all, then his properties were nationalized and finally the court itself was abolished (ibid: 26733–5). The emperor had been deposed in all but name and on 12 September he was removed from power completely and a new revolutionary government installed, the Provisional Military Administrative Council – (PMAC). A *coup d'état* of a special drawn-out type had taken place (O'Kane 1987: 32–3). A revolution was to follow in its wake, borne high on an urban mass movement (Clapham 1988: 40). Through the revolutionary terror, the military was to arrive triumphant over the new order.[1]

The revolutionary government installed on 12 September 1974, the PMAC, was effectively the Derg under a new name though its chairman General Aman was not a Derg member. Aman, too sympathetic both to the old order and the Eritrean cause, was murdered on 22 November. He was replaced by Brigadier General Teferi Banti, also not a member of the Derg, though both his vice-chairmen were members, first vice-chairman Major Mengistu Haile-Miriam, second vice-chairman Major Atnafu Abate (Clapham 1988: 42–5). It was Mengistu who was eventually to establish the revolution.

The revolutions so far considered have shown that it is not unusual for an army or army personnel to play an important part in establishing a revolutionary government. The Ethiopian group differed, however, in significant respects. These soldiers were not high-ranking soldiers who had gained power through battle in civil war, as had Washington and Cromwell. The Derg ranged only from lieutenant-colonel down to private, the majority being non-commissioned officers (Erlich 1986: 24).[2] They were soldiers from the existing state forces, and not a revolutionary army which had formed from a guerilla movement as in China, Cuba or Nicaragua. They, like the Bolsheviks in October 1917, had come to power through a *coup d'état* but in Russia the soviets had formed around workers and peasants as well as soldiers and sailors. Furthermore, Trotsky's Military Revolutionary Committee had formed within the Petrograd Soviet as the military organization of the Bolshevik Party and had not developed out of the existing armed forces of the state. In China, too, the Red Army had been the military organization of the Communist Party. The Derg had no party organization, nor was it to establish one until after the Terror had subsided. Indeed, the Terror at its height raged against Marxist parties (the Ethiopian People's Revolutionary Party in particular) to achieve military dominance over the state.

SET FOR TERROR: MILITARY REGIME TO REVOLUTIONARY REIGN OF TERROR

Violence was an inherent part of the new regime from the murder of Aman, who had been opposed to the execution of prisoners, onwards. The announcement of the execution of 57 officials of the Selassie government was made two days after Aman's murder (Clapham 1988: 44). Lefort views Aman's death as the event which began 'the blood law' of the revolution, that was used to settle all crucial disputes: 'We disagree: I shall kill you to prevent you killing me first' (Lefort 1983: 81). Initially this was the behaviour of a military regime, like the many established elsewhere by *coups d'état* and initially, as violent military regimes usually do, the PMAC moved towards the establishment of a military state. On 16 November 1974 the PMAC set in motion the construction of the means for wider repression: a special court martial; changes in the Penal Code; and a law governing public order and safety (Clapham 1988: 45). On 30 September 1975 a state of emergency was introduced under which the police and armed forces were empowered to arrest without warrant and to use force (Keesing's 1976: 27654).

A military solution was applied to Eritrea. Under a political compromise Eritrea had been joined in federation with Ethiopia in 1952. Intended self-government within the federation soon turned into Ethiopian rule and in 1961 a guerrilla secessionist movement, the ELF, was organized. By 1969, Eritrea had been placed under a state of emergency and came under military rule. In 1970, the EPLF (Eritrean People's Liberation Forces) broke from the ELF and formed a more radical, less nationalist, organization opposed to the emperor's regime. Between 1972–4 the ELF and EPLF fought each other but by 1974 they had joined forces. These revolutionary upheavals in Eritrea and the experiences of Ethiopian soldiers sent against them fed the military revolts which began the Ethiopian Revolution itself (Markakis and Ayele 1978: 61–7). Aman, himself of Eritrean origin, had adopted a policy of negotiated settlement with Eritrea and by the end of September there were signs that it might work. His policy was overridden by the PMAC, however, and 5,000 additional troops were sent in to Eritrea (Clapham 1988: 44).

THE REVOLUTIONARY REIGN OF TERROR: JULY 1976–MAY 1978

The first legislation for a revolutionary reign of terror was passed on 5 July 1976 when the death penalty and life imprisonment were introduced for widely defined 'anti-revolutionary activities' (Keesing's 1976: 27914). These activities, which were additionally penalized by property confiscation, included economic crimes such as causing damage to transport and public property, attempting to leave the country illegally and accepting or offering bribes. On 13 July it was announced that General Getachew Nadew, commander-in-chief and martial law administrator in Eritrea, had been executed 'while resisting arrest', and 18 others were executed after being tried by a special military court for spying, for engaging in economic sabotage and for plotting against the PMAC (ibid). Of these Major Sisay Habte had been a member of the

PMAC. Four executions of PMAC members soon followed, two on 25 July and two on 11 August. In October 1976 a representative of the Ethiopian People's Revolutionary Party (EPRP) claimed that the PMAC had killed 1,225, tortured hundreds more in concentration camps and carried out mass executions (ibid 1977: 28222).

In October 1976 local surveillance organizations (security squads) were developed within the *kebelles* (Keesing's 1977: 28221). These urban neighbourhood associations had been set up in July 1975 as cooperatives with around 200–300 dwellings in each. Each *kebelle* had its own people's tribunal for the settling of local disputes (Schwab 1985: 32). Lefort (1983: 216) has compared these with the revolutionary committees of the French Revolution. In the spring of 1977 some of the *kebelles* began to be armed and disputes were no longer taken to the tribunal 'as long as there were other forces like the *kebelle* guards who were willing to administer justice summarily' (Singer, quoted in Schwab 1985: 32). By early 1978, 300 of these armed *kebelles* had their own prisons, torturers and death squads (Keesing's 1978: 28995).

In December 1976, the PMAC was reorganized. It was to consist of a Congress (the entire Derg), a central committee (40 members elected from Congress) and a 'permanent committee' of 17 members to supervise the 'politicisation of the masses and of the secret service' (Keesing's 1977: 28221). Mobilization was to be an important aspect of the new order. Brigadier-General Teferi Banti was to continue as president of the Derg and as commander-in-chief of the armed forces. First Vice-President Lieutenant-Colonel Mengistu Haile-Miriam was to be prime minister, whilst the second vice-president, Lieutenant-Colonel Atnafu Abate, was put in charge of the creation and organization of a people's militia.

On 3 February 1977, Teferi Banti and eight other members of the Military Council were killed by other council members for being counter-revolutionary. Whether this was planned by Mengistu himself or not remains unknown. (On 29 January 1977, Teferi Banti had broken the rule of the Derg and spoken out in favour of the need for a party coalition Democratic Front, omitting to say anything against the EPRP classed by the PMAC as an illegal, counter-revolutionary, force.) On 11 February the PMAC returned to the name of the Derg and was again reorganized, with the central committee down to 32 members and the standing committee down to sixteen. Mengistu was elected president, commander-in-chief of the armed forces and chairman of the general congress, central committee and standing committee (Keesing's 1977: 28421). Ethiopia's reign of terror was set for its peak.

From 3 February 1977 the Derg turned fully on supporters of the EPRP sending army troops and the people's militia against them. Mass arrests and executions took place and a massacre was reported in Addis Ababa (Keesing's 1977: 28421). The soldiers were empowered to carry out 'revolutionary justice', the victims were never brought to trial (Markakis and Ayele 1978: 167). At the end of April 1977, 300–500 students accused of distributing anti-government leaflets were killed by troops and peasants. Numerous assassinations occurred. The *kebelles* in Addis Ababa were brought in to assist in house-to-house searches; lists and photographs of over 700 opponents were posted in government offices. In April public executions took place and announcements of other executions were made. On 21 April a decree enabled people suspected of sabotage to be detained without trial for up to six months (Keesing's 1977: 28421). An Amnesty International report estimated that by March 8,000 people (men, women and children) were already detained as political prisoners in Ethiopia. On 1 May ('Bloody 1 May') revenge erupted into a blood bath (Lefort 1983: 196). It has been estimated that between 600–1,000 students were massacred in just one concentration camp in the days which followed (Markakis and Ayele 1978: 168).

This 'urban terrorism' as Clapham (1988: 55) classifies it had involved two rival Marxist political factions, the EPRP, which favoured a party-led revolution, and MEISON (All Ethiopia Socialist Movement), which accepted the need initially for a military path to revolution and therefore gained the backing of the PMAC (some of whom were MEISON members). In August 1976, a new Marxist party, the Ethiopian Communist People's Party (ECP), formed in opposition both to the EPRP and the revolutionary government. The EPRP, with its own military branch, the Revolutionary People's Army, launched its destabilization campaign in September 1976 to coincide with the second anniversary of the revolution. Several MEISON leaders were killed; MEISON had developed its own 'execution squads' and turned the situation in Addis Ababa into a civil war (ibid: 55–6).

In July 1977 the Derg turned its attentions on MEISON. From July, Mengistu began to develop his own party, the Seded (Flame) and MEISON members went into hiding. Hundreds of killings continued to be reported by the government, though some prisoners were released (Keesing's 1977: 28637). According to a report in the *Daily Telegraph* (London) on 3 July, by May 1977 around 30,000 Ethiopians had been either killed or imprisoned since September 1974, including

2,000 students killed in Addis Ababa at the end of April 1977 and 500 teachers murdered in a purge (ibid). Ethiopia's population is around 30 million. Over the two weeks ending October and beginning November up to 350 people were reported killed in Addis Ababa following student demonstrations protesting against the alleged executions of prisoners (ibid 1978: 28762).

THE TERROR REACHES ITS PEAK: RED TERROR, NOVEMBER 1977–APRIL 1978

On 11 November Lieutenant-Colonel Atnafu Abate, the first vice-president, was arrested and executed on 13 November for 'counter-revolutionary' crimes. The next day in a radio broadcast 'all peasants, workers and progressive Ethiopians' were told to 'strengthen the struggle against counter-revolutionaries on the land, in factories and in offices', to 'spread Red terror in the camp of reactionaries' and to 'turn the white terror of reactionaries into Red terror' (Keesing's 1978: 28761).

Accurate figures of deaths and the proportion of victims killed by the state terror are impossible to collect. Numerous government officials and supporters were assassinated (the EPRP mainly being given the blame) and in return opponents of the regime were summarily executed either by the police or death squads organized by the regime. In January 1978, the EPRP claimed 3,500 people had been 'assassinated' by the PMAC and in Addis Ababa some 8,000 people had been deported to the countryside. Three hundred *kebelles* in Addis Ababa had their own prisons, torturers and death squads empowered to arrest and summarily execute 'counter-revolutionaries'; terror of the purest form reigned; young people were terrorized into denouncing the innocent as EPRP members. The *Times* (London), in March, reported allegations of 100–150 people, mostly between the ages of 12–20, being killed every night during February and March 1978. If true, this would total 5,900–8,750 deaths, though a statement sent by the Derg was published in the *Times* on 25 March denying the story completely. An Amnesty International report published on 15 November 1978 estimated that in the area of Addis Ababa alone the Red Terror of December 1977–February 1978 had produced around 5,000 deaths, most of them victims aged 12–25. It was estimated also that in March 1978, 30,000 people had been held in prison in very poor, crowded conditions with incidents of torture.[3]

THE CAUSES OF THE TERROR: FOREIGN WAR, CIVIL WAR AND ECONOMIC PROBLEMS

November 1977–April 1978 was the period when the PMAC experienced the peak of counter-revolutionary pressure. Adding to the problems of civil war in Addis Ababa, guerrilla movements were growing in force in the provinces. In addition to the liberation movements in Eritrea, 10,000–15,000 guerrillas in the Ethiopian Democratic Union, (EDU) which was formed in March 1975 by liberal noblemen, had taken up arms against the Ethiopian army in the bordering provinces of Tigray and Gonder in the north west (Clapham 1988: 58). As a consequence, relations between Sudan, which bordered these areas, deteriorated and war threatened. Twenty-five thousand refugees were reported to have fled to Sudan (Keesing's 1977: 28423). It was with Somalia, not Sudan, though that in June 1977 war broke out when the Western Somalia Liberation Front (WSLF), with the backing of the Somali government, attacked Ethiopian troops in the Ogaden region, an area claimed as part of the 'Somali nation' (ibid: 28633). By August parts of southern Ethiopia had also been taken over by either Somali forces or the WSLF; in Djibouti, the government had made public its willingness to use French troops in defence of its newly independent country (Lefort 1983: 192); and in Eritrea, the secessionist guerrilla movements continued their offensive: 'From every direction except Kenya, Addis Ababa heard the sound of marching soldiers' (ibid).

Economic problems were acute. The harvest of 1975–6 had been bad and new famines threatened in the provinces of Tigray and bordering Wollo. Peasants had begun to hoard their produce, and as a consequence the system of trade and transport had collapsed hitting production in the new large mechanized farms. The problem of supplying the towns and the capital in particular became acute, a shortage made worse by the increase in the urban population. In the second half of 1976 prices for foodstuffs in Addis Ababa rose by 29 per cent (Lefort 1983: 192). Food production, per capita, for the years 1976–8 was 16 per cent lower than before the revolution. With respect to National Account figures, the Gross Domestic Product fell by 1.1 per cent in 1977–8, the trade deficit widened and the external debt grew (ibid: 193). Lefort remarks that the only solution was to print money, and that indeed was what the government did. Ethiopia was then and still is one of the very poorest countries in the world, with a largely subsistence economy where money plays little part, but money was extremely important in the capital and not least to the government itself. Around 80 per cent of export earnings came from coffee. Coffee production had fallen badly under the chaos of foreign and civil wars and the deficit on foreign trade grew dramatically; from US$108 million in 1974–5 it had reached US$263 million in 1979–80 (Halliday and Molyneux 1981: 103) .

In the face of the threat of war Revolutionary Committees had been set up by the Derg in April 1977 to operate a national mobilization campaign to serve the war effort (Keesing's 1977: 28421). The people's militia, established at the end of 1976, had grown and by June it had reached 80,000. In September some 10,000 ex-servicemen under the age of 60 were called up for military service. In August all workers were asked to finance the war effort with a substantial contribution from their earnings. Mengistu strengthened his control to coordinate the war and a Revolutionary Co-ordination Centre for regular troops was set up in July, followed in August by a National Revolutionary Company in Command (NRCC) (ibid: 28637). Mengistu placed himself at the head of both. The job of the NRCC was essentially to requisition for the war effort, transport and communications especially, and also to control production and supply.

The war effort succeeded, and after a special offensive Somali gains were reversed. On 9 March following negotiations conducted through US President Carter, Somali troops withdrew from Ethiopia.[4] With Somalia repelled, civil war in the Ogaden ended and the WLFN was defeated. The opposition forces in Addis Ababa had been beaten into submission both physically and mentally by the Somali war victory; now the Ethiopian army turned its attention on Eritrea, in May. By the end of 1978 the secessionist problem had been 'contained' and the Derg had achieved relative stability with Mengistu Haile Miriam, the undisputed leader of the Ethiopian regime (Clapham 1988: 62). The Terror continued throughout 1978 but by May it had passed its peak.

NECESSITY VERSUS POLICY CHOICE: LAND REFORM, NATIONALIZATION AND THE LITERACY CAMPAIGN

Ethiopia had then faced the classic conditions conducive to reigns of terror. Foreign war, civil war and economic problems with consequent insurrection in the cities. Nationalities had raised the temperature of civil war too. Through the use of force the revolutionary government had survived over a country terrorized into submission in most if not quite all of its parts. The secessionist movements in Eritrea and the Tigray continued to provide the justification for the Derg's militaristic domination. All of the bloodshed and violence in Ethiopia cannot, however, be reduced to necessity. The policies chosen by the PMAC had an independent impact. Land reforms and nationalization programmes adversely affected the economy and stirred up counter-revolution. The militaristic nature of the regime with its lack of barriers to the use of violence also played a part.

By October 1974, students and teachers had already begun to organize a mass mobilization campaign in the countryside. The National Development through Co-operation Campaign, the *zemecha,* announced in October and launched in December, took 50,000 teachers and students into the countryside to carry the message of revolution and to spread literacy (Clapham 1988: 49). Illiteracy in Ethiopia, at 95 per cent, was the highest in the world.

The first set of policies initiated by the Provisional Military Administrative Council in December 1974 was a combination of state socialist and nationalist plans ('Ethiopia First' was the slogan of the revolution; the country was to be one nation, with one culture, one religion, one language). All financial institutions and foreign companies were to be nationalized, industry was to be under state control and eventually under state ownership, and ownership of land was to belong to those working on it (Clapham 1988: 45–6). The PMAC did not impose a set of policies in the sense of a preconceived programme. There was no outward evidence of Mengistu's radicalism before 1974 and, as Halliday and Molyneux (1981: 116–17) argue, 'his subsequent espousal of a Marxist-Leninist outlook in the latter part of 1976 was … as much a response to the immediate situation as a reflection of long-standing conviction'.

In practice, in March 1975, land was not given to the peasants but was brought under state ownership. Collectives and state farms were created. Not surprisingly some of the great landowners formed a counter-revolutionary force (Clapham 1988: 47). The reforms were to have a second effect, also associated with Terrors. They exacerbated the problem of feeding the towns and the capital. At a sweep, the whole system for transferring surplus to the towns was destroyed and the cities were put on the brink of starvation; that was remedied only when a new state-controlled market system was reconstructed (ibid: 48). Whilst Paris,

Moscow and Petrograd had foreign and civil wars to at least part explain their shortages, in Ethiopia this problem of distribution was entirely self-made. The Eritreans, too were angered by shortages. Eritrea was a region traditionally incapable of growing sufficient grain to feed its population, and Addis Ababa proved incapable of filling the gap (Lefort 1983: 176). The *zemechas* 'poured oil on fire' (ibid: 103). These urban outsiders were resented and especially so in areas where the nationalities felt threatened by the 'one nation' government. Things got out of hand, too, where the students and teachers took the peasants' side in disputes with landlords and in some cases soldiers intervened against them (ibid: 112–14). It has been estimated that by April 1976 the *zemecha* campaign had cost the lives of 1,000 students (Keesing's 1976: 27912).

Beyond the removal of the big landlords, the Derg, the *zemechas* and the poor peasants shared no other interests (Lefort 1983: 114). The students and teachers were drawn more and more to anti-military Marxist organizations, which in 1975 formed the EPRP. There was also intellectual support for Marxist revolution through the military (rather than through a party) and this led to the formation of MEISON. The PMAC was itself split over these conflicting revolutionary paths. Mengistu favoured a military route, Chairman Teferi Banti a party-state revolution. It was this difference which led to Teferi Banti's death in February 1977.

In July 1975 urban land and houses owned as investments were nationalized. Similar to the peasant associations set up in the country-side, urban neighbourhood associations were set up to administer rents. These *kebelles* were intended, eventually, to be political administrative organizations. Within a year the new regime had embarked upon a series of far-reaching changes, changes from which there could be no turning back and which stirred up counter-revolution at home. Food shortages had been created in the cities, in Addis Ababa especially, and erstwhile supporters of the revolution were turned against it through the difference between theory and practice. Direct experience of military force began to win recruits for a party-directed strategy.

VIOLENCE AGAINST OPPOSITION: CIVIL WAR EXPLODES

From September 1975 widespread loss of support for the regime became clear. Of the 56,000 students and teachers who had embarked on the *zemecha* campaign, only 17,000–18,000 remained active. The Trade Union Federation (CELU) threatened a general strike unless three conditions were met; that civilians be brought into the government; that political prisoners be released; and that a proletarian revolutionary party based on Marxist-Leninist principles be formed along with other parties into a Democratic Front. The formation of a party had been promised but had never materialized. Conciliation was not attempted, instead the demands were met with force.

This was the situation which had led to the state of emergency being declared on 30 September 1975, under which the police and armed forces had been given the right to stop, search, use force and to make arrests without warrant. At the same time strikes or incitement to strike had also been made illegal (Keesing's 1976: 27654). The following day military officers had been posted as governors in troublesome areas. On 2 October a bomb explosion in Addis Ababa led to hundreds of arrests and an unknown number of killings. Further mass arrests followed on 4 October when shooting occurred near Addis Ababa University and, after yet further arrests on 4 November, CELU was disbanded (ibid). The state of emergency was lifted on 5 December but arrests continued. The estimate up to February 1976 was put at 2,000 (ibid). The military had by then also embarked on operations against the landlords and their supporters. Between 7 October 1975– 27 February 1976, 294 people were reported killed and 100 arrested. Most of these were from Wollo province (ibid: 27653).

The PMAC had rejected a policy of compromise and sent in 5,000 additional troops in November 1974, the secessionist war with Eritrea continued to heat up and in August 1975 Ethiopian troops embarked on a 'neutralization' campaign, burning houses and killing men, women and children. Estimates suggested hundreds, perhaps thousands, of people were killed. A spokesman for one of the Eritrean guerrilla movements claimed 10,000 dead in these 'genocidal operations' over the previous year (Keesing's 1976: 27653). In 1976 they claimed an additional 5,000 civilians alone had been killed (ibid).[5] In addition to the civil war in Eritrea and the rebellion of the Afars in Wollo, the Gallas were revolting in Tigray. By April 1976 disturbances had broken out in almost every other province; the government in Addis Ababa was literally surrounded with rebellion (ibid: 27912). On 5 July 1976, in the face of severe economic problems, the result of nationalization and land programmes, and faced by escalating civil war in Addis

Ababa and the provinces the PMAC had introduced the legislation which had begun the revolutionary reign of terror.

TERROR TO PERMANENT GOVERNMENT: CONTROL OVER THE COERCIVE FORCES AND FOREIGN HELP

The revolutionary reign of terror had developed as a reaction to civil war, a civil war which had essentially been stirred by the policies of the revolutionary regime itself, policies aimed at fundamental change through recourse to coercion. Compromise had been ruled out in Eritrea in favour of assault, and land reforms had brought both opposition (particularly in the regions) and chaos to the system of food distribution. New and varied oppositions, both political and economic, had developed in reaction to the military's instinctive resort to force and outright civil war had been brought to the very capital itself. Terror had been used to destroy the counter-revolutionaries (that is forces opposed to the revolution as perceived by Mengistu and the regular armed forces). This combination of policy aims and methods had ignited a civil war of such virulence that foreign war too had threatened, finally breaking out with Somalia, drawn in to support the liberation movement in the Ogaden. It had been in response to civil war not foreign war that the Terror had begun in July 1976, provoked above all by the fighting raging in Addis Ababa itself.

The peak of the terror had developed around the execution of Atnafu. Not surprisingly, given the secrecy of the events surrounding it, his death has given rise to conflicting explanations including both personality clashes (reflecting ethnic differences) and policy disagreements (over the importation of 'socialism' to Africa), the latter being especially emphasized in the Ethiopian press after Atnafu's death. There is even controversy over whether it was Atnafu or Mengistu who incited the Derg in the power struggle (Lefort 1983: 233–4). Lefort, however, offers a simpler explanation for Atnafu's execution which rests on a more thorough analysis. Atnafu was the sacrifice (one which Mengistu had not sought) needed to achieve a compromise within the Derg between the regular armed forces and the militia. Atnafu had paid the price with his life for both the success which he had had in raising the militia and the conflict with the regular armed forces which this had brought. The compromise was that 'the militarists' got their way in officially achieving complete subordination of the militia to the regular army whilst at the same time the army was itself to be subject to the authority of the Derg and therefore no longer able to impose its wishes. In essence the significance of Atnafu's death lay in its signalling the revolutionary government's struggle to gain control over the revolutionary forces of coercion themselves. In consequence of his death both the militia and the regular army were subordinated to the Derg.

Then began what Lefort (1983: 235) refers to as 'the most ferocious (and the most obscure) repression since the beginning of the revolution': 'Under cover of striking down "reactionaries" the Derg proposed to bring to heel all the organised forces still outside its absolute control'. Having attacked the political opposition focused on the EPRP, the Derg had turned, at the end of 1976, on MEISON to whom the military had earlier given its support.[6] All urban organizations, including the *kebelles* and the rural peasant associations, were brought under central control (ibid: 234–5). A clear light is thrown on this heightened 'most obscure' repression if viewed in terms of the general role of revolutionary terrors in gaining control over the coercive forces. On 16 August 1977, MEISON members of the Derg had received permission to distribute further arms to the *kebelle* security squads. A further 130 *kebelles* were immediately armed in Addis Ababa. Significantly these were only the MEISON-dominated *kebelles;* once armed all leading MEISON figures went underground. The battle with MEISON meant that if Mengistu and the military section of the Derg were to retain power (and not lose it like Robespierre and the Committee of Public Safety) they would have to gain control over the *kebelles*.

It had been Atnafu who had first 'armed the masses' of Addis Ababa in March 1977. By May, 120 *kebelles* had been armed, leaving a further 167 *kebelles* considered too great a risk at that time (Lefort 1983: 200). From the beginning, these lumpen-proletariat urban defence forces, like the people's armies of the French Revolution, had begun operating as a law unto themselves and atrocities carried out by them were not subject to central direction.[7] Control over the peasant associations and their defence squads had no doubt played its part in Atnafu's death too, for the militia had been raised mainly from the peasantry through peasant associations. These raw recruits had been resented and despised by the regular troops even to the point where the militia were shot at by the regular forces as well as the enemy and knowingly sent into battles where their death was a certainty (ibid: 214–15). Atnafu had indeed been sacrificed in the battle to gain control over the forces of coercion, a battle which had taken place whilst foreign war raged.

The end of the Somali war had not left Ethiopia with a permanent state structure. Success in gaining control over the coercive forces ensured that Mengistu and the Derg, like Lenin and Sovnarkom, held on to power, but the new state formation had not yet been established. Clapham (1988: 63) argues that by the end of 1978 'a stable framework of political order had been reimposed' with Mengistu in 'the powerful role of dominant, personal leadership in the Ethiopian political tradition'. At this point the revolution had not been institutionalized, no Marxist-Leninist Party had been developed which could have provided political organization and economic planning, central control over the economy had not been achieved.[8] A potential administrative structure existed in the towns through the *kebelles* and in the countryside through the peasants associations, but it had not yet developed (ibid). Throughout the years of terror, fear had replaced trust (Schwab 1985: 32–3) but The Soviet Union, which had provided military and diplomatic support, did provide a 'model of government' (Clapham 1988: 63).

Ethiopia, no more than any other poor country in the twentieth century, heavily dependent on a primary export such as coffee, could not close its doors on the world as Russia and China had once done after their revolutions. Initially, the PMAC had relied on aid from the USA, receiving US$23.5 million (mostly in agricultural loans) and US$12.5 million for military equipment (Keesing's 1976: 27653). Following a statement by the PMAC in February that it would in future buy arms only from socialist countries – a secret agreement had been signed with the Soviet Union at the end of December 1976 – and with Carter now president and objecting to human rights abuses, in April 1977 the USA withdrew military aid and suspended delivery of arms (ibid 1977: 28423) . In May 1977, 20 Cuban advisers arrived in Ethiopia; by then small arms had already been received from Eastern Europe and China. By April, Soviet tanks and armoured cars were arriving and, in exchange, the USSR gained a naval base on the Red Sea. The Soviet model of a single-party state was set on course (see Clapham 1988: chs 5 and 6).

The process of organizing a new political party, the Party of the Working People of Ethiopia (COPWE), was not begun until December 1979. It was a party imposed from above with Mengistu as its chairman and its key personnel the most trusted members of the Derg. Of its top leadership, the military formed around two-thirds (see Clapham 1988: 69). In Ethiopia the military had triumphed and it is tempting to make comparison with the French Terror had the Héberistes and the Paris People's Army held sway. Such a comparison must not be over-drawn, for in Mengistu the regular army had triumphed over the militia. Atnafu, like Ronsin, had paid the price of too great a success in establishing a revolutionary people's army.

A POSTSCRIPT ON TERROR

The dominance of the military in Ethiopia, the choice of coercion over conciliation, and terror's role in effecting submission to Mengistu's rule invite comparison with Cambodia 1975–9, labelled as 'proto-totalitarian' in Chapter 2. The combination of nationalism ('Ethiopia First') and socialism (nationalization and collectivization) in the ideology of the revolution adds a further parallel. It is a comparison, though, which cannot be stretched. As Clapham has commented, in drawing attention to the important role played by towns, the capital city especially, in propelling the revolution, 'It was, ultimately the revolution that made the Derg rather than the Derg that made the revolution' (Clapham 1988: 42). The Derg was led by a mass movement pushing for change, it did not constitute an organization imposing a preconceived policy of total transformation through terror to achieve domination over an atomized society. As in all revolutionary reigns of terror, from July 1976 the Derg had lashed out against opposition to itself erupting seemingly everywhere. Only with the submission of the opposition did the potential for a totalitarian state open. Even then, guerrilla movements remained active in the provinces of Eritrea and Tigray.

NOTES

1. Clapham (1988: 42) takes issue with Halliday and Molyneux's (1981: 25–31) adaptation of Trimberger's (1978) concept of a 'revolution from above'. The Ethiopian Revolution was not led by high-ranking military officers (rather most of them, along with top bureaucrats, were to be executed, exiled or imprisoned) and Mengistu himself had been only a major in the army in 1974. Clapham also emphasizes the importance of the mass movements and radical ideology of the Ethiopian Revolution which do not feature in Trimberger's conceptualization. As in the classic revolutions the Ethiopian state was essentially destroyed, not strengthened, as in a 'revolution from above'.

2.   As the exact membership was not revealed and membership seems anyway to have changed over time, there is some disagreement over rank. Markakis and Ayele (1978: 147) suggest that the Derg ranked only to major when it took power in September 1974 and installed the PMAC.

3.   For all the above newspaper and other reports in this paragraph see Keesing's 1978: 28995 and 1980: 30016 and 30019. In addition, the UN High Commissioner for Refugees estimated that in April 1979, 270,000 refugees (mostly Eritreans) were in Sudan and 30,000 in Djibouti.

4.   Clapham (1988: 61) draws attention to the 16,000 Cuban troops assisting Ethiopia but argues that it was domestic mobilization which was crucial.

5.   As for the massacres in Ireland, 1650–1, it is difficult to be sure how far these should be counted as victims of war or of state terror. It would be necessary to know both whether those killed were armed and whether the soldiers were under state orders to massacre; those killed after July 1976 who were unarmed would certainly count as victims of the revolutionary reign of terror. The execution on 13 July 1976 of Colonel Getachew Nadew, commander-in-chief of martial law in Eritrea for counter-revolution, suggests that central government did not have control over its own organizations in this area, his murder being a step towards that end.

6.   Chege (1979: 378) claims that a half of the original 120 members of the Derg were killed in 1977.

7.   For example, the Arat Kilo *kebelle* in Addis Ababa was brought under control through force when the Derg executed the chairman for atrocities (Schwab 1983: 32). There is dispute in the literature over whether or not a class analysis can be applied to Ethiopia (contrast Chege 1979 with Ottaway 1976). Certainly the old order represented the nobility whilst the Derg did not and the civil war in Addis Ababa was fought broadly between the lumpen-proletariat and rich educated people (their children mostly) but, as the discussion above has shown, at best a class analysis over-simplifies a complex situation where political disagreements cross-cut the military ranks and regional antagonisms over-rode conflicts of class interest.

8.   Schwab (1983: 38) has argued that the Derg, through support for its policies, had laid the foundations of the new state both in theory and practice in 1976, though later (p.47) he states that 'through 1978 and 1979 discussions into what form the new political entity should take went on within the Dergue, between the Dergue and civilian representatives and between Mengistu and the Soviet Union'. In contrast with Schwab's assessment of 1976 Ottaway (1976: 483) emphasized the government's separation from society: 'but unless the Derg succeeds in establishing a relationship to the social groups that have most benefited from the revolution, Ethiopia will slip towards a heavily centralised, state-controlled system, run by the military and the technocrats, without either the participation or the mobilisation of the population'.

11. The Iranian Revolution: Terror in the Islamic State

In Ethiopia the army had played a central role in the revolution and the consequent dominance of force had heightened the reign of terror. In Iran, the excesses of the reign of terror also reflected a special feature, the Islamic Republic. Not surprisingly, the literature on the Iranian revolution has sought to explain this unusual religious dimension which fits so uneasily within the accepted generalizations about revolutions: whether or not Iran contravenes the normal assumption that revolutions are progressive (Halliday 1988; Arjomand 1986); whether it can be fitted within a Marxist framework that views ideas as secondary to material conditions (Moghadam 1989); and whether it can be accommodated within currently popular generalizations developed through the comparative study of revolutions (Skocpol 1982, and the debate generated in the same issue: Keddie; Ahmad; Goldfrank).

SPONTANEOUS REVOLUTION AND THE FORMATION OF OPPOSITIONS

As in France, 1789 and Russia, February 1917, popular uprisings heralded the overthrow of the monarchy. Contrary to popular claims this was not the first time a spontaneous revolution, that is one not led by guerrilla movements, had occurred in the Third World (Ahmad 1982). There had been one in Ethiopia just five years before. In contrast with King Louis XVI, Tsar Nicholas and Emperor Haile Selassie, however, the Shah of Iran had rather weaker claims to traditional legitimacy, having been re-installed in power in 1953 by a *coup d'état* which removed the elected Mossadeq government. The coup had been staged on the Shah's behalf (deliberately out of the country at the time) by General Zahedi.[1] This close connection between the military leaders and the personal power of the Shah helps in part to explain the army's disintegration once the Shah had left Iran for exile.

228

The revolutionary forces combined in hatred of the Shah but their post-revolutionary aims contrasted sharply. As Halliday (1988: 49) remarks, 'the broad and rapidly congealed coalition of forces that overthrew the Shah was strong precisely because of its diverse and spontaneous character; it was also one of the causes of the factionalism and paralysis of the post-revolutionary period'. The Iranian Revolution, in being spontaneous, was unlike those of China, Cuba and Nicaragua where guerrilla movements had eased the establishment of revolutionary coervice forces and through civil war had built support and learnt important lessons for post-revolutionary government.

Until the beginning of 1977, the Shah's secret police force, SAVAK, had effectively paralysed opposition forces (see Abrahamian 1989: chs 5–6). Members of the banned Communist Tudeh Party and guerrillas of the left-wing Mujahedin and Fedayee organizations populated the prisons and swelled the statistics of the tortured and executed. Fear froze less militant opposition in the single-party state. A slight thaw came in early 1977 when, in response to international pressures for human rights, the Shah relaxed controls a little, but he had mistaken the immobility of fear for passive support (Nima 1983: 54). The dangers of reducing coercion in the absence of legitimacy soon became apparent and protests began to grow among intellectual and middle-class groups. These focused around two distinct centres of protest, the political and the religious.

In December 1977 political opposition groups formed the Union of National Front Forces around lasting pro-Mossadeq supporters. Inspired in the mosques by the anti-tyrannical preachings of mullahs faithful to Ayatollah Khomeini (exiled in Iraq at the time) theology students came out onto the streets in protest against the Pahlavi regime. By late 1978 the Union of National Front Forces had given its support to the religious opposition. The entry of first the working class and then the unemployed into active opposition against the Shah propelled Khomeini to prominence. In the summer of 1978, government austerity policies, which brought cuts in both wages and benefits and increased unemployment, brought the first workers out on strike; they were joined later by the unemployed in larger and larger demonstrations. The network of mosques, some 80,000 run by around 180,000 mullahs, proved the decisive organization for mass action. Normal workers' political organizations had been effectively disarmed by SAVAK, whilst the relief organizations of the mosques (*komitehs*) functioned effectively in ordering revolutionary activity; the pulpit had provided a platform for preaching against tyranny (Keesing's 1979: 29733).

Chance played a part in Khomeini's fortunes. A mass funeral following a cinema fire blamed on SAVAK coincided with religious festivals in the latter part of 1978 and together they heightened the poignancy of religion and political action for the urban poor. Recently drawn from the countryside, by the Shah's oil-led modernization programme, this group exactly fitted Wolf's generalization about the revolutionary potential of recently created workers in industry. New town-dwellers, they were but recently peasants. Wolf gives special prominence to the 'middle and free peasant' who retains family connections with the village and argues that it is the 'very attempt ... to remain traditional which makes (the peasant) revolutionary' (Wolf 1973: 292). It was second-generation migrants and poor migrants living in bad housing, but not the poorer squatters, who formed the bulk of the protestors (Kazemi 1980). What was special about Iran, however, was that 'tradition' was inextricably linked with the Shi'a islamic religion.

As demonstrations and strikes mounted, the government declared martial law which in turn further inflamed anger. From September 1978 to the end of December the country was brought to its knees by demonstrations, riots and strikes, the most important being staged by oil workers and civil servants. The economy was disrupted totally. Go-slow tactics were used when violence forced workers back to work. In early January 1979, before leaving the country, the Shah handed power over to a new government, headed by Dr Bakhtiar, which was formally sworn in on 4 January. Demonstrations continued. On 13 January the Ayatollah Khomeini, now in exile in France, announced that a Revolutionary Islamic Council had been formed in opposition to the Bakhtiar government. The Shah left Iran on 16 January and Khomeini returned to Iran on 1 February. On the 5th, Khomeini set up a provisional government, headed by Dr Bazarghan, in opposition to Bakhtiar's government. Six days later, after battles within the armed forces between those supporting Bakhtiar and supporters of Bazarghan, Bakhtiar's government fell when the military command declared in favour of Khomeini.[2]

11 FEBRUARY 1979: THE TERROR BEGINS

Whilst Bazarghan became, on 11 February, the undisputed head of the Provisional Government, from the start its power was challenged by Khomeini's Revolutionary Islamic Council centred in the holy city of

Qom. Bazarghan's power was soon to be further undermined through the Islamic revolutionary courts, revolutionary committees and revolutionary guards. Abrahamian (1989: 186) describes this as a period of dual power, the organizations of terror being controlled not by the Bazarghan government, but by the clerics through the *komitehs*, the mosque-led (many of these leaders Ayatollahs) committees which had formed to fight the revolution. The Terror began almost at once, with 600 executions followed by summary trials held by the Islamic revolutionary courts. The accused were mainly former officers of the Shah, some civilian but mainly military, and including former officers of SAVAK, the Shah's secret police. The crimes for which they were executed, in addition to 'torture, murder, treason and corruption' included 'persons convicted of sexual misdemeanours considered to violate the tenets of Islam' (Keesing's 1980: 30145). But for the inclusion of sexual transgressions, the victims fell within the usual nature of post-revolutionary reprisal.

The revolutionary guards (Pasdaran) were first formed on 5 March 1979. They were a paramilitary police force which was supposed to combine the roles of army, police force and representative of the mosque. They were also given the tasks of supporting 'liberation movements' and spreading 'Iran's Islamic revolution throughout the world' (Keesing's 1980: 30141). By May the guards were estimated at 10,000, plus 100,000 reservists.

In March the courts were suspended; they were reconstituted on 5 April with a religious judge as chairman of a bench of three. The offences of murder, torture and 'imprisonment of innocent people' were added to: encouragement of foreign influence in Iran, damaging the economy, being involved in armed attacks and 'implementing programmes against the national or public interest'. There was to be no right of appeal (Keesing's 1980: 30145–6). Executions continued. These summary trials (some lasting only 15 minutes) and executions (sometimes within four hours of sentence) were condemned by the International Commission of Jurists (ibid: 30146). At the same time many were held in prison without trial. It was estimated in March that there were over 20,000 political prisoners, included among them were a large number of Kurds. By September 1979 over 100,000 people (mainly skilled, professional and business people) had left Iran (ibid: 30147). In August 1979, SAVAMA was set up as a secret police force to replace SAVAK which had been dissolved by Bazarghan in February 1979.

POLITICAL CHANGES

The Islamic Revolutionary Council under Khomeini took steps towards forming an Islamic Republic. A referendum was held to establish legitimacy for this aim on 30–1 March. The votes recorded were over 20 million in favour and fewer than 150,000 against, but the National Democratic Front, the Fedayee and Mujahedin in addition to several other groups, including several Kurdish ones, had all boycotted the referendum. An Islamic Republican Party (IRP) was created, some Islamic laws were introduced (governing marriage, divorce, alcohol, food, dress and music). A draft constitution was also published which proposed that dominance be given to the mullahs and to Islamic law. In August 1979 an election was held for a Constituent Council of Experts to draw up the detail of the new constitution. Sixty of the 73 members elected were Islamic fundamentalists. Electoral irregularities provoked protests from opposition parties, the greatest coming from Kurdistan and eastern Azerbaijan. The Kurds, who were Sunni not Shii moslems, objected to the rigged election of two Shii clerics to represent their area and in Azerbaijan the Moslem People's Republican Party candidates claimed that they and not the IRP had won the seats (for the above see Keesing's 1980: 30143–5).

Ayatollah Montazeri (also a member of the Islamic Revolutionary Council) headed the Council of Experts. On 14 November a new constitution was introduced under which Shiism was to dominate the state and the *Wali Faqih* (Supreme Jurisprudent) was to be given supreme power.[3] Ayatollah Khomeini was the *Wali Faqih*. In January 1980 elections were held and Bani-Sadr, representing a liberal religious approach, won a resounding victory over the Islamic Republican Party candidate in the presidential elections, but in the parliamentary elections to the Islamic Consultative Assembly (Majlis) which followed in March 1980 the Islamic Republican Party gained the majority. Khomeini swung the balance by appointing the reactionary Ayatollah Beheshti, leader of the IRP, as head of the Supreme Court. By August, Rajai was appointed as prime minister against Bani-Sadr's wishes (Nima 1983: 108–9). The refusal to permit the Mojahedin's presidential candidate to stand in the presidential elections in combination with the Ayatollah's outbursts against them led to the outbreak of violence between the Mojahedin and Hezbollahi. The Hezbollah, translated literally as 'Party of Allah', were a thuggish force which had veiled links with the Islamic Republican Party. They had first made an appearance back in

1979 wielding metal bars and sticks against the minorities (Hiro 1985: 113).

COUNTER-REVOLUTION AT HOME AND FOREIGN WAR TO THE FALL OF BANI-SADR

The Shi'ite dominance which began in February with the defeat of Bakhtiar had already provoked fighting in Kurdistan back in March 1979. In the same month, disturbances had broken out in the Turkoman area where demands for regional autonomy were made. In April, Kurds and Azeri-speaking Turks clashed in West Azerbaijan causing 1,000 casualties and making 12,000 Kurds homeless (Hiro 1985: 112). Government troops sent to the area sided with the Turks and stirred up deep resentment against the new regime (ibid). Following an incident in July, fighting broke out in August between Kurdish guerrillas and the Islamic revolutionary guards. It lasted for three months; during the previous three months regional Arab minorities had staged demonstrations. These incidents were put down by force and led directly to the expansion of the Pasdaran (ibid: 113).

In March 1980, fighting again broke out in Kurdistan when, in an attempt to defeat the Kurdish guerrillas (the Peshmergas), an estimated 45,000 Iranian soldiers and some 40,000 Islamic revolutionary guards were sent against the Kurds. The Peshmergas took to the mountains and maintained control over 60,000 square kilometres of the region (Nima 1983: 123). The other nationalities proved less able to resist, however, and their uprisings were suppressed.

In July 1980 a Royalist military coup planned by Bakhtiar was foiled. One hundred and eight executions resulted between July and August and 4,500 of the military were purged (Hiro 1985: 156–7). A further attempt to re-instate Bakhtiar was made in September 1980 when Iraq invaded Iran. Following a series of cross-border military actions on the part of both Iran and Iraq, stirred up especially by the rebellions of Arab peoples in Khuzestan, in September 1980 full-scale war began between Iran and Iraq (Keesing's: 31005–6). Foreign war offered Khomeini potentially ideal conditions for mobilizing patriotic support, better even than the US Embassy hostage crisis of late 1979– early 1981, which had been used to harness anti-Western sentiments (Hiro 1985: ch.5). Both the hostage crisis and the war undermined President Bani-Sadr's power. Bani-Sadr had been appointed commander-in-chief of the armed forces in February 1980 but, following adverse fortunes in the war and his conflict with the clergy at home, Khomeini ordered Bani-Sadr's dismissal as head of the army in June 1981. Demonstrations broke out in protest but on 21 June the Majlis voted to declare the president incompetent; this was approved by Khomeini the following day (Keesing's 1982: 31504–5).

In response to Bani-Sadr's dismissal, urban guerrilla warfare and street demonstrations broke out throughout the country. The Islamic revolutionary guards and the Hezbollahi waded in; the clash led to hundreds of arrests and executions on the spot (Nima 1983: 113). Fifteen were executed on 22 June alone (Keesing's 1982: 31505). A campaign was launched against all counter-revolutionaries, defined as anyone considered in sympathy with Bani-Sadr, the Mujahedin in particular, all left-wing groups in general, plus monarchists and religious minorities. Bombings and assassinations escalated. On 28 June a bomb went off in the Islamic Revolutionary Party's headquarters leaving Ayatollah Beheshti and 27 Majlis deputies, including five cabinet ministers and six deputy ministers, dead. The Mujahedin were blamed publicly by Khomeini; 200 executions took place between late June and early July (ibid: 31506). From the end of June Khomeini took control.[4]

ESCALATION OF TERROR FROM JULY 1981 TO THE CONSOLIDATION OF THE ISLAMIC REPUBLIC

On 8 July the judges in the revolutionary courts were given powers to apply 'Islamic principles' and from then on had to be qualified in Islamic law (*shari'a*). The persecution of followers of the Baha'i faith in particular, and also Jews, began to swell the numbers of executed. On 26 July, Radjai was elected president in Bani-Sadr's place and both Bani-Sadr and Rajavi, the leader of the Mujahedin, sought political asylum in France. Mujahedin and Fedayeen guerrillas continued to fight and two victories against the revolutionary guards were reported in August, followed by some desertions from the guards (Keesing's 1982: 31508). At the same time, there were further reports of counter-revolutionary activity; exiles (including ex-president Bakhtiar) were organizing forces to remove Khomeini and a new group, Azadegan, appeared on the scene, hijacking an Iranian ship.

In August, President Radjai and Prime Minister Bahonar (the new leader of the IRP) were killed in an explosion and the chief of police died in September as a result of injuries in the blast. The prime minister was temporarily replaced in the Islamic Revolutionary Council by Ayatollah Mahdavi-Kani who had previously been in charge of the revolutionary committees and security forces. Explosions and assassinations continued throughout September, and machine guns and grenades shattered the streets of Tehran as Mujahedin youths defiantly staged street demonstrations in the run-up to the new presidential elections. In October 1981, Hajatolislam Khamenei was elected overwhelmingly. For the first time a cleric had become president; Mr Moussavi became prime minister.

In consequence of this urban violence, between June 1981 and March 1982 executions mounted, with sometimes up to 100 every day (Keesing's 1982: 31510). Most of those executed were members of the Mujahedin and nearly all were aged 18–35, some younger. Generally, they were accused of 'waging war against Allah'. On 18 September the new Revolutionary Prosecutor-General, Musavi Tabrizi, recommended that members of the Mujahedin and their supporters should be executed on the same day that they were arrested in demonstrations whenever two witnesses could be found. In Tehran, wounded rebels were to be 'finished off' where they lay (Nima 1983: 114). There are no official figures published of the numbers executed at this point. Amnesty International, reporting in 1982, estimated that 2,500 executions had been carried out between June 1981 and February 1982. The total estimate from the February 1979 revolution was given as 4,000, a figure compatible with the 1981 report made by the International Commission of Jurists, whilst opposition sources abroad put the figures much higher (Keesing's 1982: 31511).

In November 1981 fighting had escalated in Kurdistan. In April 1982 the revolutionary guards launched a major attack. Though the claim was made that this attack was directed at Iraq as part of the war campaign, it has been counter-claimed that this was in fact a direct attack on the Kurds. With over a third of the Iranian army in Kurdistan the evidence lends weight to the anti-Kurd interpretation (Keesing's 1982: 31798). On 11 April 1982, Mr Qotbzadeh, a close friend of Khomeini's when in exile in Paris and a member of the Revolutionary Council until September 1980, was arrested for a conspiracy to kill Khomeini. He was executed on 16 September and his trial led to many further arrests. Mujahedin activities continued.

Nima (1983: 114–5) estimates that in 1983 there were 50,000 political prisoners, that torture had become systematic and some 12,000–

20,000 opposition forces had lost their lives between mid-1981–1982. The total officially recorded judicial executions since the revolution stood at 4,400 by July 1982. Mujahedin sources put the figure at 5,000 just between March and the end of August 1982, with over 20,000 since July 1981. Estimates for political prisoners in July–August 1982 were put at between 30,000–50,000 (Keesing's 1982: 31798). Iran has a population of around 42 million. It was reported that no case was known of a defence lawyer being available, that prison conditions were appalling with up to 80 prisoners per cell (a cell measured 5.75 × 5.75 metres) and that prisoners were subject to horrid tortures (details are given in ibid: 31799). Though Mujahedin activity continued, the Terror had achieved its aim. Towards the end of 1982 repression was reduced and by the end of January 1983 the counter-revolutionary movement had in effect been broken.

On 22 August 1982, Ayatollah Khomeini announced that laws not in line with Islam were to be abolished and judgements were to be based on religious texts. In September laws were introduced whereby couples seen kissing were to be given 100 lashes and consumption of alcohol and homosexual practices were to be punishable by death (Keesing's 1982: 31799–800). Khomeini then began moves to crush the non-violent forces of opposition. Tudeh Party leaders, who had given their support to the Islamic Republic, began to be arrested. Public trials and televised confessions followed. By May 1983 the Tudeh Party had been banned and its members arrested, 1,000 were admitted to be under arrest in May and executions were announced; many members of the armed forces were amongst them. Baha'is continued to be imprisoned and executed after refusing to reject their faith (ibid 1984: 32690). Clashes continued with Kurdish guerrillas and in May 1983 revolutionary guards, army, air force and police units combined to launch a strong assault.

By the beginning of 1984, Khomeini's Islamic Republic had gained sufficient control over the forces of opposition that the extraordinary judicial organization of the revolutionary reign of terror could be successfully brought within the control of the permanent state. On 22 January 1984, the revolutionary prosecutor, General Musavi Tabrizi, announced that the revolutionary courts were to be brought under the control of the Ministry of Justice. Having been opposed to the integration of the revolutionary courts into the state judiciary, the prosecutor general then resigned (Arjomand 1988: 16).

In April and May 1984 election of the Majlis again took place. With 90 per cent of the candidates endorsed by the Islamic Revolutionary

Party, this election represented the consolidation of the Islamic Republic. Rafsanjani was again elected Speaker, Musavi remained prime minister and Khamenei continued as president. Khamenei was re-elected in 1985 for a further four years and he reappointed Musavi in the same year for the same period. Ayatollah Khomeini, as *Wali Faqih,* retained supreme power, a power strengthened by the solid base of the Islamic Republic.[5] Control had been gained over the forces of counter-revolution at home and central state control had been achieved over the forces of the Terror itself.

The Iran-Iraq war had brought advantages to the Islamic Republic in its control over coercion. Kurdish opposition had been attacked under the guise of the war effort. The war conditions had furnished the opportunity for the Pasdaran to grow in strength and expertise in both local and foreign disturbances, whilst the Iranian army was kept busy in a purely foreign war. By the time the Islamic Republic had become fully consolidated, that is by spring 1984, it could rely fully on its own Islamic revolutionary forces. Foreign invasion provided ideal conditions for mobilizing patriotic support amongst the people, and especially so in regions where the Shi'a religion and its crusading zeal predominated. As early as 16 August 1979, Khomeini had begun making stirring speeches to 'all oppressed Moslem peoples' to 'overthrow the corrupt and tyrannical governments in the Islamic world' (Keesing's 1980: 30141).[6] Foreign invasion also provided ideal conditions for justifying demands for unanimity within the government. Opposition could be cast in the mould of counter-revolution and war conditions could then be used to strengthen the Islamic Republic over political opposition.

THE HOLD ON POWER: ISLAMIC POLICIES AND THE ECONOMY

Success in hanging on to power rests not only on the capacity of the revolutionary regime to destroy all opposition forces and gain full control over the institutions of force, it rests also on support. The numbers and nature of opposition to a revolutionary regime depend on a mixture of circumstances, some forced upon the government and others resulting from the regime's chosen policies. Revolutionary Iran had faced the conditions normally faced in reigns of terror. Iran had fought a foreign war, had faced uprisings in the regions amongst

Kurdish and Arabic nationalities and had faced strong political opposition at home with serious urban guerrilla campaigns. The regime had
managed essentially to avoid serious uprisings amongst either the large
property-owning community which had caused so many problems in
Cuba and Nicaragua for example, or amongst the ordinary working
people in rural and urban areas (generally associated with the problem
of feeding the cities), which had caused such upheaval in France,
Russia and Ethiopia.

In Iran, as in Nicaragua, the new revolutionary government had
benefited from the concentration of wealth which had accrued to the
overthrown Pahlavi regime. The fortunes of the Pahlavi Foundation
constituted 20 per cent of the total assets of all privately owned firms
in Iran (Hiro 1985: 132). These funds were swelled by the confiscation
of properties owned by the executed and properties were also confiscated from those who left the country. In March 1979 Khomeini had
established the Mustazafin Foundation which was given the task of
managing these assets, Mustazafin literally means 'deprived' (ibid:
107). The aim of this foundation was to help the needy through what
was, in effect, a redistribution of wealth through welfare programmes
directed at the poor. For example, poor families were moved into the
vacated houses of the rich and household items were given away or
auctioned for their benefit. The Foundation grew to incorporate, by
1983, nearly 500 companies, manufacturing, trading and agricultural,
and came to employ over 85,000 people. In 1984 alone the Mustazafin
Foundation built 50,000 housing units for letting to the under-privi-
leged (ibid: 253).

Welfare programmes were carried out through other means. A
Housing Foundation was set up and in June 1979 a Reconstruction
Crusade was developed to bring aid to the countryside. In this it was
helped by volunteers from the towns. Programmes included literacy
campaigns, the building of roads, bridges, drains, schools, clinics;
assistance was also given to farming, fertilizers, tractors and the like.
The Islamic message was spread at the same time. In its first two years
the crusade claimed to have built 8,000 miles of roads, 1,700 schools,
1,600 public baths and 110 health centres (Hiro 1985 254; Arjomand
1988: 143). The crusade was formed into a government ministry in
February 1984.

In addition to the Reconstruction Crusade, Khomeini set up a network of Relief Committees in the rural villages. In the summer of
1980 a further education movement had developed, followed by the

University Crusade which closed universities until they could be re-opened with Islamic, not Western, texts. This period, 1980–3, has been described as a cultural revolution (Hiro 1985: 255). Campaigns were also launched against drugs, drink and vice of any kind.

Whilst the Islamic regime has, reasonably, been compared with Robespierre's rule of virtue, the capacity of the Islamic revolutionary government to address the material hardship of the ordinary people bears no comparison with Robespierre's failure to square the circle of wage and price restraints. In stark contrast to Robespierre's disastrous cuts in maximum wages in July 1794, in Iran legislation increased workers' wages by 60 per cent and a system of price protection for essential needs was introduced to cushion the poor from inflation. Though under pressure of war wages were eventually frozen the subsidies continued (Moghadam 1989: 93). As early as May 1979, £70 million per month was being set aside to relieve the 2.5 million unemployed (Keesing's 1980: 30147). A similar approach was adopted in the treatment of war victims and their families following the start of the Iran–Iraq war in 1980. A Foundation for the War Victims and a war reconstruction fund were set up; pensions and compensations were generous (Hiro 1985: 239).

These emphases on the deprived and the programmes which followed were part of the tradition of Shii Islam. Here lay the appeal of the mullahs' mosque sermons against tyranny, injustice and extreme wealth. In bourgeois revolutions, such as the French Revolution became, the claims of the poor proved incompatible with the emphasis on the rights of private property. In socialism and Communism, the opposite is the case, the claims of those owning private property must be sacrificed in the interests of those who sell their labour. For the Islamic Republic there was no such contradiction. The right to hold private property was at all times upheld (Hiro 1985: 262). Excess and extravagance are despised in Shiism but small-scale rentier and entrepreneurial activities are welcomed. The nationalization of banks and insurance companies had taken place in June and July 1979 but only large and medium-sized industries had been taken over (Keesing's 1980: 30147). Provision for state, cooperative and private sectors had been included in the constitution and the Council of Guardians had emphasized respect for private property and business initiative in Islam (Moghadam 1989: 92). Faced with the pressures of war and the drain on the economy which war inevitably brought, many of these earlier nationalized industries were returned to the private sector after 1982 (ibid: 93).

In addition to Pahlavi property, the Iranian revolutionary regime had another economic advantage, oil. Though oil price fluctuations and inequalities in wealth distribution had played an important part in the causes of the revolution, oil production itself remained capable of generating surplus. Initially the revolutionary regime faced a sharp decline in production, at little more than 25 per cent of pre-revolutionary levels (Keesing's 1981: 31015). The war with Iraq had an immediate and devastating effect too, for crucial oil installations were bombed by Iraq. At one point, oil-refining capacity was cut by half. By May 1981, however, production had increased. In 1982–3 oil exports had risen again to US$23,000 million and Iran's budget showed a surplus of US$6 million in March 1983. Industrial production had not recovered its pre-revolutionary levels but agricultural production had outstripped 1978 figures. Even foreign debts incurred before the revolution were beginning to be repaid by 1983 (ibid 1984: 32692). By the spring of 1984, with the civil war at an end, the Islamic Republic had achieved both central control over the forces of coercion and the material basis for support.

CONFLICTS AND POLICIES: WAR AND THE FALL OF BANI-SADR

There has been a tendency in the literature on the Iranian Revolution to characterize the choices for the outcome of the revolution as between Marxist and Islamic states (see Moghadam 1989). In this analysis the willingness of the Communist Tudeh Party and Mujahedin to work with the Khomeini/Bani-Sadr Islamic Republic is viewed as misdirection:

> The entire left was preoccupied more with fighting imperialism and excoriating the US than with building socialism and a united left front. Had there been unity in the ranks, and a left–liberal alliance for a democratic and secular republic (rather than liberal collaboration with clerics in government), the trajectory of the revolution would arguably have been much different. (ibid: 88).

Certainly the outcome of the Iranian Revolution was not inevitable, but it seems doubtful that the alternatives open to it were other than a more liberal form of Islamic revolution. The Mujahedin guerrillas, who played the crucial role in the 'mini civil war' as Moghadam

(1989: 83) calls it, after Bani-Sadr's fall, were from the start an Islamic movement.[7] The Mujahedin-e Khalq, first formed in 1965, was an egalitarian Islamic movement which in 1975 split into two, Muslim and Marxist-Leninist. Both called themselves Mujahedin but in the end the Marxist-Leninists joined with some Marxist groups and formed the Paykar shortly after the revolution began (Abrahamian 1989: ch.6).

Essentially the Mujahedin were against the traditional Islam of Khomeini and, in particular against the 'reactionary dictatorship' of the Islamic state installed by Khomeini. They were opposed to the growth of the revolutionary guards, the role of Hezbollah and the dictatorial treatment of the nationalities. Rajavi, the leader of the Mujahedin and favoured by the Kurds, was not permitted by Khomeini to stand in the presidential elections of February 1980; Rajavi therefore chose to recommend support for Bani-Sadr instead. This was understandable. Bani-Sadr as a member of the Islamic Revolutionary Council had been in favour of holding a referendum in Kurdistan on self-rule and supported enlightened economic policies (Hiro 1985: 152). It was Bani-Sadr who had been the major force behind the nationalization programmes and welfare and employment improvements for the poor. As a member of the Committee of Experts who had drawn up the constitution he had also been responsible for the bill of rights which it contained (though in practice later ignored) and had been over-ruled on the attempt to include the principle of 'divine unity' which, had he succeeded, would have acted as a brake on Khomeini's power (ibid: 149).

Khomeini and Bani-Sadr were not in agreement on important issues. The elections of the Majlis in March and May 1980, when the Islamic Revolutionary Council had been replaced, provided the basis for Khomeini to assert his power over Bani-Sadr who had been overwhelmingly elected against the IRP candidates in January 1980. The IRP and its supporters formed a majority in the parliament. In the end, Bani-Sadr's removal was necessary for the consolidation of the Islamic state.

The first step had come in April 1980 when Khomeini went against Bani-Sadr's attempt to achieve a quick end to the US hostage crisis. The second step followed in August with the appointment of the IRP-backed Rajai as prime minister against Bani-Sadr's wishes. The losses incurred in the early months of the Iran–Iraq war provided the opportunity to remove him altogether. The war also provided the opportunity for the revolutionary guard to be strengthened and expanded. This too went against Bani-Sadr's wishes, for his preference was for the regular army to be developed. He attacked the IRP for its dictatorial and violent policies, including the use of torture in prisons and the role of the Hezbollah, at last acknowledged to have connections with the IRP (Hiro 1985: 171). When Iraqi troops invaded Kurdistan in November 1980, Khomeini, on religious grounds, over-ruled Bani-Sadr's wish to employ only the army in the counter-offensive and ordered that the Pasdaran also be used. The war situation ensured the growth of both the army and the revolutionary guard.

A further, crucial, split occurred between Khomeini and Bani-Sadr in March 1981. Having met the Iraqi advantage in troops by January 1981, Iran was repelling Iraqi advances by March. Potential existed for a negotiated peace as proposed by the UN Security Council, the Non-Aligned Movement and the Islamic Conference Organization (Hiro 1985: 173–4). Bani-Sadr was sympathetic to these moves, Khomeini was not. On 5 March, the anniversary of the death of Mossadeq, so admired by Bani-Sadr, a rally of 100,000 people was held at which Bani-Sadr spoke. His address to the gathering was made against Khomeini's expressed wishes. Hezbollahis disrupted the rally and Bani-Sadr used the opportunity publicly to expose their links with the IRP, the revolutionary *komitehs* and the Pasdaran.

Khomeini had then gone into religious retreat and Bani-Sadr had hit out in his newspaper against the developments in the regime; 'The question is whether the Pahlavis are to be replaced in the Islamic Republic by those wielding clubs' (Hiro 1983: 175). Khomeini re-emerged with a compromise solution aimed at investigating the accusations of torture. In defence of the war effort, however, public political speeches were banned and the findings of investigations into torture went against Bani-Sadr's claims. The combined effect of the reports and the ban on public speeches silenced Bani-Sadr for a while. These undercurrents against repression, however, remained and Mujahedin activities continued. Bani-Sadr's newspaper along with others were closed down on 6 June 1981. On the 9th, Hezbollahis took over the presidential headquarters and so began the removal of Bani-Sadr through impeachment in the Majlis.

Whilst the Iran-Iraq war formed an important background to the downfall of Bani-Sadr, the battle between Bani-Sadr on the one hand and Khomeini and the IRP on the other had been over the dictatorial nature of the Islamic Republic. Bani-Sadr's fight had essentially been against the institutionalization of terror, against the domination of the Islamic revolutionary guards (Pasdaran), the Hezbollah, the revolutionary committees and the IRP. The terror had begun in early 1979 before the outbreak of the war (September 1980) and it had reached its peak after Bani-Sadr's dismissal. The terror was at its worst not during September 1980–March 1981 when war fortunes were at their lowest but between June 1981–May 1983 when they were high. The policy of terror had not been necessary in the face of foreign war, rather it had been instrumental in the setting up of the traditional Islamic Republic of Khomeini's vision.

Skocpol, examining the extent to which the Iranian Revolution could be fitted within her generalisations about 'States and Social Revolutions', has remarked on Iran's good fortune, in comparison with France, in not being plunged into further foreign wars (Skocpol 1982: 279). There is, indeed, no denying that defeat in foreign war has potential for destroying governments, and not only new revolutionary ones. In Iran, the war proved not only an advantage to Khomeini but was actively encouraged by his appeals to Iraqis (a majority of whom were Shii) to overthrow President Saddam Hussein and his Sunni-Muslim dominated Ba'athist government, described by Khomeini as 'non-Muslim' (Hiro 1985: 166). Relations between the two countries quickly deteriorated; diplomatic relations broken off in June 1980. Certainly, the disagreements between Bani-Sadr and the IRP, in suggesting easy victory, made Iran a more tempting target for invasion by Iraq (ibid: 167). On the other hand, the evidence has suggested that without the war Bani-Sadr could have tipped the balance against the IRP and thereby kept the terror within bounds.

THE BALANCE BETWEEN POLICY AND NECESSITY

The new revolutionary government in Iran had faced a foreign war from September 1980. The Sandinista government in Nicaragua had, too, faced foreign war on two fronts but there the government had succeeded in avoiding a reign of terror. Nicaragua had had the immediate benefit of Somoza's properties, but so too had Iran benefited from the vast Pahlavi family fortunes. Furthermore, Iran's economy had far greater potential for producing surplus than had Nicaragua's crop economy. Like Iran, Nicaragua had had problems in its regions, but these problems had not escalated into civil war, and a comparable 'mini civil war' had not broken out in the towns as it had in Iran, reaching its peak between mid-1981–mid-1983 and continuing into 1984. In this, events in Tehran between 1981–3, seemed remarkably similar to those in Addis Ababa, 1976–8. Iran, like Ethiopia, Russia and France before, had faced the disadvantage of civil war breaking out after the revolutionary regime had come to power.

In practice, however, the civil war in Iran had been comparatively weak. Only in Kurdistan had a base for alternative government been established. Ironically, the dispute between President Bani-Sadr and the traditional clergy served to weaken the development of a full civil war. The president, in sympathy with Kurdish demands, nationalization and welfare programmes and peace with Iraq, represented the potential alternative to a dictatorial Islamic state. The role of Khomeini as Supreme Jurisprudent, aloof yet in control, enabled the piecemeal dismemberment of Bani-Sadr's power whilst allowing for the coercive forces of the future state to develop. Though candidates were scrutinized by Khomeini and his decisions tipped the balance towards IRP members and clerics, elections produced the desired effect of weakening opposition, just as the election had in Nicaragua.

Whereas in Nicaragua, however, civil and human rights legislation had bolstered the government's democratic claims, in Iran the opposite tack had been employed. Almost immediately upon coming to power in February 1979, Khomeini had begun to introduce the organs for Terror. In the strength of the Iranian economy and the weakness of the civil war had lain the potential for a moderate Terror. The continuation of the war had undermined this economic strength just as it had in Nicaragua. Economic problems had grown until in 1986 an Emergency Plan had had to be introduced (Moghadam 1989: 93). Whilst the foreign war had forced economic austerity and political centrality, continuation of the war against Bani-Sadr's wishes had reflected a policy chosen rather than simply backed into. The treatment of prisoners and excess of executions equally reflected choice. Further proof of this was to be found in the continuation of executions beyond 1984 and in the protests against the inhumanity of the regime, which began to be voiced clearly by other Ayatollahs.

DIVISIONS WITHIN THE ESTABLISHMENT

Executions did not stop with the consolidation of the Islamic Republic in 1984 though, from then on, executions were carried out not under laws designed against counter-revolutionaries and implemented in revolutionary courts but under Islamic laws carried out through the Islamic state judicial system. Guerrilla movements, in Kurdistan especially, continued, though at reduced levels, and the Iran–Iraq war carried on, too. Execution, imprisonment and torture of those unconnected with the war and guerrilla movements were also reported, in particular executions of Baha'is and those accused of corruption and vice. Amnesty International put the number of executions for 1985 at 400 including Baha'is (Keesing's 1985: 33950).[8] Opposition to treatment of prisoners was voiced by Montazeri as early as November 1984. Probably out of respect for Montazeri, in the summer of 1985 the revolutionary prosecutor in Tehran was replaced, as too were some prison officials at Tehran's Evin prison, and during 1985–6 around half of all prisoners were released (ibid 1986: 34700). Indeed at that time some open criticism of government was encouraged.

At the end of 1985, Ayatollah Montazeri was designated successor to Khomeini on the latter's death. It is difficult to say whether this focused Khomeini's attention on Montazeri as his main opponent or not. Certainly the trial and execution of Hashemi, the brother of Montazeri's brother-in-law, for 'waging war against Islam' and being 'corrupt on earth' damaged Montazeri's standing and the execution was viewed within Iran as having some connection with power struggles (Keesing's 1987: 35541–2). Whatever the exact connection, the IRP was disbanded in June 1987 on the grounds that it had become, in Khomeini's words, 'an excuse for discord and factionalism' (ibid: 35542). At the very least, the end of the IRP helped to turn attention away from the demonstrations against the war staged by the revolutionary guards in Tehran in May 1987.[9]

The Gulf war was stepped up later in 1987 and in November one of the five Grand Ayatollahs, Qomi, who had been under house arrest since 1985, spoke out against the war, declaring it un-Islamic and sinful. He also spoke out against repression, directing particular attention to the treatment of prisoners and the accusation that innocent people were being executed. Arrests followed. By the spring of 1988 other Ayatollahs were calling for an end to the war and violent anti-Khomeini demonstrations took place, leading to a ban on public marches in May 1988 (Keesing's 1988: 36054). Elections were held for the Majlis in April and May 1988. Rafsanjani was again elected Speaker and appointed commander-in-chief of the armed forces, deputizing for Khomeini. In July 1988 a ceasefire was concluded for the Iran–Iraq war and from then to the beginning of 1989 the numbers of executions increased.

The war had brought victory to neither side but was very damaging to Iran fighting a holy war, for Allah had not seemed to bring favour to Shii over Sunni Moslems. Again, however, the war seems to have been used for the purpose of suppressing political opposition. Most of those killed in the latter half of 1988–9 were already in prison, locked up, with or without trial, as opponents of the regime. As before, the Mujahedin figured high amongst the executed. The UN Commission on Human Rights mentioned 200 Mujahedin killed at Evin prison on 28 July 1988 and a total of 860 bodies of executed prisoners being transferred to a cemetery on 14–16 August. Amnesty International estimated that several thousand prisoners had probably been killed. Mujahedin estimates put the figure at 5,000. It was also reported that a fire on 26 October at Evin prison had probably been a deliberate mass execution. Several hundred 'drug traffickers', an expression considered to be a veiled term for Montazeri supporters were also executed (Keesing's 1989: 36629–31).

In November 1988 a number of clergymen, all supporters of Montazeri, were executed. This came after Montazeri's public declarations in October against torture and execution as un-Islamic: 'Islam is based on principles of forgiveness and compassion, but we have yet to learn this from the prophet's nobel legacy' (Keesing's 1989: 36631). Montazeri also attacked the government's economic policies. Whether bowing to pressure of opinion or simply now that he was assured of total control, in January 1989 Khomeini appeared to change position; he defended 'reformist theologians' and attacked the Council of Guardians for indulging in theological debates at the expense of the practicalities of politics. In February, marking the tenth anniversary of the Islamic Republic, an amnesty was announced for all but 900 prisoners, those remaining being mainly left-wing militants (ibid). In March 1989 Montazeri resigned as Khomeini's successor.

It was not Islam in general, nor even Shi'ite Islam in particular, that had led to the excesses of Terror in Iran. Rather those excesses followed from the vision of an Islamic Republic as first theorized and then adapted practically by Khomeini. As Bani-Sadr, the Mujahedin, Montazeri and Qomi had shown, it was not a vision shared by everyone.[10] The subjection of the political to the spiritual had necessitated the rejection of opposition, in whatever form it took. In the end, even the IRP, sponsored by the Islamic government itself, had been dispensable.

COMPARATIVE PERSPECTIVES

The Iranian Revolution has been compared with Robespierre's Republic of Virtue (Skocpol 1982: 279), a comparison which is entirely understandable in view of the important moralizing aspects of the revolution. Essentially, however, the two cases are direct opposites of each other. In France the peoples' armies, the equivalent of the Pasdaran, had been involved in a de-christianization programme fundamentally opposed to traditional religion. Those armies' more thuggish elements, perhaps the equivalents of the Hezbollah, had dispersed masses, broken up churches and destroyed religious edifices. In essence, the Jacobin Terror in both its anarchistic and state forms had represented the dominance of the political over the religious rather than the reverse which characterized Iran under the Ayatollahs. The appeal to reason made by Robespierre had been an attempt to distil the moral order, which had once rested on Roman Catholicism, from the residue of corruption and injustice into which the church (with its strong monarchical connections) had fallen in revolutionaries' eyes.

If there is a parallel with Iran it is perhaps the English Puritan Revolution, where religious and moral legislation preoccupied the short-lived Barebones parliament and where minority religious groups, such as the Shakers, Quakers (and Presbyterians), were persecuted and some executed. A parallel exists here with the treatment of the Baha'is and Jews though the scale of deaths was far greater in Iran and the Barebones parliament lasted less than a year. The anti-Catholic dimension of the Puritan Revolution and the consequent Terror in Ireland draws a more important source of comparison. The war against unbelievers in the true Christian God has similarities with the war against the unbelievers in the true Allah against the Sunni-dominated government of Iraq and against the Sunni-Kurds and Arabic minorities. The religious war ruled out compromise and was used to justify the barbaric treatment of prisoners.

There is a sense in which both the Puritan and the Islamic revolutions looked both backwards and forwards at the same time. Both looked back to the religious texts, the true faith as found in religious teachings (see Halliday 1988: 34). In these could be found justification for overthrowing absolute monarchies. The Divine Right claimed by Charles I could be denied only where interpretations of the true faith and therefore the true God were in dispute. The Shah was an easier target in the light of the existing political challenge to his legitimacy following the coup against Mossadeq. In challenging traditional Islam, through westernization, he had taken upon himself the claim that he held the true interpretation of the Shi'ite religion. Looking back to traditional texts gave strength to the Shah's overthrow. At the same time, both revolutions were modern too, in as far as both proposed a political system quite different from what went before and a social system lopped off at the top. For both, the elected parliament (in Iran, the Majlis) was to be the crucial debating chamber and the source for initiating legislation with a handful of 'guardians' to oversee proceedings, the Star Chamber and the Council of Guardians. Unlike in China and Russia neither revolution had aimed at total social transformation, both had limited their aim to that of removing the top layer of society, the very rich, without greatly disturbing the lower layers.

Arjomand has labelled the Islamic Republic both fascist (1986) and totalitarian (1988). The fascist label seems unnecessary once the totalitarian label is adopted, for totalitarian regimes have been compatible with both Communist (Stalin's USSR) and fascist (Hitler's Germany) ideologies. Rather than adopting Arjomand's unconvincing argument that fascism is revolutionary, and squeezing Khomeini's vision of an Islamic state into the fascist category, it would seem preferable to view it as a third type of ideology suitable for a totalitarian state. It fits Arendt's insistence that totalitarian regimes draw on ideologies which are not new to the regime, though the proof that the Islamic Republic in fact constituted a totalitarian state requires detailed analysis. The arguments put forward in this chapter, in identifying the years 1979– spring 1984 as a revolutionary reign of terror, clearly challenge the claim that Iran had a totalitarian regime before 1984. With the suppression of opposition and central control over the organs of state, by the beginning of 1984, then certainly the way was open for such a regime to be developed. As argued at various points in this book the end of a revolutionary reign of terror offers no guarantee that state violence will cease after the establishment of the permanent state.

There is then one comparison above all which has been missed in the literature on Iran, though by implication, in drawing comparison with the Jacobins, it has been there. The rule of the Ayatollahs in Iran has passed through a revolutionary reign of terror with parallels in England, France, Russia, China, Cuba and Ethiopia. This recognition again draws attention to an important theoretical conclusion: the temporary institutions of Terrors should not be confused with the permanent structures of state-building. Temporary institutions (such as the revolutionary courts) can be subsumed within permanent state ministries but revolutionary institutions can be disbanded, too. The IRP is just the last in a long line of revolutionary organizations sacrificed in the search for permanent government.

NOTES

1. For particularly good and full analyses of pre-revolutionary Iran see Halliday (1979) and Arjomand (1988).
2. For the above paragraph see Keesing's 1979: 29733–45.
3. These ideas on the role of the Supreme Jurisprudent followed from Khomeini's book *Wilayat e Faqih*. See Arjomand (1988: 148–9) who argues that at the time of writing the book Khomeini had only a vague idea of the nature of the intended state. See Zubaida (1982) for a detailed examination of Khomeini's doctrine of government. Zubaida confirms (p.153) that Khomeini seems to limit the role of government to the collection of taxes and to punishment. Khomeini was also given power over the appointment and dismissal of high-ranking members of the armed forces, the judiciary and candidacy for the presidency. The Supreme Jurisprudent was to represent the legitimacy of the regime' and could intervene either directly or indirectly through the Council of Guardians (Keesing's 1980: 30145).
4. For a full account of the role played in the revolution by the Mujahedin, see Abrahamian (1989). The Mujahedin were generally sympathetic to the theological thinker Shari'ati rather than Khomeini. The meeting with Khomeini in 1975 probably caused the split within the Mujahedin into the Islamic and non-Islamic (Marxist) factions. Khomeini was judged by the non-Islamic group as 'reactionary' (see Abrahamian 1989: 149–51). See Zubaida (1982) for the crucial differences between Khomeinis' and (the more revolutionary and more modern) Shari'ati.
5. See Keesing's 1985: 33948 and 1986: 34699. Arjomand (1988: 155) dates 'the definite consolidation of the theocratic regime in Iran' as 15 December 1982. By this date, he argues that armed opposition had been 'largely destroyed'. Given the continuing problems with the Kurds and attack on unarmed opposition (members of the Tudeh Party especially) yet to come, Arjomand's date seems premature. As the general lessons of revolutionary reigns of terror have shown, true consolidation could not be achieved whilst the extraordinary organizations of the terror retained a level of independence from the central state.
6. Such utterings against US agents had also inspired the students' takeover of the US Embassy in Tehran (see Hiro 1985: ch.5).
7. The Fedayeen also played a significant part, though they were less dominant than the Mujahedin. The Fedayeen were Marxist-Leninist, (see Abrahamian 1989).
8. The Mujahedin claimed in September 1984 that since June 1981 the total executions had reached 10,031 with 9,000 of them Mujahedin 'members or sympathisers' (Keesing's 1985: 33950). By September 1985 the estimate had reached 12,000 executions. The number of political prisoners in September 1984 was put at 120,000. Estimates of executions made by the UN Human Rights Commission published in early 1987 put the figure at 7,000 (ibid 1987: 35543).
9. Arjomand (1988: 171–2) argues that the revolutionary guard was the only organization of the Islamic Republic which had 'ideological problems' with the regime. The guards seemed to be opposed to the more conservative Ayatollahs.

Though Arjomand does not say so, presumably there was then sympathy within the guard for Montazeri.

10.   Appositely, Montazeri remarked on 12 February 1989, 'the people of the world thought that our task in Iran was to kill people' (Keesing's 1989: 36631). Montazeri also opposed Khomeini's stand against Salman Rushdie (The *Guardian*, 30 March 1989).

PART V
Conclusions

12. Comparative Lessons from Revolutionary Terrors: The Establishment of the Revolutionary State

Ethiopia and Iran, like England, France, Russia, China and Cuba before them passed through a revolutionary reign of terror: a stage of revolution which rests on laws which proscribe counter-revolution, so widely defined that the innocent are drawn in, in ever larger numbers, and stipulates execution for some and imprisonment for others which in practice, through the squalor of conditions at least and deliberately cruel treatment at worst, condemn many more to death through disease and suffering; a reign of terror which does away with the niceties of procedure and introduces summary justice where time is inadequate for gathering evidence, where defence counsel and appeal courts are absent and where the witnesses for the suspect's crime can also be at one and the same time the force that arrests, prosecutes, judges and executes the suspect. The innocent are drawn in and justice becomes arbitrary; a regime which constructs in order to carry through these revolutionary laws and punishments, a machinery of terror – revolutionary police and secret police forces, revolutionary courts or tribunals and prison systems hurriedly constructed for the crisis of counter-revolution.

Each Terror was not the same, but similar enough in construction of its coercive institutions for the administration of summary justice: institutions to gather information and to round-up suspects, courts or tribunals to administer revolutionary justice and the growth of a system for the detainment, correction or execution of the accused. In France these comprised the local surveillance committees, the people's armies, the Representatives on Mission, the revolutionary tribunals and, towards the end of the Terror, the police bureau. Ships and warehouses were brought in to serve as makeshift prisons, prisons in which droves of people met their death and from which thousands more were led to execution. Above all this was the political structure of the Terror itself, the Committees of Public Safety and General Security.

A classic example of a reign of terror was found in the Russian case. There the Cheka combined the tasks of the surveillance committees, the people's armies and the revolutionary tribunals. There the VeCheka (the Moscow Cheka) carried out the role of the Committee of General Security; above the Cheka was Sovnarkom, the Russian equivalent of the Committee of Public Safety. In Russia, prisons were supplemented by labour and concentration camps. In China a secret police force developed under the Ministry of Security (Gonganqu) that permeated deeply into society through urban local committees and rural local governments. *Yundong* (mass mobilization movements) were developed to flush out counter-revolutionaries for trial before local people's tribunals. A system of camps for punishment and re-education were developed under the Ministry of Security, and above this was the Government Administrative Council and regional military control.

In Cuba, G2 developed from military intelligence and became the organization in charge of surveillance; under G2, the civilian branch of the militia, the local Committees for the Defence of the Revolution (CDR), played their part as informers. Military tribunals were used to try the accused and as the prisons bulged, buildings such as old fortresses were put into use. Above these, Castro held control over a coalition government and a country divided into military regions. In Ethiopia, the military courts, the *kebelles* and the soldiers (and for a time the people's militia) gathered information, arrested suspects and administered summary justice. Over these, the Provisional Military Administrative Council (PMAC), later returning to the title of the Derg, held revolutionary power. In England, too, the military, the New Model Army, played its part in capturing and administering 'revolutionary justice' in Ireland, and in England an effective intelligence system was introduced. In the English Revolution it was the Rump and Barebones parliaments that presided over the Terror. Lastly, in Iran it was the Islamic Revolutionary Council which held sway over the Islamic revolutionary courts, the revolutionary committees (*komitehs*), the revolutionary guards (Pasdaran), the Hezbollah and SAVAMA. There, as in other reigns of terror, the numbers of executions rose and prisons were stretched beyond capacity.

Each of these reigns of terror had defined its own counter-revolutionaries. Those who had held power in the old order whether members of the aristocracy or simply torturers were certainly amongst them, but each Terror had added new groups, not members of the old élite but ordinary people. In the Chinese Revolution, for example, under the 'regulations regarding the punishment of counter-revolutionaries' of February 1951, in addition to the obvious counter-revolutionaries – those actively engaged in rebellion, espionage, supplying military equipment, being a former Nationalist and belonging to a secret society (normally a sign of being a Nationalist) – people who refused simply to pay taxes, to hand over grain or 'carry out any command' were classified as counter-revolutionaries. In France, under the law of suspects, suspicion alone of having counter-revolutionary opinions was enough; similarly behaviour such as withholding grain or supplies could be taken as evidence of opinion. In Russia speculators, hoarders, peasants withholding grain, petty blackmailers (bagmen) could be shot on the spot, and there, too, labour crimes (like failure to turn up to work) could also count as an act of counter-revolution. Similarly in China, under the three and five antis movements, work crimes had been made acts of counter-revolution and thought itself the basis for public denunciation. In Ethiopia damaging transport or public property was a counter-revolutionary crime as was attempting to leave the country. As in Iran, being young could be sufficient to be considered a counter-revolutionary and so lead to execution. In Cuba attempting to leave the country with more possessions than the ungenerous basic minimum permitted was considered a counter-revolutionary act (though in Cuba's mild terror imprisonment, not execution, would be the prescribed punishment).

In Iran, as in England, acts of counter-revolution included membership of religious groups and sexual behaviour too, whilst in France celebrating mass became a counter-revolutionary act. In England celebrating Christmas was for a time banned and being an Irish Catholic living in the wrong part of Ireland became counter-revolutionary during the Puritan Revolution. In Iran, intellectual opposition to Khomeini's vision of an Islamic state became classed as an act of counter-revolution because it declared war on Allah himself. Groups in dispute over religious interpretation, both Christian and Islamic, and nationalities, Kurds, Eritreans and the Irish, had all become groups against whom Terror had raged. Class conflict had certainly played its part, against big landowners and the very rich especially, but the Terror had cut across classes too and, as in the case of the rural–urban conflict brought on by starvation, it had cast poor against poor. Terror had struck out

against counter-revolution whence-so-ever it had come and in whatso-
ever form it had taken.

THE CAUSES OF REVOLUTIONARY TERROR: TOWARDS NEW UNDERSTANDING

This work had begun with a tentative hypothesis about revolutionary
reigns of terror which focused on the importance of the timing (pre- or
post-revolutionary takeover), the virulence of civil wars and the inter-
play between the crisis faced by the revolutionary regime and the
policies implemented by the revolutionaries. The hypothesis contra-
dicted existing hypotheses in two important ways: It claimed that
domestic counter-revolution was of greater importance to Terrors than
were foreign wars (national more important than international factors)
and that revolutionary reigns of terror might not represent a necessary
stage of revolution, unavoidable against the pressure of a law-like set
of crisis conditions. The proposition allowed that crises faced by revolutionary governments were to some degree self-made, reflecting the
policies chosen by the revolutionary regimes. It followed from the
emphasis on policy choice that along with the question of necessity it
was important also to consider excess both in the toll of victims and in
the nature of the suffering. Given the prime importance of civil wars,
however, only where civil war had occurred before the revolutionary
overthrow would the revolutionaries, if they so wished, stand a chance
of avoiding a reign of terror. In focusing both on civil war and excess,
attention was drawn especially to the value of guerrilla movements
which came to power not only having defeated the counter-revolutionary forces of the old state but also with the vital support gained
through their good behaviour, and understanding of people's needs.
This consideration itself drew attention to the important difference
between guerrilla movement revolutions and spontaneous ones.

The analysis and comparative lessons drawn from the cases lent
weight to these propositions and contributed further understanding.
France, Russia, Iran and Ethiopia all had spontaneous revolutions where
virulent civil wars had broken out after coming to power. There reigns
of terror had raged. In the Puritan Revolution, too, civil war had
erupted in Ireland after the revolutionaries had come to power, and
there also Terror had reigned, yet in England where civil war had been
fought before takeover events had proved very mild in comparison.

America and Nicaragua, where reigns of terror were avoided, had both fought civil wars before the revolutionary regime attained power and in both cases the revolutionary programme was moderate. Cuba and China, too, fought civil wars before the revolutionaries came to power, civil wars, furthermore, propelled through guerrilla movements. In Cuba, faced with organized counter-revolutionary movements within and around the Camagüey province and, of all revolutions, the most dependent economy, the Terror was kept mild. In China, where the most fundamental revolutionary changes of all were implemented, a reign of terror had developed, how anarchic it is impossible to say; but the differences between the old and newly liberated areas had shown clearly the advantages of civil war in reducing the virulence of reigns of terror before coming to power.

The array of people's actions and attitudes classified as counter-revolutionary – nationalities, religious groups, bagmen and the like as well as rich landowners, businessmen, torturers and so on – demonstrates that revolutionary ideology certainly played a part, as did consideration of the economic problems faced by the revolutionaries. Whilst inherited from pre-revolutionary society, made worse by the revolutionary upheaval itself and exacerbated by the crisis of civil and foreign wars, economic problems were, in part, caused by the policies introduced and the methods employed by the revolutionaries themselves. Ethiopia has proved the most glaring example, where revolutionary policies brought starvation to cities, Addis Ababa in particular, through a breakdown in distribution following agrarian reform. In France, on the other hand, the problem of distribution had been essentially inherited from long before 1789; the problem of feeding Paris had existed for a century. In France, though, as in Russia, choice of force in extracting supplies and grain from peasants exacerbated the crisis against which Terror raged.

Consideration of the fundamental nature of reforms introduced by the revolutionaries has also shown that relative considerations need to be taken into account, in particular inherited economic conditions. In Nicaragua the vacancy of Somoza lands eased the impact of agrarian reforms and helped the Sandinistas, prior to takeover, to reduce potential counter-revolution after coming to power. International economic aid from a variety of sources had also been forthcoming. Along with their revolutionary ideology (a mixed economy and a government of national unity, elections and human rights) and their advantage of victory through civil war, the Nicaraguans avoided a reign of terror.

America was similarly fortunate. There the war of independence had beaten opposition, the revolution had not sought fundamental change and the economy had been strong. In England victory in civil war, a buoyant economy after 1650 and an avoidance of far-reaching economic and social reforms had made terror almost negligible. In Ireland, however, where the policies introduced were fundamental and civil war raged, the Terror was virulent. Iran too had faced a strong economy and there, as in Ireland, religious and nationalist policies added to the Terror.

Foreign war played its part in these revolutions but it was secondary to the problems of civil war, the combined armed and unarmed insurrections faced at home. For France, Greer has long established the relatively greater importance for the reign of terror of civil over foreign war; France had not been drawn into war through international pressures, the National Assembly had earlier chosen to embark on foreign war in order to detract attention from problems at home. In Russia foreign powers had played but a minor role in comparison with the civil war, and the Polish war had been turned into a revolutionary war by the Bolsheviks as part of their revolutionary policy. As in the English Revolution and the Dutch war, the Iranian Revolution and the war with Iraq, the Ethiopian Revolution and the war with Somalia, these were not wars impressed upon the revolutions by the force of international circumstances. In England the Navigation Acts had been actively provocative to the United Provinces. In Iran, before the war, Shii Moslems everywhere had been urged to rise against the Sunni government of Iraq and actions against the nationalities at home had drawn Iraq towards war; the war had also proved invaluable in the battle to dislodge Bani-Sadr. In Ethiopia, too, Somalia had been drawn in to defend the liberation movement in the Ogaden and in Ethiopia a raging civil war had led to foreign war. It had been in China and Cuba that international pressures impinged directly on the revolution. In China the Korean war had burst upon the new revolutionary regime and in Cuba foreign invasion threatened through to the spring of 1961. Yet it was Cuba, where the mildest terror occurred, that stood out for being most constrained by international pressures, and Nicaragua even under the pressure of the Contra war did not sink into a reign of terror.

The view taken by the literature on reigns of terror as dictatorships backed into through the necessity of crisis, with a particular emphasis on international factors, seems to reflect a failure to view revolutions as a study of politics, that is to say as the study of the institutions of government and of the policy process, a view of the policy process which includes changes not only demanded by groups within the population (the workers starving in the towns and peasants dying in the countryside, the nationalities wanting independence and so on) but also initiated directly by government in accordance with revolutionary ideology. Even in modern democracies policies do not only originate with the people. Having initiated revolutionary policies, revolutionaries, like any government, must assess reaction in order to judge the degree of popular support that the policies have and respond accordingly. The choice is essentially between adjustment of policies to gain additional support or the use of coercion. As the cases in this volume have shown, demands will grow or subside in reaction to government policies and the methods employed to implement them.

THE CRITICAL PERIOD AT THE END OF CIVIL WAR

Investigation into the importance of civil wars in pushing terrors to their peak has drawn attention to the importance of domestic insurrection after the armed civil war has been brought under control. The need to respond with practical solutions to the economic problems which so often underlie such insurrections becomes very important where people face starvation, in the capital city most especially. Lenin's introduction of NEP has proved the clearest example of this for it constituted a change in policy. Governments do not, however, rely only on support, they rely also on force. Sometimes that force is naked, demands are brutally suppressed; at other times, most notably in modern democracies, the passage of time enables force to remain a threat covered by laws.

These reigns of terror were periods when revolutionary governments wrestled with crisis, mostly civil not foreign, and used terror in response. Whilst the crisis situations were real enough, some at least of the threats faced were the direct result of the revolutionary governments' own policies. The more transformatory the revolutionaries' aims and the more coercive the methods adopted, the more excessive the terror became. To some extent this was a vicious circle: the outbreak of civil war led to terror in defence of the revolution but civil war was itself, in part at least, likely to have been provoked by government policies, whether policy aims or the methods chosen to carry them through, or some combination of both; these policies were in turn likely to be, in part, a response to the crisis situation. The very urgency of the revolutionary crisis, which required quick actions, urgent decisions and the creation of laws and institutions, with inadequate preparation or time for gradual implementation, heightened the problem of control over the Terror.

Whilst the temporary period of the Terror potentially laid the foundations upon which permanent order could be built – the introduction of revolutionary policies through which support could be strengthened, the suppression of opposition through revolutionary laws and the construction of new coercive forces (the army, judiciary, courts, police, and sometimes secret police) – it offered no guarantee that the leaders of the Terror would themselves establish the new revolutionary state. The very speed of events, the newness of the institutions and the heat of the crisis situation itself meant that the new revolutionary forces of coercion operated in part at least beyond the revolutionaries' control. If control over the forces of coercion created for the Terror failed, the revolutionaries lost the capacity to hang on to power. With the civil war over, terror had lost its justification and emergency government needed to be replaced by a permanent revolutionary state. That process, however, had required that central control be gained over those revolutionary institutions of terror themselves. Failure to do so meant loss of support.

In both France and Russia, as the civil war had been brought to an end, domestic insurrection had broken out in protest both against economic policies and terror. In France, Robespierre had failed to gain control over the terror and over the Committee of General Security in particular. In Russia, through party organization and flexible economic policies, Lenin had succeeded in bringing the Cheka under central control. Party organization proved crucial in China, too, and in Iran the Islamic Revolutionary Party, along with the *komitehs* was used to establish and then gain control over the forces of coercion of the new Islamic state. In Ethiopia, however, the army destroyed the militia and gained control over the armed *kebelles* largely by force, and at the other extreme, in Cuba, Castro succeeded in running down the professional army and building a volunteer force, the people's militia, largely through popular support. In America where a revolutionary reign of terror was avoided, a professional army had been deliberately rejected from the start. In England, Leveller dissension within the New Model Army was put down with force by loyal members of the military.

The view of Terrors taken by this study, siding with Brinton, has not been that of tightly reined dictatorships but rather of temporary regimes pivotal to success in the establishment of revolutionary regimes. The evidence has confirmed this view: in all cases where revolutionary reigns of terror developed, those Terrors eventually gave way to new government structures: in France, the Committee of Public Safety ended with Thermidor; in England the Barebones parliament was replaced by the Protectorate, itself replaced by the restoration of a constitutional monarchy (as indeed, for a time, was the French Republic). In Russia, China, Cuba and Ethiopia temporary government over Terror gave way to a Communist Party state. In contrast to Russia and China, where the party had played an important part in the revolution and came to prominence over military organizations necessary in times of crisis, in Cuba and Ethiopia following alliance with the USSR, a party was built after the revolutionary overthrow. Whilst China had gained some help from the USSR after its revolution, that had some influence on state construction, in Cuba and Ethiopia relations with the Soviet Union were decisive. As emphasized in both these cases the Marxist-Leninist model of the revolutionary state had been introduced from outside rather than emerging from within the revolution itself. As in Ethiopia with Seded, party construction during the reign of terror proved temporary in Iran. Without external constraint the Islamic state was established through the Islamic Revolutionary Party which was later disbanded.

Originally included to emphasize the role of public support, consideration of the three guerrilla-movement revolutions, China, Cuba and Nicaragua, has also demonstrated the special advantage which these revolutions had in establishing the revolutionary forces of the new state. The movements themselves provided the forces for the new army, new police force, the reshaping of the judiciary and courts, and for China and Cuba the new secret police. China had the double advantage of a party–guerrilla force, but it has been Nicaragua where a reign of terror was avoided that has afforded the most significant lesson. There the FSLN kept control over the coercive forces, the army and police, and maintained a plural system in other arenas. The Nicaraguan case seems to have demonstrated most clearly of all that the established state rests on a mixture of coercion and support.[1]

THE STATE BASED ON SUPPORT AND COERCION: MARX AND WEBER

There is of course nothing new in this emphasis on importance of support combined with state control over the coercive forces. It is to be found in the Marxist analysis where, at each stage of evolution (Asiatic, ancient, feudal or capitalist), the state represents the interests of the owners of the means of production, the ruling class, and acts as an instrument of coercion against the majority. In the context of the 1848 revolutions, for example, Marx discusses state power in terms of the police, army, courts and bureaucracy and declares the police to be 'the ultimate expression of the old state' (Marx 1973: 205). It is to be found in Engels' distinction between the 'political state', the machinery for the coercion of people, and 'the simple administrative functions of watching over the true interests of society' to be established after the proletarian revolution in the theorized non-coercive, non-class dominated Communist society (Engels 1874, 'On Authority', in Feuer 1969: 522). These themes are expanded upon by Lenin in 1917 in *The State and Revolution* (McLellan 1986: ch.4) where, building on Marx's 1875 *Critique of the Gotha Programme*, Lenin argues that during the period of transition between capitalism and Communism, the dictatorship of the proletariat will retain new revolutionary forces of coercion, 'a new machinery of organized armed workers' (ibid: 256) to be used by the majority against the minority. However, in line with the Marxist tradition Lenin maintains that this 'special machinery for suppression will gradually cease to exist' (ibid: 235).

For Marxist thinkers, whilst the state rests on a combination of support and coercion, prior to the proletarian revolution support is limited to the minority ownership class; during the transitionary dictatorship of the proletariat support comes from the majority but excludes the old ownership class; and in the final stage, the Communist society, support is total and therefore in this one society the state has no need of coercion. It is hardly new to point out that the coercive organs of the state did not 'wither away' in the USSR and that such was the case for these other revolutions too. The cases have also drawn attention to an aspect of state formation not considered, the need to gain control over the new revolutionary forces of coercion themselves (the terror machine in any case developed far beyond Lenin's conception of a 'people's militia' – see Lenin, 'The April Theses', 1970: 37). This was a problem which Lenin was to face after 1917.

The revolutions covered have nevertheless confirmed, up to a point, the advantages of a Marxist perspective. Consideration of the interests served by the policies introduced by these revolutionary governments has proved particularly instructive. Comparison between cases where policies of fundamental material transformation were introduced, in China, Russia and Ethiopia especially, and economically more moderate revolutions, such as America, England, Nicaragua, Iran (and Cuba to begin with), has drawn valuable attention to the inherent class conflicts involved and brought understanding not only to the question of support but also to the development of alienation, which sometimes produced active and new bases of counter-revolution. In this sense Skocpol's (1985) heavy insistence (see Cammack's 1989 criticism) on the need to view states in operation separate from class analysis is misplaced. Where revolutionary governments are guided in their policy-making by class interests (which is especially likely to be the case where the revolution has installed a Communist Party) and where classes are capable of acting 'for themselves', then new revolutionary regimes will be obliged to respond to their needs. The introduction of NEP in Russia was surely such a response – to the demands of the middle peasant as much as to the proletariat.

At the same time the revolutions covered here have also shown that class interests are neither the only crucial base of support and social conflict nor the only inspiration for policy-making. In England and Ethiopia military interests were served; more generally, national differences and religious divisions also played their part. In Iran the mullahs' religious interests were served by the revolution whilst the Baha'is and Sunni Kurds lost out. In England it was religious minorities, and most especially the Irish Catholics, who bore the brunt, whilst in Ethiopia it was the Eritreans. In France, whilst the clergy had formed part of the ruling class, peasants simply wishing to practise their faith had faced terror. Even in Nicaragua the special interests of the Miskito Indians had to be addressed and in Russia vital support amongst the nationalities was won through policy choices. In general, the stronger the support gained, from wherever it came, the less the state needed to rely on coercion; indeed it was this very consideration that first directed attention to the importance of policy-making and civil war (counter-revolution at home), in this study of Terrors.

It is in Weber's work that a study of this combination of more general support and force as bases of the state is to be found. In his 'Politics as a Vocation' (1918), Weber opens with an acceptance of

Trotsky's declaration at Brest–Litovsk that 'Every state is founded on force' (Gerth and Mills 1970: 78) and defines the state as 'a human community that (successfully) claims the *monopoly of the legitimate use of physical force* within a given territory' (ibid).[2] In this light, the need for revolutionary governments first to gain control over the forces of counter-revolution, armed civil war most especially, and then to gain control over revolutionary terror exercised outside of the law, turns out to be exactly what would have been predicted. Crucially though Weber (ibid) expands on this and generalizing for all time adds the dimension of obedience:

> Like the political institutions preceding it, the state is a relation of men, a relation supported by means of legitimate (i.e. considered to be legitimate) violence. If the state is to exist, the dominated must obey the authority claimed by the powers that be.

Weber then asks the questions 'When and why do men obey? Upon what inner justifications and upon what external means does this domination rest?' In answer he offers three 'legitimations of domination' – rational, traditional and charismatic. The rational form is based on laws and rules designed to ensure equal treatment to guarantee the smooth running of a modern society. People are motivated through reason to support governments based on rational authority, that is to obey their laws, for such governments deliver the goods, ensure the smooth working of society and support fair play, for rules are consistently applied and not dependent on whim or favouritism. Traditional authority is based on custom and traditions, and motivation to obey comes through habit. Charismatic authority is based on devotion to an individual and support is motivated by emotion. The individual's charisma, literally 'gift of grace', is a gift from God, something with which the charismatic leader is born.[3]

Charismatic authority in its pure form arises in times of stress, and obedience to the charismatic leader relies neither on force nor administrative machinery, though in time a 'routinization of charisma' will occur with the re-establishment of bureaucracy. Charismatic domination is inevitably transitory for, as a 'gift of grace', charisma cannot be transferred but rather dies with the leader. Furthermore, as a basis of long-term support it is inherently inadequate; followers want stability eventually, and demands for change necessitate the machinery to implement it. Routinization, the development of administration and norms, towards the traditional or rational form of domination inevitably begins before long.

These bases of legitimate authority are ideal types; in reality domination normally rests on a mixture of the three. Today, for example, modern liberal-democracies best approximate the rational form of domination but politicians are likely to have a calling to politics offering an element of charismatic leadership within the rational–legal framework and constitutional monarchs may legitimate the authority of the state through attachment to tradition. Bureaucracies, for Weber, exist both in traditional and modern societies, both kinds of society rest on administration, but the bureaucracies contrast. The ideal type of bureaucracy, the epitome of bureaucracy, is rational and is to be found in modern legal–rational societies. Such bureaucracies administer on the basis of rules, are hierarchical, recruit on achievement and have a career structure. They are in essence politically neutral, thoroughly professional organizations which serve the government rather than seeking to manipulate it for their own ends. Traditional bureaucracies are the reverse. They are appointed on the basis of ascription rather than achievement, rules are regularly flouted and bureaucratic position represents not a career but a sinecure. Over time, for Weber, there is movement though not a smooth movement, not least because of the interruption of charismatic domination, towards rationalization, towards societies regularized by laws and rules with neutral career bureaucracies.

It follows from Weber's analysis, given that bureaucracies exist both in traditional and modern societies and develop through the routinization of charisma, that a concentration on the development of bureaucracy by the revolutionary state, such as found in Skocpol (1979), represents a misplaced focus for study of revolutions and state construction. Rather focus should, as this study has shown, be directed towards monopolization of the coercive forces and development of the bases of support. Coercive forces will, of course, develop their own bureaucracy, just as bureaucracies will grow, in order to implement policies which necessitate substantial administration. For Weber, bureaucracies would grow faster under socialist and Communist governments (as they did in Cuba, China and Russia) and less fast where independent, competing, economic and political organizations exist, as found in 'leadership democracies', characterized by mass parties competing for parliamentary election through leadership (for above see Beetham 1987: 62–71.) It also follows from Weber's claims for the rationalization of society, which brings with it the growth of bureaucracy, that bureaucracies can act in their own functional interest (ibid 1985: 72–79). Essentially, though, the level of the growth of bureaucracy will be affected by the policies implemented by revolutionary government; it follows that it is important to examine the kind of authority which bureaucracies serve: traditional, legal–rational or the charismatic. Within this, Weber argues that class interests could be an important aspect of analysis but so too could considerations of status group interests and personal power.

It is the Cuban revolution government which approximates most closely to the charismatic type of domination. Castro, lacking party organization and with a guerrilla army only two years in the making, held the revolution together through the strength of his personality and personal attachment as its Saviour. This was why the cabinet met rarely and the routinization of charisma into the single-party state, in spite of the importance of PSP members in INRA and of the considerable alliance with the USSR, in fact took many years to establish. It was also this very considerable level of support, obedience based on charismatic authority, which kept the terror mild. In China and in Russia, where charisma was also present, in Mao more especially, these party-based revolutions approximated more closely the legal–rational type. Communists, as Castro had learnt, are good at organization.

Governments of the English, American and Nicaraguan revolutions in their different ways rested on legal–rational domination, and in these non-Communist revolutions the state avoided the rapid bureaucratization seen in Russia and China. Though Cromwell, unlike Emperor Bonaparte, renounced the chance to be made king in the Protectorate, obedience to the new revolutionary governments rested partly on traditional domination. Nowhere was this more clearly the case, however, than in Iran, where the traditional Shi'a Islamic religion formed the basis of support, but even there legal–rational domination, in the form of the establishment of Islamic laws and provisions for the deprived also played a part along with a degree of charismatic authority to be found in Khomeini. Lastly Ethiopia stands out from the rest, furthest from Cuban revolutionary government, in spite of the eventual development of similar state construction along the Soviet model. There, whilst both traditional and legal–rational authority were mixed in the new revolutionary state, with perhaps some elements of charisma, domination rested above all on force. The country was cowed into submission.

Whilst broadly fitting within Weber's analysis of the state these revolutionary examples challenge his views. Weber does not give to revolutions the importance credited to them by Marx for whom they represent the crucial events of history through which an outdated mode of production is replaced by a new. For Weber they are just one of a number of crisis situations out of which the charismatic type of domination emerges. The Nicaraguan revolution, where no charismatic leader ever emerged, most clearly challenges this analysis. In drawing attention to civil wars and reigns of terror, the cases have also shown how crucial it is for revolutionary governments to institute and gain control over new forces of coercion; this also weighs against exclusive attention being drawn to the charismatic leader. In emphasizing the use of force, the difficulty of differentiating between manufactured charisma and genuine God-given charisma is also raised most clearly so in the case of Mengistu.

In practice there is an inherent problem in applying Weber's conception of legitimacy, which stems from the relationship between attitudes and behaviour. Laws might be dutifully obeyed, for example taxes paid on time and low crime rates. Such behaviour, however, cannot prove indisputably the existence of supportive attitudes. People may obey governments through recognition, for example, that under threat of death it would be pointless not to do so, whilst at the same time refusing to accept the regime's authority as legitimate, that is, based on rational, traditional or charismatic domination. In the Ethiopian Revolution the regime came to rest essentially on obedience through force. The government was seen as the legitimate authority in the sense that it became accepted that no other group could challenge the regime, but genuine support was absent among large sections of the population. Indeed, in Eritrea and Tigray province resistance movements have continued. As all the cases of reigns of terror have surely demonstrated, obedience, for some sections of the population at least, is to be found in behaviour only and not attitude. As Parkin (1982: 75) has argued for non-revolutionary examples, 'structures of authority which rely more upon coercion than upon willing compliance are excluded from Weber's typology of domination'. Parkin would also wish to know against whom the state's monopoly of violence is to be used and would wish for a distinction to be made between, say, totalitarian regimes and democracies (ibid: 73).

It is Weber's failure to distinguish between different sections of the people that in fact presents his greatest weakness and, in this, again it is Nicaragua which poses the greatest challenge to his views. For Weber those who obey domination are viewed as a mass, not subgroups of interest with differing capacities to influence the new revolutionary regime from below (see Beetham 1985: 102–13). As Beetham explains (ibid: 106), for Weber:

> Policy is always determined by a few, who then involve others only to the extent that their support is judged necessary, a principle which is as true of democracies as any other form of government. The mass only becomes involved as a result of initiatives from above, never from below; their role is limited to that of response.

In Nicaragua a real attempt had been made to establish the regime on the basis of power, in Arendt's sense of governments 'empowered' by groups of people to 'act in their name' (for Arendt power does not rest on force, rather power and violence are opposites – Arendt, 'Communicative Power', in Lukes 1986: 64). It is a theme similar to Luxemburg's requirement for 'mass action'. (For an excellent brief exposition see Nettl 1969: 157–8, fn.1.) In a true democracy (Luxemburg's ideal Communist state) power comes from the people, it is not imposed upon them.

There is, then, a crucial difference between obedience generated from above and support empowered from below. In revolutions, mobilizations directed from above have played an important part, most clearly seen in China in the mobilization campaigns. Mobilization was also involved in Robespierre's Republic of Virtue and the worship of the Supreme Being. In Iran, it was conducted through the mosques, and in Ethiopia through the *kebelles* and peasant associations. In practical studies it may not always be easy to differentiate between mobilization and support thoughtfully given but they are theoretically quite distinct. It follows that to the legal–rational, charismatic and traditional bases of legitimate authority should then be added two other ideal types. As for the existing three types, in reality these too would feature in combination with the others. The fourth type could be termed 'mobilized authority', obedience cultured from above through propaganda and coercion. States most closely approximating this ideal type would be totalitarian regimes. The fifth type could be called 'empowered authority', support (obedience is too passive a term) through active participation, open debate and freedom of thought and action. States most closely approximating this ideal type would be genuinely representative pluralist (not élitist) democracies.

As the Nicaraguan case has shown it is possible to separate power based on genuine plural representation from the force needed for the establishment of the new revolutionary state by restricting single-party control to the coercive forces of the state. This was achieved in Nicaragua only after a virulent civil war had been fought, before the overthrow of the old regime; through a party-guerrilla movement with widespread plural, active and spontaneous support. Nicaragua has come closest of any revolution to Luxemburg's ideal mass action. The government there had set out to avoid a reign of terror and had actively resisted charismatic leadership. Unless the circumstances faced there prove unique, the construction of the revolutionary state in Nicaragua has offered a new model, one to replace the Marxist–Leninist party state.

Whilst a reign of terror can be avoided after revolutionary takeover, a monopoly of coercion must as for all states, revolutionary or not, form part of the basis of established government. As these revolutions have shown, along with that monopoly of force must also be found support; support which is based on some combination of charismatic, rational, traditional or empowered authority and sometimes mobilized obedience too.

NOTES

1. For arguments similarly applied for military governments see O'Kane 1989.
2. See also Tilly (1985) for a view very similar to Weber's in his emphasis on the state's monopoly of violence. Interested in state-making, Tilly concentrates on foreign war. He pays some attention to potential opposition at home but does not consider support. It follows that his view is challenged by the findings of this work.
3. For this and the following exposition of Weber's views, in addition to 'Politics as a Vocation' (Gerth and Mills 1970: 77–128) see also ibid: 196–264) and Weber (1964: 324–86).

APPENDIX: MEXICO 1911–34

The Mexican revolution is one further case which needs to be considered, for there as in Nicaragua a reign of terror was avoided. Whilst the Diaz regime was brought down by battles between competing armies in a brief civil war, a very violent civil war broke out after 1911 and was not ended until 1920. For this, Mexico poses a potential counter-example to the claimed importance of the timing and virulence of civil war. The Mexican revolution, 1910–20, was not a 'great' revolution. It was neither caught up in foreign wars nor did it set off in its train the inspiration for revolutions elsewhere. Indeed, the most notable aspect of the Mexican revolution was its incapacity to establish a revolutionary regime at all. It was the introduction of reforms by Cardenas many years later, between 1934–40, which reflected the revolutionaries' demands, Zapata's in particular, that most justifies the classification of the Mexican case as a revolution. The incapacity to establish the revolutionary state seems not to falsify but to reinforce the conclusions generated here: centralized control over the coercive forces in combination with support are the essential bases for the establishment of the state.

There has been a mistaken notion that as a Latin American country the Mexican Revolution can simply be lumped in with other more recent revolutions in Central and South America and, more broadly, the Third World. Skocpol (1979: 287–9) makes passing reference to Mexico in terms of the usual points about developing countries: colonial heritage, military government – under Diaz 1870–1911 described as a 'tenuously centralized and military feeble prerevolutionary regime' (ibid: 288) – and the post-colonial problems of shifts in US foreign policy and the flows of European and US foreign investment. These points are important to Skocpol for they permit her to separate Mexico from generalizations developed for the three central cases to her work, France, Russia and China. Essentially Mexico is one of those countries 'with significantly different political histories located in more dependent international positions' (ibid: 289). Yet Wolf (1973) has successfully included the Mexican case along with the Russian and Chinese revolutions within generalizations about the causes of 'peasant wars'.

Certainly Mexico had a Spanish colonial heritage though the country had gained its independence back in 1821. America, after all, had only gained its independence from England in 1776 and had yet to fight a civil war in 1861 to establish itself as the United States of America. The USA in 1910 was not yet the international economic and military power which it was to become after two world wars. Mexico in 1910 was not a specialized producer of exports for the rich North Atlantic capitalist countries of the world, as Third World countries which gained their independence after World War II have generally become. Indeed in 1910 the terms of trade, the quantity of imports which can be purchased for a set level of exports, were in favour of countries exporting agricultural products and importing manufactured goods (Singer 1950: 477). Certainly the investment of foreign capital was crucial to Mexican development but the economy became increasingly diversified and industrialized. Though one-seventh of Mexico's lands were owned by foreign interests (mostly US, Spanish and British) Mexico operated a system of free trade (Vernon 1963: 50). Furthermore Diaz managed to maintain considerable independence for Mexico through playing foreign investors and their governments against each other, while investments were attracted to Mexico because the Diaz regime was viewed as stable and therefore a safe bet (Wolf 1973: 15). Mexico achieved remarkable economic growth. Based on figures for 1900 the Gross National Product had, by 1910, increased by 37 per cent (ibid: 47). Economic conditions there simply do not compare with the stagnant economy which Cuba had faced in the 1940s and 1950s.

In respect of social factors and the state, there are parallels with the great revolutions. The distribution of wealth was seriously skewed; by 1910, 80 per cent of peasants were landless (Vernon 1963: 49). As in Russia, large factories developed, concentrating textile workers particularly; mines expanded employment and production and railway construction grew apace in Mexico. There, unlike in Russia, however, industrialization was not state engineered but was encouraged within a system of *laissez faire* (ibid: 42). The army had fallen into disarray, though there it happened through lack of foreign wars in which to fight and corruption within the hierarchy (Atkin 1972: 71). Diaz also ruled over a bureaucratic state which relied on force; in 1910, the state employed nearly 75 per cent of the middle class and in the countryside the police force was supplemented by the *rurales,* a thug force recruited from the criminal elements of society (Wolf 1973: 14–15). In its corruption and system of privilege the large Mexican state resembled that of China before the 1911 revolution and France with its sale of offices under Louis XIV. Whilst a country unlike these classic cases in that it lacked an aristocracy, by 1910 land laws, introduced from 1856 onwards, had created a concentration of large estates into the hands of a few politically powerful families (ibid: 15–17).[1]

Armies and Government in Change

The revolution which broke out in Mexico in November 1910, like the
classic Russian and French cases, was spontaneous. Strikes had disrupted production from 1880 onwards, the worst being in 1906 and
1907 (Atkin 1972: 21). Rebellions broke out in the rural areas too.
Such protests had been violently suppressed by Diaz's highly coercive
state. It was the action of a liberal landowner, Francisco Madero,
which opened the way for the revolution. Objecting to yet another
rigged re-election of Diaz, Madero published a plan for free and fair
elections and declared himself provisional president. From such
unpromising beginnings a revolution grew and became centred around
two revolutionary armies raised in response to Madero's stand, by
Villa in the north and Zapata in the south. By May 1911 Diaz had
resigned and Madero had taken his place.

The revolution released demands for land reforms from Zapata's
forces and for labour reforms from Villa's forces to which Madero's
constitutional revolution was ill-matched. Order was not restored and
rebellion grew. Relying on the state army, Madero soon exposed himself to a military coup which installed Huerta in power in February
1913. Carranza took on Madero's constitutionalist mantle and Obregón
raised an army against Huerta. Villa returned from exile and Huerta
soon faced a civil war fought by four separate armies led in turn by
Zapata, Villa, Carranza and Obregón, though through the summer of
1913 Obregón's troops allied themselves loosely under Carranza's
Constitutionalist banner and Villa's army fought alongside the constitutionalists. In July 1914, his army defeated, Huerta was forced to
resign and Carranza took over as president.

Carranza's first task was to win over Zapata and his army, though
by September the split between Carranza and Villa was already deep
(Atkin 1972: 244). A convention intended to settle the revolution was
begun in October 1914 with delegates from all four revolutionary
armies. By November it had agreed to replace Carranza with Gutiérrez,
a Madero supporter, but Carranza refused to retire until Villa had
retired first. Villa however refused to go until after Carranza had gone,
and Mexico slipped back into civil war (ibid: 252). Zapata's forces
moved into Mexico City and in December, after talks with Villa, the
two armies joined forces (ibid: 258). The lines of civil war had become
sharply drawn between Villa and Zapata (the Convention) versus
Obregón and Carranza (the Constitutionalists). In January 1915,

Gutiérrez fled and in the changing fortunes of civil war Mexico City, located within Zapata's south, was to change hands several times. Not until August 1915 did Carranza regain control.

Carranza then set out totally to destroy Zapata's and Villa's forces. Without consciously setting up a reign of terror, through laws and institutions designed to carry out 'revolutionary justice', Carranza unleashed terror on the population using the army, headed by General González. Villages and crops were burnt to the ground, every man found was hanged and women and children were driven into detention camps. This was indeed summary justice (Atkin 1972: 330; Knight 1990 Vol. 2: 366–7). Zapata struck back with equal viciousness against González' soldiers (Atkin 1972: 330). Zapata was eventually lured to his assassination in 1919. The battle against Villa's troops was equally ferocious but less easily pinned down, and Villa's army was finally defeated by American cavalry in 1919.[2]

In March 1917, a few days after revolution had brought the provisional government to power in Russia, elections were held and Carranza won a resounding victory from a narrow electorate (Atkin 1972: 320). He was formally installed as president in May. Carranza's major success was the establishment of a constitution, first published in February 1917, under which rights such as the eight hour day, minimum wages and the abolition of peonage were to be given to workers and peasants. The constitution, however, was at best implemented extremely slowly and at worst ignored, and it fell to Cardenas between 1934–40 to fulfil the social and economic ambitions of the revolution. Carranza was replaced as president in 1920 by Obregón. Obregón had gradually drawn support from Carranza during the election campaign until, in April 1920, General González, the commander of the country's largest military force (22,000 men), declared against Carranza. With little army support remaining, Carranza fled the capital to learn that the rest of the army had also deserted him. In May, Carranza too was assassinated and de la Huerta was elected interim president. It was he who achieved the final peaceful settlement of the civil war. The remaining Zapata forces laid down their arms when de la Huerta offered them the land they had taken during the revolution (Atkin 1972: 347). In July 1920 a peace pact was finally signed with Villa. Villa retired to the farm that he was given (where he was assassinated in 1923) (Wolf 1973: 44). One by one de la Huerta settled the smaller rebellious groups, and after trial González left for the USA. In September 1920, Obregón was elected president and sworn in as November turned into December.

Obregón's presidential rule settled the revolution and 1920 is generally taken as the end. Rebellion broke out, however, in the run up to the next presidential election, with the army split between support for de la Huerta and Calles, Obregón's preferred candidate. The revolt was crushed and in 1924 Calles was elected president. Violence flared again in 1928 when another army revolt erupted over Obregón's candidacy for the election (Madero had begun the revolution with a protest against Diaz's re-election). Only 15 days after his election Obregón was assassinated. To avoid further outbreak of civil war the National Revolutionary Party (PNR) was formed in 1929 by Calles, who had succeeded Obregón as president. Its formation was intended to establish political order but as Philip (1988: 99) remarks 'the political order remained unstable and central control fragile for many years'.[3] The key posts within the PNR were mostly given to local power-holders, who happened to be mainly generals. These military–political leaders continued to hold considerable local power and some even had armies (ibid: 100). The party, though, played a crucial role in centralizing power and over time state governors who did not bow to the state were removed from office, sometimes by force. In China the Communist Party had achieved this with somewhat greater speed, after 1949!

Cardenas, elected president in 1934, inherited and consolidated this central party-state and under his presidency the promise of the revolution was realized with deep and wide-ranging social and economic reforms. Large land-holdings, (*haciendas*) were finally broken up, mainly into the form of village communities, with the land distributed to the peasantry and the political and economic power of the landlords displaced. In the 20 years 1914–1934 only 17 million acres of land were distributed; under Cardenas, during the six years 1934–40, the figure was increased by a further 41 million acres. Mexican capitalists benefited at the expense of foreign shareholders, oil fields were nationalized and workers, peasants too, were drawn into support of the regime through unionization (Wolf 1973: 45).

Comparative Perspectives and Lessons

The Mexican Revolution had been played out rather like the events of the Russian revolution with different winners at crucial points. Whereas General Kornilov's coup had failed and set in trail the successful Bolshevik revolution, in Mexico General Huerta's had succeeded.[4] The civil war which gripped Mexico was, as in Russia (on the White side at least), fought by armies which failed to unite into a single force. There, unlike the Reds' firm base in and around Moscow, the Mexican revolutionaries failed to establish a safe area for government. In Mexico too it was not the radicals, Zapata and Villa, who emerged as victors in the civil war but the Constitutionalists Carranza and Obregón. Zapata and his peasant army had played a part similar in many ways to the anarchist Makhno and his peasant forces. Like Makhno's forces, crucial in support of the Bolshevik revolutionaries for much of the civil war, Zapata's forces played a critical role in securing the Constitutionalists' power. Once relatively secure the Constitutionalists then turned, as had the Bolsheviks, against the peasant anarchist army. Makhno based far from Moscow and with more limited support had posed a rather easier target.

The Mexican revolution between 1910–20 had cost around 1.5 million lives (Philip 1988: 99), perhaps as many as 2 million (Wolf 1973: 44) and certainly no lower than half a million (Calvert 1973: 168) out of a population of only around 14–15 million. Yet the revolution had never passed through a revolutionary reign of terror. The closest it had come had been under Carranza when detention camps had been set up in the attempt to destroy Zapata's support. Local surveillance organizations had not though been developed in the villages and towns; a secret police force like the Cheka or revolutionary army acting as a police force had never developed; revolutionary courts had never been established to carry out 'revolutionary justice'; and the arbitrary laws of terror had not been introduced to stamp out counter-revolution.

In not developing a revolutionary reign of terror in the face of a virulent civil war, the long delay in establishing a revolutionary state with central control is entirely consistent with expectations which follow from the arguments generated in this work. As France, Russia, China, Cuba, Ethiopia and Iran have clearly shown, it is essential to gain central control (Weber's 'monopoly') over the forces of coercion. Failure to have a reign of terror itself though requires explanation. The evidence of ruthless willingness to use violence, rules out the possibility that this followed, as in Nicaragua, from a deliberate policy of avoidance, though as proclaimed Constitutionalists this may at times have played a part in resisting the introduction of Terror's laws and organizations. With Mexico City changing hands so many times, under Madero, Huerta and Carranza until the end of 1915 and the surrounding areas deep in civil war, a solid base for terror organization never existed. Had armed civil war been brought to the very doorstep of

Moscow itself it seems impossible to believe that the Cheka could have functioned effectively. Then, as in Mexico, the civil war in Russia might not have been fought to a decisive end. Indeed the competing armies in Mexico had fought five times for Mexico City (Wheatcroft 1983: 67, see also the map p.68–9 for the 'killing zone').

Importantly, in spite of the short civil war in November 1910–May 1911 Mexico had lacked from the beginning the advantages offered by the guerrilla movement to civil war path to revolution. There was not one revolutionary armed force but two and then four and other smaller forces besides. China after the 1911 revolution too had faced the same problem. There was no party organization capable of drawing these forces together, no guerrilla movement which had won widespread support and crucially not only had it been impossible to gain control over the coercive forces but they had also represented competing bases of support. With Mexico's economy so different between the north (cattle-ranches and cowboys) and the south (crop-production and peasants), the land reforms demanded by Zapata had held little interest for the north (Wolf 1973: 36; Dunn 1989: 56). A similar problem had faced Castro in and around the Camagüey province, but in Mexico these bases of support had split the country in half. In Mexico too the armies had changed sides. Zapata with a vast army and critical basis of support, had been essential to the establishment of the revolutionary state. By comparison Makhno's forces had been weak and regionally confined and crucially they had also been distant from Moscow.

In Mexico a firm base for a reign of terror, the temporary revolutionary state in the face of civil war, had been absent. Until the civil war had been brought to an end and control gained over the multiple coercive forces of the revolution the revolutionary state could not be established. Through a long-drawn-out process of establishing a party, the PNR, and then gaining control over local military-political leaders a state monopoly of force was eventually achieved. Cardenas from 1934 through implementation of promised policies increased support, the other crucial ingredient of the established state.

NOTES

1.   It is interesting to note that Goldfrank whilst playing down the importance of Diaz' initiative in encouraging foreign investment accepts that Diaz 'played off' European against US relations (1986: p.107) and in spite of Skocpol's objections offers an explanation for the Mexican Revolution which fits within Skocpol's

general explanation for France, Russia and China whilst adding consideration of the 'tolerant or permissive world context' and dissident political élite movements. This was a case which Skocpol should have included to fulfil Smith's (1973: 160–2) requirement for a genuinely contradictory case (see Chapter 1, fn. 4 above).

2. In spite of constant appeals to the contrary from the US ambassador to Mexico and though war between Mexico and the US seemed imminent at times, the US government effectively kept out of the Mexican Revolution, retaining a neutral position. There were two notable exceptions. During the conference in May 1914 the US army's Fifth Brigade joined marines in Veracruz though the troops did not march on in to Mexico City (Atkin 1972: 225–6). The second occasion began in March 1916 following Villa's troops' unexpected attack on the American town of Columbus in New Mexico when American troops entered Mexico to attack Villa's army. These troops left the country at the end of January 1917 (ibid: 299–319). After this the US government remained neutral (ibid: 322) until, with World War I over, US forces were finally used against the last of Villa's forces in 1919 (ibid: 334).

3. Today that party, the Institutional Revolutionary Party (PRI) as it is now known, continues to dominate Mexico's elections.

4. See Knight (1990 Vol. 2: 94–103) for particular discussion of Huerta as Mexico's Kornilov. Knight defends the view of Huerta as counter-revolutionary.

Bibliography

Abrahamian, E. 1989, *Radical Islam: the Iranian Mojahedin*, I.B. Taurus and Co. Ltd., London.

Adelman, J.R. 1985, *Revolution, Armies and War: a Political History*, Lynne Rienner, Boulder, Colorado.

Ahmad, E. 1982, 'Comments on Skocpol', *Theory and Society*, Vol.11: 293–300.

Alden, J.R. 1969, *A History of the American Revolution: Brinton and the Loss of the Thirteen Colonies*, Macdonald, London.

America's Watch Committee 1985, Report: 'Human Rights in Nicaragua: Reagan, Rhetoric and Reality', excerpts re-printed in Rossett and Vandermeer (eds) 1986: 122–9.

Arendt, H. 1958, *The Origins of Totalitarianism*, George Allen & Unwin, London.

———— 1973, *On Revolution*, Penguin, Harmondsworth.

Arjomand, S.A. 1986, 'Iran's Islamic Revolution in Comparative Perspective', *World Politics*, Vol.38, No.3 (April): 383–414.

———— 1988, *The Turban for the Crown: the Islamic Revolution in Iran*, Oxford University Press, New York.

Atkin, R. 1972, *Revolution! Mexico 1910–20*, Panther, London.

Aylmer, G.E. (ed.) 1983, *The Interregnum: the Quest for Settlement 1646–1660*, Macmillan, London.

Azicri, M. 1988, *Cuba: Politics, Economics and Society*, Pinter, London.

Barron, J. and Paul, A. 1977, *Peace with Horror*, Hodder & Stoughton, London (first published as *Murder of a Gentle Lady*, Reader's Digest Association, USA).

Beetham, D. 1985, *Max Weber and the Theory of Modern Politics*, Polity Press, Cambridge.

———— 1987, *Bureaucracy*, Open University Press, Milton Keynes.

Belden, J. 1973, *China Shakes the World*, Penguin, Harmondsworth.

Berresford Ellis, P. 1975, *Hell or Connaught! The Cromwellian Colonisation of Ireland, 1652–1660*, Hamish Hamilton, London.

Black, G. 1986, 'The 1972 Earthquake and After: Somocismu in Crisis', in Rossett and Vandermeer (eds) 1986: 189–202.

Blackburn, R. 1963, 'Prologue to the Cuban Revolution', *New Left Review,* Vol.21, October: 52–91.

Bonachea, R.E. and Valdés, N.P. 1972, *Cuba in Revolution,* Anchor/ Doubleday, New York.

Bonwick, C. 1986, 'The American Revolution as a Social Movement Revisited', *Journal of American Studies,* Vol.20, No.3: 355–73.

Booth, J.A. 1985a, *The End and The Beginning: The Nicaraguan Revolution,* Westview, Boulder.

———— 1985b, 'The National Governmental System' in Walker (ed.) 1985: 29–44.

Bourgois, P. 1986, 'Nicaragua's Ethnic Minorities in the Revolution' in Rossett and Vandermeer (eds) 1986: 459–72.

Bradley, J.F.N. 1975, *Civil War in Russia 1917–20,* B.T. Batsford Ltd., London.

Braudel, F. 1985, *Civilisation and Capitalism 15th–18th Century. Vol.2: The Wheels of Commerce,* Fontana, London.

Brinton, C. 1965, *The Anatomy of Revolution,* Vintage Books, New York.

Brockway, F. 1980, *Britain's First Socialists: the Levellers, Agitators and Diggers of the English Revolution,* Quartet Books, London.

Brower, D.R. 1989, '"The City in Danger" The Civil War and the Russian Urban Population' in Koeneker *et al.* 1989: 58–80.

Brugger, B. 1981, *China: Liberation and Transformation 1942–1962,* Croom Helm, London.

Bunyan, J. and Fisher, H.H. 1965, *The Bolshevik Revolution 1917–18,* Stanford University Press, Stanford.

Calvert, P. 1973, *Mexico,* Ernest Benn, London.

———— 1986, 'Terror in the Theory of Revolution' in N. O'Sullivan (ed.), *Terrorism, Ideology and Revolution,* Harvester, Wheatsheaf, Brighton: ch.2.

Cammack, P. 1989, 'Review Article: Bringing the State Back In?' *British Journal of Political Science,* Vol.19: 261–90.

Carr, E.H. 1964, *What is History?* Penguin, Harmondsworth.

———— 1966, *The Bolshevik Revolution 1917–23,* Vols 1 and 11, Penguin, Harmondsworth.

Carter, M.P. 1982, 'The French Revolution: Jacobin Terror', in Rapoport and Alexander (eds) 1982: ch.6.

Castro, F. 1968, 'History will Absolve Me' in F. Castro and R. Debray, *On Trial*, Lorrimer, London.

Central American Historical Institute, 1986, 'Nicaragua 1984: Human and Material Costs of War' in Rossett and Vandermeer (eds) 1986: 264–70.

Chavarría, R. E. 1982, 'The Nicaraguan Insurrection: An Appraisal of its Originality' in Walker (ed.) 1982: 25–40.

Chege, M. 1979, 'The Revolution Betrayed: Ethiopia 1974–79', *Journal of Modern African Studies*, Vol.17, Part 4: 359–80.

Chesneaux, J. 1973, *Peasant Revolts in China 1840–1949*, Thames & Hudson, London.

―――― 1979, *China: the People's Republic 1949–1976*, Harvester, Brighton.

Chomsky, N. and Herman, E.S. 1979, *After the Cataclysm*, Spokesman, Nottingham.

Clapham, C. 1985, *Third World Politics: an Introduction*, Croom Helm, London.

―――― 1988, *Transformation and Continuity in Revolutionary Ethiopia*, Cambridge University Press, Cambridge.

Close, D. 1988, *Nicaragua: Politics, Economics and Society*, Pinter, London.

Cobb, R. 1987, *The People's Armies – the Armées Revolutionnaires: Instrument of the Terror in the Departments April 1793 to Floreal Year 11*, Yale University Press, New Haven.

Conquest, R. 1968, *The Soviet Police System*, The Bodley Head Ltd., London.

―――― 1971, *The Great Terror*, Penguin, Harmondsworth.

Coraggio, J.L. 1986, *Nicaragua: Revolution and Democracy*, Allen & Unwin, Boston.

Davies, J.C. 1962, 'Towards a Theory of Revolution', *American Political Science Review*, Vol.27, no.1: 5–19.

Davies, N. 1975, 'The Missing Revolutionary War: the Polish Campaigns and the Retreat from Revolution in Soviet Russia, 1919–21', *Soviet Studies*, Vol.27, No.2: 178–95.

Debray, R. 1968, *Revolution in the Revolution?* Penguin, Harmondsworth.

DeFelice, G. 1980, 'Comparison Misconceived: Common Nonsense in Comparative Politics', *Comparative Politics*, Vol. 13, No.1 (October): 119–26.

Downs, C. 1985, 'Local and Regional Government' in Walker (ed.) 1985: 45–64.

Dumont, R. 1970, *Cuba: Socialism and Development,* Grove Press, New York.

Dunn, J. 1989, *Modern Revolutions: an Introduction to the Analysis of a Phenomenon,* Cambridge University Press, Cambridge.

Economist, 5 September 1989: 53–4, The Economist Newspaper Ltd, London.

Edwards, L.P. 1970, *The Natural History of Revolution,* University of Chicago, Chicago.

Erlich, H. 1986, *Ethiopia and the Challenge of Independence,* Lynne Rienner, Boulder, Colorado.

Evans, P.B., Rueschemeyer, D. and Skocpol, T. 1985, *Bringing the State Back in,* Cambridge University Press, New York.

Fagg, J.E. 1965, *Cuba, Haiti and the Dominican Republic,* Prentice-Hall, New Jersey.

Fairbairn, G. 1974, *Revolutionary Guerrilla Warfare: the Countryside Version,* Penguin, Harmondsworth.

Fanon, F. 1969, *The Wretched of the Earth,* Penguin, Harmondsworth.

Fehér, F. 1987, *The Frozen Revolution: an Essay on Jacobinism,* Cambridge University Press, Cambridge.

Femia, J. 1972, 'Barrington Moore and the Preconditions for Democracy', *British Journal of Political Science,* Vol.2: 21–46.

Ferguson, E.J. 1972, *The American Revolution: a General History 1763–1790,* Dorsey Press, Illinois.

Feuer, L.S. 1969, *Marx and Engels: Basic Writings on Politics and Philosophy,* Fontana/Collins, London.

Footman, D. 1961, *Civil War in Russia,* Faber & Faber, London.

Friedrich, C.J. and Brezezinski, Z.K. 1965, *Totalitarian Dictatorship and Autocracy,* Harvard University Press, Cambridge, Mass.

Geras, N. 1989, 'Our Morals: the Ethics of Revolution' in Miliband *et al.* (eds) 1989: 185–211.

Gerson, L.D. 1976, *The Secret Police in Lenin's Russia,* Temple University Press, Philadelphia.

Gerth, H.H. and Mills, C.W. 1970, *From Max Weber: Essays in Sociology,* Routledge & Kegan Paul, London.

Gilbert, D. 1988, *Sandinistas: the Party and the Revolution,* Basil Blackwell, New York.

Goldenberg, B. 1965, *The Cuban Revolution and Latin America,* George Allen & Unwin, London.

Goldfrank, W.L. 1982, 'Commentary on Skocpol', *Theory and Society,* Vol.11: 301–4.

———1986, 'The Mexican Revolution' in Goldstone (ed.) 1986: 104–17.

Goldman, M. 1967, *Literary Dissent in Communist China,* Harvard University Press, Cambridge, Mass.

Goldstone, J.A. 1980, 'Theories of Revolution: the Third Generation', *World Politics,* Vol.32, No.3: 425–53.

——— (ed.) 1986, *Revolutions: Theoretical, Comparative and Historical Studies,* Harcourt Brace Jovanovich, San Diego.

Gonzales, E. 1974, *Cuba under Castro: the Limits of Charisma,* Houghton Mifflin, Boston.

Gorman, S.M. and Walker, T.W. 1985, 'The Armed Forces' in Walker (ed.) 1985: 91–118.

Gray, J. 1990, *Rebellions and Revolutions: China from the 1800s to the 1980s,* Oxford University Press, New York.

Greer, D. 1966a, *The Incidence of the Terror during the French Revolution: a Statistical Interpretation,* Peter Smith, Gloucester, Mass.

——— 1966b, *The Incidence of the Emigration during the French Revolution,* Peter Smith, Gloucester, Mass.

Gregor, A.J. 1982, 'Fascism's Philosophy of Violence and the Concept of Terror' in Rapoport and Alexander (eds) 1982: ch.7.

Guevara, C. 1969a, *Guerrilla Warfare,* Penguin, Harmondsworth.

——— 1969b, *Reminiscences of the Cuban Revolutionary War,* Penguin, Harmondsworth.

Guardian, 2 and 8 November 1989, Guardian Newspapers Ltd., London.

Gurr, T.R. 1972, *Why Men Rebel,* Princeton University Press, Princeton NJ.

Halliday, F. 1979, *Iran: Dictatorship and Development,* Penguin, Harmondsworth.

——— 1988, 'The Iranian Revolution: Uneven Development and Religious Populism' in Halliday and Alavi (eds) 1988: ch.3.

——— and Alavi, H. (eds) 1988, *State and Ideology in the Middle East and Pakistan,* Macmillan, Basingstoke.

——— and Molyneux, M. 1981, *The Ethiopian Revolution,* New Left Books, London.

Hampson, N. 1986, 'From Regeneration to Terror: the Ideology of the French Revolution', in N. O'Sullivan (ed.), *Terrorism, Ideology and Revolution,* Harvester, Wheatsheaf, Brighton: ch.3.

———— 1988, *Prelude to Terror: the Constituent Assembly and the Failure of Consensus 1789–1791*, Basil Blackwell, Oxford.

Harding, N. 1981, *Lenin's Political Thought*, Vol.2: Theory and Practice in the Socialist Revolution, Macmillan, London.

———— 1984, 'Socialism, Society and the Organic Labour State' in N. Harding (ed.), *The State in Socialist Society*, Macmillan, Oxford.

Hill, C. 1969, *The Century of Revolution 1603–1714*, Sphere, London.

Hingley, R. 1970, *The Russian Secret Policy: Muscovite, Imperial Russian and Soviet Political Security Operations 1965–70*, Hutchinson, London.

Hinton, W. 1968, *Fanshen: a Documentary of Revolution in a Chinese Village*, Vintage, New York.

Hiro, D. 1985, *Iran under the Ayatollas*, Routledge & Kegan Paul, London.

Hobsbawm, E.J. 1986, 'Revolution' in R. Porter and M. Teich (eds), *Revolution in History*, Cambridge University Press, Cambridge.

Huberman, L. and Sweezy, P.M. 1969, *Socialism in Cuba*, Monthly Review Press, New York.

International Commission of Jurists, 1962, *Cuba and the Rule of Law*, Geneva.

Kazemi, F. 1980, *Poverty and Revolution in Iran*, New York University Press, New York.

Keddie, N.R. 1982, 'Comments on Skocpol', *Theory and Society*, Vol.11: 285–92.

Keesing's Contemporary Archives, 1950–88, Keesing's Publications, Longman.

Keesing's Record of World Events 1989 (re-named above).

Kemp, T. 1971, *Economic Forces in French History*, Dennis Dobson, London.

Kerber, L.K. 1980, 'The Limits of Politicisation: Arnerican women and the American Revolution', in Pelenski 1980: 54–74.

Knight, A. 1990, *The Mexican Revolution* Vols 1 and 2, Nebraska University Press, Lincoln.

Koenker, D.P., Rosenberg, W.G. and Suny, R.G. 1989, *Party, State, and Society in the Russian Civil War: Explorations in Social History*, Indiana University Press, Bloomington and Indianapolis.

Krejcí, J. 1983, *Great Revolutions Compared: the Search for a Theory*, Harvester, Wheatsheaf, Brighton.

Lacqueur, W. 1979, *The Terrorism Reader: an Historical Anthology*, Wildwood House, London.

Lefort, R. 1983, *Ethiopia: an Heretical Revolution?* Zed Press, London.

Leggett, G. 1981, *The Cheka: Lenin's Political Police,* Clarendon Press, Oxford.

Leiden, C. and Schmitt, M. 1973, *The Politics of Violence: Revolution in the Modern World,* Prentice-Hall, London.

Lenin, V.I. 1970, *The April Theses,* Progress Publishers, Moscow.

Lévesque, J. 1978, *The USSR and the Cuban Revolution: Soviet Ideological and Strategical Perspectives 1959–1977,* Praeger, New York.

Levytsky, B. 1972, *The Uses of Terror: the Soviet Secret Police 1917–70,* Coward, McCann & Geoghegan, New York.

Liebman, M. 1972, *The Russian Revolution,* Vintage Books, New York.

Lodge, J. (ed.) 1981, *Terrorism: a Challenge to the State,* Martin Robertson, Oxford.

Louie, R. 1964, 'The Incidence of the Terror: a Critique of a Statistical Interpretation', *French Historical Studies,* Vol.3 (Spring): 379–89.

Lowenthal, D. 1968, 'Review Essay' on Moore (1969), *History and Theory,* 7: 257–78.

Lucas, C. 1973, *The Structure of the Terror: the Example of Javogues and the Loire,* Oxford University Press, London.

Lukes, S. 1986, *Power,* Blackwell, Oxford.

Lyons, M. 1978, *Revolution in Toulouse: an Essay on Provincial Terrorism,* Peter Lang, Berne.

McAleavy, H. 1972, *The Modern History of China,* Weidenfeld & Nicolson, London.

McAuley, M. 1989, 'Bread without the Bourgeoisie' in Koenker *et al.* 1989: 158–9.

McLellan, D. (ed.) 1986, *The Essential Left,* Counterpoint (Unwin), London.

MacIntyre, A. 1973, 'Ideology, Social Science and Revolution', *Comparative Politics,* Vol.6, April: 321–42.

Malle, S. 1985, *The Economic Organisation of War Communism, 1918–21,* Cambridge University Press, Cambridge.

Markakis, J. and Ayele, N. 1978, *Class and Revolution in Ethiopia,* Spokesman, Nottingham.

Martin, J.K. and Lender, M.E. 1982, *A Respectable Army: the Military Origins of the Republic, 1763–1789.*

Marx, K. 1973, *The Revolutions of 1848: Political Writings Vol.1,* Penguin, Harmondsworth.

Matthews, H. 1969, *Castro: a Political Biography*, Allen Lane, Penguin Press, London.

Mawdsley, E. 1987, *The Russian Civil War*, Allen & Unwin, Boston.

Maxfield, S. and Stahler-Sholk, R. 1985, 'External Constraints' in Walker (ed.) 1985: 245–64.

Medvedev, R. 1979, *The October Revolution*, Constable, London.

Meisner, M. 1977, *Mao's China: a History of the People's Republic*, The Free Press (Macmillan), New York.

Michels, R. 1962, *Political Parties*, Free Press, New York.

Miliband, R., Panitch, L. and Saville, J. (eds) 1989, *Revolution Today – Aspirations and Realities*, Socialist Register, Merlin Press, London.

Mills, C.W. 1970, *The Sociological Imagination*, Penguin, Harmondsworth.

Moghadam, V. 1989, 'One Revolution or Two? The Iranian Revolution and the Islamic Republic' in Miliband *et al.* 1989: 74–101.

Moore, B. jr. 1969, *Social Origins of Dictatorship and Democracy: Lord and Peasant in the Making of the Modern World*, Penguin, Harmondsworth.

———— 1972, *Reflections on the Causes of Human Misery*, Penguin Press, Allen Lane, London (Beacon Press, Boston, Mass).

———— 1978, *Injustice: the Social Bases of Obedience and Revolt*, Macmillan, London.

Nettl, P. 1969, *Rosa Luxemburg*, Oxford University Press, London.

Nima, R. 1983, *The Wrath of Allah*, Pluto Press, London.

O'Connor, J. 1972, 'Cuba: its Political Economy' in Bonachea and Valdés 1972: ch.3.

O'Kane, R.H.T. 1987, *The Likelihood of Coups*, Gower, Aldershot.

———— 1989, 'Military Regimes: Power and Force', *European Journal of Political Research*, Vol.17(4): 333–50.

O'Sullivan, N. 1983, *Revolutionary Theory and Political Reality*, Wheatsheaf, Brighton.

———— 1986, 'Terrorism, Ideology and Democracy' in N. O'Sullivan (ed.), *Terrorism, Ideology and Revolution*, Harvester, Wheatsheaf, Brighton: ch.1.

Ottaway, M. 1976, 'Social Classes and Corporate Interests in the Ethiopian Revolution', *Journal of Modern African Studies*, Vol.14, Part 3: 469–86.

Palmer, R.R. 1941, *Twelve who Ruled: the Year of the Terror in the French Revolution*, Princeton University Press, Princeton.

Peckham, H.H. 1974, *The Toll of Independence,* University of Chicago Press, Chicago.

Pelenski, J. 1980, *The American and European Revolutions: 1776– 1848,* University of Iowa Press, Iowa.

Philip, G. 1988, 'The Dominant Party System in Mexico' in V. Randall (ed.), *Political Parties in the Third World,* Sage, London, ch.5.

Polan, A.J. 1984, *Lenin and the End of Politics,* Methuen, London.

Ponchaud, F. 1978, *Cambodia Year Zero,* Allen Lane, London.

Price, H.E. 1977, 'The Strategy and Tactics of Revolutionary Terrorism', *Comparative Studies in Society and History,* Vol.19, No.1: 52– 66.

Price, R. 1975, *The Economic Modernisation of France,* Croom Helm, London.

Rapoport, D.C. and Alexander, Y. (eds) 1982, *The Morality of Terrorism: Religious and Secular Justifications,* Pergamon, New York.

Rigby, T.H. 1979, *Lenin's Government: Sovnarkom 1917–22,* Cambridge University Press, Cambridge.

Roberts, P.C. 1970, 'War Communism: a Re-examination', *Slavic Review* (June): 239–61.

Rooper, A. and Smith, H. 1986, 'From Nationalism to Autonomy: the Ethnic Question in the Nicaraguan Revolution', *Race and Class,* Vol.27, No.4: 1–20.

Rossett, P. and Vandermeer, J. (eds) 1986, *Nicaragua: Unfinished Revolution,* Grove Press, New York.

Roots, I. 1966, *The Great Rebellion 1642–1660,* B.T. Batsford Ltd., London.

Sakwa, R. 1988, *Soviet Communists in Power: a Study of Moscow During the Civil War 1918–21,* Macmillan, London.

Sartre, J-P. 1960, 'Ideology and Revolution', *Studies on the Left,* Vol.3.

Schama, S. 1989, *Citizens: a Chronicle of the French Revolution,* Penguin, London.

Scheer, R. and Zeitlin, M. 1964, *Cuba: an American Tragedy Prelude to Revolution,* Penguin, Harmondsworth.

Schram, S.R. 1971, *The Political Thought of Mao-Tse-Tung,* Penguin, Harmondsworth.

Schurmann, F.H. 1968, *Ideology and Organisation in Communist China,* University of California Press, Berkeley.

Schwab, P. 1985, *Ethiopia,* Frances Pinter, London.

Scott, W. 1973, *Terror and Repression in Revolutionary Marseilles,* Macmillan, London.

Sinclair, A. 1970, *Guevara,* Fontana/Collins, London.

Singer, H.W. 1950, 'The Distribution of Gains Between Investing and Borrowing Countries', *American Economic Review,* Vol.40.

Sivard, R.L. 1985, *World Military and Social Expenditure,* World Priorities, Washington D.C.

Skidmore, T.E. and Smith, P.H. 1984, *Modern Latin America,* Oxford University Press, New York.

Skocpol, T. 1979, *States and Social Revolutions: a Comparative Analysis of France, Russia and China,* Cambridge University Press, Cambridge.

——— 1982, 'Rentier State and Shi'a Islam in the Iranian Revolution', *Theory and Society,* Vol.11: 265–83.

——— 1985, 'Bringing the State Back In: Strategies of Analysis in Current Research' in Evans *et al.* 1985: 3–43.

Smart, N. 1974, *Mao,* Fontana/Collins, Glasgow.

Smelser, N. 1962, *Theory of Collective Behaviour,* Routledge & Kegan Paul, London.

Smith, D. 1983, *Barrington Moore: Violence, Morality and Political Change,* Macmillan, London.

Smith, S.A. 1983, *Red Petrograd: Revolution in the Factories 1917–18,* Cambridge University Press, Cambridge.

Soboul, A. 1974, *The French Revolution 1787–1799, vol.1: From the Storming of the Bastille to the Fall of the Girondins, vol.2: From the Jacobin Dictatorship to Napoleon,* NLB, London.

Sutherland, D.M.G. 1985, *France 1789–1815: Revolution and Counter-revolution,* Fontana, London.

Sydenham, M.J. 1965, *The French Revolution,* B.T. Batsford Ltd., London.

——— 1974, *The First French Republic 1792–1804,* B.T. Batsford Ltd., London.

Talmon, J.L. 1955, *The Origins of Totalitarian Democracy,* Secker & Warburg, London.

Taylor, S. 1984, *Social Science and Revolutions,* Macmillan.

Thomas, H. 1967, 'Middle-Class Politics and the Cuban Revolution' in C. Veliz (ed.) *The Politics of Conformity in Latin America,* Oxford University Press, Oxford: 249–77.

——— 1971, *Cuba or the Pursuit of Freedom,* Eyre & Spottiswoode, London.

Thornton, T.P. 1964, 'Terror as a Weapon of Political Agitation' in H.H. Eckstein (ed.), *Internal War: Problems and Approaches,* The Free Press, New York: 71–99.

Tilly, C. 1978, *From Mobilization to Revolution,* Addison-Wesley, Reading, Mass.

———— 1985, 'War Making and State Making as Organized Crime' in Evans *et al.* 1985: 169–91.

Townshend, C. 1986, 'The Process of Terror in Irish Politics' in N. O'Sullivan (ed.), *Terrorism, Ideology and Revolution,* Harvester, Wheatsheaf, Brighton: ch.5.

Trimberger, E.K. 1978, *Revolution from Above: Military, Bureaucrats and Development in Japan, Turkey, Egypt and Peru,* Transaction Books, New Brunswick, NJ.

Trotsky, L. 1963, *Terrorism and Communism,* Ann Arbor, Michigan.

Ulam, A.B. 1969, *Lenin and the Bolsheviks,* Fontana, London, 1965 (USA: *The Bolsheviks,* Martin Secker & Warburg, 1965).

Valenta, J. and V. 1985, 'Sandinistas in Power', *Problems of Communism,* September–October: 1–28.

Vernon, R. 1963, *The Dilemma of Mexico's Development: the Role of the Private and Public Sector,* Harvard University Press, Cambridge, Mass.

Vickery, M. 1985, *Cambodia, 1975–1982,* Allen & Unwin, London.

Walker, T.W. (ed.) 1982, *Nicaragua in Revolution,* Praeger, New York.

Walker, T.W. (ed.) 1982b, 'Introduction' in Walker (ed.) 1982: 1–22.

Walker, T.W. 1985, 'Introduction: Revolution in General: Nicaragua to 1984' in Walker (ed.) 1985: 1–26.

Walker, T.W. (ed.) 1985, *Nicaragua: the First Five Years,* Praeger, New York.

Walter, E.V. 1972, *Terror and Resistance: a Study of Political Violence,* Oxford University Press, New York.

Wardlaw, G. 1989, *Political Terrorism: Theory, Tactics and Counter-Measures* Cambridge University Press, Cambridge.

Weber, M. 1964, *The Theory of Social and Economic Organizations* (ed. T. Parsons), The Free Press, New York.

Weiner, J.M. 1975, 'The Barrington Moore Thesis and its Critics', *Theory and Society,* Vol.2: 301–30.

Wheatcroft, A. 1983, *The World Atlas of Revolutions,* Hamish Hamilton, London.

Wilkinson, P. 1974, *Political Terrorism,* Macmillan, London.

1986, *Terrorism and the Liberal State,* Macmillan, Basingstoke.

Wolf, E.R. 1973, *Peasant Wars of the Twentieth Century,* Faber & Faber, London.

Woolrych, A. 1961, *Battles of the English Civil War*, B.T. Batsford Ltd., London.
——— 1982, *Commonwealth to Protectorate*, Clarendon Press, Oxford.
Worden, B. 1974, *The Rump Parliament 1648–1653*, Cambridge University Press, London.
Wright, D.G. 1974, *Revolution and Terror in France*, Longman, Harlow.
Young, Brigadier P. and Holmes, R. 1974, *The English Civil War: a Military History of the Three Civil Wars, 1642–1651*, Eyre Methuen, London.
Zubaida, S. 1982, 'The Ideological Conditions for Khomeini's Doctrine of Government', *Economy and Society*, Vol. 11: 138–72.

Index

absenteeism, worker, 92, 103, 106
Act for the settling of Ireland 138
Addis Ababa 211, 212, 216, 217, 219, 221, 222, 223, 224, 244
agrarian reform laws
  in China 199–200, 202
  in Cuba 158, 159, 161, 163–4
  in Nicaragua 181–2, 188
  see also land reforms
aid, 106, 112, 162, 163, 170, 171, 178, 180, 189, 225
  see also loans
Allied Forces 97, 98, 100
All-Russian Central Executive Committee of the Congress of Soviets *see* VTsIK
All-Russian Congress of Soviets *see* Congress of Soviets
All-Russian Extraordinary Commission for Combatting Counter-Revolution and Sabotage *see* Cheka
Aman, Andom, General 212, 213, 214
America *see* USA
American Revolution 6, 37, 38, 39, 42, 43, 117–29, 166–7
  see also Reign of Terror, revolutionary, absence in America
anarchical/anarchistic terror 14, 20, 23, 24, 25
  in America 122, 125, 150
  in China 202
  in Ethiopia 224
  in France 59, 75, 77, 78
  in Mexico 273
  in Nicaragua 188, 198
  in Russia 92, 97, 110
Angka Loeul (Angkar) 29–30, 32
appeal 61, 90, 91, 200, 231

ARDE (Democratic Revolutionary Alliance) 183
Arendt, H. 19, 21, 31–2, 117–18, 268
armées revolutionarie *see* people's armies
army, regular 201, 213
  Cambodia 32
  Cuba 153, 157
  Ethiopia 211–13, 215, 223–5, 226
  Iran 228, 230, 234, 242
  Mexico 271, 274
  Russia 88
  see also National Guard
army, revolutionary, *see* Constitutionalists; EPS; guerrilla movements; militias; New Model Army; Pasdaran; people's armies; People's Militia; popular militias; Red Army
arrivages *see* supply
assassinations 97, 170–71, 216, 217, 234–5
  attempts 79, 97, 159
  plots 141, 161, 180, 235, 273, 274
Assembly *see* Constituent Assembly
assignats 58, 70, 121
Atnafu Abate 213, 215, 217, 223–5, 226
Azerbaijan 232, 233

bagmen 95
Baha'is 236, 245
Bakhtiar, S. 230, 233, 234
Bani-Sadr, A.H. 232, 233–4, 241–3
Barbados 134, 139
Barebones Parliament 129, 130, 139, 140
Basic Statute (Nicaragua) 173
Batista, F. 152, 151–5, 160

291

Bay of Pigs 159–60, 161
Bazarghan, M. 230, 231
Beheshti, Ayatollah 232, 234
black market 105, 106, 122
Bolshevik Party 82, 88–9
    policies 96, 98, 101, 103, 106–7
Bolsheviks 51, 88, 90, 97
Bordeaux 65
Brest-Litovsk Treaty 96–7, 100, 114, 264
Brinton, C. 4, 6, 36–9, 44–9, 53–4, 78, 82, 87, 118–20, 130–31 143, 261
Brissotins see Girondins
Britain
    and American Revolution 119, 120, 121, 122, 123, 125, 126, 127, 128
    see also English Revolution
bureaucracy 73, 264, 265–6
    centralization (bureaucratic) 50, 51, 54 fn3, 71–3, 271
    for coercion 77, 92

cabinet (Cuba) 155, 158
Camagüey 153, 155, 156, 159
Cambodia 26–34
Cardenas, L. 270, 273, 274
Cardona, Miró 155, 157, 159, 165
Carolinas 120, 125
Carr, E.H. 7–8, 99, 102, 104
Carranza, Venustiano 272, 273
Castro, Fidel 7, 155, 157, 158, 164–5, 266
Castro, Raul 156, 158
CAUS (Labour Action and Unity Confederation) 182
CDS (Sandinista Defence Committees) 175–6
Chamorro, Pedro J. 170
Chamorro, Violeta 174, 180, 186
charismatic authority/domination 158, 264–5, 266, 267
    routinization of charisma 264, 265
Charles II 129, 131, 133, 134–5, 136, 145
Cheka 51, 91–5, 97, 102, 108, 109, 110, 111, 114

abolition of local chekas 92
    functions 92
China see Chinese revolution
Chinese Communist Party (CCP) see Communist Party
Chinese revolution 6, 7, 49, 52
    (1911–49) 192–5
    (1911) 276
    see also Reign of Terror, in China
Chomsky, N. and Herman, E. 30–31
CIA 159, 181, 183, 184, 189
citizens' committees (America) 122, 126, 141
civil armies see people's armies
civil war 6, 7, 8, 10, 13, 23, 42, 45, 54, 149, 204, 229, 256–7, 258
    in America 128
    in Cambodia 27
    in China 193, 194, 203, 204–5
    in Cuba 166
    in England/Ireland 131–2, 142
    in Ethiopia 216, 218, 223
    in France 60, 63–8, 69, 76, 82, 94, 95
    in Iran 233–4, 240, 244
    in Mexico 270, 272, 273, 274
    in Nicaragua 169–73, 178–9, 187, 189
    in Russia 51, 90, 94, 95, 97, 98–99, 100–101, 102, 107, 109, 113
class
    analysis 50, 64–66, 144, 150, 153, 192–3, 221, 227 fn7, 263, 266
    conflict 87, 91 95, 98, 102–3, 104, 166, 200, 221, 238
    absence of in Nicaragua 182
    struggles 42–3, 45, 48
Cobb, R. 73–5, 79
coercion 7, 8, 74, 259
    see also violence
collective farms 104, 220
collectivization 195
colonies (13 states of America) 119
commercialization 107
commissions, civil and military (France) 60–61

Committee of General Security 59, 60, 62, 75–6, 77, 79, 80, 82, 83
Committee of Public Safety 59–60, 62, 73, 75, 76, 77, 78, 79, 80–81, 82, 83
Committees for the Defence of the Revolution, CDR (Cuba) 160 166, 167
communism 53, 114
    and Cambodia 28, 33, 35 fn6
    fear of in Cuba 158, 163
    ideal society 262, 268
    and peasants 29
    world 101
    see also Communist Party; Marxism–Leninism
Communist Liberation Army *see* Red Army, China
Communist Party
    in China (CCP) 192, 193, 196, 202, 204
    in Cuba 157, 158, 163, 164, 168
        see also Popular Socialist Party (PSP)
    in Iran *see* Tudeh Party
    in Nicaragua (PCN) 182–3
    in Russia 109, 111–113
        see also Bolshevik Party
compensation bonds 159, 177
    see also money
concentration camps 21, 94, 95, 215, 216
confiscation of property 80, 122, 133, 137, 138, 157–8, 159, 160, 177, 181–2, 183, 185, 200, 214, 238
    see also land, confiscation by state
Congress, America, 119, 121, 122, 126–7
    provisional congresses 119, 120, 123
Congress of Soviets 89, 97, 111
conscription/conscripts 60, 65, 68, 71, 88, 134, 142, 184
Constituent Assembly (France) 58, 69, 82
Constituent Assembly (Russia) 89
constitution 90, 118, 128, 154, 173, 201, 232, 239, 273

constitutional church 74
Constitutionalists (Mexico) 272
Continental Army 120, 127–8, 142
    supply of 121, 122
continental currency 121
control over the revolutionary coercive forces 5, 13, 76, 77–80, 81, 83, 110–11, 113, 150–51, 156, 165, 167, 176, 188, 205, 209, 224–5, 236, 237, 240, 262, 264
Convention (France) 58, 59, 73, 75
Convention (Mexico) 272
Contras 183, 184, 185, 186
COPWE (Party of the Working People of Ethiopia) 225–6
COSEP (High Council of Foreign Enterprise) 171, 180, 182, 183
Costa Rica 171, 172, 182, 183, 185
Council of Experts 232, 241
Council of Guardians 239, 246, 249 fn3
Council of Labour and Defence *see* STO
Council of National Economy *see* Vesenkha
Council of People's Commissars *see* Sovnarkom
Council of State, England 129, 135
Council of State, Nicaragua 173–4, 176, 180
    see also national unity government
counter-revolution 7, 9, 19, 47–9, 53, 144, 202, 237, 254–6
    in China 197–8
    in Cuba 158–9
    in England 133–6, 144
    in Ethiopia 214, 218, 220
    in France 58–9, 60, 61
    in Iran 233–4, 235
    in Nicaragua 176, 179–80, 181–4
    in Russia 90, 91, 103
    see also domestic insurrection; insurrection; rebellions; riots
counter-revolutionaries 60, 62, 70, 97, 215, 220, 234
criminal courts, department 61
crisis, revolutionary 5, 68

see also economic crisis

Cromwell, Oliver 3, 7, 129, 133, 135, 139, 140, 141

Cuba
and Ethiopia 225, 227 fn4
and Nicaragua 178, 179, 180, 189
see also Reign of Terror, in Cuba

Cuban Revolution, to overthrow 6, 7, 152–5

cultural revolution, Chinese, compared with Cambodia 28

Czech Legion 98, 99

Danton, Georges 69, 78, 79

death penalty 61, 62, 79, 99, 110, 115 fn6, 123, 138, 173, 184, 187, 214

death squads (Ethiopia) 215, 216, 217

deaths in Mexican Revolution 275

deaths of patriots 123

debt crisis 132–3, 142–3

dechristianization 74, 76, 78

Declaration of Independence 118, 120

decrees of Sovnarkom 90, 91, 102, 104

decrees of Feb 1958 in Sierra Maestra 156

defections 158, 183

Democratic Kampuchea *see* Cambodia

demonstrations 88, 108, 211–12, 217, 229, 230, 233, 245
see also strikes

Derg 212, 213, 215, 216, 217, 221, 223–4, 225, 226, 227 fn8

devaluation of currency 58, 68

dictatorship of the proletariat 87, 98, 262

distribution 72, 88, 104, 105, 220–21
see also supply

districts 73, 76

domestic insurrection 42, 88, 109, 131
see also civil war; insurrection; rebellion; riots

Drogheda 134, 137

dual power 88, 89, 231

Dzerzhinsky, F. 110, 115 fn4

economic and social emergency, Nicaragua 182

economic boom 121

economic crisis 8, 46, 66, 68–9, 71–3, 80, 88, 96, 108, 120, 121, 132–5, 162–3, 177, 218–19, 257

economic determinism 69–71

economic reconstruction 176, 199, 238

economy
in America 121–22, 126
in China 201
in England 132
in Ethiopia 218–19, 225
in Iran 229, 230, 240, 244
in Ireland 141
in Mexico 271, 276
in Nicaragua 178, 182, 189
in pre-revolutionary Cuba 152–3, 162, 168 fn1
in pre-revolutionary France 72–3
see also economic crisis

Edwards, L.P. 4, 6, 36–44, 47–9, 53–4, 63, 64–5, 78, 87, 93, 118–20, 130–31, 140, 244

Eighth Route Army 194

elections
in America 128
in Cuba 152
in England 136, 145 fn7
in France 58, 59
in Iran 232, 236, 241, 245
in Mexico 273, 274
in Nicaragua 172, 173, 183, 184–5, 186, 188, 190 fn10
in Russia 89

emigration *see* exiles

empowered authority 268

Engagement Act 135

England *see* Britain

English Revolution 6, 38, 42, 43, 51, 117, 129, 143–4
see also Reign of Terror, revolutionary, in England/Ireland

EPS (Sandinista Popular Army) 173, 176, 179, 183

Eritrea 212, 214, 218, 219, 220, 221, 222, 226

Eritrean Liberation Front, ELF 212, 214

Eritrean People's Liberation Front, EPLF 214

establishment of the revolutionary state 13, 82–3, 111–13, 139–41, 150–51, 167–8, 201–2, 225–6, 236–7, 241, 248, 269, 270, 274, 276

Ethiopian Democratic Union (EDU) 218

Ethiopian People's Revolutionary Party (EPRP) 213, 215, 216, 217, 221

Ethiopian Revolution 6, 226 fnl, 267
to overthrow 211–12
see also Reign of Terror, revolutionary, in Ethiopia

excess in reigns of terror 24, 70, 83, 110, 114, 209, 244, 246

execution squads *see* death squads

executions 23, 25, 62–3, 77, 78, 91–2, 93–4, 110, 119, 125, 136, 139, 156, 157, 166, 196–7, 198–9, 213, 214–17, 229, 231, 233, 234, 235–6, 244
see also victims of reigns of terror

exiles 58, 122–3, 126, 141, 158, 159, 160, 161, 166, 168 fn4, 172, 181, 187–8, 231, 234
see also refugees

factory committees 104

famine 68, 72, 106
see also economic crisis; starvation

FAO (Broad Opposition Front) 171, 172, 173, 174

FARN 179, 183

FDN (Nicarguan Democratic Force) 179, 181, 183, 184, 190 fn10

fear 16, 17, 37–8, 94, 225, 229
see also Reign of Terror, revolutionary; terror

Fedayee 229, 232, 234

Federalist Revolts 65

feeding cities and towns 103, 109, 126, 220–21, 236, 257

feudal
dues 58
laws 69
mode of production 65, 113, 211

Fidelistas 155, 164

five antis movement 200

food detachments/food committees 102, 104

force *see* coercion; violence

foreign aid *see* aid

foreign invasion 8, 43, 159, 165, 181, 193, 277 fn2
threat of 100, 183
see also Bay of Pigs; foreign war

foreign relations 178, 180–81, 225, 271
see also Britain; Cuba; USA; USSR

foreign war 7, 45, 50, 51, 53, 54, 258
absence of in Mexico 271
and America 120
and China 199, 201
and England 131, 137, 141, 145 fn8
and Ethiopia 218, 223
and France 58, 66, 67, 68, 69, 70, 76, 82, 88, 95–6
and Iran 233–4, 237, 239, 243
and Nicaragua 181, 183, 184
and Russia 88, 95–6, 100, 101, 113

French Revolution 6, 37, 42, 43, 45, 49, 50, 52, 57, 86–7, 88, 113, 119
to overthrow 58–9
see also Reign of Terror, revolutionary

Friedrich, C. and Brzezinski, Z. 19, 34 fn2

FRS (Sandinista Revolutionary Front) 183, 184

FSLN (Sandinista Front for National Liberation) 169–74, 175, 176, 179, 184, 191 fn13

G2 (Cuba) 156, 160, 166, 167

Georgia 120, 126

Germany
under Hitler 19, 21, 30, 31
and Russia 96–7, 101, 103

Girondins 58, 59, 66, 69
González, General R. 273
Government Administrative Council
(China) 196, 201
GPP (Prolonged Popular War) 170
GPU (USSR) 110, 111, 116 fnl2
Greer, D. 57, 62–9, 70, 78, 92–4
Group of Twelve 170, 174
guerrilla campaign in Ireland, Tories, 138
guerrilla movements 6, 8, 10, 108, 127, 128, 209, 229, 261
in Cambodia 27, 35 fn5
in China 192–6
see also Red Army
in Costa Rica 182
in Cuba 152–5
see also July 26 movement
in Ethiopia 214, 218
in Iran 229, 233, 234, 241
in Nicaragua 169–73, 179
see also FSLN
Guomindang 51, 192, 193, 194–5, 197, 203

Havana 155
university 153
Héberistes 78, 79
Hezbollah 232–3, 234, 242
history 11
hoarding 61, 72, 73
Hobsbawm 8, 14 fn1
Honduras 179, 181, 183
Human Rights Policy in Nicaragua 173, 177, 187, 189
Human Rights organizations 229
reports of 171, 174, 175, 181, 186–7, 189, 217, 231, 235, 246
Hunan 192–3

ideology 9–10, 50–51, 205, 239, 257, 259
in America 118, 128, 142, 145 fn4
in Cambodia 28–9
in China 195–6, 201, 203, 204
in Cuba 153–4, 161, 163, 167
in England 142, 144, 145
in Ethiopia 220–21, 226

in France 69–71, 83
in Iran 231, 232, 234, 236, 238–40, 248, 249 fn3
in Mexico 273, 274
in Nicaragua 173, 179, 188, 191 fn13, 195
in revolution 4, 10, 50, 52, 53
in Russia 87, 88, 98–106
in totalitarianism 21, 33, 46
see also Communism, Marxism–Leninism, nationalism
illiteracy 177, 220
see also literacy campaigns
impressments 122, 128
incidence of terror, geographic 67
Indians 171, 180, 181, 183, 186, 187, 190 fn8
Indulgents 78
industrial workers 103, 105, 106, 108, 229
see also urban workers
inflation 58, 85 fn9, 88, 105, 121, 196, 218
INRA (National Institute of Agrarian Reform) 158, 168
insurrection 58, 68–9, 102, 136, 189, 258
see also civil war; domestic insurrection; rebellions; riots
Integrated Revolutionary Organization (Cuba) 168
intelligence system
in Cuba 166
in England 136
see also secret police
International Court of Justice 185
international economy (international trade) 52, 53, 114
international pressures 49, 69, 114, 189, 204, 258
Iranian Revolution 6, 177
to overthrow 228–30
see also Reign of Terror, revolutionary, in Iran
Iran–Iraq war 233, 235, 237, 240, 241, 242, 243, 245–6
Ireland 37, 129, 130–31, 132, 133–4, 137–9, 141, 144–5, 145–6 fn9

Islamic Consultative Assembly *see* Majlis
Islamic Fundamentalists 232
Islamic Law 232, 234, 236, 244–6
Islamic Republic 228, 232, 237, 241, 242
Islamic Republican Party, IRP, 232, 234, 236–7, 242, 245, 246
Islamic revolutionary committees *see* komitehs
Islamic Revolutionary Council 230, 232, 241
Islamic revolutionary courts 231, 234, 236
Islamic revolutionary guards *see* Pasdaran
Italy (under Mussolini) 19, 34 fn4

Jacobins 50, 52, 53, 59, 66, 82, 86–7
 see also Reign of Terror, revolutionary, in France
Japan
 and China 51, 193–4
 and Russia 97, 98
Jiangxi Soviet 193, 195
July 26 Movement 152, 157, 158, 164
junta (Nicaragua) 174, 176, 181

Kampuchea *see* Cambodia
kebelles 215, 216, 217, 221, 224, 225, 268
Khamenei, S. Hajatolislam 235, 237
Khmer Rouge 26, 27, 28
Khomeini, R., Ayatollah 229, 230, 232, 233, 234, 235, 237, 241–3, 245
komitehs 229, 242
Korean war 199, 201
Kronstadt rebellion 107, 109
kulaks *see* peasantry
Kurds/Kurdistan 231, 232, 233, 235, 236, 241, 242

labour camps 93, 95, 198
labour conscription 105, 106, 107, 114
land

confiscation by state 58, 83, 104, 122, 133, 137, 138, 160, 177, 181–2
 see also confiscation of property
reforms 69, 83, 106, 158, 164, 181–2, 193, 195–6, 199–200, 220
 see also agrarian reform laws
seizures by peasants 88, 212
 avoidance in Nicaragua 182
Las Villas 155, 156, 158–9
Law of 14 Frimaire 75–77, 78
Law of 22 Prairial 60, 62, 65, 79–80, 81
Law of Suspects 61, 66
laws of Terror 19, 23, 255
 in China 197–8
 in Cuba 156, 157–8, 165
 in England 135, 138
 in Ethiopia 214, 216
 in France 60, 61, 62, 66–7, 72, 75–7, 79–80
 in Iran 231, 235
 in Ireland 138–9
 in Russia 90, 91, 97
Laws of Ventôse 77
leases 107
Left SRs *see* Social Revolutionaries
legal-rational authority *see* rational authority
Leggett, G, 92–5, 98–9, 102
legitimacy 128, 152, 229
legitimate authority, legitimations of domination 3, 264, 267
Lenin, V.I., 86, 88, 89, 97, 98, 99, 103, 107, 109, 112–13, 116 fns 10 and 13
 theory of state 262
levée en masse 71
Levellers 131, 132, 133, 145 and fn5
liberated areas (China) 193, 194, 199, 203
liberated zone (Cuba) 154
 absence in Nicaragua 179
Lindet, Robert 73, 76, 81
literacy campaigns 160, 162, 178, 181, 219–21, 238
 see also zemecha

loans 178, 181, 225
local government network 197, 201
Long March 193, 195
loyalists 119, 120, 123, 125, 126
Luxemburg, Rosa 268, 269
Lyon 37, 38, 43, 61, 65–6, 67, 72, 73, 78, 79

Majlis 232, 234
Makhno, N. 95, 100–101, 275
Managua 171, 172
Manchuria 193, 194
Mao, Zedong 192–3, 195, 196
Maoism 204
Marseilles 43, 65
martial law 108, 109, 110, 214, 230
Marxism–Leninism 4, 50, 109, 204, 220–21
Marxist analysis 4, 50, 112–13, 118, 262–3, 267
Marxist ideology 102, 105
   see also communism
mass line 195
mass meetings 198
mass mobilization campaigns (China) 201, 202, 203, 205 fn4, 268
   Ethiopia *see* zemecha
mass movements in China *see* Yundong
mass society 30, 31, 32
Matos, Hubert 156, 158, 160
Maximum, law of 61, 72, 73, 74, 76, 83, 121
MDN (National Democratic Movement) 174, 180, 183
MEISON, All Ethiopia Socialist Movement 216, 221
Mengistu, Haile-Miriam 213, 215, 216, 219, 220, 221, 223, 225, 226, 267
Mensheviks 89, 97, 108, 111
Messianism in reigns of terror 46, 50
method 11–13, 117
Mexican Revolution 53, 54 fn3, 270–71
Mexico City 273, 275–6
middle peasants *see* peasantry
military administrative areas (China) 196, 201–2

comparison with Mexico 274
military commands in Cuba 156
Military Council (Ethiopia) 215
military courts (Cuba) 156, 160–61
military operations in Russian civil war 91
   see also army
military regimes 32, 213–14
military revolt in Ethiopia 211–12
Military Revolutionary Committee of Petrograd 88, 90
   provisional MRCs 90, 91
militia (Cuba) 157, 176
militias (America) 91
Miskito Indians *see* Indians
mobilization for war 50, 51, 53, 71–3, 74, 114 fn2, 215, 219
   see also war effort
mobilized authority 268
modernization 230
money 105, 133, 196, 218
   see also assignats; compensation bonds; continental currency
Monimbo 171
monopoly of force 264, 269
   see also control over the revolutionary coercive forces
Montazeri, Ayatollah 232, 245, 246, 250 fn10
Moscow 88, 90, 95, 96, 97, 108, 110
mosque network 229, 268
Mossadeq, M. 228, 229, 242
Moussavi, M. 235, 237
MPU (United Peoples Movement) 172, 174
Mujahedin 229, 232, 234, 235–6, 240, 246, 249 fn4
mullahs 229
Musavi Tabrizi, Prosecutor General 235, 236
Mussolini *see* Italy
Mustazafin Foundation 238

Narkomprod 102
National Assembly 184, 190 fn10
National Convention *see* Convention
National Democratic Front (Iran) 229, 232

National Directorate of FSLN 176, 179, 180, 182, 187
National Guard (Nicaragua) 169–70, 171, 172, 173, 174, 178–9
National Institute of Agrarian Reform *see* INRA
National Revolutionary Company in Command, NRCC 219
National Revolutionary Party (Mexico) *see* PNR
national unity government (Nicaragua) 172, 176
nationalism 33, 143, 220
Nationalists; Nationalist Party *see* Guomindang
nationalities 87, 97, 100–101, 210, 220, 221, 222, 233
nationalization 104, 159, 163, 177, 182, 212, 220, 221, 239
Nazi Germany *see* Germany, under Hitler
necessity 6, 8, 40, 70, 109, 149, 163, 199, 205, 258
New Democracy 195, 196, 199
New Economic Policy 106–7, 109, 110
New Model Army 38, 132–3, 135, 138, 142, 145, 146 fn10, 176
New York 120, 123, 125
Nicaraguan Revolution 6, 7, 169–73, 190 fn11, 267, 268
as new model of revolutionary state 269
see also Reign of Terror, revolutionary, absence in Nicaragua

oath of allegiance
in America 122, 125
in France 59, 60, 61, 74
see also Engagement Act
obedience 264, 267–8
Obregón, Alvaro 272, 273
Ogaden 218, 219
one-man management 104
opposition 5, 7, 8–9, 10, 103, 128, 170–71, 229
within Communist Party 111
see also counter-revolution; counter-revolutionaries

Organic Law 196
Ortega, Daniel 170, 174, 181
Ortega, Humberto 170, 182
outcome of revolution *see* revolution

Paris 61, 79
executions in 65
supply of 74, 76, 80, 81
Paris Commune 59, 80
Paris People's Army 62, 74, 76, 78, 79, 80, 84 fn6
Paris Revolutionary Tribunal 60, 62, 79, 81
party organization 52, 53, 112, 114, 170, 179, 201, 225
debate over in Ethiopia 221–2
lack of in England 140
lack of in France 82–3
party-state *see* single party state
Pasdaran 231, 233, 234, 235, 236, 237, 241–2, 245, 249 fn9
Pastora, Eden 170, 182, 183, 184, 185
patriots 119, 120, 125, 126
peace negotiations 91, 96–7, 185–6, 189, 242
peace treaty (1782) 121, 125
see also Brest-Litovsk Treaty
peasant associations (Ethiopia) 221, 224, 225, 268
peasantry 28–30, 53, 83, 88, 95, 99, 102–3, 104, 106, 152–4, 167, 192–3, 224, 230, 271
see also communism
people's armies (France) 62, 73–4, 76, 80, 102
People's Commissar of Justice to the Soviet 91
People's Commissariat for Food Supply *see* Narkomprod
People's Liberation Army *see* Red Army, China
People's Militia (China) 201
People's Militia (Ethiopia) 215, 216, 219, 223–5
People's Republic of China 196
People's Tribunal (Ethiopia) 215
People's Tribunals (China) 200–201
Petrograd 88, 89, 90, 96, 97, 103, 108

Petrograd Soviet 88
Phnom Penh 23, 31, 32
pluralism 175, 176, 179, 184, 269
pluralist democracy 268
PMAC (Provisional Military Admin-
    istrative Council) 212, 213–14,
    215, 216, 217, 218, 220, 222
PNR (National Revolutionary Party,
    Mexico) 53, 274, 276
Poland 100, 101, 113, 115–16 fn9
police 59, 62, 75–6, 91, 156, 173,
    179, 201, 231
police bureau (France) 79–80
policy choices and chosen policies of
    revolutionaries 6, 8–10, 44, 48,
    52, 53, 70, 78, 80, 82–3, 95–
    107, 109, 110–11, 112, 114,
    121–2, 142–3, 145, 149–50,
    161–5, 167, 173, 177–8, 181–
    2, 184–5, 187–8, 190 fn8, 199–
    200, 201, 220–21, 222, 223,
    237, 238–43, 244, 257–8, 259,
    276
    see also ideology
policy process 50, 110–11, 259
Politburo 112
popular militias (Nicaragua) 176, 181,
    182
Popular Socialist Party (PSP, Cuba)
    157, 158, 164
popular tribunals (anti-Somozista)
    185
population 63, 94, 122, 138, 166, 172,
    199, 217, 236
power 5, 9, 23, 237, 268
Presbyterians 135, 136, 138
press censorship 183, 185, 242
prisons and numbers of prisoners 22–
    3, 63, 93, 161, 198, 229, 231,
    245
    sentences 160, 173, 174, 215
    treatment of prisoners 63, 93, 110,
        123, 160, 165, 185, 186,
        213, 217, 235–6, 245, 246
Proletarian Tendency 170
proletariat *see* industrial workers
Protectorate 129, 140–41
protests 158

see also demonstrations
proto-totalitarian state 33–4
    Cambodia as an example 26–32
Provisional Military Administrative
    Council *see* PMAC
provincial congresses *see* Congress
PSP *see* Popular Socialist Party
public trials 157, 197, 236
punishment of rebels 64, 67, 68, 94,
    160
Puritan Revolution *see* English
    Revolution

Quakers 122, 150
Qom 231
Qomi, Grand Ayatollah 245

Rafsanjani, H. Hojatolislam 237, 245
Rajai, M.A., prime minister 232, 234,
    241
Rajavi, M., Head of Mujahedin 234,
    241
rational authority, domination 264–5,
    266
rationing 88, 105
rebellions 68, 107, 149, 272
    Irish 138
    see also civil war; domestic insur-
        rection; insurrection;
        Kronstadt rebellion; riots
Reconstruction Crusade of Conduct
    (Iran) 238
Rectification Campaigns (China) 196
Red Army
    China 7, 193, 194
        see also Eighth Route Army
    Russia 51, 91, 100–101, 115 fn5
refractory clergy 61
refugees 31, 177, 191 fn12, 218, 227
    fn3
    see also exiles
Reign of Terror, revolutionary 5, 149–
    51, 209
    absence in America 37, 38, 39, 42,
        43, 118–19, 122–5, 141–2
    absence in Mexico 275–6
    absence in Nicaragua 173–89,
        243–4

causes: tentative hypothesis and development of 6–10, 13, 149–51, 209–10, 256–61
  Brinton's explanation 44–7
  Edwards' explanation 40–44
  Skocpol's explanation 49–54
  end 47, 52, 77–80, 81
  fear in 37–8
  general comparative lessons 253–6
  in China 49, 52, 196–205, 254, 255
  in Cuba 155–7, 160–67, 254, 255
  in England/Ireland 38, 42, 43, 51, 129–46, 247, 254, 255
  in Ethiopia 214–26, 254, 255
  in France 37, 42, 43, 45, 49, 50, 52, 57–85, 247, 253–4, 255
  in Iran 231–47, 254, 255
  in Russia 3, 7, 42, 43, 45, 49, 51, 53, 86–116, 254, 255
  machinery of 253–4
  nature 19–20, 22–6
  organization 22, 37–9, 141
  problems for study 24–6
  see also terror, State
religious toleration in England 132, 135–6, 143
religious zealousness in England 136–7, 140
Representatives on Mission 60, 61, 62, 76, 77, 79
repression by state 7, 19, 170–72, 190 fn5, 202, 213–14, 222, 229, 230, 245–6
  see also terror, state
requisitioning 90, 99, 102, 104, 105, 107, 113, 114, 198, 200, 219
  see also impressments; supply
resignations 158, 161, 180, 182
revolution
  causes 3
  nature 5, 14 fn1, 118, 209–10, 226, 258–9
  outcomes 3–4, 7, 10, 52, 53, 114, 240, 266
  see also under separate cases
revolutionary armies (France) *see* people's armies

revolutionary armies (in Mexico) 272, 273, 274, 276
Revolutionary Directory 153, 157
revolutionary justice *see* summary justice
Revolutionary People's Army (Ethiopia) 216
revolutionary reigns of terror *see* Reign of Terror, revolutionary
revolutionary tribunals 22
  in France 61, 77, 79, 84 fn3
  in Russia 90, 91
  see also Paris Revolutionary Tribunal; People's Tribunals; popular tribunals; special tribunals
riots
  in England 132
  in France 58, 180, 182
  see also civil war; domestic insurrection; insurrection; rebellions
Robelo, A. 174, 180, 183
Robespierre, Maximilien 52, 59, 69, 70, 79, 82, 86, 113, 239
Roman Catholics 78, 134, 138, 142, 143
Ronsin, C.-P. 62, 78, 226
Rump Parliament 129, 131, 132, 136, 139, 140
Russia *see* USSR
Russian Revolution 6, 7, 37, 42, 43, 45, 49, 51, 53, 87–9, 119, 167
  comparisons with Mexico 274–6
Russian Socialist Federal Soviet Republic (RSFSR) 90, 112

sabotage 43, 90, 161, 197, 216
Sandinista Defence Committees *see* CDS
Sandinista Front for National Liberation *see* FSLN
Sandinista Popular Army *see* EPS
Sandinistas *see* FSLN
sans-culottes 52, 53, 71
SAVAK 229, 230, 231
SAVAMA 231
Scotland; Scottish war 129, 130, 131, 132, 134–5, 136, 138

security squads (Ethiopia) 215
secret police 20, 21, 91, 110, 156, 175, 197, 229, 231
secret societies 197–8
Seded 216, 261
sedition 66–7
Shah of Iran 228, 229
Shi'a Islam 230
Sierra Maestra 152, 153, 156, 159
single party state 111–13, 167–8, 201, 225–6, 229, 261, 274
    avoidance 188
Skocpol, T. 3–5, 7, 36, 49–54, 69, 71–2, 78, 81, 82, 84 fn1, 85 fn9, 109, 113–14, 144, 189, 204, 205 fn1, 243, 263, 265, 270, 276–7 fn1
slaves 123
Soboul, A. 68, 69, 80
Social Revolutionaries 89, 97, 99, 111
social science theories 8
soldiers committees (Ethiopia) 212
Somalia 218, 219
Somoza, Anastasio 169, 177
Soviet model *see* single party state
Soviet Union *see* USSR
Soviets 89, 90, 91, 104
Sovnarkom 89–90, 91, 97, 99, 104, 109, 111, 112, 114, 115 fn4, 116 fn13
special tribunals (Nicaragua) 174, 175, 177
Stalin, I.V. 112, 114
    and China 201
    Russia under Stalin 19, 21, 30
    see also totalitarian regimes
starvation 31, 66, 88, 90, 102, 103, 107, 108, 116 fn15, 126, 132, 137, 211, 220
    see also economic crisis; famine
state-building 49, 53, 113, 248
state control of farms in Nicaragua 182
state control of industry in France 52, 73, 82
state controlled market system in Ethiopia 220–21
State Council (China) 201

state of emergency
    in Ethiopia 214, 222
    in Nicaragua 177, 183, 185
statistics on terror *see* terror, State; victims of reigns of terror
Statute on Rights and Guarantees for the Citizens of Nicaragua 173, 174, 184, 187
statutes against Roman Catholicism 138
STO (Council of Labour and Defence) 104, 105, 114–15 fn2
strikes 88, 108, 153, 170–71, 172, 211, 222, 229, 230, 272
    General Strike (Cuba) 154
    see also demonstrations
Students Revolutionary Directory *see* Revolutionary Directory
Subsistence Commission 73
Sudan 218
summary justice 22–3, 25, 59, 61, 78, 91, 93, 110, 165, 166, 215, 216, 231, 234, 235, 253
Sunni Moslems 232
supply, supplies 62, 66, 69, 72, 73–4, 76, 80, 82, 88, 90, 96, 102, 109, 200
    to towns 218, 219, 220, 221
    see also Addis Ababa; distribution; feeding cities and towns; Moscow; Paris
support 13, 81, 113, 167, 175, 178–9, 188, 201, 203, 205, 237
    loss of 221–2, 229, 233 240, 259, 267, 268, 269, 274
Supreme Being and Festival of the 52, 78, 80, 268
Supreme Court (Iran) 232
surveillance committees (France) 60, 61, 62

Talmon, J.L. 34 fnl, 70–71, 82
Tambov provinces, rebellion 95, 107–8
tax in kind 105, 108, 114
    fixed 106
taxes 76, 121, 128, 133, 137, 195, 198

Tchiang Kai-chek 193, 194, 195
Tenth Party Congress 106, 109, 110
Teferi Banti 212, 215, 221
Tehran 235, 244
temporary government 76, 82, 89, 111, 114, 140, 150, 261
Terceristas 170, 174
terror 13, 21
    State terror 17, 18–22, 33–4
      under Batista 157
      under Carranza 273
      under Nationalists 196–7
      under Somoza 171
      see also repression by state
terrorism 16–18, 19, 34 fn3, 78
Thermidor 77, 80
thought reform (China) 200
three anti's movement 200
Tigray 218, 220, 222, 226
Toleration Act 135, 143
torture 23, 155, 156, 171, 173, 174, 215, 218, 229, 235, 242
totalitarian regimes 19, 20–22, 23, 31, 32, 34 fn2, 46, 226, 248, 267, 268
totalitarianism *see* ideology; totalitarian regimes
Toulon 43, 67, 68, 73, 84 fn5
trade unions 104, 108, 111, 182, 200, 212, 222
traditional authority/domination 228, 264–5
transportation 59, 63, 139
Tribunal *see* Paris Revolutionary Tribunal
tribunals in Cuba 156
Trotsky, Leon 43, 86–7, 98, 99, 112, 116 fn13, 264
trusts 104, 107
Tudeh Party 229, 236, 240

UDN (Nicaraguan Democratic Union) 179, 183
Ukraine 94–5, 96, 100, 101, 116 fn15
unemployed 103, 105, 127, 177, 229, 239
unemployment 66, 88, 95, 103, 105, 168 fn1, 229

Union of National Front Forces *see* National Democratic Front
urban workers 121
Urrutia, Dr 155, 157, 158
USA
    and Cambodia 27, 31, 32
    and China 194, 197, 199
    and Cuba 154, 157, 159–60, 162–3
    and Ethiopia 219, 225
    and Iran 177, 233
    and Mexico 270–71, 273, 277 fn2
    and Nicaragua 170, 171, 177, 178, 180–81, 184, 185, 189
USSR 112
    and China 194, 198, 199, 204
    and Cuba 159, 162–3
    and Ethiopia 225

Vecheka *see* Cheka
Vendée 37, 43, 59, 63, 65, 67, 68
Vesenkha 104
victims of reigns of terror 24, 117
    in America 119
    in Cambodia 26–7
    in China 198–9
    in Cuba 161, 166
    in England/Ireland 139, 141
    in Ethiopia 214–28
    in France 62–8
    in Iran 235–6
    in Russia 92–5
    see also executions; prisons
Vietnam and Cambodia 27, 28, 32, 33
Villa, Pancho 272, 273
village organizations 196
violence 5, 6, 13, 21, 25, 45, 75, 118, 122, 123, 144, 213, 220
    see also coercion
virtue; Republic of Virtue 78–9, 81, 247, 268
VTsIK 89–90, 97, 99, 104

wages 66, 72, 80, 88, 105, 107, 239
    see also Maximum
Wali Faqih 232, 237
war *see* civil war; foreign war

war casualties
  in America 123
  in Nicaragua 186
war communism 51, 87, 103–6, 108, 109
war damage in Nicaragua 177, 190 fn7
war effort 103, 122–8, 200, 219, 237
  see also mobilization for war
War of Independence 117, 119
war trials 155–7, 174–5
Washington, George 118, 119, 120
Weber, M. (analysis of the state) 263–9
West, France *see* Vendée

Western Somalia Liberation Front (WSLF) 218, 219
White Army 93, 94, 100–101
Wolf, E R 230, 270
Wollo province 211, 212, 218, 222
Worcester 136
workers *see* industrial workers; sans-culottes; urban workers

year zero 26, 27
Yundong 198, 200, 202

Zapata, Emiliano 270, 273, 276
zemecha 220, 221, 222
Zulu state 33, 116–40